ALIEN HORSEMAN

An Italian Shavetail with Custer

J. C. Ladenheim

HERITAGE BOOKS
2007

HERITAGE BOOKS
AN IMPRINT OF HERITAGE BOOKS, INC.

Books, CDs, and more—Worldwide

For our listing of thousands of titles see our website
at
www.HeritageBooks.com

Published 2007 by
HERITAGE BOOKS, INC.
Publishing Division
65 East Main Street
Westminster, Maryland 21157-5026

Copyright © 2007 Jules C. Ladenheim

Other books by the author:
Custer's Thorn: The Life of Frederick W. Benteen

All rights reserved. No part of this book may be reproduced or transmitted in any form or by any means, electronic or mechanical, including photocopying, recording or by any information storage and retrieval system without written permission from the author, except for the inclusion of brief quotations in a review.

International Standard Book Number: 978-0-7884-2383-3

CONTENTS

Illustrations	v
Introduction	vii
Acknowledgements	ix
Prologue	xiii
Chapter I - The Cadet	1
Chapter II - The Conspirator	25
Chapter III - The Assassination Attempt	51
Chapter IV - French Guyana	73
Chapter V - Civil War	97
Chapter VI - Regular Army Commission	117
Chapter VII - A Cavalry Officer	131
Chapter VIII - Dakota Territory	153
Chapter IX - The Little Bighorn Campaign	181
Chapter X - Custer's Wing	217
Chapter XI - Reno's Battles	229
Chapter XII - De Rudio's Adventure	249
Chapter XIII - Soldiering	265
Chapter XIV - Nez Perce	275
Chapter XV - Court Of Inquiry	287
Chapter XVI - Captain	301
Chapter XVII - Final Days	315
Bibliography	327
Index	335

Illustrations

Birthplace of Carlo De Rudio
De Rudio Requests a Smoke
Charles A. Dana Letter
Medical Disqualification Document
Dr. R. Taiszky Letter
Charles De Rudio, 2nd Lieutenant
George A. Custer, Lt. Colonel
Miles W. Keogh, Captain
Tom Custer, Captain
De Rudio Fleeing the Lakotas
John Martin, AKA Giovanni Martini
Curly, Young Lakota Scout
Marcus A. Reno, Major
Frederick Benteen, Captain
Samuel D. Sturgis
Charles De Rudio, Captain
Charles De Rudio and Daughters
Carlotta De Rudio
Officers on Maneuvers in Indian Territory

All photographs and documents located after page 180

INTRODUCTION

Charles De Rudio was fond of recounting his adventures, around the campfires and in the parlors of the officers' quarters. He had many colorful stories, gathered from his experiences on both sides of the Atlantic. So that the reader can place them in proper historical perspective, the background to these exciting events has been briefly outlined. A detailed description would seem to be unneeded -- whole libraries are devoted to struggle for the unification of Italy; three thousand volumes and papers to the Little Bighorn Battle. My narrative centers around De Rudio and the several worlds he lived in. But as spectacular as his adventures may appear, most of his later years were spent in dull, monotonous, thankless soldiering. Hence, frontier army service must also be depicted, so that his life can be better understood. Since this is primarily the story of De Rudio, many subordinate officers of the 7th Cavalry go unmentioned.

There are no monuments erected to the memory of Major (Count) Charles C. De Rudio, USA, (Ret.). Although he gave his youth to the cause of Italian liberty and spent thirty-two years of unblemished service in the United States Army, the best we offer him is a small plot of consecrated ground and a moment of reflection. For the early life of De Rudio, I have relied on the work of Cesare Crespi,[1] which, in turn, appears to be based on an unpublished autobiography, written shortly before De Rudio's death. It is grandiose, replete with prejudices and at times quite imaginative and self-serving. With regard to the infamous attempt on the life of Napoleon III, De Rudio's story is selective and therefore incomplete, representing as it does, his recollections of events about which he was not fully informed. Notwithstanding, I have presented his account, often with unstated reservations, since there is no reason why history's accepted versions cannot be challenged by a slightly impeachable eyewitness.

Notes

1. Cesare Crespi, *Per la Liberta!* (San Francisco: Canessa Printing, 1913)
2. Cesare Marino, *Dal Piave al Little Bighorn* (Belluno: Tarantola, 1996)
3. Charles K. Mills, *Charles C. De Rudio* (Mattetuch and Bryan, NY: J. M. Carroll, 1983)

Acknowledgements

My task has been facilitated by the recent biography by Cesare Marino.[2] Not only did he bring to the study a mastery of both Italian and American history, but also a seminal knowledge of Native American anthropology. Unfortunately, since his work was written for the Italian public, it contains much material of scant interest to an Anglo-American reader. This has emboldened me to restudy the life of De Rudio and to retell his story. The DeRudio genealogy, as well as the description of the polemics leveled against De Rudio in his closing years, has been briefly summarized from Marino's account, allowing me to apply myself to matters of greater interest.

The short biography of Charles K. Mills[3] here deserves mention, as a reliable reference for De Rudio's military service.

During the course of the study, I have used the library facilities of the Military Academy at West Point, the Military History Institute at Carlisle, Pennsylvania, the Widener Library of Harvard University, the library facilities at the University of California at Berkeley, Farleigh Dickinson University and Ramapo College. I express my thanks for their kindness and help. The reference librarians at the public libraries of New York, Brooklyn, Newark, N.J., Teaneck, N.J., Johnson Public Library of Hackensack, N.J., the State Historical Society of North Dakota, the Biblioteca Nazionale di Torino, the Settore Sistema Bibliotecario Urbano di Torino, the Museo Civico

(Belluno) and the Biblioteca Nationale (Venezia) were of great assistance. The U.S. National Archives in Washington, D.C. was kind enough to let me examine the military file of De Rudio, which was indispensable to this work. Anna Daniel at the Mohave Museum Institute of History at Kingman, Arizona helped me trace the activities of Hercules De Rudio. Coleen C. Bowman and Lee Rutledge at The Lincoln Memorial Shrine at Redlands, California replied to queries. Mark J. Kenneweg, of the Fort Abraham Lincoln Foundation, helped by furnishing a map of the fort. Howard Bogess, a Crow historian, recounted family recollections.

Teresa Avila of the periodical department of the San Jose Library; Jeff Malcomson, archivist to the Arizona State Library; Geneviere Troka of the California State Archives and David N. Durant of Nottingham, England all assisted this work and I use this opportunity to thank them.

Mr. Kim Allen Scott, of the Montana State Library was kind enough to furnish me with selected letters of Lt. Gustavus Doane in the Burlingame Special Collection. It is my understanding that Mr. Scott will shortly publish a life of this splendid and sadly neglected officer, whose life is an inspiration to anyone contemplating a military career. I express my thanks to Kitty B. Deernose, museum curator and John A. Doerner, chief historian, at the Little Bighorn National Monument, who allowed me to use the library. Mr. James Moske, of the manuscript department of the N.Y. Public Library, facilitated my examination of the Custer letters in the Merington Collection. I deeply appreciate the assistance generously given me by Willie Peters, of the Crow reservation, who took me to Crow's Nest, traveled with me the trail to Little Bighorn and gave me the benefit of his knowledge of the region. Jason Pitsch was most gracious in indicating the probable locations of Major Reno's skirmish lines and helped me arrange an inspection of the route of Reno's retreat.

Lastly, I wish to thank Dr. Walt Lewis for his helpful suggestions and express my appreciation to Dr. Eric D. Ladenheim for his assistance in collecting data and for his invaluable comments on firearm ballistics, to Leslie Wolfinger, my editor, and to Jean Ganley, my secretary.

PROLOGUE

On an early morning in 1845, a small public coach was drawn up in a cobbled square in Belluno, an ancient mountain town, sixty miles north of Venice. Among the passengers waiting to board the *vettura,* were two brothers, nineteen and thirteen years of age, wearing the uniforms of an Austrian cadet. The older rested his hand on the shoulder of his brother, playfully squeezing it, as if to reassure him. They were surrounded by family members who took turns repeating last minute instructions and slipping small gifts into their knapsacks. The usual contract with the coachman had already been signed by their unhappy father, providing for the expenses of transport, lodging and meals along the way. He paid the customary half-fare in advance, with the understanding that the remainder would be paid by the older brother on their arrival at Treviso, forty miles distant. The older boy would then negotiate the fares with a new *vetturino* for the next segment of the trip. The cost of the entire journey to Milan would be about twelve dollars for each, apart from gratuities, supplements and occasional tolls.

After the baggage had been loaded, the passengers took their seats in the battered coach, and, with a crack of the whip and a flurry of handkerchiefs, shouts and tossed kisses, the journey began. For the two brothers, the trip was the beginning of a new chapter in their lives.

They had mixed feelings about their uniforms and newly chosen profession. In the end, it was their uncle who had persuaded them that they had no prospects in Belluno, while the

Austrian Army would offer unlimited opportunities. In time, they might even become a colonel, like him. Besides, they lacked the aptitude for higher study; and commerce was unthinkable for a nobleman's sons.

The younger boy, Carlo, watched as his beloved Belluno disappeared in the mountains, turning his head away from his brother, to conceal his moist eyes. Once outside the city, the ancient road became bumpy and rutted, so that the distance traveled in an hour seldom exceeded three miles. The coachman stopped at inns along the way to change horses. Some of the nags could barely draw the coach, and when they approached a hill, the *vetturino* had to rent additional horses or mules; whereupon, he demanded extra payment. Passengers took turns perching out of the windows, on the lookout for highwaymen, who were known to rob coaches and make off with the baggage. Often, Austrian soldiers blocked the road demanding petty gratuities, which all but the cadets were required to pay. No sooner were the soldiers were left behind, when the passengers would begin to curse loudly and glare at the brothers' uniforms.

At Treviso, the weary travelers were deposited at a scruffy inn on the outskirts of the city, where they would be fed and lodged, according to the terms of the contract. Having completed his scheduled trip, the coachman collected the remainder of the fares and climbed back into the coach, grumbling about the tips. The travelers soon commenced a torrent of complains about the food, the damp beds and the lice and flees, which would continue throughout the journey. Better accommodations were available to the passengers in the diligence coaches, who stopped at well-known inns, but the fares far exceeded the slender means of the boys' parents.

At daybreak, the older brother, Achille, made arrangements with another *vetturino* to continue their journey. The coach traveled from sunrise to dusk, with two to three hours set aside at noon, to rest the horses and the coachman. Toward nightfall, as the party approached Vicenza, the coach was again stopped by Austrian soldiers, and documents and baggage were leisurely inspected. The examination halted when the passengers took out their purses. On through Verona, and along Lake Garda, the coach sped, amidst the pleasant landscapes of Lombardy. The boys sat back on their worn seats and tried to arrange in their minds the amazing sights they had seen. A week passed as the succession of coaches brought them closer to Milan. At last they spied the lofty spires of the great cathedral in the distance, and their two hundred and fifty mile trip drew to an end.[1]

The coach rode briskly into the busy city, rattling loudly on the flat stone pavement, as if to proclaim its arrival. The brothers gazed in awe at the architectural splendors and marveled at the dense crowds, the clean white houses and the wide elegant streets. The *vettura* finally came to a stop and, with great excitement, the weary brothers alighted. After settling up with the coachman, the new cadets straightened their uniforms, dusted each other off and made arrangements with a porter to have their trunk taken to the Military Academy of St Luca. As they followed on foot behind the *facchino* laboring with their baggage, small boys jeered at them and men spat on the ground.

Notes

1. I have found this book particularly helpful in depicting pre-railroad Italian transportation. Paul R. Baker, *The Fortunate Pilgrims* (Cambridge, MA: Harvard University Press, 1964), pp. 30-91, 237.

I
THE CADET

Belluno rises up from a rocky plateau at the juncture of the Piave and Ardo rivers, with lofty Mt. Serva in the distance. From the earliest times, the town was a regional trade center for the mountain villages, scattered along the valleys of the two rivers. Forests of larch, spruce, pine and fir were the town's principal assets. From Belluno came the piles on which Venice was built.

Belunum appears to have been of Celtic origin. Druso, stepson of Augustus, conquered the region in 15 B.C., and the Emperor Tiberius used it as a staging point to crush the Celtic resistance in the valleys of Switzerland and the Tyrol. Some of the soldiers remained in the province, and their descendants, in common with the other alpine peoples of the South Tyrol, adopted a language called *Ladin*, a mixture of Latin and mountain Celtic. This was also spoken by the people of Belluno, somewhat blended with the Venetian dialect.

Following the fall of Rome, temporal rule passed through a long succession of sovereigns, beginning with the bishops, and followed by the dukes of Trevino, Austria and Milan. In the early 15th Century, Venice easily gained control of Belluno, bringing to it security and construction.

With the rise of the Ottoman Empire and the discovery of new routes to the east, the fortunes of the Venetian Republic entered a gradual and protracted decline. Napoleon ended the pretense of a Republic and brought Venice and the province of

Venetia under his rule. He introduced a new codex of law, educational reform, conscription and the expropriation of church property. These innovations lasted for a mere decade but remained indelibly fixed in the memory of the young intellectuals. In 1815 the Congress of Vienna set about to undo the changes. Instead of restoring independence to Venice, it chose to assign rule to the Austrians. Thus, Lombardy, Belluno, Venice and Venetia found themselves under Hapsburg sovereignty, which was expected to provide stability to northern Italy.[1] France was returned to the Bourbons, and the rich duchies of northern Italy were doled out to deserving princes.[2]

In an effort to purge their domains of Bonapartism and to restore the old order, Metternich and his allies instituted, and brutally enforced, many repressive measures. These included police surveillance, arbitrary arrest, rigid regulation of the press, and control of education.

The Bellunese are proud people with few loyalties beyond their town and kin. One of the leading families of Belluno was the De Rudios. Theirs was an old name, of historic more than distinguished ancestry, going back to the 13th Century. The name was originally Nosadani (Noradano, Nosodano), later changed to De (Di) Rudio, perhaps for the Porta Ruga, the local gate, which stands at the end of the main street of the old town.

The family seems to have obtained its patent of nobility for services to Belluno, rather than from the ownership of large estates, or from any exceptional service to a sovereign. It participated in the town's defense and contributed to its buildings and fortifications. The family spread over the province, earning renown in distant places as lawyers, army officers, or prelates. The De Rudio physicians were especially celebrated. "God protect you from the prognostications of De Rudio," quipped one wit. In time, their venerable patent of nobility was confirmed by Venice, Udine and even by the Austrian throne. Their coat of arms was a panel of gold land silver, traversed by a red band with three silver roses.[3]

Over the years, the De Rudios returned to Belluno. They

continued to be a respected family, with no great financial resources to encourage pretensions. They were known for their fierce tempers. A forebear is said to have shot a knife sharpener with a harquebus for making too much noise. Another relative died in Russia, with Napoleon's twenty-seven thousand Italian contingents. Yet another served as prefect in Venetia during the Consulate and First Empire.[4] In the latter half of the 18th Century, the prefect, Ercole De Rudio, built a summer home a mile outside of Belluno, filling it with French furniture. This soon became a permanent family residence. His son, Ercole Placido De Rudio, embellished the otherwise modest structure with a singularly inappropriate cupola and double rows of columns surrounding the portico, giving it a simulated Palladian appearance. The garden was salvaged from the grounds of a nearby church that had been recently demolished.[5]

In 1825, Ercole Placido De Rudio married Elisabetta de Danini, the daughter of the Austrian military commandant in Belluno. There is a hint of scandal in the union, the suspicion being that Elisabetta conceived the first child, Achille, out of wedlock and was forced into hasty marriage arrangements. Among other reasons, this was a source of lasting discord between the two families.[6]

But apart from the dispute, the fortunes of the De Rudio family were already in decline. Ercole Placido de Rudio seems to have done little to earn a living, content to spend his life in patrician idleness. Although he had some training as a lawyer, he did not practice the legal profession. This, his son attributes to the consequences of Ercole's publicly proclaimed hostility to Austrian rule, all the more singular, since his brother-in-law was town commandant. Ecole, in the De Rudio tradition, was not a man to conceal his feelings. A violent anti-Papist, he once publicly smashed a bust of Pope Pious IX with his walking stick.[7]

The first credible challenge to the Matternich order came in 1830. Louis Philippe of Orleans succeeded in displacing the Bourbon Charles X in a rather tepid popular uprising, but elsewhere in central Europe and northern Italy the insurrections were easily put down.

Austria was an immense empire extending from Transylvania to Switzerland, from Cracow to Dalmatia. The diversity of languages, religions and nationalities, as well as the slowness of early 19th Century communication, multiplied the difficulties of administration. Yet, there were features that helped to cohere, among them, the remarkable centralization of the government. Another was the dreaded certainty that the Austrian Double Eagle was never reluctant to use force.

Such was the state of affairs when on August 26, 1832 Carlo Camillo De Rudio was born in Belluno, in the province of Venetia.

Carlo appears to have been the third of seven children, although the records of the first born, Achille, are somewhat uncertain.

The boyhood of Carlo was as buoyant as could be imagined for the son and heir of a patrician family. From childhood on, he was inseparably attached to his older brother, Achille, and to his younger brother, Guistiniano. They swam in the Ardo River and roamed the brooding and mystic mountains. Men doffed their hats to them. Carlo received his schooling from Father Bastiano Barozzi, a fiery liberal and patriotic priest of patrician Venetian family, whose politics were very much to the count's liking. Even so, the boy's education was not extensive nor was he much inclined to study.[7]

Carlo had a swarthy complexion, for which he was given the nickname "blackie" (*il Moretto*). He also had his father's temper. Family tradition recalls a fight with a youngster who had insulted his pretty sister, Luigia.

Carlo spent many hours in the company of his uncle, Fortunado Domini, the commandant of the garrison of Belluno. The colonel was determined to rid his nephew of the rebellious sentiments, which had been instilled in him by his father and the priest. When Colonel Domini was transferred to Palmanova, near Trieste, Carlo was taken along to cleanse his brain.[8]

The Cadet

On returning home, the effort was unrewarded Carlo again came under the sway of the patriotic and revolutionary fervor of Fr. Bastiano.

While Europe stagnated under Austrian rule in the late 1830's, nationalism was stirring among the European intellectuals and held out to the poor an instrument for redressing their many grievances.

With armed resistance of no avail, dissent found expression in secret societies, one of which, the Carbonari, pioneered the revolutionary underground movement.[9] It was dedicated, among its many and sometimes inconsistent tenets, to the overthrow of Austrian rule. At its height, the organization had fifty thousand members. Absolute secrecy was a requirement, assassination and murder its instruments. Traitors and informers were accorded special treatment.[10] Once indoctrinated, the member could never be free of his obligations. Their feared flag was red, blue, and black. Membership ranged from cutthroats to a few cultured aristocrats of liberal persuasion. They plotted assassinations and insurrections across dirty tablecloths and even attracted foreign support. Lord Byron is said to have aided the Carbonari, by hiding weapons in his apartment.[11]

Members of the Carbonari especially delighted to follow the adventures of Louis Napoleon, nephew of the late Emperor, who was thought to have joined this secret society.[12] He made no effort to refute the impression that his early plots to destabilize the French government were aided by the Carbonari.[13] One such plot was the sophomoric attempt to suborn the garrison of Strasbourg. He was seized and, but for the astute bribery by his mother, would have lingered in prison. Following another unsuccessful attempt in Boulogne, Louis Napoleon was sentenced to life imprisonment. After six years in the fortress of Ham, he escaped and was soon back at work, plotting behind closed shutters.[14]

Colonel Domini succeeded in obtaining appointments for Achille and Carlo to the Military Academy of St. Luca in Milan. Graduation would lead to a commission in the Austrian Army and quasi-respectability for the offspring of an impoverished and rebellious father. An heir seldom abandons the family hearth, but in Carlo's case, there was no appreciable estate to detain him in Belluno. And so, the brothers arrived in Milan in 1845.

Nothing in Belluno had prepared them for the loathing they encountered from the Milanese.[15] For three years they lived in a city under foreign occupation. They witnessed the abuses of drunken soldiers, felt the anger of the Milanese at having to yield the sidewalks to the military; sensed their fury at seeing their women insulted or abused; at having to wait months or years for a response to a petition or application; at being compelled to fund the extravagances of Vienna. One fourth of all Austrian revenue came from Lombardy-Venetia.[16] Since Lombard taxes paid for the upkeep of the garrison, the Milanese boycotted the heavily taxed tobacco. All to no avail. With glee, the Austrian officers blew cigar smoke in their faces.[17]

Similar revolutionary fervor had long been smoldering all throughout Europe, mounting with each fresh incident of repression, until at last the fury burst upon the distainful and ill-prepared authorities. The Revolution of 1848 had arrived!

Matternich fled for his life from the mobs of Vienna. Led by Kossuth, Hungary cast off Austrian authority. In Naples, Ferdinand II (King Bomba) of Naples-Sicily was compelled to grant a constitution. In Paris, after a bloody street war in which no fewer than ten thousand citizens had been killed or wounded, Louis Philippe and his umbrella were expelled, and the Second Republic came into being.

For Louis Napoleon, the disorders offered a unique opportunity. He quickly journeyed to Paris and threw himself into the political maelstrom. Favored with his imperial name and with no complicity in the blood bath of June, he enlisted diverse support in a bid for the Presidency and was elected by a five to one margin.[18] Once in office, Louis Napoleon lost no time in solidifying his position with popular measures. By entrusting the clergy with public education, he obtained the critical aid of the Church.

The Cadet

Nowhere in Europe was clamor for change greater than in Milan, where countless dissatisfactions had driven the people to a violent mutiny. Stationed within the city were four Austrian brigades, under the aged Fieldmarshal Count Radetzky.[19] Cut off from supplies, he ordered his troops to fall back to the walls and the castle. After first shelling the densely populated working district. The rebels responded by constructing hundreds of barricades to trap the retreating troops.[20] Men, women and children fell on the soldiers with whatever weapons or tools were at hand, hurling rocks, boiling water and bottles.[21]

On March 21, 1848 the insurgents surrounded the Military Academy of San Luca and demanded surrender. Under the terms of a truce, those cadets who desired to return home were allowed to depart in peace. The brothers chose to remain with the Austrian Army. Their further stay in Milan was brief. Following four days of fighting, Fieldmarshal Radetzky and his thirteen thousand troops were driven from the city.[22]

Northern Italy promptly joined the struggle against the Hapsburgs. In Venice, the Republic of St. Mark was proclaimed. Charles Albert, King of Piedmont Savoy, an implacable foe of Austria, now entered the war with his disciplined army. Uncertain of the outcome in Milan, he waited until the fighting had resolved before taking the initiative.[23] In Rome, news of the Milanese uprising was received with unabashed joy. Pope Pius IX, who recently had been elevated to the throne of St. Peter amid great republican expectations, mobilized the Papal army to take to the field against the Austrians.

Radetzky desperately strove to maintain discipline in a dispirited army, strung out for fifteen miles in torrential rain.[24] Armed with muskets, Carlo and Achille followed the retreating Austrians. Soon the boys were horrified witnesses to the conduct of troops in forced withdrawal. On leaving Milan through the Porta Roma, they saw a soldier bayonet a Lombard woman and her infant.[25] Carlo leveled his musket at the killer, but his brother checked him. Acts of rapine, pillage and murder were repeated.

Women were burned alive and thrown down wells. Many of these acts of cruelty were ascribed to Croat troops, who, according to De Rudio, were especially detested.[26]

Since reinforcements from Austria were not expected until the opening of the alpine passes in the spring, Radetzky sought a position which could be easily defended. He chose a region in the north Italian plain called the Quadrilateral, thirty miles on the broadest side. On each border was a large fortress, offering a stronghold to prevent entry into the Quadrilateral by a pursuing army.[27]

When the boys reached Brescia, twenty miles to the east of Milan, they found their uncle in command of the city. The cruelty of the Austrian troops in Brescia again shocked them. When their uncle questioned them about their loyalty, they made clear their contempt for the conduct of his soldiers. The colonel railed at their reply, but chose not to discipline them.[28]

At Castelnuova, a hundred miles east of Milan, barricades thrown up by the townspeople halted the Austrian advance. After destroying the obstacles, the army ravaged the city. Again, acts of violence and cruelty were repeated. The boys witnessed the shooting of a girl, who was fleeing a burning house. This monstrous cruelty helped shape their decision.[29]

When the army finally reached Verona, ten miles to the east, Radetzky set about to reorganize his troops. The two cadets were offered commissions in the Austrian Army and their choice of regiments. Without hesitation, they rejected the offer. The command predictably took offense, and, without their uncle to protect them, the brothers were arrested as renegades and sent off to Gratz, Austria. There, they were held at the military college.

While the boys passed the weeks in custody, great armies were on the march. No fewer than four took to the field against the Austrians. The largest was the forty-five thousand soldiers of Charles Albert of Piedmont-Savoy, which approached the Quadrilateral from the west. The House of Savoy had ruled the Kingdom of Piedmont Sardinia for eight centuries.[30] Their army was of respectful size, consuming almost three quarters of the kingdom's revenue, although the kingdom was not wealthy, nor its agriculture extensive.[31] Charles Albert was widely regarded as the most liberal monarch of Europe, but his reputation was based more on perception than on fact. He had, however, voluntarily granted a constitution.

From the south, three smaller armies moved to engage Radetzky: The Papal Army; the Bolognese Free Corps Provisional Army; and the Neapolitan Army, led by Ferdinand II of Naples (King Bomba). The common goal shared by the leaders of all four armies was their determination to prevent further Austrian expansion into the Italian peninsula.

Pope Pious IX had begun his papacy amid great liberal acclaim.[32] As time passed, the anti-clerical elocutions of the Republicans disturbed him, and he began to fear the prospects of an insurgent victory. As a result, he ordered the Papal troops to be withdrawn from the campaign.[33] This was sufficient reason for King Bomba to recall the Neapolitan army. Left in the field to support the Piedmontese was the Bolognese Free Corps Provisional, a volunteer army with little formal training.

At Vincenza, forty miles west of Verona, the Bolognese Army bravely attempted to prevent the second Austrian Army from joining Radetzky, but the Austrian troops bypassed the town and a union was achieved. Radetzky now had seventy thousand troops to face the Piedmontese. A hesitant and timid Charles Albert chose to invest Austrian fortifications, rather than engage the enemy on open ground. On July 24, 1848, while the Piedmontese were besieging Mantua, Radetzky penetrated the Piedmont line[34] and defeated Charles Albert at Custozza, compelling him to sue for an armistice.[35] Radetzky was happy to oblige, since troops were urgently needed to quell the disturbances in Vienna and Hungary. A detachment of Austrian soldiers reentered Milan and quickly subdued the uprising.

Venice continued to hold out against the Austrians. A third Austrian Army fell on the city and prepared to lay siege.

Meanwhile, in Gratz, the two cadets were released from their detention. The Austrian Minister of War, acceding to family appeals, had given permission for the cadets to return home. They should have gone back to Belluno, but, instead, chose to offer their services to Venice.

Venice was not an easy city to invest or to capture. But food was its Achilles heel. Although Venice, ever since the attack by Genoa in 1380, had maintained an agricultural presence on the mainland to guarantee its food supply, the northern plain was difficult to defend.[36] The gateway to the fertile tableland of Venetia was Vincenza, eighty miles to the west, and its easy capture by the Austrians in 1848 sealed the fate of the Venetian bread basket.[37]

From the sea, the Austrian Navy began a close blockade of the city, but small Venetian vessels managed to slip through. On land, the Austrian Army could now be brought up to the littoral. The city retained a vital railroad bridge to the mainland and also occupied the fortress of Marghera, a *tete du pont,* two miles inland. These outposts spared the city from long-range bombardment, even when the enemy buried the cascabel end of their canon in the sand for maximum trajectory. Bombing with hot air balloons, likewise, was ineffective.

Carlo and Achille reached Venice from the north, after a long journey on foot. They were overjoyed to see their mentor, Fr. Barozzi, now a chaplain in a student battalion. They sought out Fortunato Calvi, a family confident and admirer of Luigia De Rudio, a man whose portrait Carlo would hang on the walls of his home until the day he died.

Colonel Calvi, a Venetian, had been a regular officer in the Austrian Army, stationed in Vienna. Heeding the call for the liberation of Italy, he formed an army of five hundred irregulars and for six months fought the Austrian Army in the upper valley of the Piave River, known as the Cadore, until they ran out of ammunition. He then hurried to the defense of Venice.

Calvi now commanded a force of four thousand volunteers, many of whom had served with him in the Alps and on Lake Garda. The boys promptly enlisted in Calvi's legion.[38] Sadly, Achille is said to have died of Cholera shortly after the boys

The Cadet

arrived in Venice. (There is a strong suggestion that Achille may have died in Belluno from wounds sustained in the storming of the military academy, and that, for the sake of his narrative, Carlo preferred to have his beloved brother remembered for a role in the defense of Venice.)[39]

In view of his cadet's training, De Rudio was made a sergeant and assigned to lunette #13, one of the earthwork defenses outside of the main fortification of Malghera. This was no meaningless appointment. As long as Venetian troops held Malghera, the city would be safe from bombardment.

The youth was soon to demonstrate his mettle in a sortie on Mestre on the October 27. Mestre was a town two miles to the north of Malghera, sitting astride the road to Padua. According to available information, the town was lightly held, since swamp fever had caused many Austrian troops to be withdrawn.

The plan called for a frontal attack on Mestre by two thousand Free Corps Provisional troops, led by Felice Orsini, who had been in command of lunette #12.[40] Sergeant De Rudio served in Orsini's column. A second column would cross the two and a half mile railway bridge onto the Padua road and attack Mestre from the south. Another detachment of riflemen in gondolas would negotiate the shallow inlets south of the bridge and cut the Padua road even further to the south, to block the aproach of Austrian reinforcements.

Felice Orsini was born to a revolutionary father and educated as a lawyer. Imprisoned for sedition by the Papal government, the vigorous and handsome patriot was pardoned by Pope Pious IX, soon after his election to the Papal throne. At the outbreak of the revolution of 1848, Orsini joined the Free Corps Provisional and soon distinguished himself as a brave and capable leader, rising to the rank of captain. Following the defeat of the Piedmont army, Orsini and his Free Corps soldiers rushed to Venice to continue the fight.

The attack began in early dawn with the marshland covered by mist. Orsini's column set off in waist-deep water. It soon came upon a fortified redan, blocking the way. Enemy artillery fire commenced, wounding fifteen Venetians with grapeshot. The column pushed forward, when it became apparent that the enemy artillery could not depress its angle of fire. Using bayonets, the Venetians drove off the artillerymen and captured the cannon. After drying their muskets, the soldiers proceeded to Mestre, where they captured the post office, without loss of life. Orsini then led his men over an eighteen foot wall into the citadel. A fierce engagement ensued, in which four hundred of Orsini's men were killed or wounded. In the end, the citadel was taken, and six hundred prisoners and several fine bronze cannon captured.[41] Suddenly a messenger arrived, with word of the approaching Austrian army. The Venetian troops quickly withdrew, without gaining an inch of territory.

De Rudio returned to his duties in lunette #13, having experienced his first taste of battle. He did not bask for long in his new found glory. As battery sergeant, he had been ordered to withhold fire, because of the severe shortage of artillery ammunition. An enemy barrage erupted, wounding one of his sentries, whose screams filled the lunette. This was too much for the sixteen-year-old warrior. He grabbed the flintlock lanyard from the gunner and fired the cannon. The other guns followed suit.

The young sergeant was put on report and ordered to appear before Colonel Calvi, charged with a breech of discipline. Because of his youth and inexperience, he was let off with a warning.

While Venice struggled to maintain its defenses, Rome was immersed in turmoil. The Pope's decision to withdraw the Papal Army had proven calamitously unpopular, and the Pontiff quickly lost the public esteem he had once enjoyed in abundance. In an effort to placate public opinion, Pious IX embarked on an ambitious program of conciliation, but these acts came too late to quiet mounting public outrage. In the end, the Pope was compelled to flee Rome in disguise and seek asylum with King Ferdinand II of Naples in the frontier fortress of Gaeta.[42]

The Cadet 13

A republican junta was promptly set up and a Roman Republic proclaimed. From Gaeta, the Pope issued an appeal to the Christian powers for help to restore him to the throne of St. Peter.[43] Appeals for assistance also went out from the Roman republicans. Venice dispatched to Rome her unneeded troops. A call went out to the Bolognese Free Corps, fighting in the north. Garibaldi was summoned from the Lake region, where he had been campaigning since his arrival from South America. Charles Albert, who alone had an intact army, was in no position to help. He had imprudently suffered a second defeat at Novara at the hands of the Austrians and had been compelled to abdicate in favor of his son, Victor Emanuel II.[44]

Who would lead the Republic of Rome? Mazzini, the scholarly republican standard-bearer, was the popular choice. The son of a distinguished professor of anatomy at the University of Genoa, he had studied for a career in the law. Mazzini had early joined the Carbonari, but finding that organization too burdened with local issues, he founded *Young Italy,* Giovine Italia, devoted to revolutionary nationalism. Their flag was red, white and green, as was the Masons. The excessive flummery of the Carbonari was simplified. Italians would achieve liberation of Italy; foreign help was not required. As with the Carbonari, assassination was a legitimate tool to expel the oppressor. Early in his career, Mazzini had asked the King of Piedmont-Savoy to lead the battle, but anti-monarchy sentiments had since overtaken him.[45] In 1837 Mazzini had been forced to flee to London, but he continued to lead the *Young Italy* movement from exile. He devised many simplistic plots, many of them futile, with scant benefit to the cause. Following the declaration of the Republic of Rome, Mazzini hastened to the city, which he saw for the first time and was promptly elected to a triumvirate, in charge of city affairs.[46]

Back in Venice, the noose tightened, as thirty thousand Austrian soldiers and sixteen ships surrounded the city. Word reached Venice of the second defeat of the Piedmontese Army at Novara[47] and plunged the populace into deep gloom. A typhoid epidemic swept the inhabitants, killing four thousand people. Food became scarce, and rumors were rampant. Finally, Malghera was captured and the arches of the railway bridge blown up. The Austrian artillery could now be brought up and the bombardment begun.[48]

The city was in a panic. Distraught mobs gathered in the Piazza San Marco. The Minister of War, Giovanni Cavedalis, ordered Colonel Calvi to clear the square. Sergeant De Rudio was given a detachment of soldiers and ordered to disburse the crowd, by whatever means were necessary. When the mob saw the soldiers, commanded by a sergeant in an Austrian uniform with white cape and plumbed shako,[49] they feared the worst. De Rudio tried to reassure the crowd that he was there, not to shoot them, but to protect them from the order of Cavedalis![50]

This *gaffe* promptly reached the ears of the authorities, and the sergeant was again sent for. This time his family connections could not save him. Calvi informed him that Minister Cavedalis had demanded that the beardless sergeant be punished for his intemperate remarks.

In vain, De Rudio tried to explain. Colonel Calvi had already decided that De Rudio had to leave Venice. As a friend of the family, and of Luigia De Rudio, in particular, he may have been looking for an excuse to send him out of the city. With one hundred thirty thousand mouths to feed, he told him, Venice has more need of bread than of soldiers. Rome needs him more! He ordered De Rudio to Chioggia, an island in the southern lagoon, fifteen miles to the south.[51] From there, small coastal boats would take him through the Austrian blockade to Ravenna. Calvi gave the young soldier a letter to a friendly official, who would help him find passage. With great sadness, De Rudio bade farewell to the doomed city, destined to succumb at the end of summer.

By the time De Rudio reached Chioggia, a bench warrant for his arrest, signed by Cavedalis, had preceded him. De Rudio was promptly clapped into a prison overflowing with deserters, but so lax were the guards, that he had little difficulty in escaping. He

The Cadet 15

made for the beach, and boarded a vessel, carrying soldiers bound for Rome.

In Ravenna, his uniform got him arrested, this time as an Austrian deserter. While arrangements were being made to return him to Venice, De Rudio swapped his uniform for peasant clothing and slipped out of the city.[52] He set out for Rome, easily eluding the Austrian troops in the Venetia district. The long journey southward and across the Apennines was tiresome but uneventful. At the end of April 1849, he spied the dome of St. Peter in the distance.[53]

In the five months since Pious IX's departure, Mazzini had been firmly entrenched as a virtual dictator and had been showering the city with flowery proclamations.

Louis Napoleon followed the Roman scene with keen interest. Anxious to gain the support of the French Catholics before the forthcoming elections for the Chamber of Deputies, Louis Napoleon resolved to restore Papal rule by whatever force was necessary.

The French Army embarked in Marseilles on April 22, 1849 for a two day passage to Civita Vecchia, forty miles north of Rome.[54] It was allowed to disembark upon assurances from General Nicholas Oudinot that its purpose was to protect Rome from the Austrians.[55] Mazzini was puzzled by its arrival, but had no reason to doubt the intentions of Louis Napoleon, who, after all, was said to be a close confederate of the Carbonari. Little did Mazzini suspect how indifferent Louis Napoleon was to Italian interests.

The defense of Rome was entrusted to Giuseppe Garibaldi. He had arrived in Rome on April 27 at the head of his legionaries, which by this time had swollen to over one thousand. This redoubtable leader had been born in Nice to a seafaring family, and sailed as mate or master until his thirty-first birthday. He spoke Ligurian and French, with Italian, Spanish and German as acquired languages. Initiated into the *Young Italy*, he also a member of the Saint Simonian socialists and the Freemasons. For twelve years he had fought in Brazil,

Uruguay and Argentina, first as a sea captain and after 1843, as a general in the defense of Montevideo, where he had formed his famed red shirt legion.[56] The shirt, in fact, was a red smock, reaching halfway down to the knee.[57] It had been ordered for the workers in the slaughterhouses of Buenos Aires and had been awaiting export when Garibaldi seized the shipment.[58] If nothing else, Garibaldi was resourceful. He once transported a ship fifty miles overland with two hundred oxen, then launched it to attack a city.[59] He returned to Italy in 1848 with sixty-three legionaries, fought a guerilla war in the north, and learned that he had been elected a deputy in the Roman Government.[60]

Garibaldi saw immediately the danger of attempting to defend Rome from behind its walls. The city had eighteen miles of fortifications,[61] which could be attacked at any point. To withstand thirty thousand well-armed French, Garibaldi had but thirteen thousand badly armed irregulars.[62] Sound tactics require the defenders to occupy strong points outside the city and engage the enemy on his approach. Garibaldi proposed this, but the triumvirate demurred. Our army is too weak, they protested. Instead, the city would defend its walls, as did Rome of old.

Garibaldi pondered the direction of the enemy approach. To attack from the east, the attacking army would have to penetrate the city through narrow streets and bloody barricades, causing irreparable damage to many important historical structures.[63]

More likely, the attack would come from the west, which lay closer to Civita Vecchia, the port of French debarkation. The western city was enclosed by the Papal Wall of Urban VIII, which ran from the Tiber River in the north, around the Vatican and alongside the indigent Transtevere section to the Tiber River in the south. Inside the walls and parallel to it was a narrow elevation called the Mount Janiculum, considered to be an excellent position for the placement of Roman artillery. Outside the walls was a hill, which overlooked and dominated the Papal wall and the road approaching the city. Of the two lare manor houses built on the hill, the Villa Corsini, "the house of four winds," was the more strategically placed.

Oudinot ordered a surprise march on Rome. Although he had no reason to doubt the French intentions, Mazzini took no chances. As the French Army approached the walls, fully expecting to march unmolested through the gates into the city, the Roman Army opened fire. Belatedly, Oudinot found that the gate through which his troops were supposed to enter had been sealed up for centuries! Without scaling ladders or cannon, he was compelled to retire with sizable losses. Garibaldi wanted to pursue the enemy and drive him into the sea, but was restrained by Mazzini, who attributed the French attack to an error in communication. He had been informed that a French truce envoy was already on his way to Rome.

Upon De Rudio's arrival in Rome, the young warrior was taken into the Garibaldi legion and saw immediate action on April 30, in the battle outside the Papal walls, which had sent Oudinot into retreat.[64]

General Oudinot now adopted another ruse. He applied for, and received, a fifteen day armistice, ostensibly to arrange an amicable settlement. Meanwhile, he awaited the arrival of French reinforcements. To further disguise his intentions, Oudinot sent an absurd message to the Austrians, warning them to stay away from Rome.

Word reached the city of the approach of Ferdinand II's Neapolitan Army from the south. Garibaldi's legion was immediately dispatched to halt their advance, but nominal command was given to a Roman, lest the world believe that Rome had to saved by a foreigner.[65] De Rudio went along with Garibaldi's troops, in a detachment of youngsters, some of whom were no more than twelve to fourteen years of age.[66]

At Valettri, twenty-five miles southeast from Rome, Garibaldi's forces were initially repulsed by the Neapolitan cavalry. Planting himself in the middle of the road to block the retreat of the Roman cavalry, Garibaldi was knocked to the ground. Heedless of the thundering hooves, the company of youngsters ran up and dragged him to the roadside.[67] Fortunately, his injuries were not serious. Inspired by the bravery of their leader, the Roman lancers rallied and drove the enemy back to Naples.

That evening Garibaldi visited the boys in their bivouac to thank them for their provident rescue. De Rudio had the opportunity of seeing his hero at close hand, as he circulated among the youngsters and joked with them.

At the end of May, General Oudinot notified the Roman government that he was about to terminate the armistice. On June 3, *prior* to the date of termination, Oudinot began his attack. Foreseeing that the Villa Corsini, on the hill overlooking the walls, was the key to the assault, he attacked the villa and caught the defenders asleep.[68] Oudinot immediately strengthened his position and brought up artillery.

Garibaldi quickly realized the gravity of the situation. Only the prompt recapture of the villa could save the city. He assembled his forces at the Porta San Pancrazio, the gate in the Papal wall, a quarter mile from the Villa Corsini, and ordered them to retake the Villa. This meant moving uphill across an open field, over a high wall, through an exposed garden, up a long driveway flanked by high hedges and finally up the stairs of the Villa, while under constant fusillade from sharpshooters and cannon.[69]

The fighting went on for seventeen hours. The Roman cannon continued to fire at the Villa, at times endangering their own troops. Time and again, mounted on his white horse with enemy fire grazing his bullet-ridden poncho, Garibaldi ordered his men forward.[70] A few Roman soldiers reached the garden, some the steps. The Villa was even captured but retaken by the French within the hour. The carnage was frightful. Garibaldi's troops sustained five hundred casualties, a twenty percent loss of men.[71]

De Rudio was in the thick of action. At one point, he came upon a French Officer hidden in a water closet. The officer promptly surrendered his sword. De Rudio was ordered to take him to the prisoners' holding area across the Tiber. While they were crossing the Ponte Sisto Bridge, some National Guard

The Cadet

militiamen attempted to kill the officer and throw his body into the river. De Rudio protected him, until a non-com appeared and restored order.[72]

After surrendering his prisoner, De Rudio started back to the Porta San Pancrazio, against the torrent of wounded on their way to the field hospital. The battle was still raging when he reached his unit. Bayonet charges had repeatedly failed. De Rudio's squad was ordered to capture a small villa, outside the gate. No sooner had they done this, than the enemy counterattacked and forced the Romans to withdraw through a breech in the garden wall. Four of the twelve men with De Rudio were killed. The brave youth hugged the ground, his clothing splattered with the brains of an enemy soldier who lay beside him.[73]

As dusk approached, the Garibaldi forces were driven back to the Porta San Pancrazio. The fighting, which had been raging since daybreak, now drew to a close, with the flower of Roman youth fallen on the field.

Oudinot elected not to invest Rome, since his army was insufficient to surround eighteen miles of wall. Instead, he massed his troops in the west and deployed cavalry to cut off supplies to the city.[74] Cannon, positioned alongside the Villa Corsini, shelled the city day and night.

In the days that followed De Rudio saw many celebrated patriots whom he would later recall, none more remarkable than the courageous Anita Garibaldi. Pregnant with her fifth child, she had joined Garibaldi in Rome on June 26, over his objections. In late June, the red shirts were delivered to the Garibaldi Legion and red was much in evidence on the streets.[75] The young soldier wore his shirt proudly.

After a month of siege, Oudinot began his final offensive on July 1, the commencement of a religious holiday for Saints Peter and Paul, celebrated for centuries with firework displays.[76]

The attack began with a cannonade on Garibaldi's headquarters, following which the French troops attacked the west wall, quickly overcoming the defenses on the Janiculum. Fighting spread to the streets of Transtevere, where quarter was denied the defenders.

By nightfall, the enemy had penetrated into the city. De Rudio stumbled in the dark and fell to the ground. Before he could get to his feet, he was surrounded by enemy bayonets and brought to a prisoner holding ground in the courtyard of St. Paul. Roman soldiers huddled dejectedly on the pavé, worn out from their exertions.

The young warrior had no intention of remaining a French captive. Armed with a knife that he had concealed in his clothing, he attacked a sentinel and fled through a breech in the wall. Before he could get away, a flash of lightning illuminated his red shirt. The French pounced on him and dragged him back to the holding area. There, a prisoner pointed him out, as the soldier who had killed the guard.

A drumhead court martial was quickly convened, and a French officer was assigned to defend the prisoner. Something about the defiant youngster aroused his pity, and he pleaded his case with great conviction. He emphasized that De Rudio had not given his parole as a prisoner of war and convinced the court that every prisoner has a duty to escape, by whatever means at hand.

The court martial spared the life of the sixteen year old, but ordered him jailed, pending further sentence. He remained in prison throughout the closing days of the siege of Rome, while his fate was being decided.[77]

On July 2 the National Assembly capitulated. That evening Garibaldi assembled four thousand men in St. Peter's Square[78] and, with Anita at his side, addressed them:

> "To those who wish to follow me, this what I have to offer: hunger, cold, the heat of the sun; no wages, no barracks, no ammunition but continual skirmishes, forced marches and bayonet fights. Those who love your country and love glory, follow me!"[79]

His appeal spread swiftly through the city and reached the

prison, enkindling a forlorn young captive who was awaiting his fate. Garibaldi left Rome with his two thousand man legion, most on foot, and with one small cannon. No sooner had they crossed the city limits, than the men began to desert. As the days passed without tents, food or supplies, his legion shrank. Oudinot was a harsh conqueror. Those who served the Republic were sent to prison or given life sentences in the galleys.[80] Even the physicians who cared for the wounded were punished. De Rudio prepared for the worst. The death of the French soldier would not soon be forgotten.

The young captive was marched off with three hundred other prisoners to Civita Vecchia, an ominous destination, since it meant transport to France, where he could look forward to spending years, if not his lifetime, as a convict in Toulon. Along the way, De Rudio nonchalantly ducked behind a bush, as if responding to a call of nature. The guards failed to notice him, and the line of prisoners kept moving. Miraculously, De Rudio managed to slip away. He found food in a shepherd's hut and reluctantly exchanged his red shirt for peasant's clothes. Then he set out to join Garibaldi.[81]

Garibaldi was well along the way to Venice, with his sadly depleted legion. As the days passed, popular support vanished, and his army slowly dissolved. Fever claimed the life of his beloved wife, the legendary Anita, near Ravenna. Venice was in its agonal moments, the city surrounded by an impenetrable ring of Austrian soldiers. In despair, Garibaldi released his handful of loyal followers and made his way to Genoa in Piedmont Savoy.[82] When informed of his arrival, Victor Emanuel II promptly made known that his presence was unwelcome. Off Garibaldi went in exile to the United States, to become a chandler on Staten Island in New York. Mazzini returned to London to plan further exploits, and the Pope returned to Rome, amid pomp and ceremony.

In August, a few days before De Rudio seventeenth birthday, Venice fell. He halted his journey.

Notes

1. Dana Faracaras and Michael Paul, *Venetia and the Dalomites* (London: Cardogan, 1999), pp. 44-49.
2. Cecil J. S. Sprigge, *The Development of Modern Italy* (New Haven: Yale University Press, 1944), p. 23; Michael St. John Packe, *The Bombs of Orsini* (London: Secker and Warburg, 1957), p. 4.
3. Cesare Marino, *Dal Piave al Little Bighorn* (Belluno: Tarantola, 1996), pp. 352, 253 n. 1, 2.
4. *Ibid.*, p. 353 n. 2.
5. *Ibid.*, p. 355 n. 4
6. *Ibid.*, p. 36, 356 n. 7.
7. Cesare Crespi, *Per la Liberta!* (San Francisco: Canessa Printing, 1913), p. 9.
8. *Ibid.*, p. 10.
9. Edward Elton Hales, *Mazzini and the Secret Societies* (New York: Kennedy, 1956), p. 40.
10. *Ibid.*, p. 61.
11. Herman Viola and Susan P. Viola, *Guiseppe Garibaldi,* (New York: Chelsea, 1988), p. 30.
12. William Bolitho, *Twelve against the Gods. The Story of Adventure* (New York: Readers Club, 1929), p. 14.
13. Frederick Arthur Simpson, *The Rise of Louis Napoleon* (London: Cass, 1968), p. 362.
14. Bolitho, pp. 289-294.
15. Crespi, p. 14.
16. Packe, p. 8.
17. *Ibid.*, p. 66.
18. G. P. Gooch, *The Second Empire* (Westport, CT: Greenwood Press, 1960), p. 101.
19. Packe, p. 68.
20. Crespi, p. 15.
21. Bolton King, *A History of Italian Unity 1814-1871. Vol. I* (London: Nesbet, 1934), p. 218; Edyth Hinkley, *Mazzini. The Story of a Great Italian* (Port Washington, NY and London: Kennekat: 1924), p. 95.
22. Crespi, p. 16.
23. Packe, p. 69.
24. King, p. 227.
25, Crespi, p. 17.
26. Marino, p. 37.
27. Packe, p. 69.
28. Crespi, p. 18.
29. *Ibid.*, p. 19.

30. Packe, p.3.
31. *Ibid.*, p. 8.
32. Viola and Viola, p. 48.
33. Packe, p. 74.
34. Hinkley, p. 106.
36. William Roscoe Thayer, *A Short History of Venice* (Boston and New York: Houghton Mifflin, 1908), p. 159.
37. King, p. 230, 252.
38. Crespi, p. 20.
39. Marino, p. 361 n. 23.
40. Packe, p. 84.
41. *Ibid.*, p. 88.
42. Jasper Ridley, *Garibaldi* (New York: Vicking Press, 1974), p. 265.
43. Packe, p. 93.
44. *Ibid.*, p. 94.
45. Hinkley, p. 35.
46. Dennis Mack Smith, *Mazzini* (New Haven and London: Yale University Press, 1994), p. 64.
47. Ridley, p. 273.
48. King, p. 342.
49. Packe, p. 81.
50. Crespi, p. 81.
51. Thayer, p. 151.
52. Crespi, p. 23.
53. *Ibid.*, p. 24.
54. Viola and Viola, p. 52.
55. Ridley, p. 273; Smith, *Mazzini,* p. 69.
56. Ridley, p. 215.
57. Christopher Hibbert, *Garibaldi and His Enemies* (Boston and Toronto: Little Brown and Co., 1965), p. 82.
58. Christopher Herbert, *Rome. The Biography of a City* (New York and London: Norton, 1985), p. 256.
59. Viola and Viola, p. 39.
60. *Ibid.*, p. 51.
61. Ridley, p. 288.
62. King, p. 337.
63. Hibbert, p. 70.
64. Crespi, p. 28.
65. Herbert, p. 258.
66. Ridley, p. 265.
67. Hibbert, p. 65.
68. Herbert, p. 261.
69. Packe, p. 107; Hibbert, p. 70
70. Viola and Viola, p. 55.
71. Packe, p. 107.
72. Crespi, p. 29.
73. *Ibid.*, p. 30.
74. Smith, *Mazzini,* p. 72.
75. Ridley, p. 303.

76. Hibbert, p. 89.
77. Crespi, p. 32.
78. Hibbert, p. 97.
79. Herbert, p. 261.
80. Hinkley, p. 130.
81. Crespi, p. 32.
82. Viola and Viola, pp. 59-64.

II
THE CONSPIRATOR

With the fall of the three great Italian cities, the revolution of 1848 had come to an inglorious end. But the struggle for Italian independence continued. Soldiers were transformed into conspirators and absorbed into a culture of plots, counterplots, intrigue and intramural strife. Thus began for De Rudio fifteen years of wandering, which, in the end, would leave him in poverty and despair.

De Rudio followed in Garibaldi's footsteps to Genoa, a city overrun with ten thousand political refugees. They crowded the twisted alleys and thronged the crowded cafes, gossiping, plotting and spreading rumors, under the intolerant eyes of the police. But even a conspirator must support himself, and employment was scarce.

Count Ercole de Rudio evidently had some access to the local authorities. He wrote to the commandant of the Ligurian District and, in consequence, De Rudio was offered a commission of Second Lieutenant in the plumbed mountain troops of Piedmont Savoy. From a professional standpoint, this was an excellent opportunity for an unsettled Italian youngster, even more so, perhaps, than an appointment in the Austrian Army. But the Piedmontese Army was not popular with the republican fraternity, especially after the surrender of Charles Albert at Novara; and the mountain troops were especially disliked. Genoa, *La Superba,* had hitherto been a free city that had come under Piedmont rule some thirty-four years before, with little say in the matter. And so, for the second time, the young man rejected the offer of a commission.

To support himself, De Rudio found work as a laborer.[1] One day, a riot broke out in the city cemetery, well attended by the insurgents. The mountain troops were summoned, and before order could be restored, they had taken many mourners into custody.

For De Rudio, these arrests were the final indignity. He resolved to quit that accursed kingdom, which did so little to advance the cause of Italian unity. Like Garibaldi and many other Northern Italians before him, he boarded a vessel and set out for America with only a few coins in his pocket. Among his fellow passengers was a young man named Trolli, "the cardinal," who shared his political sentiments. Trolli had prepared for an ecclesiastic career, but the events of 1848 transformed him into an insurgent.

Fate was at the helm. While still in the Mediterranean, the ship encountered a savage storm and was forced to put into Carthegena, Spain. The two took this detour as an omen. They decided to abandon their voyage to America and see what France had to offer.

Although an inveterate foe of the Papacy, De Rudio had no misgivings about living off the benefices of the clergy, as he and his campanion passed through Alicante, Valencia and Barcelona before crossing the French border. They came to a tavern filled with French soldiers, who were being sent to Algeria. One of the officers recognized De Rudio. He was the officer De Rudio had captured in the outhouse and whom he had later protected on the Ponte Sisto in Rome. The officer welcomed and feted the two and allowed them to follow his regiment to Marseilles.[2]

They reached Marseilles in the spring of 1851 and sought out a *Young Italy* chapter. Marseilles had the largest organized Mazzini society beyond the borders of Italy. In fact, it was here that Mazzini had founded *Young Italy* two decades earlier. Membership in other secret organizations was not exclusionary, and there was a strong bond among the members of the various societies.[3] The two young men fell in with the activities of a lodge known as the *Circle of Heaven* and were, in turn, helped by the members, who could be relied on to assist newcomers.

A month after their arrival, the police swooped down on a chapter meeting. De Rudio and Trolli were arrested as subversives. When questioned, they claimed to have come from England.

Foreigners were routinely expelled for any suspicion of seditious activity. De Rudio and Trolli were unceremoniously herded into a closed railroad car and sent off to Calais, for a trip across the channel. But they had other plans. At Dijon, they escaped from the train, eluded the police controls and made their way to Paris, arriving in June 1851.[4]

They found inexpensive lodging in a hatter's home in the suburbs of St. Antoine, where they lived frugally. A fellow Mazzinian directed them to a Jacobin lodge in Batignolle in northwest Paris, whose forty members were engaged in making paper cartridges or cartouches.

By now, Louis Napoleon had been President for three years, slowly acquiring control of the machinery of government, while he prepared to restore the monarchy. Through his appointments, he now dominated the army, the police and the civil government and had sufficient means to frustrate any potential Paris commune.

At the end of November 1851, the Prince-President readied his *coup d'etat*. He ordered the presses seized, prominent leaders imprisoned and the drums of the populist National Guard smashed, so they could not sound the alarm.[5] A final bag of gold was handed to the army leaders as a *douceur* for the soldiers.[6]

On the night of December 1, Louis Napoleon distributed his proclamations.[7] The next day, the anniversary of Austerlitz, he shut down the unpopular Assembly and arrested potential troublemakers.[8]

As soon as the *coup* became evident, barricades were thrown up. The initial response came, not from the public,[9] but from the secret societies, which alone could quickly summon their membership. Lord Byron described a barricade that was erected in a half hour with building stones, iron rails, planks, three overturned omnibuses and two upset cabs.[10] Some barricades reached to the second story,[11] an effective obstacle to any military movement. Barricades appeared in the winding streets between Hotel de Ville and the boulevards. The streets, at that time, were still narrow. A year later, General Haussmann would begin to replace them with eighty-five miles of wide avenues and boulevards.[12]

On December 2, while on their way to a Jacobin meeting, the two youths saw police and soldiers in the Bastille plaza. The police had surrounded the lodge and were arresting members. De Rudio and Trolli quickly alerted the arriving dissidents, and, together with sixteen Frenchmen, they built a barricade. So well was it constructed, that it held off a battalion of Vincennes *Chasseurs* that tried to assail it.[13]

The next day, more barricades went up, as Victor Hugo desperately tried to rally the public. Hugo had been a supporter of the Bourbon legitimists, Louis XVIII and Charles X, then the Orleanists, Louis Philippe, and, after the coup of 1851, had become a republican.[14] Resistance throughout the city was ineffective. No more than twelve hundred insurgents could be summoned, to face sixty thousand well-armed soldiers.[15]

On the third day "the massacre of the Boulevards" occurred.[16] By now, the barricades were manned, some by as many as a hundred men.[17] The most effective were along the Boulevard des Italiens and in the north of the city.

In the Boulevard des Italiens and the Place Madeleine, orders to fire on the bystanders without prior warning were given.[18] Martial law customarily requires that the senior officer first call to the people to disperse. Instead, artillery and infantry blazed away down crowded streets.[19] Barricades were blown apart. Dozens of corpses lay on the pavement. The soldiers gave no quarter. Every man who held a rifle or had blackened hands was summarily shot.[20] In Paris alone, three hundred people died, twenty-seven thousand were arrested.[21] Soon prison facilities in

France were exhausted, and nine thousand people were deported to Algeria.[22] Even there, the numbers could not be accommodated. French Guyana was hastily opened for convict settlement, and two hundred forty were sent off to populate the jungles.[23]

De Rudio and Trolli remained at their barricade until the fourth day, when defeat was painfully evident. Martial law was in force. To walk in pairs was to invite death. Bodies were strewn along the street. One grizzly scene appalled them - a water seller whose head had been blown open, with brains and lemon slices scattered over the street.[24]

French public opinion supported, not opposed, the overthrow of the Assembly. Three weeks after the coup, they voted in overwhelming numbers in a plebiscite for the new constitution, extending the length of the presidency to ten years and assigning to it many legislative powers. Thus began a series of enabling legislation, which were to culminate next year in the crowning of Louis Napoleon. He took the name of Napoleon III, since the Emperor's son, Napoleon II, had died in Vienna while serving as a colonel in the Austrian Army.

Paris had become too dangerous for the young conspirators. They hurriedly set out for Switzerland. A drunken farmer gave them a ride out of the city in his wagon. When the farmer fell asleep, the two drove the wagon, until the horse would go no further.

From a friendly innkeeper, they learned the name of the local postmaster, who was a member of a Jacobin society. They called on him with a letter of introduction, but he was not at home. Knowing nothing of her husband's clandestine activities, his wife presumed he was having an affair. She demanded to see the letter, but the two refused to hand it over. That evening, she came to their room in the inn, accompanied by two policemen, who had written orders to seize the letter. De Rudio threw it into the fire. When the policemen started to arrest him, De Rudio pointed out that their orders were to seize the letter and not the bearer. The policemen left to seek further instructions.[25]

By the time the two arrived in Switzerland, they were penniless. Unable to afford lodging, they found shelter under a fruit stand in the market. One night, a policeman stumbled over Trolli's outstretched legs. Trolli was taken into custody and promptly expelled, under the provisions of the vagabond law.

This left De Rudio wandering aimlessly about. Nights, he slept in a barrel; daytime, he ate raw turnips and smoked straw in his pipe.[26]

In Lucern, an agent tried to recruit him for service in the Papal Army. Out of whimsy or spite, the young man went along with the illegal recruitment and signed a contract *en fraud*, with no intention of serving. Instead, he notified the authorities and had the agent arrested.

Without papers, friends or money, De Rudio realized that it was only a matter of time before he, too, would run afoul of the law. He decided to leave Switzerland of his own accord. Foolishly, he set out during a snowstorm in a grueling and dangerous trek through the Alps. Trudging grimly on foot through the treacherous St. Gothard's Pass, he was at last greeted by the balmy winds of Italy.

At Varese, the weary adventurer found refuge for a few weeks in the home of Trolli,[27] while the Austrians patrolled the streets, challanging strangers. After recovering his strength, De Rudio left in April 1852 for Turin, now the home of Father Bastiano Barozzi. The priest had returned to his parish after the capitulation of Venice, but was compelled to leave quickly, to avoid arrest by the Austrian police. He had shaved his beard, donned civilian clothes and, after much travail, joined Fortunato Calvi in Turin. Calvi had been living in an attic, subsisting on a small stipend given him by the Venetian government. Dinner for him was a pennyworth of bread and fruit.[28]

De Rudio found Don Bastiano in a coffee house. The priest welcomed his former pupil and took him to see the colonel. Calvi's reception was surprisingly hostile. Quickly, the reason emerged. Rumors had been circulating that after leaving Venice, De Rudio had defected to the Austrians. The colonel had even been given the name of an informant, who claimed to have seen De Rudio shoot his own countrymen.[29] Such accusations were common in a conspiratorial society, where rumors and lies never ceased to fester.

De Rudio vehemently denied the story and provided the names of several people who were able to refute the charges. Within twenty-four hours, the young man was vindicated and welcomed back into the ranks.

Word reached them of Mazzini's arrival in Switzerland, from where he had twice been expelled.[30] He took up residence in a quiet street in Lugano, far removed from the turmoil of northern Italy. There, in one of the idyllic pastel-tinted homes surrounding the deep blue lake, he set up his headquarters. With money from the sale of bonds at his disposal, Mazzini could now revive the insurgency. He let it be known that he had an infallible plan to awaken Italy and summon the people to the cause. A revolutionary council of war was convened in Locarno, Switzerland and the ambitious plan lay before it. Colonel Calvi would be in charge of the mission. The attack would take place in Milan on Shrove Tuesday in February.[31] This would be an even vaster uprising than the one in 1848.

De Rudio was assigned the task of gathering information about the Imperial troops in Lombardy. A bogus passport was given him, listing his occupation as a silk merchant. A simple code was arranged: the number of bolts of cloth would represent the number of regiments and various colors assigned for infantry, cavalry and artillery. He was instructed to conceal the information in his pipe tobacco.[32]

His mission took him to all the principle cities of northern Italy, encompassing a distance of several hundred miles. At Mantua, he was cordially greeted by an officer of the garrison, whom he had known at the military academy in Milan. De Rudio explained that he was on the way to Belluno to see his father. His friend did not question him, nor did they talk politics.[33]

In Verona, De Rudio took lodging in an inn, *The Shield of France*, which adjoined another inn, *The Queen of England*. His third-floor room faced the courtyard and stable. Below his window, the roof of an adjacent structure sloped down to the center of the courtyard.

As the young spy was writing his report, a voice outside the door cried, "Open in the name of the law!"

De Rudio ran to the parapet and dropped down onto the adjacent roof, just as the police entered the room. He managed to hide under the eaves until the police left, then jumped onto a pile of reeking manure. He escaped through the kitchen of *The Queen of England*, leaving the cook aghast.

In Milan, he took lodging in a pensione. When darkness came, he and another lodger, an upholsterer went around in the rain, hanging up posters. Suddenly, he saw several policemen running after his friend. De Rudio threw away the placards and bolted down the street. He climbed up a tree to hide in the leafy branches, but lost his footing and fell, striking his head. Fortunate for him, the rain had softened the ground, so that after regaining consciousness, he could resume his journey. At the Ticino River, a patrol blocked the bridge, compelling him to ford the swollen river. Only by a near miracle did he avert being swept away. By the time he reached Turin, he was thoroughly exhausted.[34]

As day of the insurrection approached, De Rudio was entrusted with the delivery of the final plans to the conspirators in Milan. Arriving by train at midnight, he positioned himself under the clock in the square and was approached by a man emerging from the shadows. The appropriate signals were exchanged, and De Rudio handed over the vital papers.

The plan called for the insurgents to subdue the hundred soldiers asleep in the great castle of Francesco Sforza and seize their weapons. They would then break into the arsenal and distribute the rifles to the rebels waiting in the streets, who would take control of the city. A Republic would be proclaimed.[35]

The date chosen was February 6, 1853, carnival time for the public and payday for the military. The signal would be a light in the cathedral tower. Mazzini assured everyone that the insurrection would have public support. If Milan could hold out for a few days, he insisted, all Italy would be theirs. But a diversion was needed to cloak the attack. Lake Maggiore had been chosen.

De Rudio was ordered to collect four thousand gold lire in Genoa, then proceed to Locarno, Switzerland, on the northern tip of Lake Maggiore and deliver the money to two conspirators, Antonio Sandri and Enrico Radonich, who would give him further instructions.

The young man carried out his assignment without incident. After handing over the money, he was astonished to learn that the Austrian police almost certainly knew about the plot, obtaining the information from some recent arrests. Sandri and Radonich both felt that the attack should be postponed.

The plan was hazardous, if nothing else.[36] It involved the seizure of the steamboat *Radetzsky* that plied Lake Maggiori with a detachment of soldiers onboard. The soldiers usually left their rifles on deck, with a sentry to guard them, before going below. De Rudio and the other two were to board the ship, overpower the sentry, lock the soldiers in the hold, and turn the vessel over to the waiting rebels. Then, with the ship flying the Austrian flag, the vessel would range alongside an Austrian garrison and open fire.[37]

De Rudio traveled to Intra, Italy, on the west bank of Lake Maggiore, to reconnoiter. While seated in an inn, he heard a lookout shout, "Police!" De Rudio leaped through a window, climbed over a garden wall and rushed to the lake, hotly pursued by several policemen. He saw a rowboat on the pier and flung himself into it. Brandishing a handgun, he ordered the two oarsmen to take him to Locarno, twenty miles to the north.

Off they went, leaving the police on the landing. During the night, a fearful storm arose and De Rudio had to man the third set of oars. A squall of sleet battered the boat, compelling the occupants to pull to shore. De Rudio paid off the boatmen and added a generous tip.[38]

He rejoined Calvi and the other two conspirators in Locarno. Calvi reported glumly that the Austrians had, indeed, been alerted and that the mission had to be called off. When De Rudio insisted that the money be returned to him, so that he could deliver it to Mazzini, Radonich refused, arguing that De Rudio's responsibility ended when he was given a receipt. The young man was incensed. With a nod from Calvi, De Rudio locked the door and threatened to hold the two until the money was returned. Reluctantly, they surrendered the four thousand gold lire.

De Rudio hastened to Lugano in Switzerland, where, for the first time, he met the legendary Mazzini.[39] A tall man with high forehead and pale cheeks, he habitually dressed in black, in mourning for his country.[40] De Rudio surrendered the money, which Mazzini casually put in a drawer without troubling to count it.

Mazzini listened patiently to the report of the discouraging events at Lake Maggiore, before reminding his young follower that their primary objective was Milan, not Lake Maggiore. Meanwhile, Mazzini had already prepared an alternate diversion. It had to be carried out quickly, since February 6 was fast approaching. He had chosen the town of Varese, Italy, ten miles south of Lugano, Switzerland. Its garrison was small and its citizens patriotic. All that remained, Mazzini added, was to find the right man for the job. De Rudio promptly volunteered.[41] He was available for any campaign, however difficult, dangerous or uncertain!

That night De Rudio left for Italy, in the company of two smugglers, the Burrasca brothers, who were known for their bravery and devotion to the cause. The party came to an inn straddling the border, a regular stop for the smugglers. While they were seated at a table drinking *grappa*, a messenger from Mazzini arrived. As he read the letter, De Rudio's face turned ashen. The insurrection in Milan had collapsed! Varese was aborted![42]

De Rudio rushed back to Lugano to learn the unhappy

details.[43] On February 6, while the soldiers in Milan were sleeping off their carousing, the insurgents forced an entry into the castle. Instead of holding the citadel, as they were ordered to do, they rushed into the streets and killed several officials. Outraged, the citizens helped the police apprehend the conspirators, while the students looked on with indifference. From first to last, the attack had been a fiasco and a stain on Mazzini's reputation. Worst of all, the authorities had known of the plot and had taken counter measures. Betrayal was a recurrent problem for the conspirators. So numerous were the informers, that the police often lacked the money to pay them all.

Quickly, the long talons of the Austrian Double Eagle reached into Switzerland. De Rudio was arrested by the Swiss police and brought before a Federal Delegate. An order for his expulsion was issued, and he was given the choice of Britain or the United States. He chose Britain, to be near Mazzini.[44]

De Rudio was deported to London in April 1853 and cast penniless into a turbulent city with unfamiliar language and customs. He took up lodging in the modest inn of a Mr. Tressoldi, a generous Milanese.

Mazzini arrived the same month but in somewhat different financial circumstances. He lived on an annuity from his mother of one hundred eighty pounds/annum and a small legacy from an aunt,[45] settling into a six room apartment in the Chelsea district. In England, he had formed a *Friends of Italy* Society with eight hundred members. He corresponded regularly with many prominent people in the literary world, including Thackeray, Dickens and Robert Browning. Karl Marx was less impressed with him. He refers to Mazzini as "licking the arse of the English liberal bourgeoisie."[46] Mazzini established the National Italian Committee, to enlist the aid of prominent Englishmen. He also promoted the sale of the National Loan bonds, issued in the amount of ten million lire or forty thousand pounds, which went to fuel the insurgency. The bonds were to be redeemed after the successful outcome of the revolution. In Italy, reception for these bonds had been less than enthusiastic. Not only was their redemption uncertain, but the subscriber also risked being executed, should his purchase become known to the Austrian authorities.[47] Nine subscribers had been hanged in a pit in Belfiore.[48] As a consequence, funding for the insurgency was heavily dependant on the meager contributions from sympathetic donors.

De Rudio found work as a gardener for an exiled author named Luigi Pianciani[49] and settled down to the dull life of a poor expatriate. He began the study of the English language, doubly difficult for someone immersed in an exile society. At the time, there were forty Italian revolutionaries living in the city,[50] all of whom were known to one another. De Rudio also got to meet some of the other exiled nationalists. On one occasion, Mazzini gave him a letter to deliver to Louis Kossuth, the famous Hungarian patriot. Mazzini was a tireless letter writer, who, in his lifetime, wrote two million letters.[51] Kossuth was living near Regent Circus, in rather high style. Outside his house were carriages and servants dressed in livery. While waiting in the antechamber, De Rudio inspected the pictures on the walls. They were of Kossuth as a simple citizen; Kossuth in hunting dress; Kossuth the general - only Kossuth.

Presently, Kossuth himself appeared. He read the letter and wrote his response. The messenger was dismissed without a word of thanks. The great man had failed to impress him, and doubtless vice versa.

The day arrived when Mazzini sent for De Rudio to give him his long-awaited orders. The forthcoming campaign would be in the Alps, he explained. Not a battle but guerilla warfare! Mazzini was certain that if the rebels could hold out two to three months, all Italy would come to their support!

Curiously, the young man was told nothing of the details. Instead, he was handed a bogus passport and sent that very evening to the continent.

After a brief mail drop in Brussels, De Rudio went on to Zurich, where, in the second half of August, he delivered written instructions to Colonel Calvi.[52] Calvi was promised two thousand francs to launch the attack and additional funds afterward to safeguard the gains.

The young conspirator was astonished when the plan was revealed to him. Their objective was Belluno! The town would be taken by the same insurgents who had fought with Calvi in the upper Piave Valley, known as the Cadere in 1848.

The attack would be launched at three points. First to be taken would be the Finance Office, near the old church of St. Stephen, where only three men and a corporal would be on duty. Next, the police station would be captured. The insurgents would stage a fake scuffle outside the building, and when the door was opened, they would rush in and overpower the sleeping policemen. Lastly, the insurgents would take the army garrison. A line of marksmen would pick off the soldiers as they emerged from the building. They would then enter the barracks up a ramp and subdue the rest of the garrison.

But Belluno was just the beginning! After securing the town, the rebels would seize horses and wagons, and, disguised in Austrian uniforms, they would march on the fortress of Osoppo, a hundred miles to the east. Osoppo would give them control the Alps. By spring, all Italy will have risen up in support!

Letters outlining the plan had been sent to Luigia De Rudio, who acted as intermediary for Ercole De Rudio and Don Bastiano, both committed to the project. The priest had returned from exile in Turin, thanks to a new amnesty. Father Barozzi alone knew the location of weapons hidden in 1848 in the Cadore. The mission's success now depended on obtaining those weapons.

De Rudio left Zurich for Belluno, delivering letters along the way. At the Italian border, he again met the Burrasca brothers, who took him to Trent, where he was given another passport.

The smugglers offered to guide him through the mountains, but De Rudio chose to set out alone. The long seventy mile trek through the Dalmatians led along lonely and precipitous roads, many of them obstructed by landslides. One careless step in the dark and the affairs of tomorrow would be of no concern. De

Rudio was overjoyed at the prospect of seeing his family again, after an absence of five long years. But he was also fearful. Should he fail, his family would be the first to suffer. But failure was inconceivable! Conspirators are irrepressible gamblers.

At nightfall, he came to the Ardo River and there, spread out before him, was his cherished Belluno. Home! It began to rain, making the river unfordable. He had to risk crossing over the bridge.

He climbed the one hundred twenty steps of the Via le Scalette leading up into the town, shielding his face with an umbrella. Close to St. Stephan church, he saw a light shinning in the home of Don Bastiano and threw a pebble at the window.

Don Bastiano welcomed him effusively and immediately sent word to his father. As De Rudio began to explain his mission, the priest cut him off. Luigia De Rudio had already written Calvi. The plan had been betrayed! The police were forewarned and at this very moment were looking for De Rudio![53]

Ercole De Rudio wept for joy when he saw his son. He, too, pleaded with Carlo to abandon the project. It had no chance of success.

Carlo De Rudio realized immediately that he had to send word to Calvi and to do so quickly. He slipped out of the priest's house and found a hiding place in the north end of the town. As he lay under an old chestnut tree, planning his next move, he heard three familiar whistles.

It was his brother, Guistiniano. With him was his mother, who dissolved into tears when she saw her son. They brought the shocking news that Count De Rudio and Father Bastiano had just been arrested!

De Rudio was devastated! Since the priest alone knew where the arms were buried, Mazzini's plan was useless. De Rudio insisted that his mother return home, so that she would not be seen in his company. After a hurried and heart-wrenching parting, he heard her soft footsteps fade into the distance, little realizing that this would be the last time he would ever see her.

His brother led him to a hut high up on a mountain, the home of a mountaineer and his wife. There, De Rudio hid for several days, awaiting word from Calvi. Meanwhile, the situation in Belluno had grown even more desperate. Luigia, too, had been arrested, and there was an order out for De Rudio's capture - *dead or alive!*

With the authorities closing in, the young patriot had no choice but to leave, whatever the risk. He resolved to set out at daybreak. Meanwhile, he dare not remain longer with the old couple. That evening, he moved to a nearby cave, known to him from boyhood. No sooner had he settled in, when a patrol of soldiers came to the hut. They handcuffed the mountaineer and tied him to a chair, then demanded to be told the whereabouts of De Rudio. When the old man refused to answer, they put a noose around his neck and strung him up over a beam.

"Talk, or I'll hang you like a sausage!" the sergeant snarled.

The mountaineer's face grew livid and his tongue protruded, but he remained silent. They let him fall to the floor, and then hoisted him up again. Neither he nor his wife would speak. Disgusted, the soldiers left, convinced that the old pair knew nothing.[54]

De Rudio waited until they had gone, then hastened to thank the old couple for their loyalty. The thought of abandoning his family grieved him, and he could only hope that his father and sister would be released, once the authorities found no trace of him in Belluno. He cast his last look at his beloved town, then began the long journey back over the remote roads. The first evening in the mountains, De Rudio heard shots, and saw soldiers bayoneting a man lying on the ground that they took to be De Rudio. As it turned out, he was a smuggler who had tried to evade capture. Later, the body was brought to Belluno, and De Rudio's mother was summoned to identify it. She was brought into a large, cold room, where the covered body lay on a table. The sheet was lifted and the Countess raised her veil.

"No, this is not my son," she said quietly.

De Rudio trudged for days up and down the mountain roads,

each step taking him farther away from the town and people he loved. Mountaineers gave him food. He arrived at night in Bolzano, in the midst of its annual fair. The town was filled with festivity. Few took notice of a weary stranger in the streets.

At the local inn, he sat down to a meal at a table near the entrance. Beside the door, a notice had been posted under the Double Eagle. He saw the name of CARLO CAMILLO DE RUDIO written in large letters, and beneath it, a reward of six thousand lire for his capture - *dead or alive!*[55]

He heard people talking in *Ladin* and saw the two burly smugglers from the Trevis Valley. They immediately recognized De Rudio, but made no effort to speak to him.

A few minutes later the police entered the tavern. One of them asked to see De Rudio's passport. When he handed it over, the policeman studied it suspiciously. "I don't understand Italian," he snapped. "You'll have to come to the station."

The smugglers sprang into action. They grabbed the two policemen and knocked them to the floor.

"Beat it!" they told De Rudio.

De Rudio rushed out of the inn, with the police in hot pursuit. He ran to the square and crawled under the steps of a house, while the police combed the streets and alleys.

At first dawn, De Rudio heard voices and the rattle of dishes. As he crawled out of his hiding place, the inhabitants emerged from the house and demanded an explanation. He told them he was a livestock merchant from Switzerland, who had arrived too late to find a room.

"You're no merchant," they scoffed. "You're a deserter!" De Rudio offered no argument. The owner brought him inside and fed him, then helped him make his way to Switzerland.

Colonel Calvi was not as fortunate. Luigia's warning had failed to reach him. No sooner had Calvi crossed the border, than he and three other conspirators were arrested. On his person, the Austrians found incriminating letters.

A woman, whose home in Zurich was a meeting place for the conspirators, betrayed the colonel. In return for a lavish reward, she had furnished the Austrian police with the details of the Belluno plot.

Calvi was brought in chains to the moated fortress of St. George in Mantua, where he joined Count Ercole and Luigia. Two years later, Felice Orsini would also be sent there for a different offense.

Calvi was tried and sentenced to be hanged. Until the end, he was a source of comfort to Count De Rudio, Luigia and the other prisoners. As he was led to the gallows, he smiled at his captors, many of whom tipped their hats.

"I am ready," he said quietly.

The executioner misjudged his height. When the trap was sprung, Calvi's feet touched the ground, prolonging his agony. After pronouncement of death, he was thrown into a pit.[56]

The Count and Luigia were held without trial at the prison in Mantua for more than two years, and then released under an amnesty. Orsini had not participated in the Belluno affair, but had been captured in Transylvania in 1855, while planning to spread dissent among the Piedmont troops en route to the Crimean War. He later accomplished the seemingly impossible, escaping the grim fortress by sawing through the double bars of his cell window and lowering himself a hundred feet to the ground by strips of sheeting.

Meanwhile, the Austrian police spread a false report through its network of agents that De Rudio had betrayed Calvi and was allowed to remain at large, only with police forbearance. Planting false stories was a favored ploy for spreading mischief in the exile community. The rumor was swift to take root.

Unaware of his newly acquired notoriety, the young man journeyed to Zurich and sought out Filippo Caronti, a friend of Mazzini.[57] Active in the 1848 Revolution, Caronti had gone into exile in Switzerland. There he had married a rich lady and managed a hat factory, which gave employment to many Italian exiles. Having heard the rumor that De Rudio had betrayed Calvi, Caronti received him coolly, but gave him work, if only to keep him under surveillance. Caronti's other employees were also distant, but De Rudio had no suspicion of the cause.

Quite abruptly, the attitude of his co-workers changed.[58] The workmen became unaccountably friendly and invited De Rudio into their activities. Someone proposed a nighttime excursion on the lake - four oars, four jugs and a few songs to enliven the bitter life of an exile. Scarcely suspecting that he was marked for murder, the young man accepted the invitation. That night, as he entered the factory, he was brusquely told that the trip had been called off. From then on, De Rudio was completely estranged from the others. No one spoke to him, ate with him, or acknowledged his existence. To make matters worse, Caronti wrote to Mazzini, accusing De Rudio of petty theft. Mazzini made no effort to defend De Rudio, although he could have mentioned that De Rudio had not faltered, when entrusted with four thousand gold lire.

All this was bewildering to the young man who suspected nothing. Day after day he worked in complete silence. His life became insufferable. The time came when he could endure no more of his isolation. He decided to leave Zurich and visit Paris once again.

Since his last visit, the Second Republic had been dissolved and the Second Empire installed. The *coup d'etat* of 1852, which De Rudio had witnessed, had been hailed by Frenchmen of many persuasions and blessed by the Vatican. When, the following year, the Senate bestowed the Imperial crown on the Prince-President and his male heirs, France rejoiced. Eight million voted for the Empire, a quarter of a million against it. Louis Napoleon assumed the title of Napoleon III on December 1852, and France moved inexorably toward dictatorship. To insure succession, he married Countess Eugenie de Montijo, a Spanish woman of noble birth but not of royal blood.[59]

De Rudio arrived in Paris in December 1853 with two francs in his pocket and a letter of introduction to Mr. Zappa, a hat maker from Turin, who had previously worked at Caronti's hat factory in Zurich.

Mr. Zappa had a kind heart. He offered De Rudio a place to

stay and a mattress to sleep on. De Rudio found a job near the Bastille, working fourteen hours a day for two francs, turning the wheels of a merry-go-round.[60] Meanwhile, he continued to immerse himself in politics and the machinations of Napoleon III. To the Italian republicans, Napoleon III was the vilest of tyrants. Not only had he caused the deaths of countless Italian youths with his attack on the Roman Republic, but he also continued to thwart all hope of Italian unity by his alliance with King Victor Emanuel II. The king had shown himself to be more interested in aggrandizing his kingdom than in unifying Italy.

Opposition among the French public had been slowly increasing, as time wore on and Napoleon III moved closer toward absolutism. He shocked Prince Albert by disclosing that he rarely discussed important matters with his ministers. His arbitrary conduct of the Crimean War was soon to forebode trouble. Only because his generals refused to obey his orders, did his army escape disaster at Savastopol.

De Rudio conceived a plan to rid the world of this monster. A lone patriot would perform the assassination. He described his scheme in three letters to Mazzini, without receiving a reply. He then wrote to Luigi Pianciani, his former employer. The author discouraged the plan and went on to inform De Rudio that Caronti had publicly accused him of betraying Calvi!

De Rudio was furious at the duplicitous Caronti. Not only had he gained nothing from the Belluno affair, but also it had cost him dearly - the imprisonment of his father, his sister and the beloved Father Barozzi! The good Pianciani sent the young man one hundred fifty francs, so that he could return to Zurich and put the matter to rest.

De Rudio arrived in Zurich in May 1854 and went directly to Caronti's home. He informed the servants that he had an important message for their master and was promptly admitted. De Rudio wasted no time in confronting Caronti with a list of the lies he had been spreading. Faced with an infuriated young man determined to protect his reputation, Caronti quickly retracted his accusations. Professing his affection for De Rudio, he gave him a letter to Count Grillanzoni, the leader of the National Revolutionary Committee, withdrawing all charges.

No sooner had De Rudio left, then Caronti wrote another letter to Grillanzoni, informing him that De Rudio's irascible character and intractable anger were a detriment to the cause!

As De Rudio was leaving Caronti's home, he felt a tap on the shoulder. It was a friend, Angelo Fumagalli. He put a finger to his lips and led De Rudio to the stable, where they could talk without being overheard.

Fumagalli cautioned De Rudio about Caronti's promises. He confirmed that Caronti's employees had earlier planned to murder De Rudio and throw his corpse into the Lake. Fortunately, a cooler head had prevailed.[61]

De Rudio hurried to Lugano to present himself to Grillanzoni. It was well he did so, for Caronti's letter had preceded him. The affair was eventually explained to Grillanzoni's satisfaction, and De Rudio's reputation was restored - for the moment.

Soon word reached the exile community that Mazzini was planning another operation. The plan called for the capture an Austrian steamboat on Lake Como, then an attack near Valtellina, Italy on the Arda River. Orsini was chosen to direct the operation from St. Moritz, Switzerland. The call went out for volunteers.

Fumagalli and De Rudio traveled on foot to St. Moritz in August, arriving tired and disheveled. Orsini grumbled that instead of the two hundred men promised him, all he got was Fumagalli and De Rudio. He sent them to shepherd's hut in the Swiss Alps, where they were joined by eight others. The group spent the long days of summer cleaning and assembling a shipment of rifles. When De Rudio finished the fiftieth rifle, he whimsically scratched his initials on the lock with a screwdriver.

Suddenly, they saw a cloud of dust and the glint of weapons in the distance. A half hour later the Swiss police appeared, forcing them to flee. The rifles were confiscated.

Not until three days later did they learn that the Lake Como plot had been betrayed and that Orsini had narrowly escaped capture by the Swiss police. Austrian authories had made other arrests.

In a nearby inn, several Swiss mountain soldiers who surrounded the bed awakened them. The two were taken into custody and turned over to federal authorities. They pretended to be Austrian deserters, with no knowledge of the confiscated weapons. The commissioner sent for a rifle and pointed to the lock. On it were the initials "C.C.R."[62]

The conspirators were jailed for several long and dreary months, then brought to Berne, where the federal authorities lectured them about the gravity of a second offense and banished them "forever" from Swiss soil. Given their choice of exile, they opted for England, where Mazzinians were still welcome.

The two were provided transport to London, where on arrival they searched for some means to support themselves. These were hard times for exiles in the capital cities. Most of them were penniless and without marketable skills. They marked time, some waiting for the decisive battle in Italy, which would restore them to their rightful place in society. Others waited for an unforeseen opportunity in Britain, which never came. Always, the police followed their every movement, ready to expel them for the slightest infraction of the law.

Through his innkeeper, Mr. Tressoldi, De Rudio met a Milanese choirmaster in Drury Lane, who hired him for the chorus in a company of Italian Opera at five shillings a night. De Rudio enjoyed listening to the prominent singers and retained an interest in the opera throughout his life.

At the end of the opera season, De Rudio looked for another job. His previous employer, Luigi Pianciani, was not available, having left to visit Victor Hugo on the Isle of Jersey. De Rudio found work on the Wapping Docks, making bottle wrappings from rushes. The Industrial Revolution was then in full progress, and the London docks were undergoing enormous expansion, providing employment for unskilled labor.[63] Since travel to work was tiresome, De Rudio was obliged to find closer lodging in

Baldwin Garden at the home of a Mr. Mancherini, who was married to an Englishwoman named Booth. She came from Nottingham and was related to General William Booth, the founder of the Salvation Army.

De Rudio had two friends still living at Tressoldi's, faithful Fumagalli and a husky fellow, named Leoni. In those days, one chose friends carefully. Austria was rumored to have recruited informers from its galley convicts and sent them to live among the exiles.

As time passed, his friends became concerned when De Rudio came less often to the inn. They went to the Mancherini home at Baldwin Garden and found De Rudio engaged in giving Italian lessons to Mancherini's daughter, Sarah, age eighteen, and to Elizabeth "Eliza" Booth, a fourteen year old niece. The blond, blue-eyed Eliza had been sent to London by her father, a framework knitter in Nottingham, to learn the florist craft. Like most girls in her circumstances, she had little formal education.

"We'll soon loose him" they concluded.

Shortly thereafter, De Rudio lost his job, when the bottle factory changed hands. He sold off a few possessions and walked the streets from morning to evening, looking for work. Weeks passed without success.

One night, after returning to his room, he found a package, tied up in an intricate bundle. It contained food. Other bundles appeared on successive nights. Puzzled, he set about to investigate.

In the morning, instead of leaving his room, he hid behind a curtain and waited. Shortly before noon, Eliza entered, carrying a package. When questioned, she insisted that a well-dressed Italian gentleman had handed it to her, but had refused to leave his name. Then Sarah appeared, carrying a vase of roses. De Rudio had once mentioned that the rose was in his family coat-of-arms. They left him to sort out the puzzle.[64]

At long last Luigi Pianciani, his former employer, returned to London. Having lost the manuscript of his famous book, *The Story of the Popes*, he had resolved to rewrite it and had chosen

De Rudio to be his secretary.

With the advance in wages, De Rudio hastened to pay his arrears, but Mrs. Mancherini would not accept the money. She told him that some mysterious foreigner had regularly paid the rent. Only later did he learn that Eliza had paid it, out of money sent her to learn the florist craft.

At the time, the exile community was deeply engrossed in news of the Crimean War, which had broken out in 1844. France and Britain had come to the aid of Turkey, which was once again threatened by Russia. Even Piedmont Savoy had joined in the hostilities, more as a diplomatic gesture than as an active participant. Lacking for soldiers, the British Army had opened its ranks to foreigners living in England. Leoni and Fumagalli had decided to enlist, and they encouraged De Rudio to join them.

Eliza was devastated at the thought of loosing the young man. De Rudio did his best to discourage an attachment. "A conspirator must be solitary!" he insisted; but once she fell into his arms, his resolve melted, and his friends had to leave for the wars without him.

They were married December 9, 1855, in an Anglican parish church in Godalming, Surrey, by the Reverend Edward T. Boyle.[65] De Rudio later wrote that the wedding had been postponed out of respect to Calvi, but Calvi went to his death in July. There is a story rampant that the marriage was necessitated by Eliza's pregnancy.[66] If so, why would they want to delay the wedding? Perhaps De Rudio had second thoughts about the marriage. Or Eliza's parents may have had their own reservations. After all, apart from his obscure title, De Rudio was no great prize as a son-in-law.

The newlyweds gave little thought to settling in Nottingham. For one thing, it had few employment opportunities.[67] Stocking weaving, Nottingham's chief industry, had been devastated by French competition. De Rudio preferred to remain in London. He was a conspirator by profession, and Mazzini held the purse, meager though it was.

The long-awaited news from Mantua finally arrived. After

more than two years of imprisonment, his father and sister had been freed.

The exiles frequented a tavern on Rupert Street, near Haymarket Square. On the night of April 12, 1856 a fight broke out between a friend named Foschini, and a young man who was thought to be a spy. De Rudio tried to intervene, if only to keep away the police. He grabbed a chair to separate the two, but as he raised it, it struck the overhead lamp, and the room was plunged into darkness. He felt sharp chest pain and sunk into an anoxic coma. When he regained consciousness, he found himself in a hospital, with a probable hemo-pneumothorax, where air enters the blood-filled chest cavity. The six knife wounds were most assuredly life threatening, but he managed to survive. Foschini, who had accidentally stabbed him in the dark, went into hiding from the police.[68]

This affair did little to benefit the young man's reputation. Mazzini, who knew of the Caronti affair in Zurich but did not intervene, wrote: "Have you heard of the fracas of Foschini of Lugo? There was a brawl... *Rudio suspected of betraying poor Calvi, rightly or wrongly, I don't know.* But it all contributed to the sad business."[69]

With the police determined to sort out the tavern brawl, De Rudio thought it best to leave England. According to Marino,[70] he signed on as a sailor on a voyage to the Orient in the hope of earning money, but more likely fled to evade the police. Engaging in a public brawl would certainly be sufficient grounds for expulsion, and he now had a wife to consider. The details of the voyage are unknown, but he is said to have been abroad for a year. On his return, he and Eliza lost no time in moving to Nottingham, where his father-in-law helped him find work as a language instructor. A son was born and named Hercules after the boy's grandfather Count Ercole. There was now another heir to the title and another mouth to feed.

De Rudio might have settled down to the life of an exiled language teacher in the hinterlands of England, but for a long-forgotten letter, written five years before.

Notes

1. Cesare Crespi, *Per la Liberta!* (San Francisco: Canessa Printing, 1913), p. 36.
2. *Ibid.*, p. 39.
3. Edward Elton Hales, *Mazzini and the Secret Societies* (New York: Kennedy, 1956), p. 60.
4. Crespi, p. 40.
5. Thomas Corley, and Anthony Buchanan, *Democratic Despot. A Life of Napoleon III* (London: Barrie & Rocliff, 1923), p. 103.
6. Samuel M. Osgood, *Napoleon III*, (Boston: Heath, 1963), p. 37.
7. Frederick Arthur Simpson, *Napoleon and the Recovery of France* (London: Longmans Green, 1951), p. 130.
8. Roger Price, *The French Second Republic. A Social History,* (Ithaca, NY: Cornell University Press, 1972), p. 285.
9. *Ibid.,* p. 302.
10. Simpson, p. 145.
11. Andre Castelot, *The Turbulent City: Paris,* (New York: Harper & Row, 1962), p. 254.
12. J. M. Chapman, and Brian Chapman, *Life and Times of Baron Haussman* (New York: Brentano, 1920), p. 140.
13. Crespi, p. 42.
14. Rene Sedillot, *An Outline of French History,* (New York: Knopf, 1928), p. 319; Ernest John Knapton, *France,* (New York: Scribner, 1971), p. 401.
15. Castelot, p. 255.
16. Walter Greer, *Napoleon the Third. The Romance of an Emperor* (New York: Brentano, 1920), p. 140.
17. Castelot, p. 254.
18. Corley and Buchanan, p. 107.
19. William Bolitho, *Twelve against the Gods. The Story of Adventure* (New York: Readers Club, 1929), p. 299.
20. Castelot, p. 255.
21. Michael St. John Packe, *The Bombs of Orsini* (London: Secker and Warburg, 1957), p. 253.
22. Castelot, p. 256.
23. Simpson, p. 174.
24. Crespi, p. 47.
25. *Ibid.,* p. 49.
26. *Ibid.,* p. 49.
27. Cesare Marino, *Dal Piave al Little Bighorn* (Belluno: Tarantola, 1996), p. 50.
28. Crespi, p. 53.
29. *Ibid.,* p. 54.
30. Dennis Mack Smith, *Mazzini* (New Haven and London: Yale University Press, 1994), p. 77.

31. Edyth Hinkley, *Mazzini. The Story of a Great Italian* (Port Washington, NY and London: Kennekat: 1924), p. 151.
32. Crespi, p. 55.
33. *Ibid.,* p. 59.
34. *Ibid.,* p. 61.
35. Smith, *Mazzini,* p. 100.
36. Marino, p. 55.
37. Crespi, p. 64.
38. *Ibid.,* p. 68.
39. *Ibid.,* p. 70.
40. Packe, p. 40.
41. Crespi, p. 71.
42. *Ibid.,* p. 75.
43. Once again, the Austrians had been forewarned. Smith, *Mazzini,* p. 101.
44. Crespi, p. 77.
45. Smith, *Mazzini,* p. 95.
46. *Ibid.,* p. 90.
47. *Ibid.,* p. 79.
48. Jasper Ridley, *Garibaldi* (New York: Viking Press, 1974), p. 378.
49. Crespi, p. 77.
50. Smith, *Mazzini,* p. 90.
51. *Ibid.,* p. 82.
52. Crespi, p. 79.
53. *Ibid.,* p. 83.
54. *Ibid.,* p.91.
55. *Ibid.,* p. 95.
56. *Ibid.,* p. 105.
57. *Ibid.,* p. 106.
58. Marino, p. 67.
59. Theo Aronson, *The Fall of the Third Napoleon* (Indianapolis and New York: Bobbs-Merrell, 1970), p. 23.
60. Crespi, p. 107.
61. *Ibid.,* p. 112.
62. *Ibid.,* p. 117.
63. Asa Briggs, *Victorian Cities* (New York and Evanston: Harper and Row, 1963), p. 324.
64. Crespi, p. 128.
65. *Ibid.,* p. 136.
67. Richard Collier, *The General Next to God* (New York: Dutton, 1965), p. 27.
68. Crespi, p. 136.
69. Marino, p. 78.
70. *Ibid.,* p. 70.

III
THE ASSASSINATION ATTEMPT

Following his celebrated escape in February 1855 from the fortress of Mantua, where he had briefly shared a cell with Count Ercole De Rudio, Orsini fled to Britain and settled in Birmingham. His relations with Mazzini faltered, as he became more sympathetic to Victor Emmanuel II, even to the point of applying for a Piedmont passport. It was never issued.

At the end of 1856 Orsini was approached by a Frenchman, Simon Francis Bernard, with a plan to assassinate Napoleon III. Bernard, a physician and an early specialist in speech disorders, had long been active in the anti-Bonaparte movement. He had fought in the barricades of 1848 and later fled France to escape the guillotine. In addition to his training in medicine, Bernard had acquired knowledge of explosives. Like Orsini, he was not on cordial terms with Mazzini. Why Bernard chose Italian accomplices, rather than Frenchmen, for his plot, might be attributed to a belief that the former were more desperate and therefore better suited to a desperate undertaking.

Sometime in September 1857, De Rudio received a chance visit in Nottingham from an Italian exile. When the man passed through Birmingham, he mentioned to Orsini that he had seen De Rudio.

"By God," exclaimed Orsini. "The very man I am looking for!"[1]

Orsini invited De Rudio to London and the two met in the

Great Northern Train Station. Orsini had with him the letter De Rudio had written years ago, proposing the assassination of Louis Napoleon by a solitary killer. It was because of this letter that De Rudio had been selected. De Rudio knew from the beginning about the plot, although his lawyer later maintained that he had not been informed in advance.

This plot would be a multi-national enterprise even more grandiose than anything Mazzini had ever planned. It called for the assassination of Napoleon III, followed by a French uprising, barricades, and the proclamation of a French Republic. Orsini was to be named Commander of the French forces in Italy. A Roman Republic would be reestablished and the Church hierarchy imprisoned. To minimize the risk of detection, the identities of the participants would be known until the last moment, only to Orsini and Bernard.

De Rudio returned to Nottingham and, in the middle of November 1857, received word from Orsini, instructing him to move to London. Obediently, De Rudio and his family took up residence in a small, furnished room on the third floor of a Bateman Street tenement. Since the letter contained no remittance, he had to pawn his best clothes for money to live on. Three days later, a well-dressed gentleman called.

He was Simon Bernard, the dean of French revolutionaries in London. He looked with astonishment at Eliza and the baby, and then asked to speak in private to the young man. In a nearby park, he spoke of a hundred subjects before expressing his surprise and displeasure that De Rudio was married. Neither he nor the committee had been informed of this. Bernard begged leave to report the matter.[2]

The following day, Bernard returned with an announcement that the Committee had accepted the situation. Eliza would be paid fourteen shillings weekly, while De Rudio was abroad, and in case of a misfortune, the money would continue until his son was fourteen years old. De Rudio gratefully accepted the terms.

Bernard detailed the mechanism of the bomb. It would have many percussion caps of fulminate of mercury, so that no matter

The Assassination Attempt 53

how it landed, the bomb would explode. Detonation would be by contact rather than by fuse. It was, in fact, a hand grenade, although called a "bomb" by generations of writers. It weighed three pounds and had a spheroid casing of cast steel the size of an orange, bronzed to dull the reflection. The casing was divided into two halves, held together by a screw. The lower half had several holes, into which nipples were screwed, each one directed toward the powder cavity in the interior.

Mr. Thomas Allsop ordered the bomb casings from the Taylor Foundry in Birmingham. Some say a Baron Torrocfalda designed the bomb; others that Orsini had first seen the bomb in Brussels and had resolved to reproduce it.[3]

By the end of November, six bombs had been prepared. Orsini later reported that he had received only five. No one knows what happened to the sixth bomb. Some accounts relate that only two and a half bombs left England, and the rest were manufactured in Brussels. There are many tedious inconsistencies, so that it is difficult to reconcile all the accounts, which, for the sake of the narrative, is hardly necessary.

Bernard had English conspirators as well. These included T.D.P. Hodge of Glastonbury, a friend of Orsini; Thomas Allsop, a barrister; and George Jacob Holyoake, founder and editor of the *Reasoner, Journal of Free Thought*. There were also French and Italian accomplices, most of whom remain unknown. Allsop ordered the construction of the English bombs, he later denied knowing their purpose. Holyoake is said to have tested the bombs in a quarry.

Unknown to the conspirators, the London Police Commissioner had all three Englishmen and Orsini under surveillance and had forwarded vital information to the Paris Police, who gave it little credence.

Some aspects of the plot made De Rudio uncomfortable. He tried to discuss the matter with Mazzini, but Mazzini would not receive him. Caronti's lies still resonated.[4]

There had been other plots against Napoleon. In the latest attempt in 1857, Paolo Tibaldi and two conspirators tried to capture Napoleon III at the home of Countess Samaria. But the Emperor was too well guarded. Tibaldi was sent to French Guyana, his two accomplices to Algeria.

Preparations for the Orsini plot were completed toward the end of November. On November 28, 1857, Orsini, with beard shaven, left England as "Mr. Allsop," using his friend's passport. He carried with him in a pouch two pounds of fulminate of mercury, wrapped in a damp cloth.

Orsini first went to Brussels, where he remained two weeks. Bernard met him there, and the two inspected the bombs. Some of the casings had been brought over from England by an accomplice,[5] others possibly manufactured in Brussels. Bernard then returned to London, and Orsini left for Paris, arriving December 12, 1857.

In December, De Rudio received a letter from Orsini, directing him to go to Cambdentown to collect a suitcase and a pair of gold glasses. The "gold glasses" turned out to be fulminate of mercury.[6] Orsini had taken with him only half the fulminate, and De Rudio was to bring the remainder.

De Rudio visited the home of Miss Eliza Cheney, an attractive thirty year old intimate of Orsini. He was given a fabric carpetbag on the side of which the figure of a tiger had been embroidered.[7] In the bag was a mahogany container filled with fulminate of mercury.

In London, Simon Bernard called on De Rudio on several occasions and gave him money to redeem his clothes from the pawnbroker. On January 8, Bernard informed De Rudio that Orsini would be waiting for him the next day at the railroad station in Paris, between six and eight in the evening. In the event De Rudio could not arrive on time, he was to go to Orsini's apartment at 10 Rue de Monthabor.

De Rudio was handed fourteen shillings for expenses and a Portuguese passport issued to a Jose Antonin da Sylva, a beer salesman. Bernard promised to meet him in Paris in a few days and reassured him that the money agreed upon would be paid weekly to Eliza.

The Assassination Attempt

No sooner had the ship left the Thames, than it encountered a violent storm, delaying its arrival by twelve hours. By the time De Rudio arrived at the Gare du Nord in Paris, Orsini was long gone. De Rudio had no choice but to go to Orsini's lodging.[8] As he entered the apartment, he saw a stranger with Orsini. De Rudio immediately pretended to be a beer salesman, opening his carpetbag to display his wares. Orsini cut him off with a smile and introduced him to Antonio Gomez, a twenty-nine year old Neapolitan, with thin, reddish-blond hair and the look of a clergyman. He had fought in 1848 and served in the foreign legion. After serving a sentence in Marseilles for theft, he immigrated to England, where Allsop selected him for the plot. According to the arrangements, Gomez was Mr. Allsop's manservant and was lodged in a building close by.

De Rudio withdrew the fulminate of mercury from the false bottom and spread it on the newspaper. Orsini inspected the material.

Another knock on the door and in walked a man of medium height, with grizzled beard and a resonating voice. It was Guiseppe Andrea Pieri, a fifty year old, rough-hewn Tuscan. After serving jail time for theft, he had immigrated to France, married a Frenchwoman and served in the foreign legion. He returned to France and fought in the barricades of 1848, then in Italy as a soldier of fortune. Pieri fled to England in 1852 and settled in Birmingham. It was there he had met Orsini.

Introductions were exchanged, contrary to the original understanding. Since De Rudio had no lodging, it was decided he would stay with Pieri at the Hotel de France et de Champagne on the Rue Montmatre.

That night, Pieri kept De Rudio awake while he recounted his life story. He was separated from his wife and in love with Rosina Hartmann, a German ladies' maid, living in Brussels. The next two days the two went for long walks to pass the time. They collected two revolvers from a Parisian merchant, who had received them by railway express from London; and they bought a third. Pieri had his own revolver, an American model. These four revolvers were supposed to be their "insurance" during the escape.

January 12, the four conspirators reconnoitered the old Opera Square. They strolled along the Rue Lepelletier as if admiring the architecture, while they silently rehearsed the plan of action.[9]

De Rudio and Orsini would be standing in front of the opera, Gomez to the right, Pieri to the left. As soon as the Emperor stepped from the carriage, Gomez would throw the first bomb. If unsuccessful, and the Emperor attempted to flee into the opera, Pieri would throw the second bomb. If the Emperor tried to reenter the carriage, De Rudio would throw the third bomb. If the Emperor escaped along the Rue Lepelletier, eight unnamed patriots would be waiting for him.

Afterwards, the four would meet in the Place de la Concord for further instructions.

They spent the evening at the theater, where they saw a play about the French Revolution, climaxing in the death of a traitor. Orsini was uneasy about Bernard's failure to meet them in Paris, as he had promised.

The next day, January 13, De Rudio and Pieri went for an excursion into the countryside to fortify their spirits. Pieri droned on about his *affaire* in Brussels. De Rudio became attentive when Pieri mentioned that he had told his girlfriend that he was going to Paris to settle old scores, which may cost him his life.

This flagrant breech of security shocked De Rudio! He immediately reported it to Orsini and begged to be allowed to proceed alone. If Orsini could get him a sergeant de ville's uniform, De Rudio would throw the bomb into the carriage and finish the matter. Orsini listened attentively but changed nothing.

Final preparations were completed. Orsini slowly dried the last of the fulminate of mercury at the fireplace, holding a thermometer in one hand and his gold watch in the other. He then loaded the bombs with the fulminate, filling each until two-thirds full. Gomez helped tighten the nipples and screwed together the locking pins on the casing.

Thursday, January 14, the fateful day arrived. Orsini visited

The Assassination Attempt

De Rudio and Pieri at their room in early afternoon and gave them each two hundred francs, to be used for their escape. After he left, Pieri removed his American revolver from its holster and brandished it proudly.[10]

In the evening, they set out for Orsini's apartment. As they arrived, two strange men with upturned collars came out of his residence. This convinced De Rudio that there were others in the plot, unknown to him.

The four conspirators gathered in the apartment for their last meeting. All had their revolvers. The bombs were distributed. Orsini wrapped each bomb in a black handkerchief to keep it from slipping. He put one in both side pockets of his overcoat and gave Gomez, De Rudio and Pieri each a bomb.[11] The bombs given to Gomez and De Rudio were made in Belgium, the others manufactured by the Taylor Foundry.[12] De Rudio later stated that eight additional bombs were kept in reserve by unknown conspirators.[13]

Gomez and Pieri left the apartment separately followed fifteen minutes later by Orsini and De Rudio.

As Orsini and De Rudio made their way on foot toward the Opera, they suddenly saw Pieri coming toward them, accompanied by a stranger. He winked as he passed by. Unknown to them, Pieri had been recognized by the same inspector of the Surete who had arrested him six years before and was now taking him into custody. Not only was Pieri *hors de combat*, he had on his possession a bomb, a revolver and a dagger, without the wit to explain them away.

Perturbed but undaunted, the conspirators continued on the Rue Lepelletier to the crowded Opera Square. A man with a long mustache and upturned collar approached them.

"How are things?" the new arrival murmured.

"Tonight," Orsini replied.

The two shook hands and whispered to one another.

This fateful meeting was of great significance a half century later. De Rudio could see that there was one less bulge in Orsini's coat pockets. When the man left, Orsini asked if De

Rudio knew the man.

"Certainly," De Rudio replied. " He is Francesco Crispi."[14]

Francesco Crispi was a Sicilian and an active republican insurgent. He helped plan the successful 1848 uprising in Sicily, later suppressed by Ferdinand II.

A few minutes later the two conspirators stood before the front of the old Opera on Rue Montpensier.[15] Light blazed from the Broggi restaurant, its entrance flanked by columns. The square was crowded. Along Rue Lepelletier the spectators were chattering expectantly. Hundreds of police struggled to keep the narrow lane open for the royal cortege. Municipal guards lined the street. Gomez stood at his assigned post, tall and straight as a statue. Orsini stood at the entrance with De Rudio nearby.

Presently, the procession approached, led by a carriage carrying the court attendants. The mounted Imperial lancers followed, with their plumed hats and polished breastplates, then the metal state coach of Napoleon III, and behind it, more mounted Imperial guards. The household coach deposited its occupants and the royal coach drew up to the special entrance of the theater.

De Rudio saw the Empress rubbing the steam from the coach window with her handkerchief.[16] As the carriage came alongside the Brozzi Restaurant, De Rudio and Orsini fell to the sidewalk, and Gomez threw his bomb. It landed among the lancers in front of the royal coach. There was a tremendous roar, followed by screams and broken glass. The gaslights of the theater facade went out.[17] Blood gushed from a cut on Orsini's forehead. His black handkerchief lay on the sidewalk.

"Now you!" shouted Orsini.

Rising quickly, De Rudio threw his bomb squarely under the carriage. There was a second flash and a roar. The carriage was hurled in the direction of the theater. A wheel was blown off. Coachmen were lying on the cobblestones, and the horses were dismembered. Around them they heard shrieks, terrified neighs and splintering of glass.

Anxiously, De Rudio waited for the third bomb. Ten seconds

passed. Then a third explosion!

De Rudio felt the earth shake and heard the stampeding of horses. This bomb had exploded beneath the coach.

Spectators were thrown to the ground. The Imperial guard rushed to surround the Imperial carriage, attempting to shield the Emperor. Bullets whistled overhead. The lancers were firing at fleeing horses. Police shot at suspicious shadows. In all, one hundred fifty were wounded, eight died, two of them American bystanders.

Who threw the third bomb? Orsini maintained that it had been thrown by the Italian with the long mustache whom they had met a few minutes before on the Rue Lepelletier. Orsini had been blinded by the first explosion and compelled to set down his own bomb in a doorway.

Napoleon III survived the three explosions, protected by the iron plates of his carriage. Short and solid in build, he emerged from the coach, his hat riddled with holes and his nose bleeding. He offered his hand to the Empress and led her into the Opera to the Imperial box, amid the strains of *Partant pour la Syrie*, the anthem that had replaced the *Marseillaise*. Eugenie sat down, a few drops of blood on her forehead and her white gown stained with blood. Napoleon remained standing, amid the tumultuous acclaim of the audience.[18]

Outside, the police had regained control. De Rudio ducked into a cafe. The proprietress was occupied in conversation with her only customer and took no notice of De Rudio, until he requested pen and paper to write Eliza. After sealing the letter, he asked for a stamp. The cafe owner did not have the usual stamp but gave him four stamps of smaller denomination. After leaving the cafe, De Rudio threw his revolver into the Seine and walked back to his hotel. There was no sign of Pieri.[19]

De Rudio quickly packed his tiger carpetbag and went downstairs. While he waited for his bill to be prepared, some plainclothesmen entered. One of them demanded to see his passport. The policeman examined it and handed it back.

As soon as they left, De Rudio took a taxi to the Orleans

station, promising the driver a handsome tip if they arrived on time. He had chosen a train to Bordeau in the southeast, rather than to Calais, which would be closely watched. The train was scheduled to leave at 11 p.m, the next at 4 a.m. He arrived four minutes late.

De Rudio decided to wait at his hotel for the later train. As he left the station, a mounted detachment galloped up and surrounded the building. The travelers inside were detained for thorough search and questioning.

He walked back to the hotel and was given his old room. No sooner had he undressed, than he heard a voice downstairs, demanding to be taken to the foreigner in room fifty-three.

Quickly, De Rudio unlocked the door and jumped into bed, feigning sleep. The policemen burst in and demanded to see his passport. They studied it, then offered apologies. A half hour later they returned, this time without apologies.[20]

They indicated that his roommate was at the police station. Pieri had informed them that Antonio da Sylva was a friend. Hence, the order for De Rudio's arrest.

The police searched the room thoroughly. They found a revolver holster, but De Rudio denied knowing its purpose. They also found a doctored passport issued to an Andrea Pierney, with the *n* and *ey* altered.

Soon after De Rudio had arrived at the police station, Orsini was brought in, with a bandage wrapped around his head. He had been struck on the right temple by a bomb fragment. The police had learned his address from Gomez, who had been picked up earlier and was now on his way to the police station.

De Rudio was brought into a large room. Behind the desk sat the Prefect of Police. Also present was the Judge of Instruction and Prince Jerome Napoleon, known as "Plon-Plon", a member of the Imperial family. Prince Jerome was a rather levelheaded advisor to his cousin, Napoleon III, whose advice was not always heeded.[21]

The Judge was willing to accept the identity in De Rudio's passport but seemed doubtful when De Rudio said that he scarcely knew Pieri.

De Rudio had a ready explanation. He had met Pieri on the trip to Calais. Pieri had suggested they share a room, since De Rudio had no hotel. Asked about his movements the previous day, De Rudio answered that in the morning Mr. Pieri had taken him to the Louvre, and midday they had eaten in a restaurant on the Rue Montmatre. After the meal, he accompanied Pieri back to the hotel, so that Pieri could meet a friend.

"Who was the gentleman?"

De Rudio explained that he had never met the man. He had discretely left the room and had no knowledge of what they were discussing.

Orsini was brought in. He claimed to be Thomas Allsop, an English barrister. De Rudio denied knowing him.

The Judge questioned Orsini in English.

"What part of England do you come from?"

"From Kent."

"How far is Kent from London?"

"30 leagues"

That did it! In England they use miles, not leagues. And Orsini had mispronounced the "th" in thirty.

"You're as much English as I am a Turk," scoffed the judge, who had an excellent command of English.

Orsini saw that there was little purpose in concealing his identity. Drawing himself up proudly, he told them, "My name is Felice Orsini."

The prefect reached into a drawer and pulled out an Austrian circular. It described the dangerous revolutionary who had escaped from Mantua. "We have a good catch!" he exclaimed and ordered Orsini to be taken to a cell.[22]

Returning to De Rudio, the prefect pointed to two bombs lying on a paper. One had been taken from Pieri at the time of his arrest, the other, abandoned by Orsini at the scene. A passerby had noticed a bomb in the doorway and tapped it inquisitively with his shoe, before bringing it to a policeman's attention.

"Do you recognize these objects?" the Prefect asked.

Feigning ignorance, De Rudio reached over to pick up a bomb, but heavy hands hastily restrained him.

The young man explained that he had been sitting in a cafe when the bombs exploded. A detective was sent to the cafe. He returned, confirming the alibi, even mentioning the detail of the four postage stamps.

The Prefect allowed De Rudio to leave, but instructed him to remain at the hotel as a material witness, at the expense of the state.

Just as he was about to walk out of the station, Gomez was brought in. He had gone into the Restaurant Brozzi, after he had thrown the bomb. A waiter had seen him trying to hide his revolver and had summoned the police.

Carlo looked away, but Gomez blurted out, "We're lost!"

"You know each other?" asked the guard, puzzled.

"Of course!" replied Gomez.

They grabbed De Rudio and brought him back to the Prefect.

"I knew it!" cried the Prefect triumphantly. He ordered the young man brought to the *Conciergerie*, the holding area.

Slowly the events enfolded. Rosina Hartmann, Pieri's *petite amie*, had been persuaded by her employer to inform on her lover to the French minister in Brussels. The minister, in turn, had notified Paris of a probable assassination attempt. When Pieri had gotten off the train, there had already been an order issued for his arrest. It was only by chance that he had not been picked up until the day of the assassination attempt.

The investigation was slowly set into motion. De Rudio was brought to the *Palais de Justice* for formal identification by the owner of his hotel and the concierge of Orsini's apartment. De Rudio acknowledged his name but steadfastly denied a role in the assassination attempt. He insisted that he had visited Orsini solely to talk over old times. Concerning the reason for his false passport, he explained that the Austrian police were searching for him by name. About the assassination attempt, he knew nothing other than what he had been told.

The Assassination Attempt

The young man was taken to *Mazas*, another prison. A secret police agent was assigned to watch him and to prevent any communication between the conspirators. Later, a second agent was added to the watch.

The Judge of Instruction came to the cell, accompanied by a one-eyed street cleaner that seemed exceedingly anxious to accommodate the police. The witness declared that while on duty at the Opera at 7 or 7:15 p.m., an hour before the assassination attempt, he saw De Rudio and Orsini studying the entrance. The time was in error. De Rudio and Orsini were not in the vicinity at that hour. Perhaps, the street cleaner had seen them later but misjudged the time. De Rudio scornfully inquired how much he was being paid for his testimony.[23]

Several days passed. De Rudio was kept from contact with the outside world but was allowed to talk to his guards. He gained their sympathy by describing the hardship and suffering inflicted by the Austrians in his homeland.

The prisoner was brought to the Chancellor's office to hear an interim summary of the accumulated evidence. He was shown letters he had written to Orsini that had been seized by the English police in a raid on the Orsini premises.

The proofs almost completed, De Rudio was transferred back to the *Conciergerie*. His cell measured ten by fifteen feet and was little better than a dungeon. Light came from a small window high up in the wall and from a little peephole in the door. From his guards, he learned that the public was far from hostile, and many thought that his execution was unlikely.

One day, he was brought to a long and narrow room. Seated at a writing desk was the Judge of Instruction and beside him, the Prosecutor. Also present was a small woman, whom he recognized as Eliza Cheney, Orsini's girl friend.

Cheney had agreed to cooperate with the French police in the hope that the life of her lover would be spared. She identified De Rudio as the man who had showed her Orsini's letter and to whom she had given the carpetbag. When De Rudio denied this, Eliza Cheney pointed to Orsini's name faintly visible on the bottom of De Rudio's carpetbag. This irrefutable evidence linked De Rudio to Cheney and to Orsini.

Next, Eliza De Rudio was brought in, accompanied by an English detective. She immediately confirmed her husband's identity. The State's case was now complete and ready for trial. The judge nodded to the prosecutor and gathered his papers.

Eliza was allowed to speak to her husband for ten minutes in the presence of the English detective. Tearfully, she told De Rudio that since he had left, she had received only one pound from Bernard. They spoke in Italian, until the detective objected. When the detective left the room to arrange for an interpreter, De Rudio implored his wife to find some influential people to intercede in his behalf.

De Rudio was brought back to the Judge. Realizing his desperate situation, he suddenly blurted out: " My only regret is in not succeeding! *I threw the second bomb!"*

His admission was duly noted.

By the time he had returned to his cell, the young prisoner was thoroughly despondent. His two guards tried to cheer him up, by wagering a bottle of champagne that he would not be executed.

A defense attorney was finally assigned. He was Mathieu de la Drome, a lawyer of excellent reputation. He insisted that he be given a free hand in presenting the defense and impressed on his client the need for self-control during the trial. Since De Rudio was the youngest of the conspirators, his lawyer would appeal to the jury, by depicting the frightful poverty that drove him to the crime.[24]

Napoleon III had been following the proceedings with great interest. The assassination attempt could not have come at a more opportune time. No obstacle now remained to securing passage of the Law of Public Security, popularly called The Law of Suspects. This authorized the arrest of anyone who, for any reason, disparaged the Emperor. In effect, it was the final legislation required to establish an autocracy.[25]

The trial began February 25, 1855, in the Court of the

The Assassination Attempt

Assises of the Seine in the stuffy courtroom of the ancient *Palais de Justice* and lasted for two days.[26] The Court was packed with spectators. A strict censorship had been imposed on the journalists covering the trial. Newspapers were required to rely on the official transcript, published in the government newspapers. No mention could be made of the early revolutionary activities of Napoleon III. Government authorization was required before a newspaper could go to press. For the first offence, a warning was issued to the publisher. After two warnings, the newspaper could be shut down.[27]

The Court was composed of the President, two associate judges and an alternate judge. The conspirators were duly arraigned.

With great thoroughness, the Imperial Prosecutor outlined the details of the plot, the evidence collected and the defendants' admissions. The material was further summarized by the Presiding Judge, who spared no effort to conceal his hostility toward the four accused, especially in his references to the deaths and casualties in the Opera Square.

Gomez testified first. He had earlier agreed to give evidence for the state. The newspapers describe him as having a feeble voice, with a strong Italian accent.[28] He assigned the blame to Orsini and denied knowledge of the bomb's destructive capabilities.

Next, De Rudio maintained that he did not learn of the details of the plot until after his arrival in Paris. He told the court that he had received three hundred thirty francs for his role in the assassination attempt, but had participated primarily to rehabilitate his name among the exiles. The newspapers noted that the young prisoner substituted verbal harangues for answers to embarrassing questions.[29]

The Presiding Judge pointedly suggested that money was the motive for De Rudio's participation.

Orsini testified freely about the details of the plot, but shielded the identities of the British and French conspirators. According to his supporters, Orsini had originally planned to take full responsibility, but changed his mind when confronted with the cowardice of his accomplices.[30] True or not, he was clearly indifferent to the fate of his young, married colleague, who had fought by his side in Venice, the son of a man with whom he had shared a prison cell.

Orsini steadfastly denied that he had thrown a bomb. He testified that he handed one to an unnamed Italian in the Rue de Pelletier.[31] The judge refused to consider any noble purpose to his acts and called him a vulgar criminal. Nevertheless, Orsini seems to have evoked considerable sympathy, deporting himself with great dignity. Moreover, he was the son of a captain in the *Grande Armee* who had been captured in Russia.[32]

Pieri denied any involvement in the assassination attempt. He testified that he had been visiting Paris on family affairs and had carried the bomb only to accommodate Orsini.

On February 26, the summations were concluded. Orsini was portrayed as a heroic character by his attorney. Astonishingly, his lawyer was allowed to read a letter written by Orsini to the Emperor: "Remember that so long as Italy is not independent, the peace of Europe and of Your Majesty is but an empty dream."[33] Pieri's attorney maintained that his client had not committed any crime and should not be punished. Gomez was portrayed as a weak-willed tool of Orsini. Lastly, De Rudio's attorney stressed his client's poverty and the suffering and calumny, which had induced him to reluctantly, participate in the plot.

The verdict was returned after two and a half hours of deliberation. De Rudio, Orsini and Pieri were found guilty. Gomez was found guilty with extenuating circumstances, since he had earlier agreed to cooperate with the prosecutor. After the verdict had been announced, the defendants were permitted to make a statement. De Rudio later claimed that he had denounced the testimony of the street cleaner, but the record shows that the prisoner had asked for clemency.[34] This appeal was to save his life.

Sentence was pronounced the night of January 26, as the

clock atop the *Palace of Justice* clanged the hour. Gomez was sentenced to life imprisonment; Peri, Orsini and De Rudio, to death by guillotine.

De Rudio was brought back to his cell. The guards had already prepared the champagne.

The next day the prisoners were taken to the *Roquette*, a prison housing the guillotine. They were made to wear a straightjacket, to prevent suicide. The two agents accompanied De Rudio to his new cell.[35]

Once a day, De Rudio was allowed a walk for an hour in the courtyard, often with Orsini. The Prefect of Police hinted that his sentence might be commuted, if he agreed to name the French conspirators. De Rudio refused. It is not altogether certain that he knew who they were. He wrote to Eliza, but the letters were not forwarded.

In England, Eliza met with several public figures, among them Sir John Walter, the Member of Parliament from Nottingham, who helped her gain public support. The London *Times* had begun a petition, to which even the Commissioner of Police, Sir Richard Mayon, had subscribed. Queen Victoria, also, had been approached. Letters of supplication were sent to Napoleon III from the parents of the young prisoner, as well as from the Cardinal Archbishop of Paris. De Rudio, too, at the insistence of his attorney, addressed a plea for clemency, in which he mentioned the services of his uncle, who had died during the retreat from Moscow.

On March 11, word reached the prisoners that the Court of Appeals had rejected their appeal. That same night the platform for the guillotine was erected. From his attorney, De Rudio learned that although public opinion favored clemency, the State Council was opposed, fearing that Austria might be provoked.

The final disposition rested with the Emperor. Both Napoleon III and the Empress Eugenie appeared anxious to confer clemency. Eugenie had even received the wives and children of Orsini and De Rudio. In later years, Orsini's daughter described the great compassion shown her by the Empress.[36] A story was current that Eugenie had gone on hands and knees to beg the Emperor to grant leniency.[37]

Napoleon III and Eugenie each had their own motives for mercy. The Emperor doubtless remembered his happy years in Italy, the support shown him by the Italians and his Carbonari-aided escape from the fortress of Ham.[38] He may have recalled Andrea Orsini, the father of Orsini, who fought by his side when he and his few confederates battled the Papal Army in 1831.[39] Eugenie's girlhood idol was Silvio Pellico, an Italian who had fought to free Italy from the Austrians.

Napoleon convened a Council of State on March 12 and informed the ministers that he and the Empress desired to exercise the prerogative of mercy. The ministers sought to dissuade him, pointing to the eight deaths outside the Opera. The Cardinal Archbishop of Paris then proposed a compromise.[40] Since De Rudio was the only defendant to have asked for mercy, let him be pardoned and the other two executed.

On March 12, the evening before the execution, the chaplain and warden made their customary death visit. Orsini declined to receive confession. He had written a final letter to Louis Napoleon, in which he is said to have renounced murder as a political expedient and implored the Emperor to remember Italy.[41]

They came to Pieri. He told them he proposed to go to eternity singing. "Always the clown," Gomez grumbled.

De Rudio was next. Notice of a commutation of sentence had not yet been received. He declined an offer to visit to the chapel and refused a glass of rum. He was brought to the dressing chamber, where the back of his head was shaved up to the ears, and he donned the execution robe with a black hood.

A wet snow had begun to fall, as the last minute arrangements were completed. The square was crowded with spectators. As much as one thousand francs had been paid for vantage places in the nearby windows. Fifteen thousand soldiers were stationed in the square to keep order.[42]

Pieri was the first to be led to the red platform. True to his promise, he sang the hymn *Mourir pour la Patrie*, as the blade dropped. De Rudio was next brought up, his hands tied behind his back, barefoot in the cold snow. He expressed a wish to smoke, and his pipe was stuck in his mouth. Suddenly a man on horseback entered the courtyard. The guards and the soldiers saluted, as the rider dismounted and spoke to the authorities. He was M. De Collet, majordomo of the Empress.[43]

De Rudio was led back to his cell. On the way, he passed Orsini who had been brought up in his place. The clock on the *Roquette* sounded the hour. Orsini climbed the snow-covered stairs and the sentence was read. He listened attentively, and then shouted *"Viva l'Italia! Viva la Francia!"* His neck was fastened to the plank, the plank lowered to the horizontal and his neck secured in the lunette. The officers removed their hats. The blade fell and his head rolled into the readied basket.[44]

Later that evening the majordomo returned to inform De Rudio that his sentence had been commuted to life imprisonment. Influential people had interceded for him to the Empress. Queen Victoria, herself, had instructed the British ambassador to make a personal appeal. Since the French throne was celebrating the second birthday of the Prince-Imperial, Eugenie had been moved to seek mercy, on the behalf of a young English mother and her child.

In accordance with the judicial niceties, De Rudio was brought back the next day to the *Palais de Justice* before the highly displeased President of the Court. Letters of Imperial Patent were read, commuting the sentence to life imprisonment. When De Rudio was asked if he repented his crime, his attorney hastily objected to the question, fearing his client's answer.

"Take him away!" the judge roared. De Rudio was returned to the *Roquette*. The straightjacket was no longer required.[45]

He was allowed to exercise in the courtyard with Gomez, who apologized sheepishly for his thoughtlessness at the police station.[46] The authorities permitted sixteen year old Eliza and her infant son a final visit for fifteen minutes. The outlook was bleak. No hope of further commutation of sentence could be expected. De Rudio would soon be leaving Paris for parts unknown. As he was being returned to his cell, he blustered: "*I will be free in one year! If not, I will be dead!*"

In England, Bernard was arrested and brought to trial in Old Bailey on April 12, 1856. To placate the French government, Lord Palmerston, the Prime Minister, had brokered a bill in Parliament in which conspiracy to commit murder was made a felony. The bill passed, but on the second reading, an amendment slipped through, censuring the government for yielding to French importunacy. Lord Palmerston's government was forced to resign.[47] "If Orsini did not kill Napoleon," Karl Marx quipped, "he certainly killed Palmerston."[48]

For a while the two capitals debated whether De Rudio should be returned to England to testify, but in the end, the trial of Bernard in Old Bailey proceeded without him. Eliza gave strong testimony for the Crown, implicating the defendant, but evidence that Bernard was not in France at the time of the assassination attempt weighed heavily in his favor, as did the eloquence of his counsel, who implored the jury to defy French pressure. English opinion was strongly critical of the French dictator, despite the lukewarm entente built up by the Crimean War. Disregarding the Presiding Judge's instructions, the jury returned a verdict of not guilty.[49]

Notes

1. Cesare Crespi, *Per la Liberta!* (San Francisco: Canessa Printing, 1913), p. 138.
2. *Ibid.*, p. 141.
3. Pierre de la Gorce, *Histoire du Second Empire, Vol. II* (New York: AIMS Press, 1969), p. 215.
4. Crespi, p. 144.
5. Gorce, p. 216.
6. *Ibid.*, p. 217.
7. Crespi, p. 144.
8. *Ibid.*, p. 148.
9. *Ibid.*, p. 151.
10. *Ibid.*, p. 155.
11. Gorce, p. 219.
12. Michael St. John Packe, *The Bombs of Orsini* (London: Secker and Warburg, 1957), p. 290.
13. New York *Times,* March 20, 1881.
14. Crespi, p. 156.
15. E. A. Rheinardt, *Napoleon and Eugenie* (New York: Knopf, 1931), p. 182.
16. Crespi, p. 157.
17. Ernest John Knapton, *France* (New York: Scribner, 1971), p. 399.
18. Octave Aubry, *The Second Empire* (Philadelphia and New York: Lippincott, 1940), p. 185.
19. Crespi, p. 160.
20. *Ibid.*, p., 162.
21. Theo Aronson, *The Fall of the Third Napoleon* (Indianapolis and New York: Bobbs-Merrell, 1970), p. 24.
22. Crespi, p. 164.
23. *Ibid.*, p. 170.
24. *Ibid.*, p. 178.
25. Harold Kurtz, *The Empress Eugenie* (Boston: Houghton Mifflin, 1964), p. 107.
26. Crespi, p. 185.
27. J. P. T. Bury, *France* (Philadelphia: University of Pennsylvania Press, 1949), p. 91.
28. Gorce, p. 238.
29. *Ibid.*, p. 228.
30. Rheinardt, p. 184.
31. Gorce, p. 239.
32. Aubry, p. 16.
33. Robert Sencourt, *Napoleon III: The Modern Emperor* (Freeport, NY: Librarie Press, 1933), p. 196.
34. Crespi, p. 188.

35. *Ibid.*, p. 190.
36. Kurtz, p. 111.
37. Erna Barschak, *The Innocent Empress* (New York: E. P. Dulton, 1943), p. 102.
38. J. M. Thompson, *Louis Napoleon and the Second Empire* (New York: Norton, 1955), p. 179; William Herbert Cecil Smith, *Napoleon III* (New York: St. Martin Press, 1973), p. 100.
39. Aubry, p. 16.
40. Rheinardt, p. 188.
41. Barschak, p. 102; Kurtz, p.110.
42. Crespi, p. 198.
43. *Ibid,.* p. 199.
44. Packe, p. 281.
45. Crespi, p. 201.
46. *Ibid.*, p. 203.
47. Derek Beales, *England and Italy 1859-60* (London: Nelson, 1961), p. 11.
48. Smith, *Napoleon III,* p. 148.
49. Kurtz, p. 112.

IV
FRENCH GUYANA

In April, while Bernard's trial was in progress, De Rudio and Gomez were moved in a convict railroad car to Marseilles and from there by jail wagon to Toulon, familiar from the early pages of *Les Miserables*. They were issued a red jacket, yellow pants and a green beret. Mustaches were shaved and hair cut. Their life sentence had begun.[1]

The prisoners were brought to a foul subterranean bunker and chained to the wall. They slept on wood planks and spent the waking hours fighting insects. Week after week De Rudio tugged incessantly on his chain, and four times the ring had to be replaced. The guards marched him to the blacksmith's shop, his only excursion into the glare of the Mediterranean sun.

Numerous visitors came to view the notorious assassins. Gomez's wife appeared with her daughters, more to reproach than to comfort her husband. A bishop newly assigned to China visited. De Rudio refused his offer of a cross and rosary. The Czarina of Russia, en route to Nice, stopped off at Toulon to view the convicts. She tried to give them money, but the guards would not permit it.

After seven months in this gruesome hellhole, De Rudio was brought before the commandant and informed that the authorities had decided to move the prisoners out of metropolitan France. He and Gomez would be leaving for French Guyana. Should De Rudio reveal the names of his French accomplices, he would be freed immediately. Otherwise, he will be dead in two to three years.

De Rudio declined to name them. It is unlikely he knew their identity, since Orsini had withheld this information. The next day, October 21, 1858, the two prisoners were brought on board the steamer *La Durr*, bound for French Guyana with a cargo of two hundred convicts. He and Gomez were taken down to a cage in the hold, almost a sentence of death, but once the ship cleared port, the captain moved them out and even allowed them up on deck occasionally. He was an Orleanist, a supporter of Louis Philippe, and made no effort to conceal his contempt for the upstart Emperor. The ship put into Santa Cruz in the Canaries to take on water. It remained in port for two days with hatches battened down on the sweltering convicts, before departing for the Ile Royal.[2]

To the northwest French Guyana is separated from Dutch Guyana by the Maroni River and from Brazil to the southeast by the Oyapock River. The territory has about two hundred miles of coastline on the Atlantic Ocean. Colonization began in 1626, with a group of French farmers from Rouen. Before the project was discontinued in 1789, over ten thousand had died.[3] For many decades, there had been no further attempts at settlement, but by 1852 the prison overcrowding in metropolitan France prompted the French government to again attempt colonization, this time with prisoners. No thought was given to rehabilitation. Convicts were sent to serve their sentence or to die, preferably the latter. "Dry guillotine" was the apt description given by Victor Hugo. Of the seventy thousand prisoners sent there, three quarters died before their sentence ended. Moreover, after completion, the liberated prisoner was compelled to remain in the colony for a period of time equal to his sentence.

The two large prison settlements on the mainland were St. Laurent on the Maroni River and Montagne d'Argent, on the Oyapock. A small, favored prison settlement in Cayenne existed chiefly to provide labor for the commercial capital.[4] The prisoners, who were deemed incorrigible or had committed crimes in the prison settlements, were sent either to the jungle camps, where they died quickly; or to the Isles du Salut, three small islands ten to fourteen miles off the coast, for a slower death. The largest of these islands was the Ile Royal, where the convicts were worked to exhaustion. Nearby, was St. Joseph, which was used for solitary confinement. Devil's Island, the smallest and a former leper station, was infrequently used, because of poor access.[5]

The *La Durr* anchored at the Ile Royal and disembarked the two hundred convicts. Gomez and De Rudio and one hundred other prisoners were transferred by steam launch to the mangrove coast of the Montagne d'Argent, twenty miles from the mouth of the Ojapok River, near the Brazilian border. The date was December 1, 1858.

There had once been a free settlement in the Montaigne d'Argent, where coffee had been cultivated. The prison commandant lived in the planter's home, and the convicts were housed in the produce sheds.

The new arrivals were assembled before the commandant, an ex-major of marines, who called out the names. When he came to De Rudio, the official who had delivered the prisoners handed him a letter. The commandant read it carefully and studied De Rudio. "You are going to leave your skin in this penal colony," he sneered and let it be known that if De Rudio tried to escape, the convict who killed him would be given immediate freedom.

Each prisoner was issued a straw hat, a pair of wooden clogs, clothe pants and a brown blouse, with his number stamped on the back. He was housed in a shed with fifty other convicts. Nights, he slept in a hammock, beset by swarms of blood-sucking insects.[6]

De Rudio was assigned to hard labor. His job was to fell the large trees and carry the trunks back to the prison settlement. The daily quota was one cubic meter of timber for each convict. Those unable to meet the quota were assigned additional work the following day.

Weeks passed and the prisoners settled into the fearsome

convict routine. Conditions around them could scarcely be imagined. The labor was exhausting, the air fetid, the heat intolerable, the insects merciless and the food barely able to sustain life. Every moment of the waking day, he dreamed of fleeing the hell of Montagne d'Argent. From the depths of despair, he searched for a means of escape; any means, however impractical.

De Rudio had heard somewhere of the dugouts used by the Indians in the interior of French Guyana. If he could make one, he mused, he might be able to go fifty miles upstream on the Opapok River to the town of St. George on the Brazilian border.[7] Then what? He would have to travel five hundred miles across the Amazon basin to Balen, on the coast. The path would take him through disease-infested jungle overrun with malaria, yellow fever and parasites, to say nothing of the snakes and wild animals. If he reached Balen, would the Brazilians keep him or send him back? That worry, he would save for later. Meanwhile, he would need help. Where could he get it? Thus far, he knew no one whom he could trust.

One day De Rudio was assigned to a ten-man gang to off-load cattle from a Brazilian sailing ship. The roadstead shelved, so that the ship had to anchor three miles off shore and run the cattle over the side. The convicts stood waist-deep in the water and drove the cattle to shore with whips and shouts.

It was late at night before De Rudio returned to his shed. The mess captain, who was supposed to have saved his supper, was asleep. When De Rudio awakened him, the man cursed him angrily. None of the others intervened.

The next day, as the mess captain was carrying a large pot of soup, De Rudio tripped him, sending him sprawling and knocking the pot from his hands. The guard immediately ordered fifty lashes for each man, but the other prisoners begged him to overlook the matter. Since no one was injured, the guard let the matter slide. From then on, De Rudio was accepted by the team. They shared a common misery and formed a mutual bond that strengthened as the weeks wore on. His reputation stamped him as a man worth listening to. He boldly disclosed his plan and was soon satisfied that the others would join him in an escape. He also approached Gomez, but Gomez was hesitant.

For two months, he and his team left their shed at night and crept into the jungle. They felled a large tree and hollowed out the trunk with firebrands. Troops of monkeys came to watch, attracted by the light and the smell of the resin. Fortunately, the smoke could not be seen in the darkness. Night after night they toiled, consumed by insects, exhausted by their labor, raked by hunger. De Rudio proved to be a capable leader of desperate men.

At long last, the work was completed. The dugout had a beam of seven feet and a length of twenty-five feet. They dragged it to the river and launched it. Wonder of all, the dugout floated! All that remained was to make the sail and paddles.

That very night their sentinel began to have violent tremors. When he tried to urinate, he had difficulty. The prisoners laughed uproariously. Then the sentinel began to spit blood, and in two days he was dead.

Other convicts began to complain of high fever and shaking. They too died. Yellow Fever had struck! One by one, all nine members of his team succumbed. The epidemic was lightening swift, taking prisoners and guards alike and quickly emptying the camp. Of the six hundred guards and prisoners, all but sixty-three perished. The convicts grew weary of throwing the bodies into a quicklime pit, at times when there was still life in them.

To the commandant's chagrin, De Rudio showed no symptoms. Then the commandant's wife and his two children died, and he lost interest in De Rudio. He, too, was found dead on the floor of his cellar, his gums covered with blood. Like the others, the commandant was thrown into the pit. De Rudio helped dispose of the body.[8]

News of this calamity reached Paris. To forestall a public outcry, the Minister ordered the survivors sent to the Ile Royal.

The steamship *Abeille* soon arrived, and the few survivors were taken on board, among them De Rudio and Gomez. From the deck of the steamer, De Rudio looked back at the loathsome Montagne d'Argent and remembered the dugout he had left behind.

The convicts were brought to the Ile Royal, where they had first disembarked. The island has the form of an eight with the residences, hospital and church on the larger loop and the sheds on the smaller loop. On the curve were the barracks.

Conditions on the island, five degrees north of the equator, were scarcely more healthful than on the mainland. Medical attention was ineffective; work was even more demanding and the food no less meager. Guards were everywhere and punishment swift and deadly. De Rudio was assigned to the blacksmith's shop. Week after week he labored almost nude before the furnace, his muscles on fire, his skin desiccated like a prune, half-starved on the best of days.

From the very first moment De Rudio set foot on the island, his thoughts were on escape. He had no great imagination. When shown a tree trunk at the Montagne d'Argent, he thought of a dugout canoe. On Ile Royal, as he moved along the beach, he saw a rowboat bobbing in the water and thought of escape by sea.

No one before had successfully escaped from the Iles du Salut *(And None Since!)*[9] Cleverer men than De Rudio had failed or abandoned the attempt. Undaunted, he set to work on a plan.

One of the prisoners was a Roman named Morbioli, who had been sentenced to ten years for killing a man who had seduced his sister. From Morbioli, De Rudio learned of the previous escape attempts.[10] Thirteen years before, some thirteen prisoners seized a pilot boat and sailed away. Everyone assumed their escape had succeeded, but later the boat was sighted with only three living convicts. They had eaten the others!

And there had been two other attempts. Twelve prisoners had set out on a raft made from driftwood. A whirlpool had broken it in two. One part washed up on shore and the twelve prisoners were captured. They were promptly returned to custody and put into pits, where they all died. The other eight prisoners drifted toward shore, but their half of raft had became trapped on a shoal, called a *vice*. By the time they were found, crabs had devoured their flesh.

Paolo Tiboldi made the third attempt. Like De Rudio, he had been sent to French Guyana for an attempt on the life of Napoleon III. He escaped by boat with ten men, but the boat foundered on the first night. Brought back, they received sixty lashes and were put into pits for six weeks, exposed to the sun and weather. Tiboldi remained for thirteen years in the prison colony until freed through the intervention of prominent people. He was later to write a popular account of his imprisonment, but there was no mention of De Rudio.[11]

To be successful, the escape had to be planned when the steamship *Arbeille* was at sea; otherwise the ship would quickly hunt them down. Also, some way had to be found to immobilize the four gunboats at anchor in the harbor. Each had a three pound cannon mounted in the bow. Lastly, De Rudio had need of a sea-worthy boat, provisions, a sail, a crew and a navigator, and all these had to be found on a small island under constant surveillance by guards and informers.

He began to look around for accomplices. Gomez had been sent to a prison settlement on the mainland and was not available. De Rudio never saw him again. De Rudio got to know two very helpful Roman convicts: a tailor named Morelli, who might be able to make the sails; and Morbioli, a boatman, whose job was to polish the cannons on the gunboats. It was Morbioli, who had told him about the escapes.

Obtaining provisions was the first task. To accumulate sufficient food from their meager rations was clearly impossible. Fortunately, De Rudio came to know a French vicar, condemned to life imprisonment for murder. The vicar carried with him at all times a green Bible, in the lining of which he had concealed twenty thousand francs. In return for a place in the boat, the vicar was willing to provide the money to buy food and supplies.

Where could he find a seaman who could navigate? De Rudio had met a Frenchman, named Cousins, an ex-harbor man and mariner, who had been condemned to life imprisonment. It was Cousins who captained the dinghy that De Rudio had seen when he first came to the Ile Royal. The boat was used for fishing, and the catch went to supply both guards and convicts.

He approached Cousins cautiously, and to De Rudio's great delight, the mariner agreed to come along, preferring the perils of the sea to a life in hell. De Rudio now had a boat and a navigator. Next, he needed the crew. In the weeks that followed, he studied the dozen Italian convicts carefully and selected five for their loyalty and endurance. When they heard what he was planning, they readily agreed to his conditions. With the vicar's money, he was able to accumulate provisions slowly and furtively, so as not to excite suspicion. Then, one night Morelli summoned him to the storehouse and showed him six large canvas hammocks, which he had sewn together. They had a sail![12]

While the plans were moving forward, the frigate *Amazon* arrived from France with startling news. At long last, Italian unification had begun -- UNDER VICTOR EMANUEL II! And without the help of Mazzini and the other conspirators!

Two months after the assassination plot, Napoleon III reversed his policy toward Italy. Brokered by Count Cavour, the Piedmont premier, the Emperor had devised a plan to lure Austria into a war with Piedmont Savoy. Once hostilities had begun, Napoleon III promised to come to the aid of Victor Emanuel. All the advantages would be on the side of the alliance -- especially transportation. Piedmont had a fine railroad system, Austria only a single tract line between Vienna and Milan; and that had a gap of seventy miles.[13]

The armies met in the decisive battles of Magenta and Solferino, in which Austria suffered enormous losses.[14] Instead of pursuing the enemy, Napoleon III did a *volte face* and called for an armistice! He had in the interim sensed danger from Prussia whose troops were massing in Coblenz and Cologne.[15] A defeated Austria would strengthen Prussia at France's expense. As a sop to the outraged Victor Emanuel II, Piedmont was given

French Guyana 81

Lombardy, Toscany and the Duchies, in exchange for Nice and Savoy, which were French speaking and considerably smaller.[16] So the unification of Italy was advancing, while De Rudio languished in his tropical hell.

The *Amazon* also brought word of a royal amnesty. The governor assembled the convicts in the square, to read them the names of those receiving Imperial pardons. It took only a few minutes for the prisoners to realize that the list contained the names of only Frenchmen. De Rudio and his Italian friends were devastated, but not surprised. If ever there were a reason to escape, they had one now!

At the beginning of December, Cousins reported that the preparations were completed and that they would soon be ready to leave. A few days later, the *Abeille* departed on its scheduled trip to Cayenne. As he watched the disappearing wake of the ship, De Rudio knew that the time had arrived!

At 5 p.m. he slipped out of the blacksmith shop and began to round up his crew. Word was sent to Morbioli in the gunboats. Morelli, the sailmaker, was in the hospital with a fever and could not come. The vicar, too, had to be left behind. Once at sea, the others would have slit his throat for the money concealed in the green Bible.

While the prisoners were at evening meal, De Rudio and his six companions carried the provisions down to the beach. De Rudio waited patiently on the strand, and the others, armed with knives, hid behind rocks. Offshore, the fishing boat was returning. De Rudio held up a five-franc coin, to signal the fishermen to put in for a private sale of the surplus fish. As Cousins hove the boat onto the beach, the convicts rushed out from behind the rocks. They boarded the dinghy, easily overpowering the fishermen, who offered only token resistance, so that they could later insist that they were taken under duress. After loading the provisions, they shoved off and headed out to sea.

From shore came the shout, "Man the cannon!"

As the crews of the gunboats rushed to their vessels,

Morbioli, the boatman, grinned broadly. He had earlier removed the oarlocks from the gunboats, so they could not follow in pursuit.

The dinghy rounded the western part of the island, cheered on by the convicts from shore. But instead of steering toward the coast, Cousins put out to sea. He explained that the *Arbeille* would soon be after them and would expect the boat to make for the Dutch Guyana or Brazil.

They sailed north by the stars, a small boat with eleven men bobbing on the deep, sending swells, carried along by a brisk offshore wind. Dawn found them on the high seas, tossed and rocked by the mounting waves. A fierce storm overtook them, battering the boat with mountainous grey seas. For two days and three nights the convicts pumped for their lives or bailed with their palm hats and wooden clogs. On the third night, a dense fog appeared. Suddenly a Dutch sailing ship crossed their bow and gave the convicts the scare of their lives. Cousins desperately threw over the rudder to prevent a collision.

By the next day, the storm had cleared. The exhausted crew made sail and broke out the food. For days, they had tasted only sips of rum. But when they opened the stores, they found the drinking water and other provisions had been spoiled by the brine.[17]

This called for an immediate change of plans. Cousins altered course southwest, to the nearest landfall. They spied a wisp of smoke on the horizon, and the men panicked, fearing that the *Arbeille* might be overtaking them. But the smoke disappeared. After a day of hard sail, the starving and thirst-crazed men reached a roadstead on the coast.

They came to a small cove where several slaves were hauling barrels and mending nets, closely guarded by a white man. The convicts beached the boat and sent De Rudio to speak with the overseer. He told De Rudio that they were in Dutch Guyana.

At the mention of Dutch Guyana, the convicts rushed back to their boat and pushed off, ready to endure any hardship rather than risk falling into the hands of the Dutch authorities. It was here that other escapees from St. Laurent had been captured and sent back for merciless punishment.

Days passed, as they sailed along the coast, beating against the west-blowing trades, with only a wisp of sail to shelter them from the blazing sun. Suddenly the dinghy broached to, and the bow plunged but did not move, its keel seized by some mysterious force. The convicts were paralyzed with fear.

Cousins turned deathly pale. There were caught in a *vice*, a mud shoal that held the boat, as if it were sunk in quicksand. Sandbars and mudflats can pose a hazard as much as fifteen miles from the coastline.[18] With no time for explanations, Cousins ordered the men over the side to prop up the boat and keep it from sinking into the mud.

"If the tide ebbs, we're dead!" he croaked hoarsely. "If it makes, we may be saved!"

For hours they stood up to their chest in the mud, with crabs biting their flesh and the tropical sun beating mercilessly down on them. Then the tide came in, and slowly the boat was released, as if from a vacuum. The crew climbed back into the dinghy, bloody and exhausted from their labors.

For two days, they sailed to the northwest, following the coastline, thirsty, starving and blistered by the sun. Suddenly, a small black cutter flying the British flag put out from shore to intercept them. It fired a shot and Cousins immediately hove to, too weak to offer resistance. The captain was a black man, who hailed them in English.

He demanded to know if they were carrying duty goods. De Rudio told them who they were and where they had come from.

The captain was astonished. "You mean you have come a thousand miles in that piece of wood?" he asked incredulously.[19]

From the captain, they learned their position. They were near New Amsterdam on the Berbick River, in British Guyana. He immediately sent over water and hardtack to revive them, but refused to take them onboard his trim craft, because of their filthy condition. The crew of the cutter showed great compassion for the escaped convicts. They showered them with gifts of tobacco and waved cordially as the convicts rowed off.

The boat entered the turbid yellow waters of the mouth of the Berbick River. They passed a fishing smack, manned by two Portuguese fishermen who were casting nets. A half hour later they were in New Amsterdam.

British Guyana was first colonized by the Dutch, who constructed a system of dikes, floodgates, irrigation and drainage works in the low-lying coastal areas that reclaimed the rich alluvial lands for crops of tobacco, cane and cotton. In 1815 the Council of Vienna gave the colony to the British, at the same time the French regained French Guyana. The Dutch had introduced slavery, but when the institution was finally abolished by the British in 1838, few freed slaves would work for their former masters. Agriculture declined. Indentured workers had to be imported from Portugal, China, West Indies, Africa, and finally from India, but lack of manpower, especially the skilled craftsmen, remained a chronic problem.[20]

A launch approached from shore. On board was the governor, a Mr. Melville, an elderly gentleman with white sideburns, accompanied by a dozen policemen. He had caught sight of the dinghy while out for a walk and had assumed the men had been shipwrecked. When De Rudio explained who they were, the governor had difficulty believing him.

The convicts were brought to the police station. There, they were given clean clothing and served a glorious meal. Bread, ham, cheese and beer were laid out before them, which they devoured in deep silence, while the police joked about their appetite.

The governor later paid a visit to the police station, accompanied by some citizens of the town. He spoke to the convicts in French.

"You are in a land that respects those who seek asylum," he told them. "Respect the laws and the land will show you hospitality. But you must give us a guarantee--to work."

He asked each convict, not their name nor their sentence, but the kind of work they did. As each convict told him his trade, the governor assigned him to one of the citizens. De Rudio's turn came, and he explained that his profession was the sword. He had been educated in the Military Academy of St. Luca in Milan. When De Rudio told him his name, the governor shook his head. "The Count De Rudio is dead!" he insisted. Word had reached them that the celebrated assassin had died in the epidemic at the Montagne d'Argent.

De Rudio was about to reply, when a handsome, young mulatto gentleman intervened and said in French, "If your Excellency will allow me, I will put him up in my house. I will be his guarantor."

He was the physician of New Amsterdam, the owner of the local newspaper and a correspondent for the London *Times*. De Rudio followed him home and was introduced to his wife, a delightful convent-educated Belgian girl, who spoke fluent French and Italian. She welcomed him and showed him great hospitality. Listening to her play the piano after dinner brought tears to his eyes.

Suddenly, someone rushed in with news that a French warship had sailed into the mole.

De Rudio excused himself and ran down to the harbor to see the ship. It was the *Abeille*. She had been sailing up the coast to Venezuela, searching for the convicts. On her way back, she had passed the Portuguese smack off New Amsterdam and had been told of the dinghy's arrival.

On deck were two guards who had been taken along to identify the convicts. When they saw De Rudio on the wharf, they called to him: "Hey, you with the bomb! Come on board and take your medicine!"

That evening the Governor sent for him. With great trepidation, De Rudio accompanied a police officer to the government house. In the room with the governor were the captain of the *Abeille* and the two guards. The guards immediately identified him.

"That's him! That's Count De Rudio!"

On hearing confirmation of De Rudio's identity, the

Governor said to him: "*Count* De Rudio, I doubted your story, and now I beg your pardon." Turning to the Captain, he addressed him coldly, "The English do not grant extradition for political prisoners!"

Furious, the captain stormed out of the room with the two guards.[21]

The appearance of the French steamship had thrown the other convicts into a panic. During the night, they managed to slip away on a boat bound for Venezuela. The next morning the *Abeille,* too, weighed anchor, but it left behind a spy, to keep watch.

Now that De Rudio's presence was known to the French, New Amsterdam was no longer a safe haven for the escaped convict. Plans were made to return him to London, preferably on a British man-of-war, since a merchant ship might be boarded.

His host spread word that De Rudio had gone off with a gold prospecting party into the interior and had been massacred by the natives. Gold, in fact, had earlier been discovered near the Guyana-Venezuela borders.[22] The doctor sent the story to the London *Times*, where Eliza saw it. Doubtless, she was perplexed, since she had previously been informed of her husband's death in the epidemic at the Montagne d'Argent. The story had one benefit, in that the French spy departed.

Word reached New Amsterdam that the arrival of the British man-of-war would be delayed. Accordingly, arrangements were made for De Rudio to sail on an English merchant brig, the *John Ramilly*. To keep his passage secret, he was logged in as a crewmember and instructed to remain in his stateroom until departure. As a departing gift, the governor gave him a Bible, bound in black Moroccan leather. This was to remind De Rudio to whom he owed his deliverance.

On Christmas Eve De Rudio bade farewell to his generous hosts and boarded the brig. The *John Ramilly* was scheduled to make the crossing in three weeks, but so fierce were the north Atlantic winter storms, that the trip took all of two months, with crew and passengers forced to live on half-rations. When the ship finally arrived in the Thames estuary, the passengers saw many wrecks littering the banks.

On February 29, 1860, the *John Ramilly* tied up in Gravesend. De Rudio left the ship with a few shillings in his pocket, given him by the second mate. He went directly to the offices of the London *Times* to report his arrival and to thank them for their efforts on his behalf. He then set out to find Bernard, so that he could obtain money to send for his wife.

His first stop was the *Cafe Suisse* in the west end, frequented by the French exiles. There he met his friend Rossi, who had been with him in the raucous brawl in which De Rudio had been stabbed.

"Is that you?" he asked incredulously, unwilling to believe his eyes.

De Rudio cut short his many questions and asked to be brought up to date. Rossi told him about the Old Bailey trial, and how, since then, Bernard had been strutting around London, proclaiming that Orsini would never have failed but for De Rudio's treachery!

De Rudio listened with mounting fury, then rushed off to find Bernard. He found him in a cafe near Leicester Square, another popular roost for French exiles. When Bernard caught sight of De Rudio, he stared in astonishment. De Rudio reached out and grabbed him by his mustache. "I'm not a ghost!" he growled. "The whole country is going to hear the truth!" He released him quickly, before someone could summon the police and stormed out the door.[23]

De Rudio lost no time in writing to Eliza in Nottingham. Next, he sent word to Mazzini but received no answer. Nor did Mazzini send for him. Bernard's falsehoods had found an attentive ear. The following evening, he ran into Bernard in Leicester Square. Trembling with fear, Bernard led him into a pub, where they could further discuss the matter.

Bernard refused to accept responsibility for De Rudio's travails, nor would he offer help. Compensation? For what? Eliza had testified for the prosecution, and it was no thanks to her that he had been acquitted. As far as Bernard was concerned, the matter was closed -- permanently! Rebuffed, De Rudio turned to the English committee. Holyoake would not receive him, and Thomas Allsop sent him a paltry five pounds, to close the books. The Englishmen were distancing themselves from the Orsini affair.

The mail from Nottingham brought startling news from Jane Booth, his mother-in-law. Eliza was in London, staying with the Mancherinis, while looking for work. No sooner had De Rudio read the letter, than the doorbell rang and in walked Eliza. Having heard some extraordinary rumors, she had stopped by to ask Rossi if he had any news of her husband. De Rudio grabbed her in an ecstatic embrace and squeezed the breath from her frail ribcage, as he swung her wildly around the room. For how many eternities had he dreamt of this moment! She alone had stood by him! *And he had made good his promise!*

Reunited with his family by the most astonishing circumstances, De Rudio set about to create a decent life for them in London. This proved no easy task with the lies Bernard had been spreading. Most distressing of all was the falsehood that the French authorities had deliberately allowed De Rudio to escape, to reward him for his services. The nightmare of Zurich was being repeated.

Rossi introduced him to a journalist, a Mr. Kinner, who wrote an article about his trial and subsequent escape. Kinner arranged a series of lectures starting in Nottingham and later in Derby, Birmingham, Manchester and Leeds.[24] The reception by the public was lukewarm, and there was little financial gain. No mention of the lecture appeared in the Nottingham newspapers,[25] where one would have expected some notice, since De Rudio had lived there and the Booth family was long established in that city. Elsewhere, one account tells of an attendance of twenty-five in a hall for one thousand.[26] Around this time, perhaps in preparation for his lecture tour, De Rudio began to grow his fashionable mustache and goatee, which he would henceforth retain.

Several events helped to restore De Rudio's reputation. A convict who had known of him in French Guyana had come to England. He let it be known that De Rudio was detested, rather than favored, by the prison authorities. Then Mazzini, who had been asked to impartially review the matter of De Rudio's guilt, publicly stated that such a review was unnecessary, since his innocence was beyond question. Finally, Bernard, his chief accuser, had absconded with funds entrusted to him, mooting his accusations against De Rudio. Bernard was later to become insane.

De Rudio's exoneration had little effect on his poverty. He remained abjectly poor, and Eliza was pregnant with their second child. Their living conditions were abominable. In a letter to Holyoake, he pleaded: "Many a day we have been without any thing to eat--without coal to warm us."[27]

De Rudio found a poorly paid laborer's job polishing marble in a stone factory. He tried to sell the rights to his story to Holyoake, but although part of it was later used, De Rudio received nothing.[28]

On Christmas Eve his second child died, after only a few weeks of life. The couple had nothing in their tenement room that could be used to prepare the infant for burial. All he could do was to dry Eliza's tears.

The news from Belluno was equally depressing. His mother was gravely ill, his father in desperate financial circumstances, and Luigia forced to work at menial jobs.

Meanwhile in Italy, events were proceeding with lightning speed. Garibaldi had conquered Sicily and then the Kingdom of Naples. After first establishing himself as dictator, he relinquished his domain to Victor Emanuel II and retired to Caprera, an island off the coast of Sardinia. With this one *beau geste*, the Kingdom of Piedmont was transformed into the Kingdom of Italy. The monarchy triumphant, Mazzini and Garibaldi had henceforth to adjust or retire. In England, interest in the revolutionary Italian movement had waned, especially interest in the Orsini affair, as De Rudio had seen from his lecture series.

De Rudio gave some thought to returning to Italy, although he continued to detest King Victor Emanuel II. Venetia was still in the hands of the Austrians and Rome still under Papal and French rule.

A Piedmont ship, the *Vittorio Emanuele II*, arrived in English waters. Its captain was empowered to embark Italian exiles that desired repatriation. After much deliberation, De Rudio decided to return to Italy. In order to avoid notoriety, he gave his name as Carlo Nosodano, instead of Carlo Camillo de Rudio, Count of Nosodano.

He was summoned for an interview at the Italian consulate. No sooner had he entered the room, than a man whispered in the consul's ear. De Rudio was told to come back the next day. When he returned, the Consul angrily accused him of using a false name.

In vain, De Rudio explained that he had a right to use his ancient family appellation.

"Sorry," he was told. "No place for you."[29]

De Rudio was bitterly disappointed but soon came to realize that had he returned he would have been handed over to the French. Victor Emanuel and Napoleon were now close allies. Prince Jerome, Plon-Plon, had married Clothilde, the daughter of Victor Emanuel II.

The destitute family man searched endlessly for better employment. He was, after all, a soldier with some battle experience. Poland offered possibilities. A rebellion had broken out in 1863, and Czar Alexander II was taking measures to repress it. The call had gone out for patriots interested in fighting for the Polish cause, and De Rudio made known his interest.

Word of his intentions spread quickly through the exile community. At long last, a letter from Guiseppi Mazzini arrived, inviting De Rudio to a meeting. Mazzini had been dividing his time between Italy, Lugano and London. The unification of Italy under a liberal monarchy had undercut his position. Unlike Garibaldi, he had little support among the upper classes, and the working class found him too esoteric.³⁰ Although his followers in the Italian legislature continued to respect him, they, too, had strayed from his leadership. Mazzini was gravely ill. He was anxious to set things right with those who deserved better of him, and none more so, than his faithful follower from Belluno.

He began by inquiring about Orsini's last moments and wondered if Orsini had mentioned his old friend. De Rudio described the scene at the prison as Orsini was led to the guillotine. Mazzini listened sadly to the story, and then explained the purpose of the meeting. He had been told that De Rudio was considering fighting for the Polish cause. He wished to dissuade him, since his efforts would be wasted. The Polish situation was untenable. Russia will divide the Polish patriots and keep them from succeeding.

But in America, he continued, an epic struggle was enfolding between the armies of slavery and emancipation. "Go to the United States!" he thundered. Without giving De Rudio a chance to argue, Mazzini quickly added: "AGREED! YOU LEAVE FOR THE UNITED STATES!"

Mazzini sketched the American political scene and stressed the nobility of the northern cause, which coincided exactly with the objectives of *Young Italy*. He gave him a list of men to contact, then sat down at his desk and wrote letters of introduction. One letter De Rudio carried with him the rest of his life:³¹

London 21 January 1864
I beg to recommend to all those American citizens who sympathize with me, Charles Rudio, brave, energetic, resolute and prepared to defend the cause of Emancipation.
He deserves to be helped.

Joseph Mazzini.

The exile community was not saddened to learn of De Rudio's departure. The great suffering he had endured had been a thorn in its conscience and his poverty, an embarrassment. Mazzini, himself, who had steered De Rudio westward, was of little financial help. When asked to contribute to his departure expenses, he gave one pound: "It will also be cheaper in the end," he wrote, "because if he stays, I would have to help him often."[32] This was hardly Mazzini's most generous moment.

Holyoake contributed a poncho, to keep De Rudio warm on his ocean voyage. In one of the pockets, De Rudio found a biscuit, cognac and some eau de cologne. These had been safety rations, in the event that Holyoake had to spend a night in jail. The eau de cologne doubtless proved useful during the sea voyage.

February 8, 1864, as all London was preparing to welcome Garibaldi on his triumphant good-will visit, De Rudio bade good by to Eliza and their young son and embarked from Liverpool on the *S. S. Virginia,* bound for New York.

The vessel carried three hundred sixty six passengers, mostly poor Irish and English steerage, and a few Germans. Although less loathsome than the sailing packets, steerage conditions on the steamships were still frightful. Passengers were given a small shelf space to sleep on, slop that passed for food, buckets for the body wastes. Below deck, the smell was indescribable. Illness abounded.[33]

Yet, the spirits of the immigrants soared, as they prepared for their new life. For De Rudio, the trip was an awakening. He boarded the ship as a thirty-two year old failure, a ridiculed conspirator, an improvident husband and father; but inspired by the fierce determination of the desperate people around him, he, too, looked hopefully to the future. Henceforth, his energies would be directed toward securing a respected place in the land of opportunity, however arduous the obstacles that lay ahead.

Eliza returned to her mother's home in Nottingham to await word from her husband. His trip took a fortnight. The ship arrived on February 22, 1864. The customs register at Castle Garden in New York lists a Charles Rudio, age thirty-three, male, mechanic, native of Germany.[34] With his waxed mustache and goatee, De Rudio may not have wanted to be listed as a laborer and chose the occupation of "mechanic" to describe his last job of cutting and polishing stone. "Germany" might have been a bureaucratic error, although the passenger lists were usually surprisingly accurate; or it might have been an instance of the conspirator's habitual effort to disguise his identity, just as De Rudio had done at the Italian consulate in London.

Notes

1. Cesare Crespi, *Per la Liberta!* (San Francisco: Canessa Printing, 1913), p. 206.
2. *Ibid.*, p. 210.
3. Alexander Miles, *Devil's Island. Colony of the Damned* (Berkley, CA: Ten Speed Press, 1988), p. 13.
4. *Ibid.*, p. 36.
5. *Ibid.*, p. 33.
6. *Ibid.*, p. 75.
7. Crespi, p. 210.
8. *Ibid.*, p. 214.
9. The escape in *Papillon* by Henri Carrière is considered to be largely fiction of a composite of the accounts of other prisoners. Miles, p. 119.
10. Crespi, p. 216.
11. Paolo Tibboldi, *Da Roma A Cayenna* 3rd edition, Rome: Topografico Italiano, 1888. (Microfilm: Widener Library Harvard University Film W13029)
12. *Ibid.*, p. 220.
13. Thomas Corley, and Anthony Buchanan, *Democratic Despot. A Life of Napoleon III* (London: Barrie & Rocliff, 1923), p. 213.
14. Herman Viola and Susan P. Viola, *Guiseppe Garibaldi*, (New York: Chelsea, 1988), p. 81.
15. Corley and Buchanan, p. 215.
16. Janet Penrose Trevelylan, *A Short History of the Italian People* (New York: Pittman, 1956), p. 357; Cecil J. S. Sprigge, *The Development of Modern Italy* (New Haven: Yale University Press, 1944), p. 35.
17. Crespi, p. 226.
18. *Guyana, Visual Geography Series*, (Minneapolis, MN: Lerner Publication, 1988), p. 12; Miles, *Devil's Island*, p. 98.
19. Crespi, p.229.
20. *Guyana*, p. 30.
21. Crespi, p. 233.
22. *Guyana*, p. 32.
23. Crespi, p. 236.
24. *Ibid.*, p. 239.
25. The newspapers have been searched by Mr. David N. Durant.
26. Daniel Magnussen, *Peter Thompson's Narrative of the Little Bighorn Campaign of 1876* (Glendale, CA: Clark, 1974), p. 246.
27. George Jacob Holyoake, *Sixty Years of an Agitator's Life* (New York and London: Garland, 1893) volume 1, p. 38.
28. Cesare Marino, *Dal Piave al Little Bighorn* (Belluno: Tarantola, 1996), p. 158.
29. Crespi, p. 258.
30. Derek Beales, *England and Italy 1859-60* (London: Nelson, 1961), p. 31.
31. Crespi, p. 262.

French Guyana

32. See Melvin Maddocks, *The Atlantic Crossing* (np: Time-Life, 1981) for complete description of an Atlantic Crossing in the mid 19th Century.
33. Holyoake, p. 39.
34. Passenger List of Vessels arriving in New York 1820-1887; list numbers 15-129, Jan. 9 – Feb. 27,1864 (microfilm roll 237) National Archives and Record Service, General Services Administration, Washington, D.C.

V
THE CIVIL WAR

By the time De Rudio landed in New York, the tide of battle had begun to favor the North. General Ulysses S. Grant had been summoned from the West, to take command of the entire Union Army. Declining to remain at a desk in Washington, he chose instead to accompany the Army of the Potomac into the field. While he hoped for a quick and decisive victory, failing that, he was prepared to pursue the campaign, until the enemy could be worn down by attrition. The Union Army now numbered two million, twice the strength of the South.

The Italian community that De Rudio found in New York was quite different from that in Switzerland or England. For one thing, although profoundly sympathetic to the cause of Italian unity, they were not Mazzinians. Conspiracies and assassinations were quite repugnant to them. An attempt to found a Mazzini tabloid in New York had failed. The sole Italian newspaper was *L'Eco d'Italia,*[1] edited by G. F. Secchi de Casali, located at 298 Broadway. It defended the immigrant's interests and offered lively accounts of Garibaldi's activities. Garibaldi had lived intermittently in the United States during the early 1850's, where he had made many friends.

New York had a small Italian population of about two thousand,[2] which came chiefly from northern Italy.[3] Since many had arrived destitute, a Committee of Italian Political Refugees had been organized to provide relief. An unknown number of

Italian children had drifted into the vast subculture of homeless children on the streets of the city. They had been indentured to a bureau in Paris and upon arrival at New York, were forced to play musical instruments on the streets late into the night. Other were made to black boots, sell flowers, or sweep crossings.[4] But the city had hoards of street children of other nationalities.

Although the Italian immigration was small, there was a certain resentment against the immigrant. Many were thought to be revolutionaries, who had been offered the choice of America or jail. Others were condemned for their Roman Catholicism.[5] But the Italian community, too, had its share of anti-Papists. In 1853-4 Monsignor Gaetano Bedini, the Papal Nunico, visited the United States. It was rumored that he had been responsible for the death of Ugo Bassi, chaplain in Garibaldi's army. The *L'Eco d'Italia* severely censured him, prompting an attack on his person by seventy-seven Italian patriots in NewYork.[6] A most visible and well-applauded contribution of the Italian community in New York prior to the Civil War came in 1853 at the N.Y. Universal Exposition, where the stunning Italian exhibit dazzled the spectators. The following year the Academy of Music was established, which brought many renowned Italian singers and musicians to the music-hungry New York public and helped popularize the Italian opera.[7]

De Rudio found modest lodging in the City of Brooklyn. He is known to have made the acquaintance of a Mr. D. Minnelli, an Italian instructor at Columbia College, probably a fellow Mazzinian, on whom he came to rely. Doubtless he also contacted other Mazzinians and, since he was a Mason, may have visited Masonic lodges. He showed his letters to anyone he thought could help him and let it be known that he was seeking a commission in the United States Army.

De Rudio soon learned that procuring a commission in 1864 was considerably more difficult than it had been in the early years of the war.

Having worn the red shirt in Rome, he might have been directed to the 39th N.Y. Infantry Regiment, the so-called

"Garibaldi Legion." Alexander Ripetti, who fought with Garibaldi in 1848, merged some Italian drill groups into one company of Italian Guard. In April 1861, there was a further consolidation of three companies of Germans, three of Hungarians, the Garibaldi guard and one company of Spanish and French volunteers. Later, there were additions of the Netherlands Legion, Polish Legion and First Foreign Rifles, all of whom went to form the 39th N.Y. (Garibaldi) Regiment,[8] so that the Italian contribution was quite diluted.[9]

Most regimental officers were elected, and even those appointed by the governor, had to be acceptable to the soldiers.[10] While regiments were being formed, commissions were comparatively easy to come by, but by 1864, new commissions were awarded chiefly by merit promotions, and rarely from gubernatorial appointments or from written examinations. Since the Garibaldi 39th Regiment was Italian in name only, De Rudio had no inside track for obtaining a commission in that regiment.

Italians served with other units of the Union Army. One hundred became officers and three rose to the rank of Brigadier General.[11] A private Italian military academy for aspirant officers was established early in the war. The enrollment fee was one hundred dollars and the course ran for six months. Some of the graduates did serve as commissioned officers. The founder, Count Luigi di Cesnola, went on to active military service in the 11th N.Y. Cavalry. He was captured at Gettysburg and after ten months of imprisonment, was paroled by the Confederates.[12]

De Rudio lost no time in hunting up Horace Greeley, editor of the N.Y. *Tribune*. Greeley had visited Genoa and Turin in 1851 and came away sympathetic both to Mazzini and the monarchy. Moreover, like De Rudio, Greeley was a Mason and numbered among his many friends Secretary of War Edwin Stanton and Abraham Lincoln. Although an early supporter of the President, Greeley may have later antagonized him, by personally offering to negotiate a peace settlement with the Confederacy.[13]

De Rudio paid his respects to Greeley and presented

Mazzini's letter. Greeley read it and offered immediate assistance. He wrote letters of introduction to public figures in New York and Washington, setting into operation the patronage network. The next three months were busy times for De Rudio, as he sought out public figures and solicited support. Carlos di Secci, a language teacher, requested on De Rudio's behalf a letter of recommendation from Charles Sumner, the Senator from Massachusetts. Judge Advocat John A. Bingham, formerly an Ohio Congressman, obliged with a letter for De Rudio. A very important contact was made with Rev. Henry W. Bellows, an official of the U.S. Sanitary Commission. Rev. Bellows was pastor of the First Unitarian Church of New York, founder of the Century, Union League and Harvard Clubs, and organizer-founder-president of the U.S. Sanitary Commission, which supervised the medical care of the army.[14]

The Rev. Bellows, in turn, addressed his own letter of introduction to General George Washington Cullum:[15]

> General George Washington Cullum
> U.S. Sanitary commission
> New York, March 31, 1864
>
> My dear General
> Count Carlo de Rudio, a Venetian, brings me excellent letters from England, accrediting him as a soldier and a gentleman. If you can in any proper way, facilitate his pursuit of a military position, you will greatly oblige
> Yours very truly
> Henry W. Bellows

Meanwhile the sad news reached De Rudio that his mother had died in the hospital at Belluno. The family was living in great poverty, and he was powerless to help.

De Rudio decided to follow up the letters with a trip in June to Washington. He called on many important officials, and, despite polite receptions, he found himself no closer to a commission. Washington was an expensive city, and, as his slim purse began to shrink alarmingly, he was compelled to borrow fifty dollars from F. V. Knapp, a member of the Sanitary Commission and an associate of the Rev. Bellows.

De Rudio had begun to realize that his chances for a direct commission in a volunteer regiment were poor. He had no gubernatorial connections, and no newly formed company would elect him. The best way to a commission might be in a black regiment.[16]

In the spring of 1863, the War Department had organized a system for the selection of officers to serve with the black troops. The Adjutant General established selection boards in several large cities. In Washington, the president of the board was Major General Silas Casey, a veteran of the Mexican War.[17] Initially forty-seven percent of the candidates were rejected as unfit. For those civilian and military candidates requiring special instruction, a free thirty-day course was given in Philadelphia, dealing with tactics, mathematics and drill evolution. One in four candidates eventually received a commission.[18]

De Rudio may have been referred directly to the Casey Board by someone in Washington:

"Under authority of the Secretary of War, you are hereby permitted to appear for examination before the Board now sitting at No 212 d "F" Street, of which Major General Silas Casey is President..."

He appeared before the selection board, underwent an examination and was found to be qualified:[19]

War Department
Adjutant General's Office
Washington, D.C. June 30, 1864
Count Carlo De Rudio
Washington D.C.

Sir:

I have respectfully to inform you that the Examining Board of which Major General Silas Casey is President report you qualified for a Second Lieutenant.

In accordance with the rules of the Department you will be appointed a Second Lieutenant U.S.Colored Troops, in term and as soon as the interests of the service will permit. (signed) C.W. Foster, Asst Adjt. Gen. Vols.

Successfully completing the examination was no guarantee that a commission would be forthcoming. This soon became apparent to De Rudio, when weeks passed without notification from the War Department. The army may not have been especially anxious to accept another foreign candidate, of which there were many, for a regiment that might have difficulty understanding even a native Yankee officer.

De Rudio returned to New York to further discuss his predicament with his sponsor. Greeley now proposed a different approach. He reasoned that De Rudio might find it easier to secure a commission, if he were already in the army. Moreover, should he offer himself as a substitute, he would receive a handsome financial incentive. And no one needed money more than De Rudio!

Congress had enacted a draft law in 1863 for ages twenty to forty-five, but allowed a temporary exemption until the next lottery drawing to anyone who paid three hundred dollars to the government; and permanent exemption for the draftee who furnished a substitute. The current emolument to the substitute was a thousand dollars. Many thought this law unfair to the poor. In the summer of 1863, a violent riot had erupted in New York, reflecting dissatisfaction with the war in general and with the draft in particular. Dissention quickly turned into a race riot, and it was the African-American who next drew the wrath of the rioters. A dozen black residents were murdered, and an orphanage for black children was sacked and burned.[20]

Charles C. De Rudio, as he was hereafter called, let it be known that he was prepared to offer his services as a substitute. An agreement was struck with Mr. William B. Ross of Brooklyn, who had been called up the summer of 1864 for service in the 79th Highlanders. The money proved to be a bonanza for De Rudio, enabling him to send for his family. He gave some cash to Mr. D. Minnelli, the language teacher, to pay off his debts and look after Eliza, once she arrived in New York.

Eliza, Hercules and her infant, born after De Rudio's departure, left from Liverpool on July 4, 1864. This can be learned from a letter written by her mother to George Holyoake, in which she complained that her daughter had been a great burden and had left her in poverty.[21] Clearly, Eliza's stay in Nottingham had not been a pleasant one. After the usual horrible sea journey, she arrived in New York in mid-July, where, doubtless, she was met by her husband and apprised of his plans.

The 79th Highlanders, in which De Rudio had enlisted, was a volunteer infantry regiment originally composed of people of Scottish descent. Early in the war, it sported bagpipes, Scottish plaid tartan pantaloons (undress) and kilts (dress). After Ft. Sumter, other nationalities joined, so that its Scottish origin became less evident.[22] At the expiration of their two-year enlistment, the soldiers patriotically volunteered for a third year. The regiment survived the First Battle of Bull Run and saw service at Antietam, Fredericksburg, Vicksburg, Tennessee, the Wilderness and Spottslyvania.[23] More than two-thirds of the regiment had been lost to death, illness and casualties. During the early seige of Petersburg, it had been stationed at Ft. Stedman,[24] occupying the far right segment of the Union line. At the end of July, most of the regiment was sent back to New York to be mustered out, but a cadre of one hundred enlisted men, who had not yet completed three years of service, were retained to help with the reorganization. While the regiment was undergoing its month of basic training, the regiment was stationed on Hart Island, offshore in the Bronx.

De Rudio reported to Hart Island on August 25, 1864. The

examining physician noted on physical examination that private De Rudio had dark eyes, black hair, dark complexion and stood 5'7" tall.[25] Moustache and goatee, which were to be his hallmark, were not mentioned, but we may presume he retained them. The enlistee signed a declaration that he, Charles De Rudio, age thirty-two, was physically and morally fit to serve for three years in the Army of the United States. An oath was then administered, in which he swore fidelity to the United States and to the President. The Count of Nosodano was now a private in the 79th N.Y. Highlanders

Captain Andrew D. Baird, the acting regimental commander, assigned De Rudio to Company A. At the conclusion of its month of training, the N.Y. 79th Infantry embarked on the steamer *Varuna* for a passage to Ft. Monroe, Virginia and thence by march to Zlinck's Station in southeast Virginia, where it rejoined the siege of Petersburg.

Grant had taken command of the Army of the Potomac four months earlier. He crossed the Rappahannock and first engaged the Army of Virginia in the Wilderness. At the conclusion of that savage battle, Grant astonished his staff by ordering an advance, personally heading up the lead column. Further battles followed in Spottsylvania and Cold Harbor, in which both sides sustained frightful losses. Following Cold Harbor, Grant crossed the James River over a mile long pontoon bridge and moved onto Petersburg, the Confederate rail junction. Unfortunately, the Union advance was delayed, so that instead of a quick victory, Grant was compelled to lay siege to the city. He could attack Petersburg from the north, and could extend his line to the east, but the siege was never an investment, since Petersburg continued to be supplied from the south by the South Side Railroad. Gradually, the siege works grew larger and more elaborate, as both sides dug deeper. It was clear to all that the fate of Petersburg would determine the outcome of the war. Worn down by the staggering losses of the earlier campaigns, the Union Army was content to continue the siege, mounting only one major effort to penetrate the Confederate lines.[26] On July 30,

1864 the Union forces attempted to breech the Confederate line by an elaborate tunneling, but the attack failed. Thereafter, Grant had to satisfy himself with sorties in force against the Confederate railroads and supply roads, slowly extending his line southward. At this point, the newly reorganized 79th N.Y. Infantry rejoined the Army of the Potomac.

On its return to duty at the Petersburg front on September 1, the 79th N.Y. was assigned to headquarters duty for the 9th Corps.[27] In addition to garrison duty at Ft. Hays, the 79th Infantry dug trenches, constructed abatis, felled timber, built corduroy roads and fortifications and performed picket and trench guard duty. In brief, the regiment was put to good use, but spared a major battle.[28] That would come later.[29]

Private De Rudio was a willing soldier. He learned quickly and showed bravery under fire during his month of service on the line. On several occasions he volunteered for hazardous duty. Once, as messenger, he carried in his mouth a cartridge case containing a ciphered message written on cigarette paper. He crossed the enemy lines under fire, avoiding capture.[30] He carried out other dangerous assignments, which came to the attention of his officers. As an enlisted man, Pvt. De Rudio had difficulty "fitting in". The young nobleman wrote to a patron, complaining of the course behavior of some of the soldiers.[31] The moustache, goatee and accent may have set him apart from his rough-and-tumble comrades in the 79th Infantry.

Pvt. De Rudio lost no time in pursuing his plans for a commission. He obtained from his commanding officer a testimonial, and, on 31 August, he asked that it be forwarded to the Adjutant General, Bureau of Colored Troops, together with other attestations of good moral character and standing. Had De Rudio not previously passed the Casey examination, he could at this point have requested to be sent to Philadelphia for special training; but as it turned out, a second examination was not required. Like De Rudio, most applicants for a commission in the USCT had previous military service.[32]

Pvt. De Rudio now turned to his supporters for help in

securing the commission. On October 5, 1864 he wrote to Pastor Frederick Newman Knapp requesting that he ask Rev. Channing to contact Mr. Dana, Assistant Secretary of War on his behalf. Charles A. Dana was a former editor of Greeley's N.Y.*Tribune,* who served early in the war as Lincoln's roving commissioner and later, as Assistant Secretary of War.[33] Dana was duly contacted. He wrote on the back of an undated letter of recommendation: "Can this man be appointed a 2nd Lieut with advantage to the Service?"[34] The note was sufficiently persuasive. On October 10, 1864 the Assistant Adjutant General, CW Foster, directed that "C.C. De Rudio be appointed to 1st vacancy of 2nd Lieut. Verbal order of Mr. Dana, Asst. Secretary of War of this date."[35]

Three days later, De Rudio received a letter from the War Department notifying him of his appointment as Second Lieutenant in the 2nd United States Colored Troops (Infantry), then stationed in Key West, Florida.[36]

All that remained was the formality of accepting the commission and detaching himself from the 79th Regiment. This he did on October 16, in a formal letter to the General Headquarters of the 9th Army Corp, requesting that he be discharged from the 79th, so that he could join the 2nd U.S.C.T (Inf).[37]

Black regiments were initially considered to be a political liability, while the loyalty of the slave-owning soldiers from Maryland, Delaware, Kentucky and the District of Columbia was in question. On August 4, 1862 President Lincoln was compelled to refuse an offer from the Indiana delegation to raise two regiments of colored troops, observing: "To arm the Negroes would turn fifty thousand bayonets from the loyal border states against us."[38] Supporters of black enlistment persevered, mindless of disappointments. Meanwhile, slavery had been prohibited in the territories, then terminated in the District of Columbia and, finally, abolished in the southern states still at war.[39] Lincoln carefully marked time, waiting for the first opportune moment. The time came on March 1863 when he wrote: The colored population is the great available, and yet unavailed of, force for restoring the Union."[40]

The United States Colored Troops were established on May 22, 1863 by General Order No. 143,[41] and a month later the first regiment was organized. In all, one hundred sixty-six regiments were raised during the war. Equality in pay and benefits was slow in coming.[42] On April 19, 1864, equal pay was authorized, but for only those black soldiers who had been freemen on April 19, 1861. This led many black soldiers to take a "Quaker oath," with fingers crossed, stating they had been freemen on that date. Not until March 3, 1865 was equality in pay established for all and, in expiation, made retroactive to the date of enlistment.[43]

By October 1864, there were one hundred forty Colored regiments in Federal service with a strength of a hundred thousand men. They were to participate in every major Union campaign between 1864 and 1865, with the exception of Sherman's invasion of Georgia. A total of thirty-seven thousand black soldiers lost their lives in battle.[44] Also to be factored in is the inestimable contribution of the black "contraband," which extricated the bulky wagons from the mud, unloaded freight trains and river boats and obligingly performed the many distasteful jobs around camp.

The 2nd USCT (Infantry), to which De Rudio was assigned, had been formed in 1863, while camped outside of Washington in Arlington Heights.[45] There, the recruit was transformed from a plantation hand into a soldier.[46] Its first colonel, Second Lieutenant James Schneider, had successfully passed a qualifying examination in algebra, geometry, trigonometry, chemistry, history and geography. When he informed the examiners he was seeking a major's commission in the USCT, he was told that his goal was too modest. Instead, they recommended a colonel's commission and with it, command of a regiment of nine hundred and fifty men.

The other thirty-six commissioned officers in the regiment included seven or eight college graduates, half of whom had seen action.[47] They had high intellectual attainments and generally were of good moral character. During training, several complaints from the slave-holding Maryland farmers were received by the War Department, accusing the regiment of enticing away field slaves. This, the recruiting officer denied, pointing out that one of his lieutenants had been murdered and four soldiers poisoned, by those unscrupulous Maryland slave owners.[48]

After its formation, the 2nd USCT had been sent from Washington to New York on November 22, 1863, for embarkation by steamer to New Orleans. The march up Broadway to Canal Street, where the ship was docked, was not without incident. A crowd followed closely behind, hurling insults at the soldiers and their white officers. This pattern was later to be repeated. The trip to New Orleans took two weeks and was thoroughly disagreeable.[49] The regiment was then sent to Ship Island, eight miles off the coast of Mississippi, guarding Mobile Gulf. There it remained for two months, during which time disease claimed the lives of three officers and twenty-four soldiers.[50] The regiment was then transferred to Key West, Florida, in the Department of the Gulf of Mexico, where it arrived February 22, 1864.

Key West had been quite prosperous before the war, its chief income derived from fishing, the manufacture of cigars, and the harvest of salt and sponges. In early 1860, it was considered the wealthiest town in the United States, per capita (slaves were excluded from the calculations). Since then, it had become an important station for the Union blockade of the southern ports. Over three hundred captured Confederate vessels lay at some time in its harbor, under the watchful protection of Ft. Zachary Taylor. The fort had been built on an island, to defend the town from pirates, but the island had since joined the mainland, after the intervening water had silted up.

The 2nd USCT was stationed at Ft. Taylor on the southwest end of the Key West, near the entrance to the harbor. At that time, a railroad ran from the fort to two market towns near the eastern end of the island. Four of the companies were billeted in the fort; another in barracks and five were encamped, awaiting completion of additional barracks.[51]

Once again, the regiment encountered hostility from the white population, many of whom had suffered financial loss from the emancipation of their slaves. Their colonel complained that since his arrival, "I have been insulted, cursed and abused everywhere."[52] A rivalry sprang up with the 47th Pennsylvania who were also garrisoned on the island. The 47th promptly petitioned to be transferred. As time passed, the inhabitants of Key West saw that the black regiment drilled better and behaved better than the white companies. Notwithstanding, until the 47th Pennsylvania left, no day went by "without one of the officers or men being struck with stones, etc."[53]

In May, four months after their arrival, Yellow Fever struck! More than half the regiment came down with the illness and four died, despite the insistence of the local inhabitants that yellow fever "seldom proves fatal to colored men." All but one officer developed Yellow Fever.[54]

To protect the health of the soldiers, the regiment was quickly withdrawn from Key West and the companies scattered to various posts along one hundred miles of the western Florida coast.

The regiment's early military record was unspectacular. In a raid on Tampa in May, they captured and destroyed five cannons. In October, they destroyed plantations and burned cotton in Bay Port.[55]

De Rudio was discharged from the 79th Regiment at Pebbles House on the outskirts of Petersburg on October 17, 1864. He proudly outfitted himself with an officer's uniform and, after "wetting down his commission," made arrangements for Eliza to join him in Florida. Arriving by ship in Key West on November 11, he reported in to Colonel John Wilder and was assigned to Company D.

Company D remained for a few weeks on guard duty in Key West and was then sent to Point Rassa, south of Tampa to serve as military police. De Rudio handled his men well and listened attentively to their complaints.

They had much to gripe about.[56] A Lt. O.A. Carpenter of D Company made off with two thousand dollars, given him by the enlisted men for safe keeping.[57] Soldiers also voiced their resentment about unequal pay, which went unremedied until 1865.[58] They criticized their obsolete muskets, which were later replaced with Springfield rifles.[59] And, too, they complained about not having black officers.[60] Black officers had served briefly in the free black militia in Louisiana, but none had been appointed to a U.S.C.T. regiment, apart from an occasional black physician or chaplain.

Eliza and Hercules arrived at Key West in January 1865, bringing with them a second child. Eliza's trip from New York had been a nightmare. During a violent storm, the ship had foundered with the loss of all their possessions, including their marriage certificate.[61] No sooner had Eliza and her children reached Key West, than the second child came down with an infectious disease and died. Elisa was required to attend to the burial arrangements by herself, since De Rudio was away at Ft. Myers, Florida. It is likely Eliza lived in the officers' quarters in Ft. Taylor, where she may have had the company of other officers' wives.

In February 1865 the 2nd USCT participated in a minor raid in Levy County, destroying commissary stores, and capturing ten men, thirteen horses and one hundred head of cattle.[62] But it was not until March 1865 that the regiment fought its first important engagement. The objective was the capture of St. Marks in the Florida panhandle, which had replaced Wilmington, North Carolina as the last Confederate seaport. The plan also called for the regiment to seize nearby Newport, cut the rail tracks to Tallahassee and finally capture Tallahassee itself. About one thousand Union soldiers participated in the expedition.

The 2nd USCT embarked on several steamships for the Florida panhandle, a distance of four hundred miles. De Rudio and Company D sailed on the *Magnolia*. After landing, the Union troops set out for Newport, but their advance was halted by the destruction of the Newport Bridge. Undaunted, the Union Army tried to seize Natural Bridge, four miles away, but the Confederate troops had already reinforced the bridge, and their artillery had ample opportunity to register their guns on the approaching Union forces. De Rudio and his men participated in the attempt to seize Natural Bridge. Since the Navy was slow to arrive, the troops could not be ferried across river, nor supplied with ammunition. Suddenly two thousand Confederate soldiers appeared, including cadets from the Florida Military Academy. They poured across the bridge, charged the Federal line and swept it back. The Union soldiers were compelled to withdraw, abandoning the wounded. In all, twenty-one Union men had been killed, including the commanding officer. The raid had been a fiasco. The Union soldiers reembarked in haste and were transported back to Key West, where the commanding officer was buried with honors and details of the raid forgotten in the official archives.[63]

In March and April of 1865, Company D was back in Punta Rossa.

By now, the war was winding down. Sherman had completed his march to the sea and Sheridan, the conquest of the Shenandoah. Grant had finally cut the South Side Railway and, as Sherman's Army approached from the south, Lee was forced to abandon Petersburg and Richmond. The Third Cavalry Division, led by Major General George A. Custer, cut off the Confederate retreat and on April 9, 1865 General Lee surrendered at Appomattox Court House. The war had ended.

Following the defeat of the Confederacy, the 2nd USCT was retained in the military district of Florida for another eight months. Enlistments in the regular army were encouraged. Black companies in time would come to comprise ten percent of the infantry and twenty percent of the cavalry. In July and August, Company D was sent to Tallahassee, Florida to show the flag. September and October saw the company "absent gathering cattle," probably confiscated from Confederate sympathizers. In November and December, the company returned to Key West

Florida, where on January 5, 1866 it was mustered out of military service.⁶⁴ The soldiers scattered quickly.

Ten days later De Rudio acquired United States citizenship. This resource, together with his war service, opened up new opportunities. On July 14, 1866, De Rudio moved his family to Washington. He lost no time in contacting Dr. Bellows, who provided him with letters of recommendation and assisted him in finding employment as a civilian clerk in the War Department. De Rudio was assigned to the Bureau of Refugees, Freedmen and Abandoned Lands, which seemed an appropriate position for a former officer in a black regiment.

The Bureau had been established to provide for the welfare of the black population in former Confederate states. General Oliver Otis Howard,⁶⁵ the one-armed "praying general," headed the agency. He had risen from second lieutenant to Major General and Corps commander in the Civil War.⁶⁶ He was thirty-five years old, born in Maine, a graduate of Bowdoin College and West Point, distinguished not only for his compassion, but also for his spirited efforts in the behalf of African Americans.⁶⁷ Since the Bureau was an agency of the War Department, General Howard ran it along military lines. He appointed his assistant commissioners from the military officers known to him. The assistant commissioners worked side by side with the army officers until 1868, when the Freedman's Bureau was terminated and its work taken over by the district military officers.⁶⁸

De Rudio was employed in the Quartermaster General's Office of the Freedman's Bureau, which handled food and supply indents for the needy southern population, both black and white. Most of his fellow clerks had been hired by the War Department, but a few came from Howard's own army staff. The Bureau was located on the corner of 19th and I St., in a house provided by Secretary of War Edwin Stanton. The Quartermaster's Department furnished the desks and chairs insuring that the decor would conform to high bureaucratic standards.⁶⁹

Doubtless, Mr. De Rudio fulfilled his duties to the

satisfaction of his superiors. He was known for his neatness, regularity, sobriety and attention to detail. Even without patronage, his performance sooner or later was certain to come to the attention of General Oliver Otis Howard.

Notes

1. Jasper Ridley, *Garibaldi* (New York: Vicking Press, 1974), p. 364.
2. Howard R. Marraro, "Italians in New York in the 1850's." N.Y. History 30, no. 2 (April-July, 1949), 181-203.
3. Olivis Allen, *New York* (New York: Athenium, 1990), p. 239.
4. Marraro, p. 14.
5. Jerre Mangione and Ben Morreale, *La Storia* (New York: Harper Perennial, 1993), p. 16.
6. Marraro, p. 12.
7. *Ibid.*, p. 33.
8. William L. Burton, *Melting Pot Soldiers* (Ames: Iowa State University Press, 1988), p. 169; Ernest McKay, *The Civil War and New York City* (Syracuse, NY: Syracuse University Press, 1990), p. 76.
9. Edwin G. Burrows and Mike Wallace, *A History of New York City to 1898* (New York and Oxford: Oxford, 1999), p. 870.
10. Burton, p. 170.
11. Mangione and Morreale, p. 17.
12. *Ibid.*, p. 18.
13. William Harland Hale, *Horace Greeley* (New York: Harper, 1950), pp. 280-6.
14. *Dictionary of American Biography* (New York: Scribner, 1936), 1:1699.
15. Appointment, Commission, Personal File (ACP): Charles C. De Rudio, Consolidated File D345 CT 1864 (CF D345 CT 1864); Pension File: Charles C. De Rudio [Eliza Booth DeRudio] National Archives and Record Service, National Archives Building, Washington, DC (NAB).
16. Joseph T. Glatthaar, *Forged in Battle* (New York: Macmillan, 1990), p. 43.
17. Herman Hattaway, *The Sable Arm* (Lawrence, KS: University of Kansas Press, 1987), p. 208.
18. Glatthaar, pp. 47, 53.
19. ACP, Charles C. De Rudio, CF D345 CT 1864, NAB.
20. Glatthaar, p. 196.
21. Cesare Marino, *Dal Piave al Little Bighorn* (Belluno: Tarantola, 1996), p. 387 n. 30.
22. Burton, p. 162; William Todd, *The 79th Highlanders,* (Albany, NY: Biandow, Barton, 1880), p. 1.
23. McKay, p. 24; Todd, p. 134 *et passim.*
24. Richard J. Sommers, *Richmond Redeemed* (Garden City, NY: Doubleday, 1999), p. 240.
25. Kenneth Hammer, ed., *Custer in 76* (Norman and London: University Oklahoma, 1988), p. 97.
26. Bevin Alexander, *Robert E. Lee's Civil War* (Holbrook, MA: Adams Media, 1998), p. 284.
27. War of the Rebellion, Series I, Vol. 42, Part II, Richmond Campaign.

Correspondence, p. 646; see also Todd, p. 480.
28. War of the Rebellion, Series I, Vol. 42, Part II, Richmond Campaign, Correspondence, p. 707; also War of the Rebellion, Series I, Vol. 43, Part I. Reports. p. 74.
29. War of the Rebellion, Series I, Vol. 42, Part I, Correspondence, p. 558.
30. (no author) "Notable Military Figure Loosing in this Battle." *Los Angeles Daily Times,* 1 November 1910.
31. De Rudio to F. N. Knapp, October 5, 1864. ACP, Charles C. De Rudio, CF D345 CT 1864, NAB.
32. Glatthaar, pp. 38, 18; Hattaway, pp. 209, 213.
33. *Dictionary of American Biography* (New York: Scribner, 1936), V:49.
34. ACP, Charles C. De Rudio, CF D345 CT 1864, NAB.
35. *Ibid.*
36. *Ibid.*
37. *Ibid.*
38. James M. McPherson, *The Negro's Civil War* (Urbana, Chicago: University of Illinois, 1982), p. 164.
39. *Ibid.,* p. 44.
40. *Ibid.,* p. 165.
41. Hondon B. Hargrove, *Black Union Soldiers in the Civil War* (Jefferson, NC: McFarnand, 1988), p. x.
42. Ira Berlin, ed., *Freedoms* (Cambridge, London: Cambridge University Press, 1982), p. 374.
43. Michael Lee Lanning, *The African American Soldier* (Secaucus, NJ: Carol, 1997), p. 50.
44. McPherson, p. 222.
45. Increase Tarbox, *Missionary Patriots. Memoirs of James H. Schneider and Edward M. Schneider* (Boston: Massachusetts Sabbath School Society, 1867), p. 127.
46. McPherson, p. 171.
47. Tarbox, p. 136.
48. Berlin, p. 212.
49. Tarbox, p. 138.
50. *Ibid.,* p.159.
51. *Ibid.,* p. 160.
52. *Ibid.,* p. 169.
53. Glatthaar, p. 196.
54. Tarbox, p. 193.
55. War of the Rebellion, Series I, Vol. XXXIV Pt. IV, Correspondence, p. 390.
56. Tarbox, p. 130; Ervin L. Jordan, Jr., *Black Confederates and Afro-Yankees in the Civil War* (Charlottesville, VA: Virginia University Press, 1955), p. 271.
57. Glatthaar, p. 89.
58. *Ibid.,* p. 171.
59. *Ibid.,* p.189.
60. Noah Andre Trudeau, *Like Men of War* (Boston: Little Brown, 1998), p. 365.
61. Marino, p. 387 n. 31.
62. War of the Rebellion, Series, I, Vol. 49, Part I. Reports and Correspondence, p. 40.

63. Trudeau, p. 365; War of the Rebellion, Series I, Vol. 49, Part I. Reports and Correspondence, p. 40.
64. Official Army Register for 1908, Government Printing Office, p. 469.
65. Henrietta Buckmaster, *Freedom Bound* (New York: Macmillan, 1965), p. 55; John A. Carpenter, *Sword and Olive Branch* (Pittsburgh: University of Pittsburgh Press: Pittsburgh, 1964, p. 105.
66. Carpenter, pp. 21-60.
67. Charles A. Wesley, and Patricia W. Romero, *Negro American in the Civil War* (Cornwells Heights, PA: Publishers Co., 1967), p. 131; Buckmaster, p. 35.
68. Carpenter, p. 137.
69. *Ibid.*, p. 222.

VI
REGULAR ARMY COMMISSION

Charles Camillus De Rudio had no intention of being permanently fettered to a clerk's stool. From the very beginning, he was determined to secure a commission in the regular army. This required careful and meticulous planning. A regular army commission was far more difficult to obtain than a wartime commission in a volunteer black regiment. Proven military mettle was the established criterion for selection, and De Rudio had less than fourteen months service in a black regiment with an inglorious record. Notwithstanding, he resolutely set out on the familiar path of contacting prominent people and assembling letters of recommendation. With no pressing concern about his family finances, he could afford to be patient, circumspect and thorough.

Why did De Rudio not apply for a commission in the regular army while he was still on active duty? It seems likely that a military candidate without two years of field duty would have been *automatically* disqualified; but the rule could be relaxed for a civilian candidate.

The ambitious clerk obtained letters from Horace Greeley, Rev. Dr. Bellows, and Congressman Henry Dawes. His former superior officers also supplied him with testimonials. General Newton, Lt. Col. John Wilder and Major Dewey spoke of his "uniform good character, faithfulness activity and attention to duty."[1]

Other prominent figures were approached. General Benjamin Butler, a political heavyweight (and a military flyweight), wrote a perfunctory letter: "I beg to draw the attention of the Secretary of War to *Captain* Rudio, an Italian, who seems to have an excellent record in the war and wishes to have a 2nd Lieutenancy." Senator Sumner, once again, provided a letter to Under Secretary of War Dana. Charles Sumner had been senator from Massachusetts since 1851 and an early supporter of the celebrated black regiment, the 54th Massachusetts.[2] Doubtless, he had a kind regard for any officer who had served with a black regiment.[3]

Letters of recommendation do not suddenly appear in the mail. One must request them hat in hand, wait, follow up, wait and hope.

With the help of his patrons, De Rudio was finally able to approach General Howard, who himself owed a part of his meteoric rise to political help. General Howard studied the documents De Rudio placed before him. He was especially interested in the De Rudio family history and asked questions about it.

Howard forwarded the recommendations to General Schriver, together with his own note:

> "Are there any vacancies as 2nd Lieutenant? It strikes me that Lieut. De Rudio is too worthy a man to lose. He is a gentleman of education and culture".

De Rudio's efforts came at a time when many thousands of volunteer offices had been discharged from military service. A few were anxious to exchange their volunteer rank for a commission in the regular army. The army needed four thousand officers at the moment, but the candidates knew from the beginning that this number would be steadily reduced in the ensuing years, and that many would later be out of work. Half the officers would not be West Point graduates. About thirteen percent would be commissioned from the ranks.[4]

Regular Army Commission

De Rudio's papers were submitted to the War Department, along with the letters of recommendation, painstakingly collected. He was classified as a civilian candidate. There was a requirement in 1866 that the civilian candidate have two years of wartime service, but this appears to have been waived in De Rudio's case. The candidate's application was duly processed by the War Department, during which time his military record was studied and his letters of recommendation weighed. Selection officers made their evaluations and their findings were presented to the Secretary of War. In De Rudio's case, the imprimatur of patronage was quite evident on the application, but this was by no means extraordinary.

The memorable day came on August 31, 1867 when De Rudio was officially notified of his appointment as second lieutenant in the regular army, subject to a review of his educational qualifications and medical status. He appeared before the first board, which examined military service and educational background. The candidate's grasp of military matters was not explored, since his service record was presumed to speak for itself. Instead, he was asked such general questions as:[5]

> How many pounds of beef, flour and coffee would you require for 10,000 men for 60 days, the daily ration being 1 1/2 pound of flour, 1 1/4 beef and 1/16 pound coffee?
> Name the principle rivers that empty into the Atlantic.
> Locate the Straits of Gibraltar.
> Name the principle events in American history.

De Rudio was able to satisfy the examiners and they passed him unconditionally.

He was then ordered to report to New York for a medical examination. There, three doctors examined him and submitted their report to the War Department. To his astonishment, their report read:

Board to Examine Officers Appointed in the Infantry of the Army No 125 Bleecker Street, New York City Sept 17, 1867

I certify on honor that I have carefully examined Charles C. De Rudio agreeably to the General Regulations of the Army, and that in my opinion he is *disqualified* from performing the duties of an Officer, on account of retraction of the right testicle, existing from his birth. (signed) MJ Sloan and Brev. Brig Gen Ash

The small congenital malformation cited in the report was a partially undescended right testicle of little medical import. The Hart Island medical examination makes no mention of it, not that wartime medical examinations were particularly thorough. Perhaps this finding was just a pretext for disqualifying him; or his role in the Orsini affair may have become known to the army selection staff; or there may have been resentment about his patronage or his accent.

A subsequent notice from the War Department Adjutant General's Office dated September 20, 1867 confirmed the calamitous news:

Sir:
I have to inform you that the Report of the Board of Examination has been in your case on account of physical disability unfavorable and that your appointment is, by direction of the President, hereby *canceled*. (Signed) D.C. Kelton Assistant Adjutant General

On the very day he learned of the decision of the Medical Board, De Rudio hastened to consult Dr. R. Tauszky, a prominent civilian surgeon, at his own expense. The surgeon declared:

"There is not the slightest deviation either in the

shape, size or direction of the right testicle, which would in the least interfere either in marching on foot, or horseback, nor in any posture...and there is not even the slightest probability that it will ever incommode him during the remainder of his life."

For good measure, Dr. Tauszky added that the patient had little danger of developing an inguinal hernia, since the opening of his internal inguinal canal was snug.[6]

The following day he was examined by a second civilian physician, Dr. Edward H. Djon, who reported that De Rudio's condition "in no way impairs his constitution power nor his capacity as a military man."[7]

Armed with these documents, De Rudio wrote G.C. Kelton, Assistant Adjutant General of the United States on September 30, 1867 and requested reexamination by the Army Medical Board, pointing out that the chief examining surgeon in New York himself had declared that he would consider another opinion. Horace Greeley and Senator Charles Sumner, who had both understood the travesty of De Rudio's rejection, personally contacted Secretary of War Stanton. The matter finally came to the attention of the Executive Mansion. William G. Moore, an aid to President Johnson, gave De Rudio a letter to bring to the Adjutant General:

> Executive Mansion
> Washington D.C. Oct. 16, 1867
>
> Dear General:
>
> The bearer, Lieut. C.C. de Rudio, is the gentleman respecting whose case I spoke to you yesterday. Having passed the required mental examination, he failed before the Medical Board at New York. He has been assured by eminent members of the medical profession, that the physical defect which caused his rejection cannot

incapacitate him from the performance of active military duty, and the fact that it did not in the least interfere with him during the war....would seem to confirm this opinion. As he has a wife and two children and was appointed, I believe, upon his military record, I hope that the rules of the service will not interdict a second examination in Mr. Rudio's case (signed) William G.Moore

De Rudio was ordered to undergo a new medical examination, not in New York, but at the office of the Surgeon General in Washington, D.C. He did this and on November 4, 1867 was notified of the result:

> Board to examine Officers appointed in the Infantry
>   of the Army
> November 4, 1867
> Sir
>
> I have the honor to inform you that you have *passed* a satisfactory examination before this Board (signed) S.P. Heintzelman Col 17th Infy President of the Board.

De Rudio was reinstated in rank, retroactive to October 25, 1867. As of that date, he was a Second Lieutenant in the U.S. Army. He donned his old uniform and awaited word of his new assignment. To add to the family pleasure, it was further blessed with the birth of a daughter, Roma Elisabetta. And his fondest hopes were realized when at long last, following the defeat of Austria by the Prussians, Venetia was given over to the Kingdom of Italy!

The army had undergone great changes since the exuberant days of the late war. Gone were the civilian plaudits -- the bouquets, banquets and baked pies. Too many military stars had risen and set on the horizon, and the streets were filled with limbless veterans, scornful of military pretensions. Economy and indifference now governed the public attitude, and few civilians made an effort to understand the current problems of the military community. The regular army was a closed society, living apart from public scrutiny. Seniority was scrupulously observed and social obligations stressed. Private income, family background, wartime service and political support were all important factors in an officer's social standing and assignments.

The peacetime army had fifty-six thousand soldiers in 1867, but its strength was expected to fall sharply each year by Congressional design, until it reached twenty-five thousand in 1875. With these numbers, the army was required to maintain the coastal fortifications, perform Reconstruction duty and provide protection for the vast expanses of unsettled country from Texas to the Canadian border and from the Missouri River to the Pacific coast.[8] A total of four hundred thirty companies manned two hundred posts.

The officer appointed from civilian life differed in many ways from the West Point graduate, who often regarded him with suspicion, if not hostility. A quarter of the civilian appointees were foreign born and many had served in foreign armies. The salary scale for all officers was the same. The pay for a second lieutenant was $1,400 per year, for a colonel $3,500. Promotion for all was excruciatingly slow, the second lieutenant requiring twenty-four years to reach the rank of major and thirty-three to thirty-seven years to become a colonel,[9] if in fact that rank were ever attained.

In early November 2nd Lieutenant Charles De Rudio was handed orders to report for duty with the Second Infantry in Louisville, Kentucky.

The Second Infantry was a celebrated regiment, first organized in Kentucky in 1791. During the Civil War it had participated in many of the campaigns as a part of the Vth Corps of the Army of the Potomac, beginning with Bull Run and continuing through Sharpsburg, Fredericksburg, Gettysburg, Wilderness and Spottsylvania.[10] After Cold Harbor, the survivors were consolidated into one company, and in October 1864 they were sent for build-up to an infantry recruit depot at Newport

Barracks, Kentucky, where they remained until the end of hostilities. In the months that followed, the buildup continued, but now a new breed filled the ranks.

The peacetime recruits were a colorful, if not a motley collection. They came from the cities, chiefly from among the urban poor and unskilled workers. In 1866 one newspaper editor remarked "a respectable American citizen would no more think of joining the Regular Army than he would volunteer for the penitentiary." Another referred to the rank and file as "bummers, loafers and foreign paupers."[11] And yet another: "the vast majority were 'bounty jumpers', blackguards and criminals of various degrees, or, at any rate, men who had sought the army as an asylum from the punishments."[12] Some signed up for free transport to the gold mines in the west, intending to desert at the first opportunity.[13] From 1865 to 1874 more than half the recruits had been born in foreign countries, especially Ireland and Germany.[14] Many had seen service in foreign armies.

The average age for first-time recruits was twenty-three. Some were illiterate; others used a false name when enlisting. The cavalry recruit enlisted for five years, the infantry recruit for three years; but after 1869 the infantry enlistment was lengthened to five years. The starting pay for a private was thirteen dollars a month, increased incrementally until it reached fifteen dollars a month in the third year.[15] This was less than the sixteen dollars paid to the Civil War private, a cause of great dissatisfaction. Payment was made in greenbacks, issued by the Federal Treasury. Since these were not fully backed by gold, merchants around camp demanded a fifteen to forty percent discount before accepting them.[16] Protests were plentiful, bitter, and usually unavailing. From 1867 to 1891 one third of all recruits eventually deserted.

After enlistment, the recruit was sent to a recruiting depot. Newport Barracks in Kentucky was one of three such depots for

Regular Army Commission

the infantry; Jefferson Barracks in Missouri served for the cavalry.[17] He was issued a surplus undress uniform usually in small size, since the Civil War contractors had tried to maximize profits.

Clothing costs were debited to his pay account. His kit included a forage cap, an overcoat, a blouse, a pair of pants, two flannel shirts, two pairs of flannel draws, two pairs of socks, one pair of mittens and a woolen blanket. Shoes were issued to the infantryman, boots to the cavalryman, if available. There was much dissatisfaction with the issue: the woolen underwear and socks caused unmerciful itching; right and left footwear were indistinguishable; the leather was too stiff to be broken in; and the brass screws through the soles caused blisters in the summer and frostbite in winter.[18]

The newcomer received four to six weeks training in elementary barracks routine. This meant drill, courtesy and review and, for the cavalry recruits, the elements of riding. Discipline was inflexible and austere. The recruit was taught to keep body and uniform clean and was given exercises to toughen him up.[19] Seldom did he get to fire a rifle.[20] Following indoctrination, he was sent to the regiment in which he had enlisted.

Second Lieutenant De Rudio traveled by train to Crittenden Barracks in Louisville, Kentucky and was later joined by his family. On November 18, 1867, he reported for duty and was assigned to Company F, Second Infantry, as assistant company commander. With the ink still wet on his commission, his quarters may have been among the least desirable on the post. His acting company commander was Lieut. William L.R. Marge, a twenty-three year old Civil War veteran from Pennsylvania, who had temporarily replaced the regular commander.

One presumes that the new shavetail experienced difficulty in adjusting to his new assignment, at least in the beginning. A company of spirited white city youths differed in many ways from a company of black soldiers recently delivered from slavery. For one thing, their speech was different, although neither could have found it easy to understand their new officer. Then again, a thirty-five year old shavetail was something of a curiosity, especially one with a waxed moustache and goatee.

There are some unconfirmed reports that De Rudio was not welcome in his unit. A newspaper article published four decades later states that the field officers swore they would not have "that man" in the regiment.[21] According to the story, De Rudio was not assigned to any specific duty for two years, but there is no indication of this in his service record.

On the contrary, Second Lt. De Rudio seems to have discharged his duties to the satisfaction of his superiors. In the summer of 1868, he was made acting company commander, when the regular company commander was on temporary duty. In the autumn of 1868, he was transferred to Lebanon, Kentucky, to serve as adjutant to the commanding officer of the local garrison.[22] Service in Kentucky was considerably more pleasant than the Reconstruction duty he was later to see in the south. Kentucky had not seceded from the Union, so that the repressive Reconstruction laws were not applied to it, although a considerable number of Kentuckians had served in the Confederate Army. The fact that there was a good response to peacetime recruitment for the 2nd Infantry might indicate that the public held the regiment in high regard.

While in Kentucky, Eliza gave birth to a girl named Italia Luigia after Carlo's sister. Eliza settled down to the dull life of a subaltern's wife in a Kentucky garrison, while her husband went about his duties. Louisville was not without its courtly charm, although, with three small children and a husband away in Lebanon, Kentucky, it is doubtful that Eliza had much opportunity to enjoy the attractions of the city.

While De Rudio was mastering the details of army life, the nation was deeply engrossed in westward expansion. Gold had been discovered in Colorado, Idaho, Montana and Wyoming;

silver in Nevada. Chicago was soon to be joined to San Francisco by rail. Hundreds of thousands of homesteaders were streaming west, lured by the promise of one hundred sixty acres for five years of work.

Congress was in remarkable agreement as to how the frontier should be guarded. With the hostile tribes scattered over an immense area, it was thought that protection could best be achieved with cavalry. Accordingly, in 1866 Congress authorized an increase in the number of cavalry from six to ten regiments, and correspondingly, it reduced the infantry regiments from forty to twenty-five.[23] Enlisted and officer infantry personnel would gradually be decreased, until the army reached a size of twenty-five thousand enlisted and two thousand officers by 1875. During this period of reorganization and retrenchment, promotions would be frozen and unfit officers weeded out.

In effect, the services of many infantry officers whose regiments were disbanded or consolidated were about to be terminated. Benzine Boards were set up to quickly eliminate the undesirables.[24] Others were placed on the unassigned list. Pay could be suspended and commissions revoked, unless the officer was assigned to a new regiment. Word was received that the 2nd Infantry was about to be merged with the 16th Infantry. Second Lieut. De Rudio, then stationed in Lebanon, Kentucky, was placed on the unassigned list, pending reassignment, reassessment or dismissal by the War Department. The list even included the commanding officer of the regiment.[25]

Officer selections and assignments were directed, not by the Commanding General of the Army, whose duties were largely confined to matters of discipline and military control,[26] but by the quasi-independent War Department, under the supervision of the Secretary of War. Selections and assignments by the War Department reflected its own concepts of service requirements and officer merit, which, in turn, were often influenced by outside pressures, brought to bear by members of Congress or by those to whom the Congressmen were beholden.[27] Without patronage, De Rudio would have been extremely vulnerable during this reorganization, since he had been a civilian appointee, with a comparatively brief and undistinguished wartime service.

Notes

1. The recommendations cited and others are found in the file. ACP, Charles C. De Rudio, CF D345 CT 1864, NAB.
2. *Dictionary of American Biography* (New York: Scribner, 1936), I:277
3. Claude G. Bowers, *The Tragic Era* (Cambridge, MA: Houghton Mifflin, 1929), p. 332.
4. Robert M. Utley, *Frontier Regulars. The United States Army and the Indian, 1866-1890* (New York: Macmillan, 1973), p.19.
5. W. A. Dobak, and Thomas D. Phillips, *The Black Regulars 1866-1898* (Norman: University of Oklahoma Press, 1995), pp. 32, 132.
6. Letter of R. Tauszky, M.D. Sept. 19, 1867. "...The abdominal rings as well as the inguinal canal on both sides and also both spermadic cords are healthy." (Signed) R. Tauszky, M.D. late a surgeon of U.S. volunteers. ACP, Charles C. De Rudio, CF D345 CT 1864, NAB.
7. ACP, Charles C. De Rudio, CF D345 CT 1864, NAB.
8. Mary Ellen Jones, *Daily Life on the Nineteenth Century American Frontier* (Westport, CT: Greenwood, 1988), p. 217.
9. Don Rickey, *Forty Miles a Day on Beans and Hay* (Norman and London: University of Oklahoma, 1963), p. 214.
10. Frederick Shaw, *One Hundred and Forty Years Service in Peace and War: History of the Second Infantry* (Detroit and Fullerton, CA: Strathmore, 1930), p. 328.
11. Jones, p. 218.
12. *Ibid.*, pp. 218, 214.
13. *Ibid.*, p. 219.
14. Rickey, p. 18.
15. Interview with Pvt. William Slaper in E. A. Brininstool, *Troopers with Custer* (Lincoln and London: University of Nebraska, 1952), p. 36.
16. Jones, p. 218; Utley, *Frontier*, p. 23
17. Rickey, p. 33.
18. Jones, pp. 219, 223.
19. *Ibid.*, p.223.
20. *Ibid.*, p. 239.
21. W. H. Robarts, "A Resurrected Infamy," *Washington Post*, 15 September 1901.
22. Cesare Marino, *Dal Piave al Little Bighorn* (Belluno: Tarantola, 1996), p. 185.
23. Utley, *Frontier.* p. 17.
24. John Upton Terrell, and George Walton, *Faint the Trumpet Sounds* (New York: McKay, 1966), p. 71.
25. Shaw, p. 333.
26. Maurice Matlof, *American Military History* Office of the Chief of Military History, 1969 (revised 1973), Government Printing Office, p. 291
27. Utley, *Frontier*, p. 32.

CHAPTER VII
CAVALRY OFFICER

Happily for him, De Rudio remained idle for no more than a few weeks, although it must have been a time of great apprehension, as he watched fellow officers reluctantly prepare to reenter civilian life. Thanks to his political benefactors, he soon received word that he was assigned to the 7th Cavalry, stationed at Ft. Riley, Kansas. By army standards, this appointment was a plum for a young unmarried officer, inured to the outdoor life and anxious to see action. For a married man, it meant serious hardship for his family, especially since the station was on the frontier, where family social life would be confined to an outlying, manure-reeking, fly-ridden collection of shabby buildings.

His enemy, henceforth, would be a brave, aboriginal people recently emerging from a paleolithic society. On the southern plains, the tribes ranged over Colorado, Kansas, Texas and the Indian Territory, oblivious of modern boundaries. Although their sympathies had been somewhat inclined towards the Confederacy, they made no concerted attacks during the Civil War. In 1868 after the discovery of gold in Colorado, wagon trains began to crowd the Smoky Hill and Sante Fe trails, disrupting the buffalo migration in the southern plains. The Nations retaliated with isolated attacks on wagon trains and ranches. Various expeditions were sent against them and thereafter, peace on the southern plains was illusory, with a temporary truce the best that could be arranged. As if the payment of gifts and annuities could assuage the many grievances of the tribes, the Medicine Lodge Treaty was negotiated in 1867, but it became immediately evident to all parties that there would be little compliance with the terms.

Warrior attacks increased with greater ferocity after construction was begun on the Kansas Pacific Railway. Responding to the pleas of the settlers and the railroad, the government rushed cavalry to the plains, regardless of its state of training. Four new cavalry regiments had been authorized in 1866, among them the 7th Cavalry. Rather than form the 7th Cavalry in the east and then move it to the plains, it was decided to organize the regiment at isolated Ft. Riley, Kansas, where even the sight of rag-tag recruits might help reassure the settlers.

More than eight hundred men were assigned to twelve companies, lettered from A to M (J omitted because of translocation). The 7th Cavalry was first commanded by Andrew J. Smith, a veteran of the Mexican and Civil Wars but upon his transfer to a command on the upper Arkansas, the regiment was given to Colonel Samuel Sturgis, whose career had stagnated toward the close of the Civil War. When Sturgis was absent on his many temporary assignments, the acting command passed to Lt. Colonel G. A. Custer, precisely as the Commanding General had intended.

George Armstrong Custer was born in December 1839 in New Ramsley, Ohio. He attended the Military Academy at West Point, where his grades were poor, especially in deportment. If he graduated last in his class, one need but recall that Napoleon finished forty-second out of fifty-eight. Custer did manage to graduate, without having been suspended. Suspension was by no means a rarity.[1] Philip Sheridan was suspended for one year, Marcus Reno for two. It seems likely that Custer, like many cadets from the north, had initially given no thought to a military career and chose the Military Academy for the free education. The entire pre-war army numbered only thirteen thousand and offered few opportunities for a bright young man. This attitude quickly changed with the outbreak of hostilities. Custer served with distinction on several staffs and attracted the attention of his superiors, as a man who could carry out an assignment. Time again, he left his staff duties and plunged into battle. Custer had eleven horses shot out from under him but sustained only one minor leg wound.[2] Promotions were rapid. In one afternoon he moved from captain to brigadier general. At Williamsport in 1863 he might have cut off Lee's retreat from Gettysburg and ended the war, had General Meade given him the requested support. By the age of twenty-six, he had helped Sheridan defeat Jubel Early in the Shenandoah, for which a grateful Sheridan gave him a division and a major-general's brevet.[3] Custer had married Elizabeth Bacon, a lovely beauty with luxuriant chestnut hair, who was to play an important role in his life and even long after his death.

At the end of the Civil War, Custer reverted to his substantive rank of captain. This meant a reduction in pay from $8,000 to $2,000 per year. His wife's modest inheritance helped to tide him over the loss of earnings. With the settlers clamoring for immediate action against the warriors, General Sheridan saw in Custer the needed qualities of a plains fighter. He used his influence to have Custer given acting command of the 7th Cavalry and with it the rank of Lt. Colonel.

Many of the officers who were to serve with Custer in the 7th Cavalry were present when the regiment was first formed, or joined it shortly thereafter. Each made his contribution, large or small. Captain Frederick W. Benteen was there since the early days. Benteen had been given H Company and retained his command for fourteen years.

Benteen was born in Virginia, but his family had since moved to Missouri. With the coming of the Civil War, he enlisted in the Union Army. A brave and resourceful cavalryman who fought in eighteen major actions, he rose in rank to Lt. Colonel and had last commanded the 137th United States Colored Troop (Infantry). He was breveted twice for valor in the Civil War and in June 1865 was recommended for brevet Brigadier

General, but the appointment never materialized. He attributed this to the enmity of a West Point clique.[4]

At the end of the war, he declined a major's commission in a black regiment (Custer had turned down the colonelcy), accepting, instead, the rank of captain in the 7th Cavalry. Benteen was a superb soldier and a strict disciplinarian who allowed his subordinates full rein, yet watched them closely. He governed by suggestion and never raised his voice, but was not a man to trifle with. Benteen was well liked and well cared for by his subordinates, especially when he was in his cups, which was not often.

At Ft. Riley, the newly formed 7th Cavalry began its training. It was first taught the basic evolutions, which included squad drill, setting up drill, dismounted drill, saddling and unsaddling, and preparation to mount. Thereafter, the soldiers began platoon and company exercises and finally battalion drill. To prepare them for the field, Custer sent them off on escort duty with the government wagon trains, under the watchful eye of a wagon master. How the soldiers envied him! Not only was he paid sixty-five dollars per month, but he also carried in his wagon the entire equipage needed to make himself "comfortable" on the trip. Even his teamsters, "mule wackers", received twice the soldiers' pay, and it was hard to find one sober.[5]

During the spring and summer of 1867 Custer had led his poorly trained regiment in an expedition against the Cheyenne and Sioux in the southern plains, between the Platte and Arkansas Rivers. His intention was to fragment the tribes and drive them onto assigned reservations.[6] The first Indian campaign, personally directed by General Hancock, known as Hancock's War, was an abject failure.[7] The enemy had been elusive, the heat oppressive, supplies inadequate and desertions rampant. In that year, one hundred forty-seven settlers had been killed and four hundred thwenty-six women carried off into captivity.[8]

Moreover, Custer found himself in a peck of trouble. Upon hearing rumors that Ft. Riley was undergoing an epidemic of cholera, Custer left his command to rescue his wife. He was court martialed and suspended from rank and pay for one year. In his absence, the Indian campaign floundered. Since General Hancock had accomplished little, General Sherman exchanged him for General Philip H. Sheridan, who had been serving in the 5th Military (Louisiana-Texas) District and had been the subject of numerous complaints from the southern whites for his stern enforcement of Reconstruction laws.[9] President Johnson wanted him removed.

As Custer looked on from his banishment, the 7th Cavalry marched out against the Cheyenne, Arapaho and Kiowas. Once again, the campaign faltered, when the tribes avoided an engagement.

Sheridan quickly determined the reason for the failures. In the summer, the army horse was no match in speed or endurance for the warrior pony, which could climb a mountain or ford a swiftly flowing river, with the greatest of ease. The pony could travel sixty to eighty miles in a day, compared with thirty to forty miles for a soldier's mount. During the winter, however, the warrior ponies were thin and weak, barely subsisting on scratch feed, cottonwood or willow bark,[10] and lacked the stamina of the grain-fed army horses or Missouri mules.[11] Nor could the pony travel great distances in wintertime without grass.[12]

Sheridan could plainly see the advantages of a winter campaign.[13] He also knew that the troops, which had been expecting to spend a comfortable winter in their cozy winter quarters, would complain bitterly when sent in the field. But Sheridan had just the man to stifle their complaints.

He waited until the autumn to summon Custer from his banishment at Ft. Leavenworth. Custer promptly rejoined his regiment, camped on Bluff Creek, thirty miles from Dodge. He drilled the men mercilessly for long hours, reorganized them, gave them target practice and replaced their tired mounts. Using a French system, he assigned to each company, horses of the same color, so that the company could be easily identified from the distance. As winter approached, Sheridan and Custer perfected their plans.

On November 12, 1868 the regiment set out from their encampment, in a foot of snow.[14] A fortnight later, guided by compass and warrior tracks, with many soldiers suffering from frostbite, Custer made his celebrated attack on the Cheyenne at the Washita River.

He led his troops undetected up to the Cheyenne village. Warrior vigilance was relaxed in winter. The warriors sat around the fire in their tightly laced tepees, under the shelter of bluffs bordering the rivers.[15] Custer did little reconnoitering; else he would have seen many other villages camped along the river. He divided his troops into four units and attacked at daybreak, killing more than one hundred three, chiefly women and children, and seizing a thousand ponies and mules.[16] A captive white woman and her infant also died in the assault. His men were armed with the Spencer .52 cal. seven round repeating carbine, well suited for Indian warfare, apart from its weight and rimfire ammunition, which made it somewhat underpowered.[17] Even so, the 7th Cavalry was lucky to escape. Rushing to repel him were two thousand warriors from the many other villages, spread out in an almost continuous line for ten miles along the Washita. Before the warriors could launch a concerted counterattack, the 7th Cavalry had departed; but not before shooting seven hundred ponies, burning a thousand buffalo robes, and destroying badly needed ammunition and supplies.[18]

Washita was an important template for the later battles, employing, as it did, the triad of surprise, divided command and simultaneous attack.

By itself, the Washita victory would have been inconclusive, had not Custer persevered. He drove his exhausted troops deep into the southern plains during the winter of 1869, in pursuit of the Cheyenne and Arapaho. When he met the hostile tribes, instead of hazarding battle, he persuaded them to report to their assigned reservations. On these considerable efforts, in which Custer showed daring, inurement to hardship and iron determination, together with the efforts of the 5th Cavalry at Summit Springs Colorado in July 1869,[19] the southern plains tribal problems had been contained. That Custer did this with poorly trained troops and a desertion rate of thirty-three percent cannot but add to his achievement.

After the Battle of Washita, Custer had his first major confrontation with Captain Benteen. The animosity shared by these two fine officers was to leave a permanent scar on the regiment. In his hasty withdrawal from the battlefield, Custer had left behind a detachment of troopers, without bothering to ascertain their fate. Later, Benteen criticized Custer in a private letter to a friend. The friend had the letter published, infuriating Custer. In revenge, Custer assigned Benteen to Ft. Dodge, knowing Mrs. Benteen was at Ft. Harker, ill and mourning the death of a child.[20] In Benteen's defense, it must be mentioned that however much he detested his commanding officer, Benteen never failed to carry out his orders, or to offer his best and honest advice, whether or not it was solicited.

Following the Washita campaign, the exhausted regiment was sent to Ft. Hays in Kansas on April 7, 1869, to rebuild as a fighting unit. While it may have been stratigically situated, Ft. Hays was hardly an ideal setting to promote discipline.

The fort had been established in 1865, to protect the builders of the Kansas Pacific Railroad, which followed the Smokey Hill Trail.[21] A short half-mile away from the fort was Hays City,[22] a wild and unruly place with gunfire echoing throughout the night. The town was filled with railroad men, toughs of all descriptions, cowmen up from the Chisholm Trail, drunks, Mexican drifters, desperadoes, prostitutes, gamblers and the worst criminals spawned on the frontier. Wild Bill Hickok lived in the town and worked both sides of the law. He also helped round up deserters, which scarcely ingratiated him to the troopers. Soldiers who visited the town did so under constant threat of robbery or murder. Nor were the servicemen reluctant to contribute to the violence. When Hickok was not in office, vigilante committees settled the subtleties of the law. A separate, ever-enlarging cemetery, familiarly known as Boot Hill, was set aside for the exclusive use of those who died from gunfire.[23]

By the time the regiment reached Ft. Hays, it was completely drained. Desertions, illness and death had left their mark, and much of their equipment had been lost, damaged or abandoned.[24] Clearly, there was an urgent need for replacements and supplies.

The soldier was issued, or allowed to purchase, a shell jacket or a sackcoat of dark blue wool, hip length; various shirts which might include a gray or blue flannel shirt, a civilian shirt, a fireman's shirt or, if he could afford it, a buckskin shirt; blue wool trousers with an one and a half inch yellow running stripe, reinforced in the seat and thigh with white canvas or burlap; metal buttons and white suspenders; a felt "Hardee" hat with turned up brim, or a kepi, or a broad brimmed campaign hat; and shoes, moccasins or high cavalry boots, if available. The kepi or "bummer" was not popular for extended field use, since it absorbed water and did not protect the neck. Only on the march, when covered by dust, did the soldiers' dress look uniform.[25]

Cold weather clothing[26] included overcoats made from buffalo hide; hats from bearskin; mittens from beaver; and gauntlet gloves from buckskin. The regimental tailor could substitute other hides if they were more plentiful. The skins were bought with regimental funds. A buffalo blanket sold for three dollars, for use in the barracks.[27]

The new man was assigned to a company and teamed up with a seasoned soldier, who taught him the routines, the trumpet calls and the standing orders.[28] He was given a horse and instructed in its care. The stable sergeant had him first ride bareback, then ride without stirrups and finally, taught him to jump over rail fences.[29] He received saber and rifle training, but, for reasons of economy, fired his rifle only a few rounds per month.

Training was supervised by the executive officer, usually a major. Custer himself was not fond of this duty. He had lost a major at Washita and needed a replacement to restore the regiment to fighting trim. A major who saw eye to eye with his own ideas would have been a treasure. Two or three majors were supposed to be attached to a cavalry regiment, but it was unusual for more than one to serve at any given time. The other(s) might be absent for years on extended duty.

Major Marcus Albert Reno reported for duty in December 26, 1868. Tall, straight-shouldered with closely cropped mustache, he was a descendant of Philippe Renault, who had accompanied the Marquis de Lafayette to America.[30] Also a West Point graduate, Mark Reno had finished with a poor record in discipline, probably because, like Custer, he did not plan a military career. Like Custer, he had distinguished himself in battle in the Civil War, with two horses shot out from under him.[31] He rose to the rank of Brevet Brigadier General of Volunteers, recommended by Sheridan himself.[32] After reverting to the substantive rank of major after the war, he served in a variety of administrative posts.[33]

Reno had married Mary Hannah Ross, a woman of well-to-do background, ill suited to frontier army life. Reno understood this and made valiant efforts to avoid being posted to the 7th Cavalry. When his orders could not be changed, Mary Hannah reluctantly took up residence and unpacked her crates of fine linens, lace tablecloths, cut glass and sterling, wholly inappropriate to life in a frontier fort and predictably the source of jealousy with Libby Custer, the colonel's lady and arbiter of social usages.[34]

In view of his brevet rank, Reno might, like Custer, have been addressed as General, but the 7th Cavalry had room for only one. In fairness, it should be mentioned that Custer's brevet of brigadier general was in the regular army, while Reno's brevet was in the volunteers.[35] Probably by design, Reno spent considerable time on detached duty; as much as could be arranged. He was away until 1870 and afterwards served with the Canadian Boundary Commission until 1875 but remained a regimental officer.[36] When he did return, there was an established coolness between him and his commanding officer.

Before setting out for Ft. Hays to join the 7th Cavalry, De Rudio sought to clarify his date of rank. He did this for the purpose of establishing his seniority over the newly-commissioned second lieutenants, thereby insuring better living quarters and other benefits. Since his commission was dated October 25, 1867, De Rudio came to believe, as had been the practice in the past that he was due for promotion when he reported to his new post. The army now took a different position. They held that because of the reorganization law of 1865, the promotion clock did not begin to tick until the day he reported to the 7th Cavalry. Consequently, his promotion to 1st Lieutenant would be delayed.

An exchange of letters with the War Department began that was to go on for several years.[37] De Rudio first wrote to the Secretary of War applying for retroactive pay dating to his first commission on 31 August 1867, rather than to 25 October 1867, the date he was reinstated. The amount involved a paltry twenty-two dollars and fifty cents. The application was denied. De Rudio next wrote to Major General E.D. Townsend, the Adjutant General of the Army, claiming rank from the date of his commission in the 2nd Infantry. This signaled the start of prolonged correspondence. The first response from the Adjutant General advised him:

> "Referring to your letter of the 5th instant...concerning your transfer to the 7th Cavalry (with)...rank from the date of your commission in the 2nd infantry, I have respectfully to inform you that (your claim) is not entertained by the Secretary of War."

Many letters were exchanged. At one point, De Rudio even requested permission to put the matter before the President. The request was ignored. The resources of political patronage were invoked. Senator Cockrell suggested to the War Department that the matter be referred to the Attorney General for decision. This counsel was disregarded. A final published opinion by the Adjutant General upholding the army decision closed the matter. Meanwhile, when his promotion to 1st Lieutenant finally arrived at the end of 1875, it was based on the date he joined the 7th Cavalry. The ruling was not devised to harass De Rudio, but was consistent with army policy. Until 1880, the officer was expected to spend his entire military life in a regiment, with promotion determined by the length of service within that regiment.[38]

De Rudio arrived by train at Ft. Hays in the summer of 1869 and reported to the (then) adjutant, Lt. Myles Moylan. Moylan was a case unto himself. Without formal education, he rose from the ranks to a captaincy of volunteers during the Civil War, and then enlisted in the regular army as a private. He became regimental sergeant major in the 7th Cavalry, before receiving his commission in 1867. Custer had taken Moylan under his wing and even put him up in his home, when the officers in the bachelor officer's quarters had frozen him out, because of his coarseness and vulgarity.[39] Often, when a man is commissioned from the ranks, he is transferred to another unit, but in Moylan's case, he was retained in the 7th Cavalry, probably at the request of Custer. Moylan married the sister of Custer's brother-in-law and was perforce a member of the Custer circle.[40]

De Rudio's reception by Moylan and the other officers of the regiment was less than cordial. To begin with, he was older than any of the other company officers. Unlike most foreign-born officers in the regiment, De Rudio had no brevet, and his wartime service was with black troops. Also, word of his European activities had preceded his arrival, and Custer and his coterie -- half of the officers of the regiment -- lost no time in showing what they thought of this foreign conspirator. Custer is said to have "raged like an angry lion" at having a man in his unit who was implicated in an imperial assassination.[41] To make matters worse, the shavetail could not even ride a horse.[42]

Almost predictably, the new officer was assigned to Captain Benteen's H Company. Since Benteen had little field duty that year, he could give this outcast his full attention. To a great extent, De Rudio owes his army career to this remarkable officer. Had De Rudio been otherwise assigned, it is doubtful he would have lasted in the 7th Cavalry, notwithstanding his patronage. For a while, Benteen was his only friend in the regiment.[43]

Benteen took De Rudio in hand and showed him how he wanted things done. De Rudio had no knowledge of horses. In fact, he never acquired a good seat, according to Benteen. He had much to learn about farriery, feed, stable inspection, drills, garrison and field sanitation, picket duties and a thousand other matters a cavalry officer was required to master. First of all, he had to learn to ride -- *army style*, and stable sergeants love to teach a green officer. But De Rudio was not unique. Half the new officers were novice horsemen. Many were from infantry regiments or appointed from civilian life.[44] Since De Rudio did not own his own horse and saddle, he was probably given a spare army mount, selected for him by a sergeant, who, if he so chose, could select the most ill tempered in the stable or might even borrow a stallion from a scout. The established penalty for a first fall was the forfeiture of a basket of champagne, but domestic champagne from St. Louis was acceptable.[45]

As the months wore on, "the Count," as De Rudio was disparagingly called, learned his trade. Benteen was protective of his protégé. Like De Rudio, Benteen, too, had served with a black regiment and was familiar with snide remarks. He was amused at first by this peculiar looking shavetail with a long moustache and goatee. Benteen himself was clean-shaven. Benteen had no great formal education, nor, for that matter, did De Rudio, but he had an impressive veneer. The foreign accent, the wild stories around the campfire intrigued Benteen, but the skeptical company commander never abandoned his reservations. A terrible liar, he wrote his wife; but Benteen learned to trust him.

De Rudio became a Benteen man, and, perhaps, for that reason, Custer never ceased to show his contempt. Six years later he wrote of him, "the inferior of every first lieutenant in this regiment as an efficient and subordinate officer,"[46] but as long as De Rudio had his company commander's support, getting rid of him would not be easy. Perhaps that is why Custer never submitted De Rudio's name to a Benzine Board, although requested by Colonel Sturgis to report incompetent officers.

Benteen detested bullies, whether or not commissioned. He broke a first sergeant for handing out cruel punishment. De Rudio served as judge advocate for the trial, a disagreeable collateral duty. The soldier was reduced to buck private, but later restored in grade.[47] Benteen did not stop with sergeants. He and Reno had a fistfight in the trader's hut. Benteen had called Reno, the notorious blusterer, a son of a bitch,[48] but the enmity seems to have been soon smoothed over. In later years, when Reno was fighting for his professional reputation, no officer gave him greater support than did Benteen, though he was not enamored of him. But that was Benteen.

Eventually, Custer had to accept this peculiar shavetail, who kept his distance and proved in time to be respectful, sober, competent, and, as shall be shortly seen, *lucky*. Other officers cursed, complained, drank to excess, gambled, chased the women or came down with venereal disease. De Rudio gave his superiors no such trouble. His wife, Eliza, was a help. Her English accent charmed Libby Custer, who was partial to all things European. She saw in twenty-nine year old Eliza a flicker of foreign allure. After all, De Rudio was a genuine count with charming manners and knowledge of good wines.[49] Who knows, his wife might someday be a countess? Libby Custer wrote of him patronizingly in 1889 in *Tenting On the Plains*, "There was an Italian who had a long strange career to draw upon for our amusement, and numbered among his experiences, imprisonment for plotting the life of *his* king."[50]

Eliza was a close friend of Kate Benteen, and Roma De Rudio was the same age as the Benteen's son, Freddie. The Benteens seemed to have an affection for this simple English mother, who struggled to raise three children on a second lieutenant's pay. Another officer might have hired an enlisted "striker", who, for five to ten dollars a month,[51] would help out around the officer's lodging, attend his horse or build a chicken coop, but a second lieutenant with a growing family and destitute parents could ill afford this luxury.[52]

The De Rudio family quickly settled down to army life. Eliza seems to have adapted, even quicker than her husband. Her life in the hideous London tenements well prepared her for the frontier fort. With the officers away for months at a time, the wives were left to fend for themselves. Despite the proximity of the post to Hays City, their activities were strictly confined to the fort. Poetry was read aloud, books discussed and maternity stories compared. Well-worn copies of Harpers *Bazaar* and Harpers *Weekly* passed from hand to hand and back again. Food was a recurrent problem. Initially, Ft. Hays had no warehouse, and supplies were left exposed to the elements, covered only by tarpaulins. The food quickly became rancid and infested with rodents. But such was the army, and the wives learned to make the best of it.[53]

The family remained at Ft. Hays through the winter 1869-70, while a favored part of the regiment followed Custer into winter quarters in the larger and more agreeable Ft. Leavenworth.

In February, De Rudio was given his first field command. He took over G Company, whose commander had been recuperating from a wound sustained at Washita. He received orders to relieve Battery B of the 4th U.S. Artillery, then stationed at Great Spirit Spring. Kansas.

De Rudio began by letting his men know that he was going to personally supervize their welfare, rather than delegate this duty. This practice was to be characteristic of his command during the remainder of his military career. He was approachable to all ranks but never failed to give his NCO's an opportunity to display their initiative, which helped cement company discipline.

De Rudio led G Company to Solomon Forks at the junction of the branches of the Homonymon River in north central Kansas. His mission was to put an end to the raids on the settlers and livestock by small bands of Kiowa, Comanche and

Cheyenne. He and G Company got off to an incredibly lucky start, which comes to an officer once in a lifetime. On the way to the assigned area, they came upon two warriors and gave chase on the high prairie. Unknown to De Rudio, the warriors had just killed some settlers and had abducted two sisters, ages eight and six. G Company pursued the braves, forcing them to abandon the girls, who were returned unharmed to their frantic parents. All this in the first week of his assignment! De Rudio was thereafter held in the highest regard by the grateful settlers.[54]

He divided his command into several patrols, each consisting of a non-commissioned officer and four enlisted.[55] During the five months of vigilant patrol, only one farmer was lost to warrior attack.[56] Other records indicate that three settlers were killed at Glen Elder settlement.[57] On one occasion, De Rudio's unit pursued two bands of braves for sixty long miles before recovering stolen livestock. De Rudio himself fell victim to one attack, when warriors crept into camp and made off with his horse.[58]

De Rudio encouraged the ranchers to form their own militia and to build sturdy houses to defend themselves, since most of the attacks came from small warrior parties. So grateful were the ranchers that one hundred of them drew up a testimonial "thanking De Rudio for his tireless patrolling in protecting them." This was certain to have been brought to the attention of Custer, if not to higher authorities. When their Solomon Forks assignment was completed, the men of G Company presented him with a cavalry saber with a gilded hilt. Custer learned of this and berated De Rudio for an infringement of regulations. No officer may accept gifts from an enlisted man![59] Nevertheless, he allowed De Rudio to keep the saber, and the shavetail wore it proudly. He took it along to Little Bighorn.

This independent command was a turning point in De Rudio's army career. His rescue of the girls became local legend, and word circulated across the southern plains. Custer reluctantly came to see a modicum of merit in his shavetail. Thereafter, De Rudio became a regular replacement for an absent company commander. On July 11, 1870, De Rudio was assigned to D Company, to temporarily replace Captain Thomas B. Weir and was later given temporary command of the H Company.

War in the southern plains was beginning to wind down, with patrols now encountering little opposition.[60] The Kansas Pacific railway had completed the tracks to Denver, and the tribes by now were confined to reservations or otherwise pacified.

Glad tidings from Europe found their way to the frontier. Napoleon III had withdrawn his army from Rome, in preparation for the war with Prussia. The city had fallen to the troops of Victor Emanuel II. At long last, Italy was UNIFIED!

In 1871, the 7th Cavalry was ordered to the south for Reconstruction duty. Congress oversaw this activity, or more precisely, the Republican majority in Congress, with the Democrats in bitter opposition.[61] Reconstruction would continue until 1877, often marked by savage violence.

The regiment traveled in day coaches, with three men assigned to two seats. Meals aboard the train consisted of bread, dried fruit, sandwiches, canned goods and coffee, served from the baggage car. After several days, the cars were in sore need of cleaning.[62] The regiment arrived in Louisville, Kentucky, and then went on to Ash Barracks in Nashville, Tennessee, which would be their "permanent" post for the next two years.

The regiment was divided up and the companies assigned to various stations.[63] Two favored companies remained with Custer in Elizabethtown, Kentucky, twenty miles from Louisville, where Custer settled into a snug little cottage. It was during his stay in Elizabethtown that Custer wrote the articles later published as *My Life on the Plains,*[64] destined to be the equivalent of a best seller back east. He was also called upon to accompany Grand Duke Alexis of Russia on a hunting trip on the plains.

Custer often visited Lexington, Kentucky to buy mounts for the regiment. The army paid $165 for horses, $185 for mules. A want ad would be placed in the Louisville newspapers for geldings, 14-15 hands high.[65] The gelding was a colt, castrated soon after the testes descended into the scrotum, usually before the age of ten months. This made the animal tractable, so that it would share the stalls with other mounts, unlike the stallion, which was often unmanageable and destructive. The officer, if he owned his own horse, rode a mare.[66] Mares were docile and hard working, but testy around estrus, which came every twenty-four days in the spring. Gestation lasted eleven months, but foals were generally dropped before the regiment left for the field.

After examination by the veterinary surgeon, the horse was put through a gallop and trot. If its performance proved satisfactory, the animal was branded with *US* on the left foreshoulder.[67] Private mounts were not branded. For this reason, when deserting, the soldier tried to make off with an officer's horse. Captain Benteen lost seven of his mounts to deserters.[68]

The other companies were sent to Tennessee, South Carolina and Mississippi, all former Confederate states. Their duties were to prove tiresome and demanding. They camped on the lawns of county courthouses, to remind the inhabitants of the power of the federal government. The locals, in turn, compared them unfavorably with the Confederate cavalry of Nathan Bedford Forrest, now grown to mythical stature. At any moment, the Federal company might run afoul of the local population. When it did, the officer in charge had to tred cautiously, since he was not always assured of support from the higher authorities.

On June 17, 1871 De Rudio led a detachment of twenty-five men from H Company to Tullahoma, Tennessee and then to Oxford, Mississippi, to protect and assist federal revenue agents. The company also functioned as process servers for the United States marshal, revenue tax collectors, and as a restraint to the Ku Klux Klan and its cognates. The latter included the Knights of the White Camellia, the White League, the Invisible Circle and the Pale Faces, all dedicated to subverting the activities of the civilian government and making life miserable for the Federal "blue bellies."

De Rudio and his detachment returned to Ash Barracks, Nashville in August. After two weeks of rest, they were rushed to Huntsville, Alabama, where they remained until the end of the year. Here, the Klan was especially powerful. As many as fifteen hundred Klansmen had earlier paraded the streets of Huntsville. Work was boring, never-ending, and potentially explosive.[69] De Rudio had experienced southern hostility during the Civil War when he had patient and well-disciplined black troops, but now he commanded swaggering white soldiers with little inclination to put up with insult. Nevertheless, De Rudio seems to have discharged his duties without falling into snares.

The company returned by rail to Nashville, Tennessee in February 1872, arriving after a weary three day journey. A week later, they left for the hinterlands of Tennessee, to help the internal revenue officers apprehend moonshiners. In May 1872 De Rudio and his detachment were ordered back to Oxford, Mississippi and then to Carroltown and Livingston, Alabama, again to assist revenue officers. They remained there for four months, before returning to Ash Barracks, Tennessee in November for winter quarters. With the coming of spring, De Rudio was given temporary command of H Company and with it, the thankless task of serving warrants, summonses and eviction notices. He performed these services with his usual patient competence and without complaint. Meanwhile, the two years of Reconstruction duty was nearing completion, and the regiment impatiently awaited word of its new assignment.

While her husband was away, Eliza gave birth in Nashville to a third daughter on October 4, 1872. They named her America Carlotta. Perhaps the choice of name reflected a symbolic reorientation for the De Rudios. The other girls were named Roma and Italia. America was also known in later life as Carlotta. By now, Eliza was thirty-two years old, deeply immersed in family and army life, as was her forty year old husband. Within their home, they spoke Italian, and she called him "Carlo."

Notes

1. Charles M. Robinson III, *A Good Year to Die. The Story of the Great Sioux War* (New York: Random House, 1955), p. 32.
2. Wayne Mitchell Sarf, *The Little Bighorn Campaign* (Conshohoken, PA: Combined Books, 2000), p.165.
3. Robert M. Utley, *Cavalier in Buckskin* (Norman and London: University of Oklahoma Press, 1988), p. 41.
4. John M. Carroll, *They Rode with Custer* (Mattetuck, NY: J. M. Carroll, 1993), p. xviii.
5. Sandy Barnard, ed., *Ten Years with Custer. A 7th Cavalryman's Memoirs* (Ft. Collins, CO: Citizen Printing, 2001), pp. 20-22.
6. Frederick F. Van de Water, *Glory Hunter* (Lincoln and London: University of Nebraska, 1934), p. 169.
7. Utley, *Cavalier,* p. 54.
8. S. L. A. Marshall, *Crimsoned Prairie* (New York: Scribner, 1972), p. 108.
9. J. G. Randall and David Donald, *The Civil War and Reconstruction* (Boston: Heath, 1961), p. 600.
10. Evans S. Connell, *Son of the Morning Star* (New York: Harper Perennial, 1984), p. 138.
11. Kenneth Hammer, ed., *Custer in 76* (Norman and London: University of Oklahoma, 1988), p. 11.
12. Lonnie J. White, *Hostiles and Horse Soldiers* (Boulder, CO: Pruett, 1972), p. 90.
13. Van de Water, p. 183.
14. Stephen Longstreet, *War Cries on Horseback* (Garden City, NY: Doubleday, 1970), p. 171.
15. Ralph K. Andrist, *The Long Death* (New York: Macmillan, 1964), p. 248.
16. Connell, p. 187.
17. Jason Hook and Martin Pegler, *To Live and Die in the West* (Oxford: Osprey, 1999), p. 22.
18. Longstreet, p. 173.
19. Don Rickey, *Forty Miles a Day on Beans and Hay* (Norman and London: University of Oklahoma, 1963), p. 8.
20. Van de Water, p. 208.
21. Robert W. Frazer, *Forts of the West* (Norman and London: University of Oklahoma, 1988), p. 54.
22. John Upton Terrell, and George Walton, *Faint the Trumpet Sounds* (New York: McKay, 1966), pp. 70, 79.
23. Barnard, *Ten Years,* pp. 100-136.
24. Mary Ellen Jones, *Daily Life on the Nineteenth Century American Frontier* (Westport, CT: Greenwood, 1988), p. 225.
25. Hook and Pegler, p. 15.

26. Jones, p. 224.
27. ACP, Charles C. De Rudio, CF D345 CT 1864, NAB.
28. Jones, p. 219.
29. Ani Frank Mulford, *Fighting Indians in the 7th Cavalry* 2nd ed. (Fairfield, WA: Ye Galleon Press, 1972), p. 26; Rickey, p. 43.
30. Terrell and Walton, p. 17.
31. Barnard, *Ten Years,* pp.100-136.
32. W. A. Graham, *The Reno Court of Inquiry* (Mechanicsburg, PA: Stackpole, 1995), p. xxix.
33. Sarf, p. 192.
34. Terrell and Walton, p. 77.
35. Utley, *Cavalier,* p. 41.
36. Graham, p. xxx.
37. ACP, Charles C. De Rudio, CF D345 CT 1864, NAB.
38. Robert M. Utley, *Frontier Regulars. The United States Army and the Indian, 1866-1890* (New York: Macmillan, 1973), p. 31.
39. Elizabeth B. Custer, *Tenting on the Plains* (New York: Webster, 1889), p. 416; Van de Water, p. 155.
40. Terrell and Walton, pp. 95, 98.
41. "From Devil's Island," *Washington Post,* 15 September 1901.
42. "No, the 'Count' was never at home on the hurricane deck of a horse" Letter from F. Benteen to O. Barry, April 1, 1899, Manuscript Collection White Swan Library, Little Bighorn.
43. Edward L. Daily, *Custer to MacArthur* (Paducah, KY: Turner, 1995), p. 31.
44. Custer, Elizabeth, *Tenting,* p. 419.
45. *Ibid.,* p. 420.
46. Sarf, p. 195.
47. Rickey, p. 139.
48. *Ibid.,* p. 142.
49. Terrell and Walton, p. 96.
50. Custer, Elizabeth, *Tenting,* p. 429.
51. Rickey, p. 143.
52. Jones, p. 220.
53. Custer, Elizabeth, *Tenting,* p. 688.
54. William Cutler, *History of the State of Kansas* (Chicago: Andreas, 1883), p. 1022
55. Daily, p. 34.
56. Hammer, p. 83.
57. Cutler, p. 1022.
58. Hammer, p. 83; Cutler, p. 1022.
59. Hammer, p. 83.
60. Van de Water, p. 226.
61. Utley, *Frontier,* p. 62.
62. Rickey, p. 241.
63. Van de Water, p. 227.
64. George A. Custer, *My Life on the Plains* (New York: Citadel, 1874). No page citation
65. Hook and Pegler, p. 58.
66. Frazier Hunt and Robert Hunt, *I Fought with Custer* (New York and London:

Scriber, 1947), p. 9.
67. Barnard, *Ten Years,* p. 140
68. *Ibid.,* p. 34.
69. Henrietta Buckmaster, *Freedom Bound* (New York: Macmillan, 1965), p. 46.

VIII
DAKOTA TERRITORY

With the restoration of peace in Kansas, Washington could next direct its attention to the northern plains, which was threatening to become the new battleground. In 1873 the 7th Cavalry was ordered to the Dakota Territory.

General Alfred Terry, commander of the Department of the Dakota, faced two vexing problems. Construction along the proposed Northern Pacific railbed was endangered, and prospectors in the Black Hills of South Dakota were being scalped. In both instances, the Lakota Sioux and their allies were responsible.

The Sioux Nation was composed of three tribes: the Lakota Sioux, the largest, inhabited the great plains; the Dakota (Santee) Sioux, dwelt chiefly in Minnesota, and the Nakota (Yankton) Sioux, lived in the southeast Dakota Territory along the Missouri.[1]

The Lakota had been on the northern plains for only a century, driven westward by the Algonquian-speaking tribes, especially the Chippewa, who had been armed by the French traders.[2] The Lakota, in turn, displaced the Crow and Blackfeet, both of whom had been dwelling on the edge of this uninhabited region.[3] Their primary draft animal had been the dog, which pulled the travois, but after 1750, the Lakota acquired horses, enabling the tribe to move onto the plains to hunt buffalo. Thus began for them an age of affluence,[4] in which they acquired extensive wealth in ponies, hides and trade articles.[5] Their skill as horsemen was legendary. Crook called them "the greatest light cavalry the world has ever known."[6]

The Lakota Sioux were made up of seven tribes. The most warlike of these were the Teton (Dwellers on the Prairie), the Oglala (To Scatter One's Own), the Unkpapa (End of the Circle) and the Brule (Burned Thighs'). Other familiar names are the San Arcs, the Miniconjou (Planters by the Water), Blackfeet and Two Kettles. Lewis and Clark had come to know their menace. The Lakota enjoyed a loose confederation with the Northern Cheyenne, who had been cut off from their southern brothers by the interposition of settlement.

Bow-and-arrow had been their primary weapon. It could be shot up to six times/minute, as far as one hundred fifty yards, with accuracy up to fifty yards. At five to fifteen yards the arrow was said to be able to pass through a buffalo, if such can be believed[7]. Around 1870, the Lakota began to acquire muskets, carbines and rifles, some magazine-fed, which added to their resources. Rifles were used for long-range sniping and carbines for rapid fire on horseback. At the time of the Sioux War, considerably more than half the warriors were equipped with firearms -- sidearms and/or long guns. Correspondingly, the Lakota shield became smaller and like the lance, was carried chiefly for ceremonial purposes.

Conflict between the Lakota and the army began in 1866, over the Bozeman Trail. This led from the Colorado's South Platte River through Lakota territory in Wyoming to the Montana gold fields. The Bozeman Trail was a shorter, but more dangerous, route than the steamship trip up the Missouri River to Ft. Benton and then overland to the mines of Virginia City, Montana. More than two hundred fifty whites died while traveling over this road. To protect the Bozeman traffic, three army forts had been constructed along the way, but the forts were inadequately manned and offered little security. The army quickly concluded that it lacked the resources to effectively protect the road and signaled a willingness to negotiate with the Lakota leader, Chief Red Cloud.

Red Cloud was an Oglala warrior and statesman, long engaged in territorial wars with other tribes. When the wagons of white settlers first started up the Bozeman Trail, it was he who mobilized the Lakota for a successful campaign against the United States Army in what was called Red Cloud's War, and it was he who negotiated the Treaty of Fort Laramie in 1868.

By the terms of the Treaty, the Lakota Sioux were guaranteed a large Dakota reservation, as well as unmolested occupation of territory north of the North Platte and between the Powder and the Bighorn basins. This land was termed "unceded," since it was not deeded to the government.[8] Further, by the provisions of the Treaty of Fort Laramie, the forts along the Bozeman Trail were to be abandoned and the Black Hills closed to prospectors. Like all treaties, the Treaty of Fort Laramie was ratified by a two-thirds vote of the Senate and signed by the President.

About four fifths of the Lakota nation settled in the great Sioux reservations in central and western South Dakota, and the remainder, three thousand Lakota and four hundred Cheyenne, roamed the unceded lands.[9] During the autumn and winter months, many reservation warriors left the reservation to join the free-roamers for the buffalo hunt in the unceded lands.

Notwithstanding the occasional attack on miners, steamboats and couriers, tranquillity on the northern plains prevailed until 1873, when the Northern Pacific Railroad drew up plans to lay track through the unceded land along the Yellowstone Valley. The tribes did not take kindly to seeing yellow survey stakes planted in their territory and regarded the proposed construction as a breach of the Treaty of Fort Laramie. Washington showed little concern for legality. Government planning rested on the understanding that any arrangement, agreement or treaty with the North American Nations was only temporary and that a way could always be found to circumvent the terms, should the necessity arise. Meanwhile, topographical survey of the railbed along the Yellowstone River had to be protected.

The Northern Pacific Railroad project was the largest single financial investment yet launched in the United States. Plans called for the railroad to eventually run from Lake Superior to Seattle, Washington. Instead of subsidizing construction with direct payment, the government provided incredibly generous land-grant acreage within an eighty mile corridor along the rail track. The difficulty encountered was that the government did not own the land, and so the railroad could not deliver title to prospective settlers. Without the sale of title, immigration was threatened, and railroad construction itself was in jeopardy, since the cash flow needed to continue operation could not be derived solely from the sale of equities or from traffic revenue; but was dependant on the sale of land.

News of their new Dakota posting reached the 7th Cavalry at their scattered stations in the South. The companies boarded trains in New Orleans and Louisville, for a trip to Memphis. There, the regiment assembled, and a lively reunion was held.[10] The men were delighted with the new mounts. Some of the officers had even acquired pedigreed blood horses, bought cheaply at the racetrack when the horse lost the race.[11] While awaiting transport, the company commanders tried to keep the soldiers busy with mounted, dismounted and saber drills, to the delight of the spectators; but after tattoo roll call, many enlisted men crept out of camp, in search of liquor and mischief in the city.

Three steamships transported the regiment and its nine hundred horses from Memphis to Cairo, Illinois, and the railroad carried them to Yankton, Dakota Territory, on the Missouri River.[12] There were long stops along the way, to water and exercise the mounts. Mrs. Custer traveled by the now popular Pullman car with "inlaid woods, mirrors and plush."[13]
She makes no mention of the other wives.

Dakota Territory

The train halted one mile from Yankton on the Missouri River, where the regiment set up camp. At the time, Yankton consisted of a few log houses and some rutted dirt roads. Eliza De Rudio and the other officers' wives found rooms at the St. Charles Hotel, a framed building, little more than a glorified barn. Here they saw a slice of life few would soon forget. The floor of the lobby was strewn with sawdust and littered with cuspidors. The walls lacked paint or paper, the carpet was threadbare, the beds springless and the furniture little more than camping outfits.[14] Eliza remained at the St. Charles Hotel with her family, apart from a four month stay in St. Paul, until the family quarters at Ft. Rice were finished.

On March 14, while waiting in Yankton for the ice to clear, the regiment experienced a frightful Dakota blizzard, the worst in seventeen years.[15] In one infantry company caught in the snow near Ft. Shaw, twenty-two men required amputations.[16] At Yankton, the families and officers were frantically rushed to the St. Charles Hotel, soldiers to lodgings, outhouses, sheds and saloons and the horses were taken to warehouses and stables. There were nine hundred horses to shelter, so the arrangements must have been hectic. Libby and George Custer, who had been living in a small cabin in camp, narrowly escaped freezing to death.[17]

The citizens of Yankton welcomed the regiment. The army wives gave the town a cachet, the soldiers' pay contributed to the local economy and the regiment made the people feel secure. When winter ended, a ball was held for the regiment. The public hall was decorated with flags and the ball well attended by the girls from the outlying homesteads.[18] During its stay in Yankton, the regiment came to know the rapidity with which news was carried by runners and signals. News of the west coast Modoc disaster was brought in by Indian runners from the reservation, "moccasin telegraph," long before word had been received by wire.[19]

With the coming of spring, the regiment was ordered to provide protection for the Northern Pacific survey party in the

Yellowstone Valley. The Lakota had rejected all requests for rights of way through their territory.[20] There had been small survey parties sent out in 1871 and 1872, without serious interference, but the Lakota had since made known their intentions to halt further work on the railbed. Judging from the experiences of the other railroads, the Northern Pacific could expect attacks on the pathfinders, if not on the main line workers, who were usually better guarded.[21]

This survey expedition was to be no ragtag affair. More than four hundred civilians would accompany the fifteen hundred soldiers, including ten companies of the 7th Cavalry. After the appearance of spring grass, the regiment would set out for Ft. Rice, five hundred miles up the Missouri, from where the expedition would begin. Steamships would carry the survey party and supplies to Ft. Rice, together with officers' wives, laundresses, and similar personnel.[22] The families were expected to take up residence in Forts Lincoln and Rice.

After a grand review by the citizens of Yankton on May 7, *Boots and Saddles!* was sounded, and the soldiers rode off two-abreast. The column began its march, thirty miles a day, four miles an hour, halting once during the day to water the horses and lunch.[23] For many recruits, this march was their first opportunity to see what soldiering was about. They rode along in the choking dust, leather squeaking, hooves clanking and mounts prancing and dumping waste, with sergeants moving up and down the endless line of march, bellowing out orders. Libby Custer accompanied the column for five hundred miles, no mean feat for a woman riding sidesaddle or bouncing along in an ambulance.

At the end of the day's march, the recruits were taught the camp routine. Company commanders were assigned their camping site, and a guidon was planted on the designated area. The men cut the reeds and grass and beat the ground to scare off the rattlesnakes. They killed as many as forty snakes in one camp. The tents were pitched in two long lines facing each other. Wagons were drawn up at either side, placed diagonally, one end overlapping the other, to form a barricade against hostile attack. After the horses and men had been fed, the horses watered and inspected, and a myriad of tasks attended to, the recruit could sit around the campfire and nurse his aches.[24]

The expedition reached Ft. Rice on June 10, 1873, after a month of hard march. Situated on the right bank of the Missouri River on a tableland one hundred feet above river level, the fort offered important protection for miners traveling by ship up the Missouri River to Ft. Benton, the head of navigation, and then overland to Virginia City, Montana. It had been originally built with cottonwood logs and earth roofs, but was now undergoing more robust construction, with timber brought up by steamship.[25] Ft. Rice was to be the permanent station for H Company, and the soldiers carefully surveyed the progress.

The steamers arrived a day or two later, bringing supplies and regimental property, and some very unhappy women. Their personal belongings had been damaged while the boxes sat on the pier at Yankton. But nothing compared with their fury, when they learned that the officers' quarters in Rice and Lincoln were still unfinished.

Libby Custer returned by railway to St. Paul by way of Bismarck, sharing with a few chosen wives the private car of the president of the Northern Pacific Railroad. Mrs. Benteen went on to Bismarck and stayed in a ramshackle hotel. Eliza and the other wives returned by ship to the notorious St. Charles Hotel in Yankton, to await the completion of the officers' quarters.

Before the Yellowstone expedition got underway, Lt. De Rudio was the first regimental officer to come under Lakota fire. In mid-June, while escorting a small party of Northern Pacific engineers up to Ft. Lincoln, his detachment was attacked by one hundred Lakota on the Heart River. His men were anxious to engage the enemy, but De Rudio wisely avoided battle, to insure that no harm came to his charges. He delivered them safely to Ft. Lincoln.[26]

H Company did not accompany the expedition for the entire Yellowstone expedition. It was ordered to guard the base camp at Stanley's Stockade, a hundred miles up the Yellowstone.[27] There it remained, swatting mosquitoes, until Custer picked it up on the return march. The assignment was dull and uncomfortable, which may have been why Custer gave it to Benteen. Or perhaps it was because of damage done to the wagons of H Company during an especially severe hailstorm.

Benteen, De Rudio and the other junior officers passed the time gossiping about Custer's shady deals. There were many such stories. Custer is said to have peddled contraband whiskey; evaded paying taxes while handling soldiers' pay; sold a trader's post to a gambling house owner for a thousand dollars. The most delectable morsel was the story that at the end of the Civil War, Colonel Sturgis found that Custer's grain and hay contracts were stupendous frauds. Sturgis immediately annulled the contracts and notified the authorities.[28]

Over the years, there would be other charges of trader irregularities leveled against the regimental commander. Custer threatened to keep his regiment away from the trading post, unless the trader gave him $3,500. To cover the bribe, Custer is said to have given the trader a bill of sale for an ambulance and four mules and two horses.[29] Also, Custer had a "working agreement" with the sutler during the Black Hills expedition.[30] And so on. Clearly, Benteen had little love for his commanding officer. How many of these tales were true is difficult to say, but it must be noted to Custer's credit that he had an implacable vendetta with traders and helped bring trader corruption to the attention of the Congress, at the peril of his own career.[31]

Major Reno did not accompany the Yellowstone expedition. He had been away on recruiting duty in New York. When he returned, orders awaited him to take two companies for duty with a border survey commission. Meanwhile, his wife Mary Hannah Reno died back east on July 10. Sadly, Major Reno was denied permission to return for his wife's burial service.[32] This refusal was neither arbitrary nor heartless. Officers were *never* granted leave when the regiment was in the field.

Apart from two sharp encounters resulting in three deaths

and two wounded, the Yellowstone expedition had not been excessively troubled by warrior attacks. Custer spent his time writing incredibly long letters to his wife (one of them 80 pages) and composing a steady stream of dispatches to the eastern newspapers, pointing up his accomplishments in the heart of the Lakota country.[33] The confluence of the Little Bighorn and the Yellowstone rivers was finally reached, and the expedition halted. It had marched fifteen hundred miles. On the way back to Ft. Lincoln, they picked up the companies left at Stanley Stockade, and the ten companies preceeded to Ft. Abraham Lincoln, now under construction. Half the regiment would remain at Ft. Lincoln, the other half would be distributed to four other forts, among them Ft. Rice, where H Company would be stationed. These forts would be permanent posts for 7th Cavalry during the next five years and a familiar part of the Custer legend. But wherever its permanent station, each company spent at least several months of the year at Ft. Lincoln.

Ft. Lincoln was very much in Lakota country, sixty miles upriver from the Standing River Sioux Reservation.[34] A small infantry garrison, composed of thirty men and a Gatling gun, was stationed a mile away in a stockaded enclosure up on a hill, to stand watch while the regiment was in the field. In the regiment's absence, the fort had been raided and animals stolen on three occasions that year.[35] One soldier reported that scarcely a week passed without an alarm being sounded.

Construction of Fort Abraham Lincoln was supervised by an infantry general (Engineers) who brought in one hundred fifty workers and seven hundred carloads of supplies from St. Paul. As late as 1876, some officers' quarters were still unfinished. For George Armstrong Custer, Ft. Lincoln was the largest and best-appointed post he had ever commanded, and his house, the finest he had lived in. Custer made sure of that. But its beginning was hardly auspicious. A fire from a faulty chimney burned the house to the ground, and the Custers lost all of their possessions on the upper floor. While their new quarters were being built, the Custers lived with Captain Tom Custer, George's brother. Their second house was even more elegant, situated in the middle of the officers' row, with a fireplace in every room and a piano to entertain the guests.

Ft. Lincoln had the usual quadrangle construction, build around a drill field, where the regular parades were held. Dress parades, performed daily during the summer months, were held outside the garrison on a level parade ground. Two miles to the north, a flat plain accommodated the tents of the visiting companies. Since grass grew poorly, quick-growing oats were planted in all three areas to hold down the dust. Even so, a dust cloud seemed to hover over the parade and camping grounds.

The barracks were strung out along the edge of the parade ground, on the long side of the quadrangle, nearest the river. Each of the three large buildings housed two companies. Opposite the barracks was the officers' row of six detached frame houses, each accommodating two families. The commanding officer's home stood in the middle of the row.

Stables for the six hundred horses were situated near the river. During the summer, the manure attracted swarms of blue-bellied flies, which vied with the mosquitoes to make life miserable; but by then the regiment had left for the field, bequeathing the torment to the infantry and the families. Custer had the well-deserved reputation for providing his men with the best horses and demanding from them the most diligent care. At reveille roll call, the horses were led out of the eight stables to be groomed by the soldiers, clad in white stable coats. Meanwhile, the stable guard cleaned the stalls. The horses were then brought back into the stable and fed. Afterwards, the soldiers returned to the barracks, which had been cleaned in their absence by the company orderlies. The hungry men removed their white stable coats, washed up and only then were they, too, fed. In the evening the horses received another one and a half hours of attentive grooming.[36]

Laundress' quarters, known as Suds Row, were easily identified by the familiar swinging clotheslines near the stables. One laundress was authorized for every twenty enlisted men, each of whom paid her a dollar per month. She also sold pies, tailored uniforms and at times rendered other services. After the puritanical Hays administration took office, her employment was terminated.

The storehouses were on the small sides of the quadrangle, facing the guardhouse and the granary. Fifty prisoners could be jailed in the guardhouse. Within the granary, a crude theater had been erected, which was used for amateur theatrics and minstrel shows. Admission was fifty cents. Each company sponsored a ball or hop at least once during the winter, attracting woman from miles around and the families from nearby Ft. Rice. Jigs and square dances were popular, as were waltzes and polkas.

There were no potable wells or cisterns in Lincoln. Water was taken from the river and hauled in barrels by water wagons. In winter, a hole had to be cut in the ice. Ice was harvested from the river and stored it in the icehouse, for use in the summer by the hospital, the infantry and the families. For his labor, the soldier on ice detail received an extra fifty cents a day and two gills of whiskey, to restore the circulation.

The hospital was situated within the stockaded infantry post, a mile from the garrison. Among its facilities, it boasted a galvanic current for the treatment of muscular aches.[37] This may have been of particular interest to De Rudio. Other buildings near the ferry landing included a barbershop, a blacksmith's shop and post office, as well as an icehouse and the log homes for the scouts.

Most important of the outbuildings were the trader's hut and the billiard rooms. These served the soldiers until taps, and the officers thereafter. A pint of beer or a gill, quarter pint of wine was allowed the soldier each day until the Hays administration, but this limit was regularly exceeded. Beer sold for eighteen to fifty cents a quart. Spirits were also available, subject to authorization by the commanding officer. A one-ounce "shot" cost a dime. The trader kept the tally with a pegboard mounted on the wall. At times when the sale of spirits was prohibited, the trader brought out a keg marked "for personal use." The contents sold for more than the "rot gut" served in the bars and brothels of Bismarck.[38] A roll of Navy Tobacco was supplied monthly to the soldier. He cut up the unused portion and used the segments for chips in the card games.

Officers could purchase unlimited quantities of spirits. Drinking was often excessive, and the amount of alcohol consumed by an officer generally increased over the years, leading to illness and poor performance. Many an officer ended up a pitiful wreck.[39] Gambling was another destructive vice, especially for Tom Custer, who was attracted to the tables across the river. Cards seemed to go well for Benteen. Adultery was prevalent, but seldom mentioned. Not even Libby Custer was immune to rumors. When the husbands were in the field, the wives were called "widows," and the young officers remaining in the garrison were expected to escort them to social functions.

The regimental band was an important boost to garrison morale. In the early days, Custer used whatever musical talent could be found in the regiment, but after 1870, musicians were recruited expressly for band service.[40] They practiced off-duty.[41] German musicians were especially well represented, nine of them serving in the 7th Calvary at one time. The bandsmen received private's pay of thirteen dollars a month but supplemented this with money earned at civilian functions. Their bandmaster, Felice Venitieri, an Italian from Turin, held the rank of warrant officer. Since he had lived in Bismarck before being persuaded to join the army, he doubtless found many lucrative occasions for the band to perform.[42]

Ft. Abraham Lincoln owed its existence to Bismarck, across the river. Together, they reflected the determination of the government to open the area to the railroad, which was expected to bring in immigrants to settle the land.

A dilapidated bridge spanned the Missouri River, forever in need of repairs, so that most of the crossings were made by wooden rowboat and later by steam ferry.[43] On the army side, the officers' wives were met by an army ambulance, which transported them three miles to Ft. Lincoln. Those soldiers who chose not to rely on the ferry schedule, made the crossing by skiff or canoe, often flirting with death on the return trip. Close by the landing on the Bismarck side, a small town, called Whiskey Point, had sprung up to cater to the soldier, who, for his own reasons, was not anxious to go into town. It had the usual rum shops, gambling halls and brothels.

Bismarck was a town of five thousand people with a single, unpaved main street and a single untidy hotel.[44] Men walked on plank sidewalks and horses ploughed through the mud.[45] The commercial buildings were cheaply knocked together, high in front with a low shanty in the rear. Bismarck had a Mason's lodge, and it is known that Custer, Benteen and De Rudio were Masons.[46] There was the predictable abundance of dance halls, gambling dens and crime holes. In the early days, when the town stood on Sioux land, it could not be incorporated and so lacked proper law enforcement. A favorite hangout of the soldiers was Mullen and O'Neill, where fights could at times be deadly. On their visit to the town, soldiers brought with them "drinking jewelry" -- iron knuckles made from horseshoe nails.[47] The crude brothels or hog ranches cordially welcomed the soldier on payday. Otherwise, he had to seek the company of laundresses or Native American prostitutes.

The early growth of Bismarck was greatly hindered by its real estate difficulties. Deeds were hard to come by, since title could not be passed until such time as the Lakota surrendered claim. Instead, most settlers purchased "contracts" from the railroad, while others claimed squatter's rights. Another obstacle to development was the shortage of lumber. Unless brought in by ship, timber had to be harvested upriver and even that was cottonwood, which readily warped, pulling out nails and causing huge cracks in the sides of buildings. Fuel was expensive, cottonwood selling for five dollars a cord and ash for eight dollars.[48]

Despite its difficulties, Bismarck was a still railhead. On June 5, 1873 the first passenger train arrived and the town came of age. A passenger could board a train and be in New York in seven days, except in winter, when rail traffic was shut down. Singers, actors, musicians trickled into Bismarck, to the delight of the army and civilian communities.

A telegraph line ran from the railroad station in Bismarck to the adjutant's office in Lincoln.[49] In addition to relaying army dispatches, the line helped the fort keep abreast of the activities in town. Relations between the military and the Bismarck were not always cordial. Citizens complained that Custer was arrogant in his dealings, especially after 1875, when the rail traffic stopped, and the army took control of the postal services. Custer, in turn, accused the townspeople of thievery. When grain was stolen from the forage building in Ft. Lincoln, he sent the 7th Cavalry into Bismarck to retrieve it. The grain turned up in the mayor's own warehouse.[50] The worst strain came when the government forbade any but licensed post traders to sell alcohol to the soldiers. According to the rumors, the wife of the Secretary of War Belknap was anxious to protect her annuity, since she received $12,000 yearly from the trader at each Missouri fort. The prohibition does not appear to have been enforced for very long.

On November 22, 1873, while at Ft. Lincoln, De Rudio was forced to take sick leave because of "Rheumatism." Apparently, the galvanic current stimulation at the hospital was ineffective. On his return in January 1874, he was assigned to administrative work at General Terry's headquarters in St. Paul, where he remained for five months, probably with his family. There would be no reason to pay two rents. At the time, St. Paul had the Merchant's Hotel, on 3rd Street.

Among De Rudio's duties was the purchase of horses for the regiment.[51] This was no perfunctory assignment but reflected confidence in his abilities. Defects in a mount were sure to be detected once the animal reached the regimental stables, and the purchaser would not soon be allowed to forget his mistakes. By now, De Rudio had five years of Benteen's tutelage, and Benteen knew horses.

In anticipation of his promotion to 1st Lieutenant, De Rudio purchased a full-dress uniform, complete with gold braid, cords, tassels, epaulettes and belt. The spiked pickelhaube helmet, large metal eagle and yellow horsehair gave it a Prussian flair, and revived memories of the European officer's dress.[52] Although De Rudio did not own his own horse, the uniform might have been a priority, since dress parades were now the order of the day during the warmer months. A photograph of the officers at Ft. Rice shows most in full dress. De Rudio cut a fine figure. He was forty-four years old, with hair flecked with gray, waxed mustache, and long narrow goatee, in the grand Napoleon III style.

While De Rudio was away on temporary duty in St. Paul, the command received word that President Grant had authorized a expedition to the Black Hills, ostensibly to find a site for a fort; but, in fact, to explore the land. Thus far, the government had respected Lakota rights in the Black Hills. Was there sufficient gold to justify a change of policy? The government was anxious to have an answer to this question.

The Black Hills lies in Dakota Territory, encompassing an area a hundred by fifty miles, covered with valleys and canyons; and dark pine trees, which gave it its name. From here, came the tribal lodge poles. Flowers grew in great abundance, and there was much game and refreshing streams. The land had been sacred to the Cheyenne and to a lesser extent to the Lakota Sioux, but neither ventured regularly into the interior. Miners in small numbers had been working the ground, dating back to the time of the Belgian Jesuit Pierre Jean de Smet in the early 19th century. Although the Treaty of Fort Laramie of 1868 had placed it off-limits to the prospectors, mining had continued unabated, despite feeble efforts by the army to exclude the gold-seekers.

De Rudio did not accompany the expedition to the Black Hills. He remained on temporary duty in St. Paul and Ft. Lincoln. Had he gone along, he might have found time to exchange a few informal words with the Italian contingent. This included the bandmaster, FeliceVinitieri, who, as a warrant officer, was almost a social equal and a man with whom De

Rudio could discuss his experiences in the London Opera. Others in the Italian contingent were Frances Lombardi, a musician; Giovanni Casella, a trooper in E Company; August de Voto in B Company and Giovanni Martini, the H Company trumpeter.[53]

The regiment left Ft. Lincoln on July 2, 1874, accompanied by scientists, topographers, geologists, naturalists, miners and newspapermen -- a long column of one thousand soldiers and civilians. Temperature hovered in the high 90's. The band was taken along, to serenade the party in the evening. On the way to the Black Hills, the regiment met a monocled Englishmen rancher, who served the officers tea in the afternoon and appeared for dinner in a dinner jacket.[54]

Once in the Black Hills, the scientists set about their work, making measurements and gathering specimens, while the troopers played baseball. Soon, abundant traces of gold were discovered, confirming the miners' reports.

The expedition spent sixty days in an invigorating excursion without encountering hostiles. Upon return to Lincoln, the newsmen immediately telegraphed word of the discovery of gold. The news was electrifying and brought a deluge of prospectors to Yankton, where stagecoaches were available to take them to the Black Hills.[55] The geologic, zoologic and paleontologic specimens collected by the expedition were sent east by railway express to waiting scientists. De Rudio later secured some marble and tried his hand at sculpture.[56] It may be recalled that he had previously worked with stone in London.

By the end of De Rudio's temporary duty in St. Paul, construction at Ft. Rice had been completed, and the De Rudio family moved into their new quarters. The buildings resembled those of Ft. Lincoln, but the amenities were vastly different.

Ft. Rice was built on ten acres, at one time enclosed by a ten-foot stockade of two inch oak planks. There were two sally ports and two 2-story bastions, with a guard stationed in each sentry box day and night. The stockade had provided needed protection during the summer, when the horse companies were in the field, but had to be removed to accommodate the needs of an expanding fort.

The officers' quarters were constructed with cottonwood planks, caulked with adobe, and finished off in the interior with lath and plaster. Each of the ten two-story units resembled Lincoln. Locally kilned brick was used for the fireplaces and chimneys, but stoves, vented to the lower chimney, did the actual heating. Doors and window frames were difficult to close, because of warping. Newspapers, magazines and old canvas lined the walls for insulation.[57] Furnishings were largely makeshift. Since the officer and his family moved frequently, they sold off their furniture at the old station and improvised at the new. Bedspreads were made from calico and were tacked onto boxes for seat covers. Rugs were fashioned from red flannel and discarded army uniforms. Families sat on campstools and ate their meals on tables, set on carpenter's horses. A complete set of dishes was a rarity.

As with all officer quarters, each unit had a privy, set up in the yard over a deep hole. When the holes filled, the privies were moved elsewhere in the yard, but the odor persisted. There was no permanent assignment of quarters. A newly arrived ranking officer was given his choice of billet, and the officers junior to him were required to move, so that the lowest 2nd lieutenant might end up in a two room NCO cottage.[58]

Across the parade ground were six one-story enlisted barracks, with sod-brick insulation. Horse companies H, M and C were garrisoned here, as well as three infantry companies. As in Lincoln, sergeants bunked in a small cubicle, privates and corporals in a large room on cots with wooden slats. Three cast iron stoves gave off heat. A three by four foot locker, containing personal property, stood at the foot of each bunk. Saber, carbine and other equipment hung on a nearby post.

Each company had its own mess and selected its own cook-and-baker for a ten day tour of duty.[59] Meals were prepared in a small kitchen off to the side of the barracks and served on wooden tables with long benches, presided over by a non-com. Provisions arrived by steamer from Sioux City. Since Ft. Rice had no railroad and river traffic shut down in winter, a year's supply of food had to be kept on hand.

The soldier ate better in garrison than did a workingman in the city. His daily ration consisted of one pound of pork or bacon, a quarter pound of fresh or salt meat, eighteen ounces of bread or twelve ounces of hardtack and a quarter ounce of corn meal. Also, for every one hundred rations, the mess was provided with eight quarts of peas or beans or ten pounds of rice and six pounds of coffee.[60] Game sometimes supplemented the diet, but hunting was usually left to civilian hunters.

Fresh vegetables sometimes made an appearance, through the valiant efforts of the soldiers and their wives, who battled grasshoppers and recurrent drought.[61] Beets and onions were dried, ground and pressed into cakes.[62] Although some families kept chickens and cows, all relied on canned food. Crystallized eggs, potatoes, tomatoes and peaches came in airtight tins.[63] Condensed milk sold for fifty cents a can.

Ft. Rice had a post school, which the De Rudio children and Freddie Benteen attended. The teacher was chosen from the enlisted ranks and paid an extra thirty-five cents a day. He was not excused from fatigue details. At some posts, the chaplain ran the school, but Ft. Rice had no chaplain. Outside the stockade, the graveyard offered a somber reminder of the sorrows of frontier army life.

The visiting regimental band often visited and gave concerts at evening retreat. "Hops" were held in the post library, but for the elegant balls, the wives were brought by ambulance to Lincoln, where they remained overnight. Captain Benteen vigorously promoted a baseball team, the *Benteen Baseball and Gymnasium Club*,[64] which competed with the other three regimental clubs and with teams as far away as Yankton. Boxing and foot races were also popular, as were horse racing, greased pig wrestling and three-legged races. There was also a German *volkslieder* singing group.

Ft. Rice was awash in alcohol. Spirits were readily obtainable inside the fort and sometimes even in the guardhouse.

They arrived in mislabeled bottles and cans or were dropped over the side of a steamboat, tied to a fishing line, to be gathered by a dealer and sold to soldiers or bartered with warriors. On the outskirts of the fort were the "whiskey ranches" and the tepee brothels.[65]

Mrs. Catherine Louse Benteen was the senior wife, when a major was not in residence. Tall and thin, she was quite the antithesis of her heavy-set husband. Benteen was passionately devoted and wrote her almost daily, when he was in the field. The Benteens were fond of Mrs. De Rudio and enjoyed playing casino with her for ice cream and cake.[66] Later, while on recruiting duty in Philadelphia, Benteen kept an eye out for housekeepers to be brought back to the fort,[67] but it is unlikely that the De Rudio's could have afforded to pay the going rate of twenty-five to thirty-five dollars a month. In all his correspondence, Benteen never uttered one sour note about Eliza, and always referred to her as Mrs. De Rudio or Mrs. De R. The two wives were confidants, which was a close relationship in a frontier fort,[68] where life is soon reduced to the monotonous routine of seeing the same faces and listening to the same stories, with an occasional whiff of scandal to titillate.

Custer spent the winter of 1875-6 in Ft. Lincoln in his snug new quarters, but H Company was not destined to shovel snow. In September six companies were ordered to Louisiana in the Department of the Gulf, for the now-familiar provost duty. Eliza and the other wives packed their belongings and vacated their quarters.

The companies left Ft. Rice on September 15, 1874 for Lincoln, with the wives and children traveling in ambulances. While waiting to board the train in Bismarck, the families were housed with the officer families. The husbands slept on tables set on carpenter horses. One wife refers to De Rudio's children as "urchins" and reports that one of them "walked down my back at night."⁶⁹

On September 29 the detachment departed by train on a journey lasting almost a week. As the snow vanished, the passengers gladly removed their winter attire. The children had a merry time running down the aisles, fighting, and nursing bloody noses and fractured teeth. Young and old ate real ice ream at all hours. Freddy Benteen and Roma De Rudio preferred the chocolate flavor.

The troops were sent to various stations in Louisiana and Alabama, where they remained on constabulary duty until the spring. Their permanent headquarters was Breaux Bridge, Louisiana at the 164th Headquarters, Department of the Gulf, about one hundred miles from New Orleans. Benteen was fortunate enough to be assigned to New Orleans, where he and his family enjoyed the amenities, especially the racetrack. Benteen owned two thoroughbreds, but did not race them; they may have been bought for stud.⁷⁰ He was a canny investor, who, unlike his fellow officers, ended his days well off.

New Orleans was a dream fulfilled for the long-deprived wives. The handsome, slightly plump Eliza enjoyed herself as never before. With nearby Jackson Barracks unprepared to receive them, the families lived in boardinghouses. While the husbands were away, the women spent the time eating delicious food, attending band concerts and theaters, and driving into the country. Eliza even had a Creole nurse for her children!

Soon the happy days were over. November brought chill, penetrating rains and unhealthy odors from the narrow streets, especially in the French Quarter. Hospital ambulances began to be seen. The dreaded QUARANTINE sign appeared on the fronts of houses, and whispers of "small pox!" were heard.

Panic swept the boardinghouse when pustules appeared on the forehead of a boarder, and by the next day he, too, had come down with smallpox. The house was quarantined. Eliza De Rudio comforted his young bride and kept her from entering the room of her dying husband. Mail could be delivered but not sent out. Mrs. De Rudio's Creole nurse managed to slip through a narrow window and mail the wives' letters. She could have caused a disaster by spreading the virus! Day and night, the Black Marias passed the boardinghouse. At last, a few days before Christmas, the quarantine was lifted, and the families could be transported by ambulance to Jackson Barracks.[71]

Louisiana had been readmitted to the Union by 1870, after ratifying the 15th Amendment, which gave the vote to the African-American man. By the time the 7th Cavalry arrived in September of 1874, the days of the northern domination were coming to an end. Many a Republican stalwart was destined to lose out in the forthcoming Congressional elections in November, when Democrats would win a majority in the House of Representatives and in the Louisiana legislature. With the disappearance of the Republican supremacy went the last vestiges of De Rudio's patronage, if it ever again were to be needed.

In Louisiana, the situation was especially complex. William P. Kellogg, a northern carpetbagger had been elected governor of the state in 1872 with the aid of an illegal returning board.[72] His opponent, a southerner, had organized armed insurrection, which the Federal military forces had been called on repeatedly to suppress. To add to the confusion, the black vote veered from the regular Republican control, and President Grant, himself, withheld political support from Governor Kellogg because of Kellogg's hostility to a relative of the President in the Custom Service. All these inconsistencies insured that the Republican civilian government could not function without close support from the Federal army.

In the rural districts of Louisiana, the white population resorted to violence,[73] spurred on by the White League, an organization that resembled the Klu Klux Klan but lacked the cape and accessories. It boasted of fourteen thousand members and in many areas was the sole authority. To keep them in check, the government had one hundred thirty federal soldiers, including H Company, stationed in three widely separated locations within the state.

General Hancock, Commander of the 5th Military District, had witnessed the erosion of power of the carpetbag government and resolved to avoid confrontations.[74] He recalled the example of his predecessor, General Sheridan, who had opposed the southern interests, only to lose favor with Washington.[75] Hancock, moreover, as a Democrat and perennial presidential hopeful, had no use for the Reconstruction Acts and fought them in many ways.[76]

De Rudio went about his business, enforcing the law with his Federal "blue bellies." Thought by some to be "harsh and peremptory," his devotion to duty was soon to be tested. While stationed for five months with a detachment of H company at Breaux Bridge, not far from Lafayette, Louisiana, he was called upon to arrest General Francoise Clouet, an old French gentleman with Bonaparte sympathies, who had flagrantly prevented his black servants from voting. According to the Force Bill of May 31, 1870 anyone who obstructed Negro suffrage was subject to imprisonment and fine.[77]

The outcry against General Clouet's arrest was prompt and far-reaching. The French colony and the French consul in New Orleans lodged immediate protests. These were more than General Winfield Scott Hancock, the thunderbolt of the Army of the Potomac, could endure. He had little desire to be enmeshed in a Reconstruction fracas, let alone a diplomatic *embroglio*. He ordered De Rudio to be confined to quarters under house arrest and issued a statement "reproving overzealous officers who seemed to think that part of their duty was to give personal offence, thus demonstrating their zeal in doing their duty." This rebuke was intended more to mollify the southern whites, than to chastise De Rudio. No further disciplinary action was taken against him, nor did an unfavorable entry appear in his Correspondence and Personal file.

The matter, unfortunately, could not be contained. Besides being a lynchpin of the southern economy, New Orleans was a world city. The Clouet affair was reported in the St. Louis newspapers, the French *Journale de les Colonies* and even picked up by the *la Provincia di Belluno!* In all instances, De Rudio was identified as a former conspirator who had escaped from French Guyana and was a serving officer in the United States Army.[78]

With the cat out of the bag, De Rudio made no public comment and wisely allowed the matter to settle down, which it did within a few weeks. Other sad news reached him. From Belluno, came word that his father had died at the age of eighty in dire financial straits. 2nd Lt. Charles C. De Rudio had now inherited the title.

De Rudio's further stay in Louisiana was mercifully short. Orders were received, returning De Rudio and his detachment to the Department of the Dakotas. He and his family left Louisiana on May 5, 1875 on a six day trip to Yankton, Dakota. In the haste of departure, Eliza had thrown their belongings into an army footlocker, together with the keys. The children's clothing protruded from the chest. A soldier hastily trimmed the footlocker with a hatchet, and De Rudio finished the job with his saber. When they arrived at their destination, the children had to wear sleeveless clothes.[79]

H Company was stationed temporarily near Ft. Randall on the lower Missouri. De Rudio was given temporary command of H Company, and Benteen, a battalion. They were ordered to lead a patrol through the Black Hills to interdict gold mining.

The battalion left Ft. Randall in July. Along the way, it visited the Ponca Indian Agency and arrested some young braves who had been stealing livestock and supplies. It then proceeded to the Black Hills. In the year following the Custer expedition, the Black Hills had been overrun with gold-seekers, whose numbers, had increased five fold. Considerable quantities of the precious metal were now being mined. For six weeks, the patrol moved back and forth along the rivers, rounding up forty-four hapless miners, whom they brought back to Ft. Randall.[80] This did little to stem the influx of prospectors, as well the government realized, but it conveyed the impression that the government was attempting to uphold the terms of the Red

Cloud Treaty. After remaining for one month in Ft. Randall, the company returned to Ft. Rice for winter quarters.[81]

Ft. Rice was overjoyed to see them. In their absence, Eliza and the other wives had been living in terror, with hundreds of warriors passing the fort daily and smokesignals seen regularly. The warrior's favorite ploy was to attack the fort, in order to divert attention, and then to make off with the cattle. During an attack, stray bullets would stream through the bedroom windows in the upper stories of the officers' quarters.

Domestic tragedy seemed to dog Benteen. While he was away at the reservation downriver, his youngest child died. A soldier was called on to make the coffin, since the station carpenter had gone off with Benteen. It was constructed with wood scraps and its interior lined with material from a wedding dress. The child was buried in the Ft. Rice graveyard, without the comfort of a chaplain. In all, Benteen lost four children while on frontier duty.[82] Their symptoms seem to suggest meningocoicol meningitis, promoting the suspicion that Benteen or his wife may have been a carrier.

Instead of improving, the living condition at Ft. Rice had been steadily deteriorating. The government had decided to phase out the fort and had ordered construction halted. Nests of rattlesnakes hibernated under the rotting floors and crawled into the rooms when the heat was started.[83]

The women put up with the hardships and dreamed of better days. The winter of 1875 was the coldest in memory and seemed to go on forever. Spring finally arrived and with it came news of profound unrest among the Lakota Sioux.

Notes

1. Harvey Markowitz, ed., *American Indians* (Pasadena, CA and Englewood Cliffs, NJ: Salem, 1995), p. 719.
2. S. L. A. Marshall, *Crimsoned Prairie* (New York: Scribner, 1972), p. 5
3. Charles M. Robinson III, *A Good Year to Die. The Story of the Great Sioux War* (New York: Random House, 1955), p. 6.
4. Jason Hook and Martin Pegler, *To Live and Die in the West* (Oxford: Osprey, 1999), p. 81.
5. Robinson, p. 119.
6. Hook and Pegler, p. 82.
7. Stephen Longstreet, *War Cries on Horseback* (Garden City, NY: Doubleday, 1970), p. 215.
8. Wayne Mitchell Sarf, *The Little Bighorn Campaign* (Conshohoken, PA: Combined Books, 2000), p. 39.
9. Peter Panzeri, *Little Bighorn 1876* (Botley, Oxford: Osprey Publishing Co., 1995), p. 8.
10. Elizabeth B. Custer, *Boots and Saddles* (New York: Harper, 1885), p. 13.
11. *Ibid.*, p. 13.
12. *Ibid.*, p. 14.
13. *Ibid.*, p. 17.
14. Katherine Gibson Fougera, *With Custer's Cavalry* (Lincoln and London: University of Nebraska, 1986), p. 213.
15. Edward L. Daily, *Custer to MacArthur* (Paducah, KY: Turner, 1995), p. 37; Hugh Lenox Scott, *Some Memories of a Soldier* (New York: Century, 1928), p. 30.
16. Edward J. McClernand, *With the Indian and the Buffalo in Montana* (Glendale, CA: Clark, 1969), p. 28.
17. Custer, Elizabeth, *Boots,* p. 29.
18. *Ibid.*, p. 30.
19. *Ibid.*, p. 36.
20. Maurice Matlof, *American Military History* Office of the Chief of Military History, 1969 (revised 1973), Government Printing Office, p. 315.
21. Marshall, p. 89.
22. Custer, Elizabeth, *Boots,* p. 37.
23. *Ibid.*, p. 47.
24. *Ibid.*, p. 42.
25. Robert W. Frazer, *Forts of the West* (Norman and London: University of Oklahoma, 1988), p. 113.
26. John Upton Terrell, and George Walton, *Faint the Trumpet Sounds* (New York: McKay, 1966), p. 92.
27. Marguerite Merington, *The Custer Story* (Lincoln: University of Nebraska

28. Custer, Elizabeth, *Boots*, p. 119.
29. John M. Carroll, *They Rode with Custer* (Mattituck, NY: J. M. Carroll, 1993), p. 254.
30. *Ibid.*, p. 256.
31. Robert Nightingale, *Little Bighorn* (U.S.: Far West Publications, 1996), p. 60.
32. Terrell and Walton, p. 88.
33. *Ibid.*, p. 122.
34. Hugh Lenox Scott, *Some Memories of a Soldier* (New York: Century, 1928), p. 31.
35. Terrell and Walton, p. 92.
36. Custer, Elizabeth, *Boots*, p. 119.
37. Ani Frank Mulford, *Fighting Indians in the 7th Cavalry* 2nd ed. (Fairfield, WA: Ye Galleon Press, 1972), p. 126.
38. Stephen Longstreet, *War Cries on Horseback* (Garden City, NY: Doubleday, 1970), pp. 154, 203.
39. Elizabeth B. Custer, *Tenting on the Plains* (New York: Webster, 1889), p. 408.
40. Daily, p. 179.
41. Don Rickey, *Forty Miles a Day on Beans and Hay* (Norman and London: University of Oklahoma, 1963), p. 113.
42. E. A. Brininstool, *Troopers with Custer* (Lincoln and London: University of Nebraska, 1952), p. 43.
43. Mulford, p. 24.
44. Custer, Elizabeth, *Boots*, p. 185.
45. Fougera, p. 62.
46. F. Benteen letter to Mrs. Benteen, July 4, 1876. John M. Carroll, *The Benteen-Goldin Letters on Custer and his last Battle* (New York: Liveright, 1974), p. 157.
47. Evans S. Connell, *Son of the Morning Star* (New York: Harper Perennial, 1984), p. 155.
48. Linda Slaughter, *Fortress to Farm* (New York: Exposition, 1972), p. 74, *et passim;* Sandy Barnard, ed., *Ten Years with Custer. A 7th Cavalryman's Memoirs* (Ft. Collins, CO: Citizen Printing, 2001), p. 207-221.
49. Mulford, p. 26.
50. Nightingale, p. 60.
51. Regimental Returns [Personnel], Regular Army Cavalry Regiments 1833-1916: 7th Cavalry 1866-1896, (microfilm 744, rolls 71-74), National Archives Building, Washington, DC.
52. Robert M. Utley, *Frontier Regulars. The United States Army and the Indian, 1866-1890* (New York: Macmillan, 1973), p. 76.
53. Vincent, Transano, "Custer's Italians," *Wild West*, June 1999.
54. Fougera, p. 185.
55. Terrell and Walton, p. 123.
56. Fougera, p. 189.
57. *Ibid.*, p. 162.
58. Custer, Elizabeth, *Tenting*, p. 372.
59. Utley, *Frontier*, p. 88.
60. Fougera, p. 193; Rickey, p. 113, Brininstool, p. 43.
61. Mary Ellen Jones, *Daily Life on the Nineteenth Century American Frontier*

(Westport, CT: Greenwood, 1988), pp. 230, 222.
62. Merington, p. 9.
63. Custer, Elizabeth, *Boots,* p. 171.
64. Jason Hook and Martin Pegler, *To Live and Die in the West* (Oxford: Osprey, 1999), p. 27; Rickey, pp. 206, 111; Harry H. Anderson, "The Benteen Baseball Club," *Magazine of Western History*, July 1970.
65. Longstreet, p. 155.
66. Carroll, *Benteen-Goldin,* p. 13.
67. *Ibid.,* p. 57.
68. *Ibid.,* p. 14.
69. Fougera, p. 200.
70. F. Benteen letter to T. Goldin, February 22, 1896. Carroll, *Benteen-Goldin*, p. 280.
71. Fougera, p. 207.
72. Claude G. Bowers, *The Tragic Era* (Cambridge, MA: Houghton Mifflin, 1929), p. 436.
73. Richard Nelson Current, *Those Terrible Carpetbaggers* (New York and Oxford: Oxford, 1988), p. 289.
74. Eric Foner, *Reconstruction. America's Unfinished Revolution 1863-1877* (New York: Harper & Row, 1988), p. 554.
75. J. G. Randall and David Donald, *The Civil War and Reconstruction* (Boston: Heath, 1961), p. 598.
76. Currant, p. 17.
77. Charles A. Wesley, and Patricia W. Romero, *Negro American in the Civil War* (New York: Publishers Co., 1967), p. 200.
78. Cesare Marino, *Dal Piave al Little Bighorn* (Belluno: Tarantola, 1996), pp. 206, 207.
79. Fougera, p. 212.
80. *Ibid.,* p. 200.
81. Regimental Returns [Personnel], Regular Army Cavalry Regiments 1833-1916: 7th Cavalry 1866-1896, (microfilm 744, rolls 71-74), National Archives Building, Washington, DC.
82. Carroll, *Benteen-Goldin,* p. 196.
83. Fougera, p. 228.

BIRTHPLACE OF CARLO DE RUDIO ON THE OUTSKIRTS OF BELLUNO, ITALY. PHOTO WAS TAKEN FROM THE ROAD.

DE RUDIO REQUESTS A SMOKE WHILE AWAITING EXECUTION.
(*WASHINGTON STAR*, OCTOBER 16, 1910)

> War Department
> Washington City D.C.
> _____ 1862
>
> Can this man be appointed a 2nd Lieut. with advantage to the service?
>
> C.A.D.

ASSISTANT SECRETARY OF WAR, CHARLES A. DANA, ARRANGES FOR DE RUDIO'S COMMISSION IN THE VOLUNTEER ARMY IN 1864.
(NATIONAL ARCHIVES)

> Board to Examine Officers Appointed in the Infantry of the Army.
> No. 125 BLEECKER Street,
> New York City Sept 17 1867.
>
> I certify on honor that I have carefully examined Charles C. De Rudio agreeably to the General Regulations of the Army, and that in my opinion he is ~~far from all bodily defect and mental infirmity, which would in any way~~ disqualified him from performing the duties of an Officer, on account of retraction of the right testicle, resulting from his birth.
>
> Wm J. Sloan
> Bvt. Brig. Gen USA Surgeon
> Examining Surgeon

DE RUDIO LEARNS THAT HE IS MEDICALLY DISQUALIFIED FOR A COMMISSION IN THE REGULAR ARMY.
(NATIONAL ARCHIVES)

New York, Sept 19th, 1867

I hereby certify that I have carefully examined 2d Lieut. C. C. de Rudio, and found that he is in my opinion perfectly qualified to perform the most arduous duties devolving upon an officer of the Army, although one of the testes (the right) has not descended as low down the scrotum as is the case on the left side (the right testis is ordinarily somewhat higher up than the left.)

There is not the slightest deviation either in the shape, size or direction of the right testicle, which would in the least interfere either in marching on foot, or horseback, nor in any posture

A LETTER FROM DR. R. TAISZKY, A CIVILIAN PHYSICIAN, ATTESTING TO DE RUDIO'S MEDICAL FITNESS FOR A COMMISSION IN THE REGULAR ARMY.
(NATIONAL ARCHIVES)

he may be regu[late] himself in performing his duties as a soldier, and there is not even the slightest probability that it will ever incommode him during the remainder of his life, since it is apparent to me, that he was born so, and this case must come under the many "vitia primae formationis," or physical peculiarities, which are found in the most robust and healthiest individuals.

The abdominal rings as well as the inguinal canals on both sides, so also both spermadic cords are healthy.

R. Tauszky, M.D.
358. West 42d street
Late A. Surgeon of
U. States, Vols.

CONTINUATION OF LETTER FROM DR. R. TAISZKY
ATTESTING TO DE RUDIO'S MEDICAL FITNESS FOR A
COMMISSION IN THE REGULAR ARMY.
(NATIONAL ARCHIVES)

Second Lieutenant Charles C. De Rudio.
He remained a 'shavetail' for 8 years.
(Brian C. Pohanka collection at the
US Army Military History Institute)

LT. COLONEL GEORGE A. CUSTER,
ACTING REGIMENTAL COMMANDER OF THE
SEVENTH CAVALRY AND A MAN OF GREAT AMBITIONS.
(DENVER PUBLIC LIBRARY. WESTERN HISTORY COLLECTION.)

Captain Miles W. Keogh.
Born in Ireland, he fought in
the Papal Wars and the Civil War
before joining the Seventh Cavalry.
(Denver Public Library. Western History Collection)

Captain Tom Custer,
Brother of the regimental commander and
twice winner of the Medal of Honor during the Civil War.
(Denver Public Library. Western History Collection.)

ARTIST'S DEPICTION OF DE RUDIO FLEEING THE LAKOTAS AT LITTLE BIGHORN WITH GUIDON IN HAND. (HARPER'S WEEKLY, SEPTEMBER 25, 1897)

TRUMPETER JOHN MARTIN, AKA GIOVANNI MARTINI, IN LATER LIFE. HE WAS DISPATCHED BY CUSTER BEFORE THE BATTLE.

Curly, a young Lakota scout.
The last witness to the Battle of Little Bighorn.
(Denver Public Library. Western History Collection.)

Major Marcus A. Reno at the time of the Court of Inquiry. Libby Custer blamed him for the Little Bighorn defeat. (Mrs. John C. Tuten Collection at the US Army Military History Institute.)

Captain Frederick Benteen in 1878.
He was thought by Gen. Hugh Scott to be
the finest officer in the army.
(Mrs. John C. Tuten Collection at the
US military History Institute.)

Samuel D. Sturgis, nominal commander of the Seventh Cavalry, shown in Brigadier General's uniform, took active command after the Battle of Little Bighorn. (Denver Public Library. Western History Collection.)

Captain De Rudio in later years, wearing aiguillette.
By now he is known as "Old Rudy."
(Denver Public Library. Western History Collection.)

The devoted father, De Rudio, with his two daughters. The photo was taken in a photographer's studio. (Denver Public Library. Western History Collection.)

Carlotta De Rudio, the youngest daughter.
(Brian C. Pohanka Collection at
the US Military History Institute.)

Officers posing for a photo while on maneuvers in Indian Territory. A somewhat thin Captain De Rudio indicated by the arrow in the second tier of horsemen.
(US Army Military History Institute.)

IX
LITTLE BIG HORN

In the summer of 1875, Red Cloud visited Washington to protest the violation of the Treaty of Fort Laramie by the miners. He steadfastly refused to allow the treaty to be altered, despite what the government thought were liberal inducements. For President Grant, this recalcitrance was unacceptable. The President was determined to end that treaty, without his actions appearing too obvious.

The reason, in a word, was gold! Following the failure of Jay Cooke and Co. in 1873, a severe financial panic had overtaken the country. This disaster was far worse than even the crisis of 1837. It was, in fact, a depression. Hundreds of factories had closed; railroad construction had come to a halt; five thousand businesses had failed and a quarter of a billion dollars gone into default. The cycle of business failures did not reverse itself in a few months, but continued relentlessly for five years.[1] According to the simplistic economic thinking of the time, only gold could halt the panic. The surface riches of California had long since dwindled, as had the supplies in Colorado and Virginia City, Montana, but Custer's report left no doubt that there were considerable quantities of gold still to be mined in the Black Hills.

President Grant devised what he thought were plausible justifications for abrogating a treaty passed by the Senate and signed by a President. It was only a matter of time before the warriors outside the reservations would disrupt train travel and telegraph communication.[2] Also, the miners' safety required that the tribes be barred from the Black Hills. Lastly, for the economic good of the country, title to the Yellowstone corridor had to be obtained from the Lakota, and no better way could be found to impose national will than to defeat the free-roamers in battle and confine them to a reservation.

A plan was set in motion. In November 1875 Inspector E.C. Watkins of the U.S. Indian Bureau completed his investigation of the Sioux country. He declared that the tribes living outside the reservation constituted a threat to western expansion.[3] Knowing that both reservation tribes and the roamers spent the winter hunting in the Powder, Tongue and Bighorn basins, the government instructed the Indian Bureau on December 1, to order all warriors to return to their reservations before January 31, 1876. The government well understood that this order would not be obeyed. Communication and movement were difficult enough in the winter months, and the winter of 1875-6 was the worst in memory.[4] Nor did the Lakota fully realize the consequences of failing to heed the ultimatum.

To show the warriors that the government meant business, the army was assigned jurisdiction over all tribes living off the reservations.[5] Preparations for a military campaign were drawn up, employing the largest military body yet assembled on the plains and the largest peacetime army since Sherman's demonstration on the Mexican border in 1865. A winter campaign was preferred, when the tribes would have difficulty escaping through the snow. The attack would be launched from several directions, to keep the Sioux and Northern Cheyenne from evading an encounter. From the south, General Crook would lead his men up from Ft. Fetterman. From the north, General Alfred H. Terry would lead a column from Ft. Lincoln in the east and also dispatch a column from Ft. Shaw in the west. The Crow and Shoshone could be relied on to help block an escape to the west. Because of difficulties with communication, an overall commander would not be named. All parties would operate independently within the confines of the general battle plan. Not only were the warriors to be driven back to the reservation, but also they were to be dealt a blow that would discourage them from ever again venturing outside.

Brigadier General George Crook, of the Department of the Platte, was a successful Indian fighter, renowned for his campaigns against the Paiute and the Chiricahua Apache in the southwest. Characteristically, he achieved success without excessive loss of life to his men or to the warriors. Born in Ohio, he graduated West Point in 1852, a classmate of Sherman. In the Civil War he commanded cavalry, spent time in Confederate captivity and ended his wartime service as Major General of Volunteers. Appointed a Lt. Colonel of infantry in the regular army, he spent his military career in Indian campaigns. In 1873, he defeated Cochise in the Tonto Basin of Arizona and won his brigadier's star.

Crook brought two innovations to the campaigns. He used wagons only to support his initial advance and to provision his supply base. Supplies were then transferred from wagon to pack mules for the final assault.[6] Crook's mules packed two hundred fifty to three hundred twenty pounds, more than twice the ordinary army load, and they traveled five miles per hour. Crook is said to have inspected each mule personally before setting out.[7]

Moreover, Crook tried to recruit his scouts from the same tribe that he was fighting. This gave him a surer knowledge of the terrain, as well as insight into the enemy tactics. Unfortunately, he could not obtain the services of Lakota scouts for the forthcoming campaign. There was another intangible reason for his successes. The warriors, hostile and friendly, respected his word.

Crook completed his preparations long before Terry. He had packers and mounts at hand, both having been brought up from the south. Even so, wagons were in short supply, because of the Black Hills gold fever.[8]

Crook was the first to move. His was the largest of the three columns. March 1, he set out from Ft. Fetterman in deep snow and proceeded up the Bozeman Trail toward Montana. At his staging area at Goose Creek, Wyoming near present day Sheridan, he transferred his supplies to a mule train. Crook also mounted his infantry on mules, which troubled the novice rider less than did a cavalry horse.[9]

The Crook column proceeded toward the Powder River. At the end of March, it scored an initial success with the capture of an enemy village, but Crazy Horse (Untamed Horse, more accurately[10]) and the Northern Cheyenne counterattacked from high ground and regained their supplies. Worse, the warriors made off with the column's beef herd. Even without large casualties, Crook sensed that he was stopped. Like the Native American warrior, Crook would seldom fight, unless the odds were on his side, and he was certain of winning.[11] Crook returned to Ft. Fetterman with his column intact, to await the spring grass before starting out again.

After refitting in Ft. Fetterman, Crook set out in May with fifteen companies of cavalry and five companies of mule-mounted infantry, three hundred Shoshone, Crow and Snake scouts, totaling thirteen hundred men. He noted smoke signals daily.[12] At Goose Creek, he transferred supplies to the mule train, before proceding north. Reaching northern Wyoming, the troops were struck by an epidemic of "inflammatory rheumatism," probably trichinosis from the uncooked or undercooked pork, but kept moving. At the Rosebud-Tongue River divide on June 17, Crook was again surprised, this time by the Lakota Sioux. Crazy Horse, Gall, and their Oglala warriors had made a forced night march from their encampment in the valley of the Little Bighorn, thirty-five miles to the west. After six hours of hard fighting, Crook suffered another defeat, with twelve killed, twenty-six wounded.

Crook's campaign was not the army's first encounter with Crazy Horse. The warrior had previously led his Oglala Lakota against Ft. Phil Kearny in the Bozeman War, and it was Crazy Horse who had enticed the ill-fated detachment of Captain William Fetterman into an ambush. This gifted mystic was a superb horseman and fearless warrior, fiercely determined to prevent encroachment on what be believed to be Lakota hunting ground. Gall, an Unkpapa chief, was as brave a warrior and a practical, respected leader, as well. He, too, had led attacks against the army in 1872 and 1873.

Crook assessed his situation. He was outnumbered, or so he thought, impeded by the wounded, and short of ammunition. He decided to return. This was seven days before the Custer engagement. As it turned out, it was fortunate he did so, for the hostiles had prepared a dangerous ambush in the Dead Canyon Gorge several miles ahead.[13] The Lakota, too, were also anxious to leave the scene, fearing in their absence that the rival Crow might threaten their village.[14] This victory served to reinforce Lakota confidence and validated Sitting Bull's vision of the defeat of the U.S. Army and the return to old times. Unaware of Crook's movements, Terry divided his command into two columns in preparation for the campaign. Colonel Gibbon would leave from Ft. Ellis and follow the northern bank of the Yellowstone. Terry would leave from Ft. Lincoln in the northeast and march overland. Both columns would rendezvous in June somewhere along the Yellowstone River and plan their further campaign, in accordance with information gathered along the way. On paper, this plan seemed fool proof. There was no apparent way the enemy could escape, since his retreat would be cut off in all directions.

Colonel John Gibbon was born in North Carolina and educated at West Point. He chose the Union cause, although his two brothers were in the Confederate army. Wounded at Gettysburg, he rose to Major General of Volunteers by the end of the war. He was a cautious, reflective officer whose hip wound continued to trouble him.

Colonel Gibbon chose Ft. Ellis as a staging area, three miles from Bozeman. His column had ten companies of infantry and cavalry, as well as the usual scouts, guides and interpreters, totaling about five hundred. Beginning March 23 several inches of snow had fallen, three weeks after Crook's first campaign got underway, Gibbon staggered his departure. Early in the march, snow blindness plagued the recruits.[15] Men lose almost total vision from exposure to the glare of sun on the snow, especially during late winter and early spring. To prevent this, the seasoned trooper blackened his face with lampblack or soot up to one inch from the eyes.[16]

Without steamships to supply him, Gibbon had to relay heavily on wagons. Trails were laboriously widened, to accommodate the supply trains. Up to a ton of freight could be carried in each civilian two-horse cart and two tons in the military six-mule team wagon. In the military team, the driver rides the off-wheel mule, and manages the team with a jerk line.[17] Mules are preferred to oxen, since they are swifter, but they require grain feed. Muleteers exalt the mule over the horse as more intelligent, harder to frighten and less likely to drink polluted water.

The Gibbon column proceeded along the more passable north bank. Steep rock and clay bluffs, twenty to a hundred feet high border the Yellowstone River. Occasionally it flows through a valley, with meadows on one or both sides. Clusters of cottonwood grow along its banks, and less frequently, ash, willow and box elder.[18] Civilian mackinaws did little to ease the supply problem. These elliptical raft-like boats had gunwales raised several feet to contain the cargo. They were manned by four oarsmen and steered by a helmsman seated on a platform. Since the boat made only one downriver trip, it carried only highly profitable goods, especially alcohol, for sale at high prices.[19]

Colonel Gibbon advanced cautiously, unwilling to be prematurely engaged, since Terry's column could not support him. He built up supply depots, rested, gathered his forces, advanced, then waited. He sent out several reconnaissance parties, which reported that a large party of Lakota was moving west from the Tongue to the Rosebud. Eventually his column reached the mouth of the Rosebud on June 14. There, Gibbons established camp and awaited the arrival of General Terry.

Little Big Horn 187

General Terry was the last to leave. His record was most unusual. He was a lawyer, who had commanded a volunteer regiment in the Civil War and later a corps, rising to the rank of brevet major general. For his gallant services in the capture of Ft. Fisher in Wilmington, North Carolina, the last major Confederate seaport, a grateful Congress voted him special thanks.[20] After the war, he was given a brigadier's commission in the Regular army.

Terry's column had the longest distance to travel. He had no contact with General Crook, nor did he know of Crook's defeat, although word of a "small skirmish" had crept back to Ft. Lincoln after Terry had left.[21] Terry had three companies of infantry as well as all twelve companies of the 7th Cavalry, wholly assembled for the first time. The regiment was under-officered and undermanned, with only forty men to a company; and a third of them were recruits.[22] There had been no time for target practice before departure.[23]

For several weeks, it appeared that Custer would not be around to lead the 7th Cavalry. It fell to Major Reno to prepare the regiment for the field. Custer had been away on leave for five months in New York, the site of the forthcoming Democratic Presidential Convention. Although he had many friends in the city, his choice of New York for furlough may have been politically motivated. He had asked for a further extension, which the Secretary of War Belknap had denied. In Custer's absence, Reno requested that he be given command, an act that did little to ingratiate him to Custer. Reno divided the regiment into two wings of six companies. He, a major, would command one wing, when Custer returned and Benteen, a senior captain, the other. By this arrangement, Reno would be assured of an active field command, rather than staff duties.

Back east, Custer found himself up to his neck in trouble. He had made the unforgivable mistake of implicating the Secretary of War Belknap and the brother of President Grant in charges of graft, relating to traders' activities. When called upon to offer proof, Custer could not substantiate his charges.

Custer was called to Washington under subpoena by a Congressional committee and later detained there by the President. Suddenly Custer's career was in peril. Instead of the flaxen-haired favorite of the Democratic press, thought to be Presidential material, Custer found himself in danger of being cashiered or placed permanently on the sidelines. Only through the intercession of General Terry, a generous man, did President Grant permit Custer to regain command of the 7th Cavalry. But it had cost Custer five weeks of wasted time. He arrived six days before the regiment's departure, fiercely determined to salvage his career.

De Rudio received the news of his long-awaited promotion to 1st Lieutenant on December 15, 1875. A bar could be added to his shoulder straps, and the back issues of the *Army Register* could now be used to paper the walls of his quarters for insulation, since they were no longer of compelling interest.

Throughout the closing days of winter, work had been progressing at Ft. Rice, in preparation for the forthcoming campaign. Horses had to be closely inspected for infirmities, bridles overhauled and four hundred horses reshod. Several extra pairs of shoes were made for each mount. Saddles required close attention. They were of McClellen type, wood base covered with black leather or rawhide, with leather side skirts. Even with oil and lampblack to retard shrinkage,[24] most wore out within two years.[25] There was no breast strap to prevent the saddle from sliding backwards, when the mount went uphill. Rust had to be scoured from the metal stirrups. After the last of the preparations had been completed, the men were given only two days to pack and store the company property.[26]

De Rudio made the march from Rice to Lincoln by ambulance. He had a saddle but did not own a horse. Benteen had lent him a revolver and had promised a mount, when they got to Ft. Lincoln.[27] With four children, De Rudio obviously had difficulty getting by on a Lieutenant's pay, but a good horse could have been bought for less than the price of his dress uniform, and less than the seventy-five to one hundred fifty dollars which Custer paid for his own horses.

The Ft. Rice battalion arrived on May 5 at the assembly ground outside of Ft. Lincoln. First Lieutenant De Rudio had every expectation of being given E Company with the gray horses, which lacked a company commander.

Custer had other plans for him. Although qualified and in grade, De Rudio was assigned to A Company with the black horses, where he would serve under Captain Myles Moylan, whose blood curdled at the sight of this quiet, cultured officer. A Company had the reputation of being wild and unruly, known in the regiment as "the Forty Thieves."[28] Over the years, Custer knew of Moylan's dislike for De Rudio, so the assignment may have been somewhat malicious. In fairness, General Terry might also have had a hand in the arrangement, since the officer who had been given E Company was a former aid to Terry in the Civil War. Under the circumstances, De Rudio could do little more than stifle his disappointment.

While at Lincoln, Moylan refused to take De Rudio into his mess, although he shared it with only one other officer. This was utterly contemptible and inexcusable behavior, unbefitting a senior officer, but about as much as one might expect from Moylan, who himself had been dealt similar treatment in the past. De Rudio had to trudge three times a day to the shack of Fred Girard, a scout-interpreter, to get something to eat. Benteen found Rudio ill-equipped: "no horse, no mess-kit, no nothing-- but my pistol to war with."[29] Benteen gave De Rudio the same horse he had lent him before, when he had served in H Company. De Rudio later returned the revolver without the holster which was lost during the battle, much to Benteen's vexation, as Benteen recounted in later years, but by then Benteen was at odds with all the officers of the regiment.

To transport heavy supplies on the Terry expedition, the army had contracted for the use of the steam ship *Far West,* a flat-bottomed, stern wheel craft, one hundred ninety feet long, drawing two feet of water, laden.[30] The government leased it for three hundred sixty dollars per day. Sidewheel steamboats had appeared on the Missouri in 1819, later replaced by the sternwheel. Navigating the Missouri could at times be a nightmare, because of the sandbars, windings, snags, and changing channels. Captains found that the river could alter its course by several miles in one week.[31]

By arrangement, the *Far West* would ferry two hundred tons of cargo and three companies of infantry to the depot at Stanley's Stockade a hundred miles up the Yellowstone. Embarking three companies was no picnic. Three hundred and fifty men had to be crowded onto the upper deck in the 98 degree sunshine and a hundred horses and mules on the lower deck, together with army wagons. The soldiers were frequently put ashore to cut wood, since the boilers required two cords of wood an hour.[32]

The Terry column left Ft. Lincoln in the morning of May 17, 1876. It had twelve hundred soldiers, Arikara scouts, civilian packers and seventeen hundred animals.[33] Also in the column were eighty-five to one hundred ten cavalry recruits who marched on foot, because of a shortage of horses.[34] The recruits were brought along to toughen them up. Some would later accompany Custer on mounts taken from the band.

The three companies of infantry and the supply train moved out first. Then Custer ordered *Mount!* and *Forward!* and led the 7th Cavalry in review, to the tunes of *Gary Owen* and *The Girl I Left Behind Me*. Alongside Custer, the standard bearer carried the huge three by five foot swallow-tailed regimental standard with crossed white sabers. Behind each company commander, the swallow-tailed, gold starred American flag was used as troop guidon, with the letter of the troop superimposed. At Custer's side, rode the regimental trumpeter. Each company had two trumpeters, one remaining beside the officer and the other riding with the first sergeant.[35] The cavalry trumpet has no valves, and its notes have a lower range than a bugle.[36] Once outside the garrison, the column halted, and the married men and officers were permitted to fall out to say their farewells.

To the people who knew him well, Custer had changed. His

experiences in Washington had shaken him badly. The day before the departure, he had cut his long golden locks with horse clippers.[37] He wore fringed jacket and dark blue shirt with a dark brimmed hat and a red silk scarf. As the column moved off, Mrs. Custer noted that the figures of the horsemen were reflected ominously in the low cloud cover.[38]

Custer was surrounded by a strong family presence on the march. With him was a nephew who worked as a drover in the employ of the beef contractor; a younger brother, Boston, who was listed as a guide; his brother, Captain Tom Custer and a brother-in-law, Lt. James Calhoun. Also along, against orders, was a local journalist, to insure that accounts of his anticipated glory would come to the notice of the important newspapers. The Democratic Convention was scheduled for June 28 in New York City, and Custer was highly regarded by the important New York *Herald*.

The column left in *HEAVY MARCHING ORDER!* Sabers were sheathed and lariat tied to the left side of the saddle. Nosebag and canteen were attached to a ring on the front right of the saddle. Blanket was rolled up in front of the saddle, leather saddlebag and greatcoat or tunic carried behind. In his haversack, the soldier kept a tin plate, knife, fork and spoon, serving kit, coffee, sugar, a box of cartridges, socks, matches, a box of hardtack (twelve crackers) and twelve ounces of salt pork. A stake for picketing his horse hung from the pommel ring.[39]

For sidearms, soldier and officer carried in a holster a six shot .45/40 Model 1872 Colt single action revolver *Peacemaker*, standard issue for the past year. It used forty grains black powder and a 255-grain lead bullet in a metal cartridge.[40] A butcher or bowie knife was kept next to the holster.[41] The soldier's long gun was the Springfield trapdoor Carbine .45/55, model 1873.[42] The bullet weighed four hundred five grains and had a muzzle velocity of 1,200 fps. The carbine could also accommodate the .45/70 rifle cartridge, which had the same caliber but was packed with seventy grains of black powder, instead of the fifty-five grains of the carbine. When fired in the carbine, the rifle cartridge had a distressing kick. Substituting the seventy for the fifty-five was an oft-practiced practical joke among cavalrymen.[43] But when hunting with a carbine, the soldier used the .45/70, for its greater range. The Springfield 1873 utilized a soft copper cartridge with an internal centerfire primer that ignited the black powder and gave off thick, lingering smoke.

Each soldier carried fifty rounds of carbine ammunition and twenty-five rounds of revolver ammunition on his person. Most preferred to carry the ammunition in a canvas cartridge belt rather than a cartridge box, but both were used. There was an additional fifty rounds of carbine ammunition carried in the saddlebag, making a total of one hundred rounds of carbine cartridges.

A repeating weapon might have been preferred by most soldiers to their Springfield single shot carbine. In the Washita campaign, they had used a Spencer repeating rifle to good effect. Army ordinance maintained that the Winchester 44/40 carbine had a shorter range and less penetration than the Springfield 45/55 carbine. The merits of the two weapons had been evaluated on the ordinance firing range, but not on horseback, nor in battle. In fact, Major Reno had been on the ordinance board. As a general rule, the military preferred accuracy to speed in its choice of weapons. All the more curious, for it provided little training in marksmanship. Not until 1872, at the urging of the National Rifle Association, did the army mandate ninety cartridges a year for practice.[44]

In addition to the 7th Cavalry, Terry also had three companies of infantry, a detachment of two 5 barrel-Gatling machine guns, Arikara scouts, two hundred wagons and a hundred fifty muleteers. In heavy marching order, each company had one wagon to transport rations, forage, cooking equipment, tents and the officer's baggage. Many of the mules were young and unbroken and those pulling the contract wagons were of poor quality.

No sooner did the column leave the fort, then rain began, and continued intermittently for four miserable days. Then the sun shone and spirits brightened. Custer retained Reno's table of organization, dividing the regiment into two six company wings, one under Reno, the other under Benteen.

The order of the march commenced early, to prevent a surprise attack. One battalion rode as advanced guard, another as rear guard each maintaining a distance of five hundred yards from the train. In the advanced guard, one company rode until it was half a mile ahead of the train, whereupon it dismounted and unbit the horses, allowing them to graze until the train had passed it and was half a mile ahead. It then rejoined the march and the next company took its place.[45] Custer rode with the advanced company to select the route and camping sites. The other two companies built bridges or assisted at the river crossings.

The wagon accompanying the forward companies carried axes, shovels, picks, iron bars, scythes, rakes and forks. At a river crossing, the forward companies cut down trees and laid the trunks crisscross. Grass would then be packed on top and dirt piled above it. Thirteen spans had to be constructed on one fourteen mile stretch.[46]

De Rudio remained in A Company under the disagreeable Captain Moylan, until Benteen took pity on him. Since Benteen had been given command of the left wing, he was authorized to have an adjutant. He chose De Rudio, removing him from Moylan's company. "None likes to serve with Moylan," Benteen wrote his wife. "With me, he [De Rudio] has nothing to annoy him--and little to do."[47] Benteen, De Rudio and another junior officer in H Company, messed together.[48]

By the end of May, the column had come to the first large river, the Little Missouri. Despite the predictions of the Indian agents, General Terry saw no signs of the Lakota Sioux. Terry had hoped to encounter them here, to avoid the necessity of a long campaign. This was not to be. He had to adhere to the original plan and join up with Gibbon.

The column passed through the Bad Lands, known to it from the Black Hills expedition. The surface was fiery red or dark brown or black, underlain by beds of coal, which may have once burned and uplifted the ground.[49] Many fossils were visible, which the soldiers collected, as had the geologists previously. June 1, two weeks out, they encountered a violent snowstorm, with snow piling up to two feet. This lasted for two days, until the sun shown, and the chinook winds melted it away. During the march, the scouts brought down much game, including deer, pronghorn, sagehens, prairie chickens and jackrabbits, which fetched handsome prices in camp.[50]

Custer selected the camping ground, and his adjutant directed the company commanders to their assigned camping places. Each camp was laid out in the familiar quadrangle, with the tents of the soldiers facing the officers, and headquarters facing the wagon train.

Horses were rubbed down and watered, then led outside the camp to graze. The firewood detail was sent out to collect wood and buffalo chips. Company wagons were unloaded, pup tents set up and mess kitchens started.

Strikers pitched the officers' three-pole Sibley tents.[51] The occupants grumbled that when the Sibley was left open, the tent filled with flies; and when closed, the heat was unbearable.[52] Next, the officers' "furniture" was unloaded. Folding cots often permitted a quick nap, before dinner. Folding chairs, folding table, iron cooking stove, and cooking utensils all made the sit-down meal more agreeable.

At *Stable Call,* one hour before sunset, horses were again watered, groomed and brushed. Hooves were inspected by the duty officer and the first sergeant; the horses fed their forage and then led into camp to be picketed.[53]

The Powder River was reached June 7, and the regiment made camp. The following day Moylan's company escorted General Terry down the Powder, where they met the steamboat *Far West* at the junction with the Yellowstone.

Terry was taken on board the *Far West* and brought to meet Colonel Gibbon, who had camped further upriver at the mouth of the Tongue. Gibbon's scouts reported that they had seen Lakota villages, situated between the Rosebud and Bighorn basins.

Terry had his own reasons for wanting to confirm Gibbon's report. Before deploying his troops for the final assault, he had to be certain that the Lakota were all accounted for. He ordered Major Reno to reconnoiter in strength with six companies. The strong scouting force would ensure that Reno could extricate his command, should he become engaged. Terry chose Reno purposely, much to Custer's annoyance, to give him an opportunity to demonstrate the merits of his two battalion wing.

Reno's exact instructions were to make a loop by going up the Powder River, move west to the Tongue, follow the Tongue down to the Yellowstone and rejoin the column. He was given pack mules and assigned five citizen packers, to teach his inexperienced men how to load and lash a pack saddle.[54] He also took with him a Gatling gun, which could fire fifty to four hundred shots per minute depending on how fast it was cranked. It often jammed at the higher speeds.[55]

Reno set off with half the regiment, and Terry moved the rest of his troops to a palisade on the mouth of the Powder River, which was to serve as a staging area.

Meanwhile, the river steamboats had brought up the supplies to the landing, where the traders promptly set up shop. Custer had not paid his men in Lincoln, hoping to discourage the sale of liquor, and so when the paymaster finally made an appearance, after an absence of four months, the sutlers did a brisk business. Officers and soldiers bought broad-brimmed straw hats, since the regular campaign hats were not available in Lincoln. They also stocked up on whiskey. One officer reported that Reno later bought two quarts of spirits. No one knows if this was the largest amount sold to an officer.

Word was received from Reno that he had found fresh tracts leading west toward the Rosebud, past a recently abandoned four hundred tepee village, probably belonging to non-reservation tribes. Contrary to orders, Reno had followed the Rosebud, instead of the Tongue, enlarging the loop of his survey. He arrived at the Yellowstone on June 20 after a creditable two hundred forty mile reconnaissance and reported to Terry that the Sioux were west of the Rosebud, between the Rosebud and the Little Bighorn.

Two important facts were unknown to Terry. This convocation of Lakota Sioux and Northern Cheyenne was the largest Native American gathering ever assembled on the North American continent. In the past, there had been other meetings at Bear Butte, just above the Black Hills. There, thousands gathered to race, wrestle, dance, sing and participate in formal ceremonials, but a year before, their meeting had been disrupted. Now, they were drawn together in huge numbers by the perilous signs that their life was coming to an end. The buffalo no longer roamed the broad prairie, but were limited to the Powder, Tongue and Bighorn basins. In the southern plains, railroads had shipped one and a half million hides and seven million pounds of buffalo tongue and hams between 1872 and 1874. So massive was the slaughter that the price of a buffalo hide had fallen to fifty cents![56] Soon, the railroad would come to the northern plains, and the Powder River buffalo would also disappear. The reservation warriors had gone off to hunt, while there were still buffalo; and to voice their concern. Fearing a reduction in the reservation's allowances and supplies from the Federal Government, the numbers remaining on the reservation were deliberately inflated by the agents.

The massive assembly was also a time for renewal and dedication. Prior to Crook's battle on the Rosebud, the famed Unkpapa medicine man, Sitting Bull, had performed the summer solstice Sun Dance, imploring the great spirits to preserve the wild animals and to send his people sufficient food. In this mystic ceremony, the shaman inserted sticks into his muscles and attached them to horsehair or lariats cords, dangling from a twenty foot pole. Suspended upright, Sitting Bull stood on tiptoe for two days. At the end of that time, he saw in his vision the defeat of the U.S. Army and the return to old times. This vision, together with the feeling of omnipotence imparted by their huge numbers, electrified the bold and braced the timid.

Also not known to Terry, was that on June 17, General Crook had sustained a second defeat, compelling him, once again, to withdraw to Wyoming. Terry's command was on its own.

Terry was not completely satisfied with Reno's report, but accepted the information, which put the tribes in the unreconnoitered area between the Rosebud and the Little Bighorn. This being the presumption, Custer would block their escape by moving up the Rosebud, then west over the watershed to the valley of the Little Bighorn, then north to the confluence of the Bighorn and Little Bighorn Rivers. Terry and Gibbon would take their troops west along the Yellowstone River to the mouth of the Bighorn. The *Far West* would ferry them across the Yellowstone, and they would then march south, up the Bighorn to its junction with the Little Bighorn, where Custer would join them.

Custer was ordered to find the Sioux, communicate their location to Terry, and then join Terry and Gibbon on June 26, in a joint attack. He was to avoid an engagement before that time, and fight, only if it could not be avoided. The two columns were to maintain contact to reinforce each other, if called upon to do so.

At least, this was the interpretation that most put on the orders, which, after all, were drawn up by a lawyer.

Terry gave Custer six of the best of Gibbon's Crow scouts. Unlike the partly agrarian Arikaras, who came from further down the Missouri, the Crows were completely familiar with the Powder-Tongue-Rosebud area.[57] The Crow was an impressive warrior, somewhat taller than the Arikara, his hair braided on the side, gathered in back and swept up in front.[58] Unlike the Arikara who wore odd pieces of uniform, the Crows kept their native dress.

Before setting out, Custer's immediate task was to trim down his column to *LIGHT MARCHING ORDER!* This called for drastic changes and careful attention to detail. For the final push, the regiment had to be in fighting trim and able to move fast. But no necessary item, however small, could be neglected, since shoe, horse, rider, battle and kingdom might all be lost for want of a ha'penny nail.

A mountain of equipment and supplies was left behind. Sibley tents were abandoned, apart from the one taken for the command headquarters. Instead, soldiers and officers would sleep under tent flies or in pup tents, two to three men to a tent.[59] Only one blanket, the saddle blanket, was authorized. Sabers were forbidden, since they rattle on the march and were thought to have little value as a weapon. Notwithstanding, De Rudio and another officer took their sabers, perhaps to kill rattlesnakes. They were kept out of sight, packed in the mule train. Later, some of the soldiers would regret not having sabers for hand-to-hand combat. The band was left behind and their horses given to some of the recruits, who, until now, had marched in cavalry boots.[60] Even so, one hundred recruits did not accompany the regiment. No cooking utensils could be brought, except for the soldier's tin cup and mess kit. Each man would carry two days cooked food supply and four days rations (twelve pounds of oats) for his horse.[61] Custer selected the best of the horses, but half were unfamiliar with gunfire or campaign.

No company mess kitchens would be taken. Henceforth, each soldier prepared his own food. He was given an ample amount of salt, so that he could eat horse meat, if it became necessary.[62] Many abandoned their overcoats, to lighten the load, gambling that they could later retrieve it. Otherwise, they would be charged for the loss.[63]

The Gatling guns were left behind, since they were drawn by condemned cavalry mounts, which might impede the march. Reno had taken a top-heavy Gatling gun on his reconnoiter, which had overturned, injuring three men. The mountain howitzer was left behind, since it was thought to be too heavy for rough country and to have too short a range.[64] Others would have disagreed, maintaining that the 12 pounder mountain howitzer Series 1840 can be broken down into parts, packed on a mule and reassembled. In fact, the howitzer was later used to good effect in the Nez Perce campaign and was retained until 1890.[65]

The three companies of infantry were not taken along, since, according to Custer, they would slow the march. Some argue that the infantry could move as fast and as far as the cavalry, without the burden of caring for horses. Also, men deployed on foot, are better able form a skirmish line. The infantrymen carry the Springfield Long Tom .45/70 rifle, which has a greater range than the carbine .45/55 and can keep the mounted warrior at a distance.

Field supplies were transferred from wagon to mule, the shorter and more compact the better. Leading the mule train was a bell mare, a gray or white mare with a bell around its neck. Twelve mules carried twenty-four thousand rounds of ammunition for the regiment. In addition, each company was given eleven mules to carry rations for fifteen days. A non-com and four enlisted men were selected from each company to care for its own mules. Despite the best efforts of civilian packers, loading was clumsy, and the packs frequently slipped.

The march got off to a bad start. On the night of June 21, while still camped at the mouth of the Rosebud, Custer and Benteen became embroiled in a heated discussion. Benteen had remarked that he hoped he would get better support than at Washita. Custer, in turn, taunted Benteen for having shot an Indian boy in battle. A warrior can be as young as thirteen years. This was a familiar argument.

The regiment left the staging area on Thursday June 22, 1876. After passing in review before General Terry in the middle of nowhere, Custer set off with five hundred ninety soldiers and scouts, understrength by two hundred men.

Terry wanted no heroics from Custer; only team play. He had given him written instructions to keep Terry informed of his movements. The orders were deliberately explicit, permitting only a minimum of discretion.

"Don't be greedy," Gibbon called out to Custer in Terry's presence. Most interpret this to mean that Custer should not try to engage the enemy before joining with Gibbon's forces. Custer may have had other ideas. The story was later told that Custer had boasted to a friend prior to returning to Lincoln, that he was going to "cut loose" and "swing clear" of his commanding officer.[66] Many portentous conversations were reported after the event, but the above was related before the Little Bighorn Battle.

Once out of sight of Terry, Custer lost no time in annulling Reno's wing assignments and notified his officers that the company commanders would henceforth report directly to him. Reno was out of a job. He had no wing nor battalion, nor any specific duty. This was a demeaning arrangement. De Rudio returned to A Company, but continued to mess with Benteen.

The regiment moved up the Rosebud Valley with its groves of wild plum and chockcherry.[67] Their goal was a thirty mile march at three mph walk gait and/or, six mph trot.

The scouts fanned out ten to thirty miles away from the column,[68] Crows rode ahead on their half-wild broncos,[69] Arikara or Rees on the flanks with their ponies.[70] The Crows looked for high elevations with good views. With their old telescopes and binoculars, they scanned the horizon for suspicious signs of the enemy, such as ravens suddenly flying upward, a wolf or coyote running out of a ravine, or antelopes or buffalo suddenly stampeding.[71]

The mule packs proved to be a problem from the start. Loads kept falling off and the mules fell behind. Trained to draw wagons, they were unaccustomed to packs and often chose to lie down. Before it can be made to stand, it must first be unpacked; and once on its feet, it has to be repacked.[72] To make matters worse, the least knowledgeable soldiers had been assigned to the mule train.

On the first day, June 22, the regiment had traveled twelve miles in four hours, when Custer called a halt. He chose a campsite with lush grass, which, in the days ahead, would be in short supply. The animals were fed a half-ration of grain. Horses and mules soon become irritable, whinnying for more feed.

After supper, the officers were summoned to the command tent. Custer seemed more benign than usual. He announced that

Little Big Horn

he was dispensing with trumpet calls, and then amazed his officers by explaining why he had refused the infantry and the Gatling guns. Explanations were unusual for him. The officers were urged to husband their rations, since the campaign might be longer than planned. Reveille would be at 3 a.m., the march to begin at 5 a.m. and it would cover no less than twenty-five miles. He himself would select campsites, but watering would be left to the company commanders. Toward the end of the meeting, he pointedly mentioned that he did not want to hear criticism from his officers. Benteen immediately asked if Custer was referring to him, but an argument was narrowly averted.[73]

At daybreak, Friday June 23, the pickets awakened the troopers. Voice commands replaced the familiar *First Call*, *Reveille*, *Stable Call*, *Mess Call*, *Strike Camp Call*, *Boots and Saddles*, *Assembly* and *Forward March*.[74]

Before mounting, the company formed a single line, and each man was given a number from one to four. This was done so that when the order to dismount was given, number four would remain on his horse, while the others would dismount and hand over their bridle reins to him. In order for one man to handle all four horses, the heavy U.S. Cavalry bridle had a strap and ring on each side, to allow the four bridles to be linked together.[75]

Custer set a rapid march of thiry-five miles per day. The terrain was fairly level, but the heat was exhausting. The column continued south, crossing and recrossing the Rosebud five times, with the packtrain continuing to give trouble.

Benteen, no longer commanding a wing, had duty watch that day. This consisted of providing protection and support for the mule train. H Company rode behind the pack animals, prodding them along. Packs kept falling off. At noon, the horses and mules were fed and watered and the soldiers ate their usual "SOB and trimmings," as Benteen called it--salt pork, hardtack, and coffee. Coffee beans were roasted in the soldier's mess kit, pounded with a rock or revolver butt and emptied into a can of boiling water.[76] The march continued until late afternoon before halting for camp. They had come forty-five miles up the river, a grueling pace.

Around them, they had seen many signs of Indian activity: cropped grass for miles around and thousands of droppings. In some places, the trail was a mile wide, plowed up by innumerable travois poles.[77] Many wickiups were visible. Wickiups are bundles of sticks forming a pyramid, around which a skin is wrapped. They provide temporary shelter for the bachelor warrior and are put up anew each day. Tepees are erected by the women and are carried with them to the next destination.

The march halted at 4:30 p.m. to allow time for the horses to graze.[78] Benteen was the last to arrive in camp. The pack train had experienced difficulty in fording the Rosebud. To protect it, Benteen had posted troops on the flanks and in the center. This was a shrewd precaution that deserved to be made a standing order. He suggested it to Custer's aide. Supper was eaten and the fires extinguished.

The next day, Saturday June 24, Custer was the first officer up. He toured the camp and, unusual for him, was pleasant to everyone, even to Benteen. The scouts had left early to reconnoiter and find fodder. They looked for grassland rich in seed and when they found some, they plucked the grass and packed it in their blankets, to be brought back to camp for feed. This was done so that the ponies would not become accustomed to army grain. All around them, they saw broken branches and recent droppings.

Early in the march, the column reached a well-grazed camp on the valley of the Rosebud, surrounded by several strange rocks. Here, Sitting Bull had performed the Sun Dance, prior to the encounter with Crook on the Rosebud.

The camp attracted much attention. The scouts inspected the large, trampled area and, from the number of poles and branches, they estimated that four hundred lodges had been present. Judging from the myriad of signs, best understood by them, they sensed that the enemy was preparing for a great battle.

Little Big Horn

Henceforth, the scouts would become increasingly wary.

At officers' call, Custer instructed the company commanders to move along different trails, to reduce the dust. The march resumed. The recruits began to complain of saddle ache. Buffalo gnats bit their faces, swelled the eyelids and ballooned their ears to the size of saucers. The scouts showed increasing reluctance to stray far from the column.[79] Custer kept reassuring them that all they were expected to do was to capture the Lakota horses, which they could keep. They could then leave. Having suffered often at the hands of the Lakota, the Arikara were deathly fearful of them; but the Crows were apprehensive only when confronted by unfavorable battle conditions.

Smoke signals were seen to the north in the direction of Tullock's Creek, where scouts of General Terry may have been waiting to hear from the 7th Cavalry. Custer deliberately withheld word of his movements, although he had been provided with a messenger whose sole job was to keep Terry informed.

The march continued throughout the sultry evening, passing innumerable lodge poles. At around 7:45 p.m. Custer called a halt at a point called Mud Creek, on the eastern foothill of Wolf Mountain. The men were ordered to keep their fires small. The mule packs were not unloaded, nor were the saddles removed. Pickets worked to prevent the animals from scattering to the lush grassland.

Captain Keogh, commanding I Company, sent word to Benteen and De Rudio that he had saved a good place for their pup tent.[80] Myles Keogh was a likeable character, with a merry grin and a profound thirst. He had been born in Ireland, the son of an officer in the 5th Royal Irish, stationed near Garryowen, which is probably how the regimental song came to Custer's attention. Keogh left Dublin University and went to Africa as a mercenary, then joined the Battalion of St Patrick in the Papal Army as 2nd lieutenant. He had been awarded the Medal of the Holy See and the Order of St. Gregory. In the Union Army, he served as aide to General George McClellan and was breveted Lt. Colonel for gallantry at Gettysburg. He had a Morgan horse named Comanche, a good army mount, but, according to some, hardly deserving of the veneration later shown it.[81]

Benteen and De Rudio finished their evening meal and were soon joined by Keogh and other officers. They sat in front of Benteen's pup tent and listened to De Rudio spinning his yarns. Benteen, who had retired earlier and who claimed to have heard the stories before, called out to them to go to sleep or at least to quiet down. He offered to bet them that they would have to march during the night. The party went on without its host.[82]

Hardly had Benteen spread his saddle blanket and laid his head back on his saddle, when the officers were summoned to Custer's tent.

Custer informed them that the Crow scouts had found a pass over the divide, with tracks leading to the Little Bighorn River, thirty miles away. He was certain the enemy would be there. Instead of continuing up the Rosebud, marking time with Terry's movements, they were going to push on during the night and follow the tracks to the Little Bighorn basin. He ordered the march to commence in an hour, so that they might cover as much ground as possible before daylight. Tomorrow, Sunday, he would find some way to conceal the column and allow it to rest up. Monday, June 26, he would attack at daybreak. He made no mention of coordinating his attack with the Terry-Gibbon column.

Towards midnight, the regiment broke camp in pitch darkness. The mules brayed, a sure disclosure to any warrior in the area. Even without the braying, a warrior in the vicinity could easily detect the column by placing his ear or his hand to the ground.[83] The march was slow and tedious. With the column stretched out for several miles, the horsemen could only follow the rattling of tin cups and the troopers' swearing. Men fell asleep in the saddle. They climbed eleven miles of gradual ascent from two thousand to four thousand feet.

Lt. De Rudio rode at the head of A Company, with a trumpeter at his side. He was ordered to the rear of the column, to hurry along Captain Keogh, the duty officer, who was with the pack mules. Keogh was having an exhausting time, helping the mule train officer extricate the animals from the morass. It took all his men and the men in the mule train to get them out.[84] (Today the morass has been drained by the Crow ranchers, so there is little visible evidence of the travails of the pack officer.)

De Rudio and his trumpeter rode for ten miles, until he found Keogh and gave him Custer's message. Keogh's answer is unrecorded. The two then started back.

Suddenly a gang of whooping "warriors" surrounded them. De Rudio drew his revolver, but before he could fire, he heard a familiar laugh. It was Captain Tom Custer. Each had mistaken the other for a warrior, but Tom Custer parlayed the error into a prank. He was a practical joker and had tried the same trick a day before on his brother Boston. It was in poor taste, but one can be lenient with a person who had twice won the Medal of Honor.

The column rode eight tortuous miles in the night before halting at 2:30 a.m. on the morning of Sunday, June 25. They had come to the foot of the divide, a ridge separating the valley of the Rosebud and the Little Bighorn.They were still sixteen miles from the Little Bighorn River. The column had drawn up on a flat bottom under a bluff. Straightway, the horses broke for a small, stinking pool, but the water was alkaline and undrinkable. The men kept the mounts under saddle, but they unbitted them and allowed them to graze, while the men held the reins. The older troopers removed the saddles and rubbed the backs of their mounts with twists of weeds, then saddled up, leaving the cinches loose and the bits unseated, so that the animals could eat whatever grass was available.[85] It had been a hard ride. Soldiers lay exhausted on the ground.

While the column rested, the scouts climbed an elevation known as Crow's Nest, almost at the center of the divide, which the Crows used on their raiding expeditions.[86] The exact mountaintop is in question. There are two peaks and a saddle. (Willie Peters, a Crow, showed me on a visit that the peak usually designated as Crow's Nest could not be easily mounted on horseback by the Crow scouts and that an adjacent peak [which we also climbed] could be effortlessly mounted and offered a similar view. Further, he says that Crow tradition identifies the second as Crow's Nest and the first as White Man's Crow's Nest.)

At first dawn, Lt. Charles Varnum, the officer-scout, saw the Lakota and Cheyenne encampment in the valley of the Little Bighorn sixteen miles away. From the size of the pony herd and the fires, he had concluded that the encampment was huge. The scouts, who knew the region thoroughly, agreed. Not only was it huge, it was unprecedented! Varnum immediately sent word to Custer.

Custer wanted to see for himself. Before leaving for the Crow's Nest, he ordered the march to begin at 8 a.m. without him. Meanwhile, the horses and men had to be fed. So parched were the horses that the oats fell from their muzzles. Almost the entire twelve pound bag of oats had been used up.[87] The soldiers ate the bacon raw, without kitchen utensils to fry the meat. They lit fires to heat up the stale alkaline water for coffee and to soak the hardtack, some of it was six years old. Unless soaked, the hardtack could have cracked their teeth.[88] The scouts atop Crow's Nest saw the fires and feared that they would be visible to the Sioux.[89]

At 8 a.m. the command moved out. The regiment traveled up the slopes and through the cuts and passes, parallel to the warrior trail, moving on sod or stone whenever possible to decrease the dust.

Custer, himself, arrived at the Crow's Nest at around 9 a.m. There, he met Lt. Varnum, atop the peak. Since he did not have field glasses, Custer borrowed an old pair of binoculars or a telescope from the scouts, to view the encampment.[90] It was shrouded in mist, so little could be seen. The mist may have been the smoke from the hundreds of campfires that were lit in early morning.[91] Custer doubted the size of the encampment, although his fourteen scouts agreed with Varnum.[92] When the guide, Mitch Bouyer, tried to convince him, Custer hinted that Bouyer was afraid.

"I am not afraid to follow you anywhere," Bouyer replied glumly, "but if we enter the valley, we will wake up in hell!"

Custer did not pursue the argument. No sooner had he returned to the column, than a troop commander belatedly reported that one of his sergeants had encountered some Lakota outriders on the trail, who fled in the direction of Little Bighorn.

The column marched uninterrupted for several miles and then halted in a wooded ravine between two high ridges. Here, Custer presumed, they would be concealed from view. Some troopers fell asleep with the reins in their hands. Others made fires to boil coffee, again to the disgust of the Crows. A warrior can hunt in the morning and travel thirty miles in the afternoon, without eating. When preparing for battle, he makes no fire, but eats raw liver, kidney or ear gristle.[93]

At around 11:30 a.m., Custer summoned his officers and ordered his company commanders to prepare for an attack on the enemy!

He explained why it was useless to hide. The warriors had known of their movements ever since they came up the Rosebud.[94] In fact, their movements may have been known since the column left Lincoln. Shod horses cut up the grass, so that even a half-blind man could track them.[95]

Custer ordered the regiment to saddle up quickly. The first company to report readiness would head up the column, and the others would follow in the order of their report. Benteen, the wily fox, had alerted his company at the moment when Custer sounded *Officers' Call*! He promptly reported his company's readiness and so headed up the column, to Custer's intense irritation. Behind him was A Company with Moylan and De Rudio. Far in the rear was the one hundred and sixty mule train. The last commander to report ready would have the dirty work of providing protection for the pack train.

At noontime Sunday June 25, 1876 the 7th Cavalry preceded in the direction of the Little Bighorn. Custer moved up and down the column, inspecting and making adjustments. Custer sent his adjutant, Lt. William Cooke, to borrow De Rudio's fine Austrian binoculars, which had been given him by an Austrian optician. De Rudio never got them back.[96]

The column advanced along the warrior trail toward the Little Bighorn. The day was beginning to heat up. The men were tired and dirty. Many had shed pieces of their uniform. Custer's worry was that at any moment the village might move, not only because of the approach of his troops, but because of problems of sanitation and the rapid exhaustion of game, wood and grass. As a rule the tribes move camp once a week to find grass and new sanitary facilities.[97] The Lakota, in fact, had been camping higher up on the east side of the river until the day before, when they had moved down river to their present location on the west bank.[98]

Custer kept the column moving rapidly and ordered the mule train to keep up. When told that some packs had fallen off the mules, Custer ordered them abandoned.

The column crossed the divide separating the Rosebud and Little Bighorn watershed. As they rode in column of four's down the dried-up tributary now called Reno Creek, Benteen and H Company were ordered to cross over to the left side, to reduce the dust raised by the iron-shod hooves.[99] Thus far, Custer had given no indication of his plan of attack. It is not certain he had one, but may have depended on "Custer's luck," which had not yet failed him. In battle, "something must be left to chance," wrote one celebrated English naval officer.

At the Rosebud Divide the column was twelve miles from the Little Bighorn River.[100] Custer ordered Benteen to reconnoiter the ground to the south. His orders were to take three companies and swing left from the line of march towards a ridge of high bluffs two miles to the southwest. If any hostiles were encountered, he was to notify Custer immediately. If none were seen, he would then *retrace* his footsteps and rejoin the regiment. This would position Benteen's battalion at the rear of the column.

These were puzzling orders. Benteen was given no guides, although there were several Crow scouts on hand, who knew the terrain well. None of the three surgeons were assigned to him. Was this just an oversight, or did Custer realize that the chances of Benteen engaging the hostiles were remote? Why have him retrace his footsteps? To bring him to the rear of the column? No one will ever know. One suggestion is that Custer wanted to keep Benteen away from the impending action, away from the dash and glory of the battle. Benteen had acquitted himself nobly in the Washita battle, but was intolerable ever since (or so Custer may have thought). Hatreds run deep in the frontier service. If Benteen were being sent to protect Custer's flank, Custer would have had him swing northwest after his reconnoiter and rejoin him further down by the Little Bighorn River, instead of having him retrace his line of march.

J. S. Gray offers an explanation. He states that Custer may have wanted to drive "satellite villages" to the main encampment.[101] In point of fact, the hostiles had been camping on the eastern bank of the Little Bighorn River, and had moved downstream to their present location on the west bank only the day before.[102] But to suggest that Custer knew this, is to credit him with extraordinary prescience, unless one postulates that the scouts had earlier discovered this and reported it to Custer and to none else.

Benteen objected to the order, as a good subordinate is obliged to do. "Would we not do better to hold the regiment compact, general? If it is really a big village, as the scouts say, we'll need all the available men"

"You have your orders," Custer replied curtly.

What we know of this curious circumstance was learned from Benteen himself, since the order was verbal. But there is confirmation. Custer repeated the orders to a sergeant, and Benteen's objections were overheard by a trooper.[103]

Benteen left the main column and went off southwest in column of two's and occasionally single file, passing over rugged, steep and broken slopes. He had no view of the Little Bighorn valley, nor did he see any signs of the hostiles. Twice Custer sent word to him to extend his search. After climbing four bluffs in a circuit of seven miles in two and a half hours of "valley hunting," he rejoined the trail lower down the Reno Creek, rather than retrace his march. In a technical sense, he disobeyed his orders. To retrace his footsteps would have put him in the middle of, or behind, the mule train. Instead, his battalion ended up a mile from Lone Tepee, about an hour after Custer had left it.[104] (see below)

The Benteen battalion then followed the Reno Creek trail an hour behind Reno and Custer. Along the way, he received messages from Custer to hurry along and bring up the pack train. Benteen also took the time to water his thirsty horses, every second of which has been begrudgingly noted by those who fault him for Custer's disaster. The van of the pack train had caught up to him. Benteen cut out two pack mules, bearing four thousand rounds and brought the mules with him.[105]

Benteen had no knowledge of what was happening to the others. He came to a junction where one trail led west to the Bighorn River and the other to the north. Crow scouts motioned him to turn to the right, onto the bluffs.[106] As he came up on the ridge, he caught a glimpse of what might have been the rear of Custer's wing, or, more likely, F Company stragglers on jaded horses. Presently, he saw the last elements of Reno's battalion making a fighting retreat across the river and up the bluffs. He ordered his battalion to form a skirmish line and, with drawn revolvers, raced to meet them.[107]

After Benteen left the column at the divide, Custer and Reno continued down on the warrior trail along Reno Creek. Well

Little Big Horn

behind them was the pack train with twenty percent of the regiment, consisting of two officers, one hundred thrity-one enlisted, eleven packers.[108]

The scout interpreter, who had been riding ahead of the column, reported to Custer that he had seen forty warriors galloping along the west bank on their way to warn the village. Custer decided that unless an immediate attack was mounted, all surprise would be lost. Custer sent word to Reno to take command of companies A, G, and M, in preparation for the attack.

"Is that all?" asked Reno.

"Yes," the adjutant replied. Reno had been given six companies on the Powder River expedition.

Reno's battalion crossed to the left side of the dried-up Reno Creek to take up Benteen's position, and Custer advanced along the right bank. This was done to decrease the dust. Toward 2 p.m. Custer ordered Reno to recross the stream at a point about five miles from the Little Bighorn, and the two units continued together, Reno in front.

They came to a recently abandoned tepee with cooking utensils and the ashes of a fire. Nearby, the scouts found a funeral pyre with the decomposed corpse of a warrior killed in the battle with Crook.

One of the scouts climbed a hill behind the lone tepee site. From there, he saw a band of warriors moving up the trail from the river, unaware of the column of soldiers. There was a brief exchange of gunfire, and the warriors fled back toward the river. Later it was learned that these warriors had been on their way to the reservation.

Custer ordered his scouts to overtake the warriors, but they refused, fearful of being led into an ambush. The scouts began to strip to breechcloth, paint their faces and put on their battle dress.[109] They passed a lariat around the lower jaw of the pony, letting it trail behind, to make it easier to catch the pony if the rider were thrown.[110]

At this point Custer concluded that the enemy would soon

learn of his approach, when the recent party of warriors returned to camp. If he were going to attack, he would have to do so immediately, to prevent the enemy from escaping.

His tactics had not changed since the days of glory in the Civil War: *ATTACK FIRST, NO MATTER THE STRENGTH OF THE ENEMY AND CUT YOUR WAY OUT, IF HE PROVES TOO STRONG!*

Notes

1. J. G. Randall and David Donald, *The Civil War and Reconstruction* (Boston: Heath, 1961), p. 661.
2. Evans S. Connell, *Son of the Morning Star* (New York: Harper Perennial, 1984), p. 166.
3. Peter Panzeri, *Little Bighorn* (Sterling Heights, MI: Osprey Publishing Co., 1995), p. 12.
4. Stephen Longstreet, *War Cries on Horseback* (Garden City, NY: Doubleday, 1970), p. 206.
5. John Upton Terrell, and George Walton, *Faint the Trumpet Sounds* (New York: McKay, 1966), p. 124.
6. Wayne Mitchell Sarf, *The Little Bighorn Campaign* (Pennsylvania: Combined Books, 2000), p. 80.
7. S. L. A. Marshall, *Crimsoned Prairie* (New York: Scribner, 1972), p. 128.
8. Charles M. Robinson III, *A Good Year to Die. The Story of the Great Sioux War* (New York: Random House, 1955), p. 58.
9. Marshall, p. 129.
10. Longstreet, p. 206.
11. E. A. Brininstool, *Troopers with Custer* (Lincoln and London: University of Nebraska, 1952), p. 339.
12. Sarf, p. 76.
13. Brininstool, p. 30.
14. Interview of He Dog. Kenneth Hammer, ed., *Custer in 76* (Norman and London: University of Oklahoma, 1988), p. 205.
15. Sarf, p. 46.
16. James H. Bradley, *The March of the Montana Column* (Norman: University of Oklahoma, 1961), p. 13.
17. Hugh Lenox Scott, *Some Memories of a Soldier* (New York: Century, 1928), pp. 53, 35.
18. Bradley, p. 36.
19. Seymour Dunbar, *A History of Travel in America* (New York: Tudor, 1937), p. 1144.
20. Robinson, p. 53.
21. Marguerite Merington, *The Custer Story* (Lincoln: University of Nebraska Press, 1987), p. 303.
22. Paul Andrew Hutton, *The Custer Reader* (Lincoln and London: University of Nebraska, 1992), p. 296.
23. Daniel Magnussen, *Peter Thompson's Narrative of the Little Bighorn Campaign of 1876* (Glendale, CA: Clark, 1974), p. 34; Terrell & Walton, p. 112.
24. Edward L. Daily, *Custer to MacArthur* (Paducah, KY: Turner, 1995), p. 73.
25. Jason Hook and Martin Pegler, *To Live and Die in the West* (Oxford: Osprey,

1999), p. 20.
26. Don Rickey, *Forty Miles a Day on Beans and Hay* (Norman and London: University of Oklahoma, 1963), p. 221.
27. Letter from Benteen to Barry, April 1, 1898, manuscript collection, White Swan (Little Bighorn) Library.
28. Rickey, p. 77.
29. Letter from Benteen to Barry, April 1, 1898, manuscript collection, White Swan (Little Bighorn) Library.
30. Sarf, p.138; Dunbar, p. 1150.
31. Dunbar, p. 1149.
32. Rickey, p. 242.
33. Robinson, p. 109.
34. Magnussen, p. 57.
35. Ani Frank Mulford, *Fighting Indians in the 7th Cavalry* 2nd ed. (Fairfield, WA: Ye Galleon Press, 1972), p. 104.
36. *Ibid.*, p. 59.
37. Frederick F. Van de Water, *Glory Hunter* (Lincoln and London: University of Nebraska, 1934), p. 301.
38. Robinson, p. 108.
39. Hook and Pegler, p. 21; Sandy Barnard, ed., *Ten Years with Custer. A 7th Cavalryman's Memoirs* (Ft. Collins, CO: Citizen Printing, 2001), p. 230.
40. Frank Barnes, *Cartridges of the World* (Wisconsin: Krause, 2000), p. 285.
41. Elizabeth B. Custer, *Tenting on the Plains* (New York: Webster, 1889), p. 475.
42. Sarf, p. 127.
43. Douglas D. Scott and Richard A. Fox, Jr., *Custer Battle* (Norman: University of Oklahoma, 1987), p. 77; Rickey, p. 211.
44. Hook and Pegler, p. 22.
45. Sarf, p. 117 for the N. R. A. reference; Daily. p. 51.
46. Robinson, p. 112.
47. Letter from F. Benteen to Mrs. Benteen, June 13, 1876. John M. Carroll, *Camp Talk* (Matetuch, NY: J. M. Carroll, 1983), p. 14.
48. *Ibid.*, p. 17.
49. Magnussen, p. 57
50. Sarf, p. 124.
51. Randolph B. March, *The Prairie Traveler 1859* (reprint; Bedford, MA: Applewood, 1993), p. 143.
52. Scott, *Memories*, p. 50.
53. Daily, p. 53; Frazier Hunt and Robert Hunt, *I Fought with Custer* (New York and London: Scriber, 1947), p. 57.
54. Magnussen, p. 63.
55. Sarf, p. 118; Rickey, p. 219.
56. Longstreet, p. 185.
57. John M. Carroll, *The Benteen-Goldin Letters on Custer and his last Battle* (New York: Liveright, 1974), p. 310.
58. Hook and Pegler, p. 112.
59. Elizabeth B. Custer, *Boots and Saddles* (New York: Harper, 1885), p. 310.
60. Sarf, p. 147.
61. Rickey, p. F222.
62. Marshall, p. 118.

63. Magnussen, p. 88.
64. Robert Wooster, *Nelson A. Miles and the Twilight of the Frontier Army* (Lincoln: University of Nebraska, 1993), p. 120.
65. Longstreet, p. 201.
66. Brininstool, p. 11.
67. Marshall, p. 124; Terrell and Walton, p. 134.
68. Scott, *Memories*, p. 33.
69. Hammer, p. 138
70. John S. Gray, *Custer's Last Campaign* (Norman and London: University of Nebraska, 1991), p. 210.
71. Scott, *Memories*, p. 33.
72. Mulford, p. 102.
73. "Benteen's Own Story," Chapter 3. Brininstool, p. 70.
74. Rickey, p. 74.
75. Magnussen, p. 117.
76. Connell, p. 150.
77. *Ibid., p. 267.*
78. Mari Sandoz, *The Battle of Little Bighorn* (Philadelphia and New York: Lippincott, 1966), p.34.
79. *Ibid.*, p. 43.
80. "Benteen's Own Story," Chapter 3. Brininstool, p. 71.
81. Edward S. Luce, *Keogh, Comanche and Custer* (Private Edition, 1939), p. 12.
82. Narrative of F. Benteen. Carroll, *Benteen-Goldin*, p. 165.
83. Sandoz, p. 48.
84. Sarf, p. 181.
85. Sandoz, p. 50.
86. Sarf, p. 179.
87. Letter from Theodore W. Goldin to Albert Johnson, November 8, 1932. Carroll, *Benteen-Goldin*, p. 39.
88. Hook and Pegler, p. 30.
89. Connell, p. 26.
90. Letter from F. Benteen to T. Goldin, February 24, 1892. Carroll, *Benteen-Goldin*, p. 214.
91. Herbert Coffeen, *The Custer Battle Book* (New York: Carlton Press, 1964), p. 51.
92. Gray, *Custer's Last Campaign*, p. 225.
93. Interview with Frederick F. Girard, Jan. 22 and April 3, 1909 in Hammer, p. 230.
94. Interview with Black Bear, July 18, 1911 in Hammer, p. 203.
95. Hunt and Hunt, p. 80.
96. Hammer, p. 84.
97. Sarf, p. 90; Scott, *Memories*, p. 56.
98. Sarf, p. 170.
99. *Ibid.*, p. 190.
100. Gray, *Custer's Last Campaign*, p. 246.
101. *Ibid.*, p. 245.
102. Robinson, p. 154.
103. Connell, p. 274.
104. Gray, *Custer's Last Campaign*, p. 264.

105. Sarf, p. 221.
106. Testimony of E. Godfrey. W. A. Graham, *The Reno Court of Inquiry* (Mechanicsburg, PA: Stackpole, 1995), p. 177.
107. "Benteen's Own Story," Chapter 3. Brininstool, pp. 79, 84.
108. Sarf, p. 188.
109. *Ibid.*, p. 190.
110 Scott, *Memories,* p. 71.

X
CUSTER'S WING May 25 (2-5 P.M)

The Crow scouts knew the terrain well. Four of them went with Custer, two with Reno. With a weed stalk, Custer's Crows sketched the Little Bighorn Valley in the dirt.[1] They showed him two fords on the Little Bighorn River, separated by four miles. On the west bank, between the fords, lay the enemy encampment with more warriors than could be counted.

Custer *might* have thought as follows. He would send Reno with his battalion over the near ford, now know as Ford A to distract the enemy. While Reno was diverting enemy attention, Custer would cross the the other ford, now known as Ford B and attack the village from the north with his five companies. Or he may have thought that Reno's sudden attack might cause the tribes to flee and that Custer could then pursue them.

This attack would differ from Washita. There, the regiment was divided, but it attacked *simultaneously* and with complete surprise. Regulation 599 of the Cavalry Tactics and Regulations of the United States Army states: "If possible, at the moment of a charge, assail your enemy in the flank or charge him in the flank when (the enemy) is engaged in his front,"[2] but this suggests a simultaneous attack.

Custer, the regimental commander, made no effort at this time to recall Benteen. To be fair, he might have believed that Benteen would shortly rejoin him, at the end of his mission.

Custer now gave Major Reno the order to attack: "Take as

rapid a gait as you think prudent and charge the village, and you will be supported by the whole outfit." Off went Major Reno with companies A, M and G. Captain Moylan commanded A Company, with De Rudio riding beside him.

Custer's wing followed behind Reno for about five riding miles, stopping off long enough to water his horses in a scum-filled pool. Before he came to the river, he turned off the trail Reno had been following and rode up a ravine to a ridge that looked down on the river. Custer set off at a trot. Presently, he heard and saw the early fighting in the valley. Custer's scouts joined him and together they viewed the encampment that extended to the north along the river. His trumpeter states that Custer stood surveying the Reno battlefield for ten minutes[3] -- twenty minutes, by another account. Messengers from Reno arrived, reporting that Reno was heavily engaged. Thus far, Reno's battalion was intact.

The regimental commander was seen leading his five companies along the top of the ridge probably just north of what came to be known as Reno Hill. Some of Reno's men reported seeing Custer waving his hat. The hat-waver was probably Bouyer, one of the guides.[4] Custer proceeded along the ridge parallel to the river past Reno Hill, in columns of two. Perhaps he climbed a hillock at Weir's Point, to survey the action across the river, but there was no need to do so, since he could see almost as well from the ridge.[5]

The huge Indian encampment was now indisputably apparent. There were at least seven Lakota tribal circles and one Northern Cheyenne circle at the far north end of the village. Horned Horse indicated that there were eighteen hundred Sioux lodges with three to four warriors each and four hundred wickiups, each with four young warriors.[6] One generous estimate has twelve thousand people in the village, with three to five thousand warriors. Gray has analyzed the matter in impressive detail and has persuasively concluded that there were a thousand lodges, containing seven thousand one hundred twenty persons, of which one thousand seven hundred thirty were warriors.[7]

Custer led his men off the ridge and rode behind it to a ravine, called Cedar Coulee, which led north, somewhat parallel to the river. Once the column entered Cedar Coulee, it was no longer visible to the encampment across the river, nor could Custer observe what was happening there. Today, an access road runs along the bluffs, parallel to Cedar Coulee. After two miles of trail, the regiment came back up to the ridge and saw a steep-walled trench called Medicine Tail Coulee, which led down to Ford B, or Miniconjou Ford. The scouts were well acquainted with this route.

By now, Custer realized that he had a hard battle ahead of him. If, at this point, he had been considering a lightning ride through the village, he would require no more than the hundred rounds per soldier, which he already had. But to defend themselves from a resolute attack by a huge hoard of warriors, his men would need the ammunition in the mule train, as well as the services of Benteen's battalion. He sent a sergeant to hasten the pack train and later dispatched an Italian trumpeter to Benteen, carrying a message to come quickly and bring up the supplies. There were three trumpeters assigned to the regimental commander. Each took turns as orderly trumpeter.[8] Custer kept the chief trumpeter with him. On this occasion he sent the duty trumpeter, a recent Italian immigrant, Giovanni Martini. He was born in Italy 1853, served as a drummer boy for Garibaldi and enlisted as trumpeter in the United States Army. A trumpeter is supposed to be able to repeat a twenty-word message verbatim,[9] but Custer's adjutant wisely took no chances. He wrote Custer's order on a piece of paper. The message was written in haste and indicates great excitement. Off went the trumpeter with the written order. Custer's brother, Boston left the pack train on his own initiative and had passed Benteen and the trumpeter on his way to join Custer. *Thus, Custer knew the approximate location of Benteen's battalion and the pack train.*

Custer's guide and scout joined him next; they had both been atop a hill observing Reno's attack. They reported to Custer that, rather than advancing or standing fast, Reno's battalion was in total retreat.[10] Custer knew then that he had *lost the opportunity to execute a two-pronged attack on the village.*

Custer was therefore in possession of all the information necessary to make a tactical decision. He could advance, halt, or rejoin Reno. As history records, he advanced. Back up on the ridge parallel to the river, his men, numbering one hundred ninety three men and thirteen officers, were again visible to the warriors in the encampment.

The sight of this force alarmed the village. Drums, shouts and bone whistles sounded and mirrors flashed. Word was sent to the warriors pursuing Reno. The warriors still in camp lost no time in crossing the river at Ford B and elsewhere up and downriver, to harass the invader until sufficient numbers of warriors could be brought up. Fords might be used when the tribe moves with women and children, encumbered with loads and travois, but when crossing alone on his nimble pony, riding bareback without bit or stirrup, the warrior can climb steep embankments, burdened by only his weapon, some dried food or pemmican and an extra pair of moccasins.[11]

Once on the east bank, the warriors rode quickly through the ravines and gullies. They dismounted at favorable positions, protected by ravines and out of firing range. There, they awaited the arrival of other tribesmen.

What did Custer do next? He was last seen by the Trumpeter Martini five hundred yards up from Ford B.[12] Stragglers from F Company might have seen something from afar, but their testimony was never solicited, so far as is known. Anything thought to have occurred after Martini's observation is based chiefly on circumstantial evidence and speculation. Somewhere in the Native American reports is a true description, but collectively, the reports are not consistent, and the accurate statement is difficult to sift from the conflicting accounts. Archaeological findings are often compelling,[13] but conclusions must be tempered by the knowledge that the warriors used captured army equipment; construction changes have altered the topography; and decades of souvenir hunters have distorted the field. The warriors themselves may have contributed to our confusion by picking up empty cartridge cases after the battle.[14] The Sioux pioneered cartridge repacking.

Numerous theories have been offered to explain Custer's subsequent movements, but only a few will be cautiously discussed. One theory states that Custer dispatched one or two companies to Ford B by way of the Medicine Trail Coulee, since he may not have been able to see the ford adequately from the curving Coulee. Actually, the ford is easily visible and quite accessible from the ridge. Custer, in his hell-for-leather mode, would have led his five companies across the Ford B through the village. Instead, as we have seen, he sent for ammunition and Benteen. He must have begun to see the difficulties of a village strike, especially with Reno in retreat. This being so, sending troops to Ford B may have been nothing more than, in military terms, a feeble *demonstration*. There could not have been many soldiers who made it down to the riverbank. De Rudio later recounted that he saw the hoofprints of only two shod horses at the river edge.[15] Curly, a young Crow scout, who had left Custer before the battle, reported that Custer reached the river and had retreated a third of the way up to the ridge, when the Sioux fell on his right and left flanks.[16] Unfortunately Curly spoke little English in the early years and the accounts attributed to him were somewhat inconsistent, owing mainly to the confusion of the interpreters.[17] In later years, Curly lived with the grandmother of Howard Bogess, a modern Crow historian, and left behind an additional oral record that deserves to be considered. Curly told the grandmother that Custer had sent a sergeant and *some* men to the river. *If* the soldiers had reached the river, they remained there only a short time, then went back up to the higher ground by another cut, Deep Coulee, to rejoin the others on Calhoun Hill. There could be only one likely reason why Custer did not lead his troops across the river -- *he was not able to*. His troops would have been too hotly engaged.[18]

The second theory is that neither Custer nor any of his troops ever got to Ford B. This accords with the testimony Spotted Bull

Horn and his wife.[19] Warrior fire, pouring at them from the west bank, kept the troops from descending to the ford. Chief Gall, who had a reputation for balanced judgement, stated ten years later that Custer never came to the river and was attacked three quarters of a mile back, near the crest of the ridge.[20] But even Chief Gall gave out conflicting interviews. Graham helps us resolve the problem: ... *"does it really matter how Custer came to the battle ridge? We know he did arrive there, because he and most of his men were found there."*[21]

When Custer realized that he could not safely cross Ford B, he must have begun to worry. If Reno were wiped out without Custer making a substantial effort to attack the village, then it would appear that Custer had sent his subordinate on a fool's errand and failed to support him. His reputation would be irreparably damaged. Perhaps Custer thought he could cross at another ford to the north of the village, with less opposition. Or perhaps he could find a better location to take up a defensive position. Or perhaps he was waiting for the tribes to flee or waiting for some unforeseen opportunity. No one can be sure of what passed through his mind.

By this time, the troops who had explored Ford B had rejoined Custer (if, indeed, they had ever gone there and if Custer, himself, had not been with them at the ford). Custer was now at Calhoun Hill with a united command.

Our next quandary. Did Custer lead his five companies north or did he take only two companies? Let us first assume he took only two companies.

Custer left companies, C, L and I, on Calhoun Hill. He would not have set off, if the Calhoun Hill companies were under attack. Mounted, the three companies offered an excellent target to the warriors concealed in the ravines and gullies, so with warriors beginning to threaten the troops, the men *may* have dismounted before the attack and hobbled their horses. Skirmish lines and defense bastions may then have been formed.[22]

With the other two companies, E and F, Custer set out to inspect another ford north of the village, if one accepts the suppositions advanced. He led the two companies along the ridge, past Custer Hill, a mile away, and then down to the north ford, another mile away. There he saw no opportunity to cross, and so he led his troops back up to the Custer Hill area. Here, he halted to await Benteen and the pack train, an additional two hundred men. It was at this point that the attack commenced on both the Custer Battlefield and Calhoun Hill, probably simultaneously, since the troops were separated by only a mile. He had his two companies dismount and take up defensive positions.

Thus, with the command divided, the five companies were in two defensive positions a mile apart. But this is not an ideal situation. A unified defense would have been more desirable, where the men would be better able to support one another and hold off enfilading fire.[23] Conversely, a divided command would be just what the warriors wanted. In the two unit scenario, the companies on Calhoun Hill were quickly overwhelmed. They fell out in two large consolidations, north and south of Calhoun Hill. Some troopers are supposed to have fled toward Custer's position and were cut down. Simultaneously, Custer was attacked and his position easily overrun. Perhaps Custer had begun to make plans to consolidate his position. Officers from the Calhoun companies were later found clumped around him. Most probably, they had been summoned for officer's call *before* the attack and had not had an opportunity to return to their men on Calhoun Hill. Or Custer may have sent word to Keogh, and what was left of his company, to join him,[24] but this is less likely.

Another scenario is that Custer led all five companies toward Custer Hill and that the troops were in the usual line of march when they were attacked and their column bisected or trisected by the warriors. The two or three sections then clumped together, dismounted and sought defensive positions. The usual extension of a three company battalion horse column in rough ground is three quarters of a mile.[25] The approximate distance between Custer and Calhoun Hills is a mile, but allowance must be made for the fact that Custer had five, rather than the three, companies. One military historian suggests that the clump around Custer resulted from a bunching up, after the wing had suddenly halted, but this does not explain the cluster of officers from the Calhoun companies.[26]

Whatever the relationship between Calhoun and the Custer companies, the warriors had been actively infiltrating the area. The warrior takes advantage of every feature of the topography to move into position.[27] Because of the gullies and ravines they could move, mounted and unmounted, with reduced exposure to gunfire. Gall and his Unkpapa warriors are reported to have surrounded Custer. Crazy Horse and his Oglala warriors are said to have engaged the three companies on Calhoun Hill and then moved to Custer Hill. But this depiction is doubtless an oversimplification. The warriors participated somewhat pell mell, without unified command. Bands and tribes chose their own targets of opportunity and their own tactics, usually -- but not always -- heeding a respected leader.[28]

A detailed description of the final moments of the battle is somewhat gratuitous, as when describing the last moments of a dying man. Chief Gall said the battle took a half-hour.[29] Graham collected fifty to sixty warrior accounts and found them impossible to form a coherent narrative.[30] The final event appears to be a frantic dash by some soldiers into a cut called Deep Ravine (not Deep Coulee), where they were run down and killed. Others maintain that this happened early in the battle. Nor does it matter much. Two hundred and eight cavalrymen died, in addition to the civilian deaths. Warrior losses was said to be eighteen, twenty-two or one hundred fifty, depending on how much credit a writer deigns to assign to Custer's defense. Dead warriors were carried off the field, so their numbers are uncertain. This much is known: seventy dead cavalry horses were found on the battlefield and two dead warrior ponies.[31] A total of two hundred twelve troopers and civilians died. If one uses these numbers to construct a ratio, then six warriors died. Howard Bogess, a Crow historian, tells of finding the remains of ten to twelve warriors a day's march from the battleground along the line of their later retreat. These might well have been the warriors who fell on all three battlefields.

While the warriors were busying themselves with the army horses and the booty, the women roamed the battlefield, mutilating the bodies and picking up souvenirs. Mutilation was a common practice in hunting societies, done to punish the dead warrior and keep him from entering the happy hunting ground in fit condition.[32] Later, the warriors not engaged turned their attention to what was left of Reno's command.

Notes

1. Mari Sandoz, *The Battle of Little Bighorn* (Philadelphia and New York: Lippincott, 1966), p. 105.
2. Robert Nightingale, *Little Bighorn* (U.S.: Far West Publications, 1996), p. 90.
3. Evans S. Connell, *Son of the Morning Star* (New York: Harper Perennial, 1984), p. 278.
4. Kenneth Hammer, ed., *Custer in 76* (Norman and London: University of Oklahoma, 1988), p. 157.
5. *Ibid.*, p.100, 103.; John S. Gray, *Centennial Company* (Ft. Collins, CO: Old Army Press, 1976), p. 344.
6. Wayne Mitchell Sarf, *The Little Bighorn Campaign* (Pennsylvania: Combined Books, 2000), p. 169.
7. John Upton Terrell, and George Walton, *Faint the Trumpet Sounds* (New York: McKay, 1966), p. 189.
8. Don Rickey, *Forty Miles a Day on Beans and Hay* (Norman and London: University of Oklahoma, 1963), p. 113.
9. Charles M. Robinson III, *A Good Year to Die. The Story of the Great Sioux War* (New York: Random House, 1955), p. 188.
10. Herbert Coffeen, *The Custer Battle Book* (New York: Carlton Press, 1964), p. 49.
11. Stephen Longstreet, *War Cries on Horseback* (Garden City, NY: Doubleday, 1970), pp. 16, 87.
12. Interview with John Martin, May 4, 1910 in Hammer, p. 105.
13. Douglas D. Scott, P. Willey, and Melissa A. Connor, *They Died with Custer,* (Norman: University of Oklahoma, 1991); also the popular work of Sandy Barnard, *Digging into Custer's Last Stand* (Huntington Beach, CA: Ventana, 1998).
14. Sarf, p. 124.
15. Hammer, p. 86.
16. Interview with Curly, August 3-4, 1909. Hammer, p. 162.
17. W. A. Graham, *The Custer Myth* (Harrisburg, PA: Stackpole, 1953), pp. 10-18.
18. Interview with Tall Bull, July 22, 1910. Hammer, p. 212.
19. Edward L. Daily, *Custer to MacArthur* (Paducah, KY: Turner, 1995), p. 69.
20. Graham, *Myth,* p. 90.
21. *Ibid.*, p. 145.
22. Edward J. McClernand, *With the Indian and the Buffalo in Montana* (Glendale, CA: Clark, 1969), p. 93.
23. S. L. A. Marshall, *Crimsoned Prairie* (New York: Scribner, 1972), p. 154.
24. McClernand, p. 93.
25. Marshall, p. 154.
26. *Ibid.*, p. 156.

27. Sarf, p. 44.
28. Jason Hook and Martin Pegler, *To Live and Die in the West* (Oxford: Osprey, 1999), p. 70; Longstreet, p. 284; Robinson, p. 195.
29. Connell, p. 303.
30. Sarf, p. 228.
31. Marshall, p. 159.
32. Sarf, p. 233.

XI
RENO'S BATTLES[1]
(3-4 p.m; and thereafter)

Upon receiving his orders, Reno led his troopers at a trot in a column of two down to the river several miles away. He had one hundred twelve men, many of whom were spring recruits. In A Company, the company to which De Rudio had been assigned, one-fourth had less than one year of service.[2] Most had never been in a hostile engagement and were poor shots and poor horsemen.[3] Also assigned to Reno were two Crow scouts, Arikara scouts, guides and interpreters. The mission of the Arikaras was to cut out the Lakota ponies. Custer also sent his aide and another officer to ride along with Reno up to the river crossing, to keep an eye on the battalion and report back.

On the way to the river De Rudio watered his horse in a small tributary. It was the same fiery mount that Benteen had lent him in Ft. Lincoln. Probably the horse watered himself, for no junior officer would willingly drop out of the march to water his horse, especially if Captain Moylan were his company commander. De Rudio also filled his canteen while the horse drank.

The Little Bighorn is a rapid tortuous mountain stream from twenty to forty yards wide, with pebbled bottom and abrupt soft banks. At ordinary times, the water is two to five feet deep, depending on the width of the channel.

When Reno reached the east bank of the Little Bighorn, he had to order a halt, so that the horses could be watered. Frantic with thirst, they would not cross until they had drunk. The soldiers made use of the halt to fill their canteens. The battalion spent ten to fifteen minutes on the riverbank, a risky interlude with the encampment nearby, but it suggests that Major Reno was not about to plunge into battle unprepared.

First to cross the river were the scouts. A few, probably the Crows, crossed at Ford A downstream, where Reno would later make his retreat.[4] They returned with the disconcerting news that their party had been observed.

Around 2:30 p.m. De Rudio galloped down the trail and into the water. In his haste to rejoin his company, he splashed Reno, who, according to some, had been drinking from a whiskey flask in the middle of the stream.

"What are you trying to do, Rudio?" he snapped. " Drown me before I am dead?"

At the ford, Reno could make out a few tepees situated at the southern end of the encampment. Reno brought his force across the river, with the water coming up to the horses' bellies, which refreshed the tired animals.

Once on the west bank, the troops passed through a two hundred yard stand of bullberry thickets and cottonwood timber bordering the river and came upon a broad level prairie, an old flood plain, pockmarked by prairie dog towns and sage clumps. It had been grazed off by the warrior ponies.[5] The battalion reformed on the flood plain.

An order was given to *"Dismount and tighten saddle-girths!"* Girths were tightened, carbines checked. The troops reformed by trumpet call.[6] Reno then gave the order *"Right front into line! Load pistols! Quick walk!"* and they proceeded in marching order in columns of four. Reno advanced first at quick walk, then at rapid trot and lastly at gallop.[7] A gallop could have been treacherous, with all the holes made by the prairie dogs. The scouts and M Company rode in advance, A Company followed, and G brought up the rear.[8] Reno rode in front twenty yards ahead and the scouts were fifty to seventy-five yards in front on the left.[9] De Rudio was fifteen yards behind Reno and saw him look back to check the formation.[10] Until then, the full extent of the village was not apparent, the view blocked by the many bends of the river. After they had gone one and a half miles, the southern end of the encampment gradually came into view.

Hidden by the bends in the river were more than a thousand tepees and wickiups, extending for three miles to the north. The Unkpapa tribe led by Chief Gall occupied the southern end of the encampment. Next were five other tribes, then the Oglala led by Crazy Horse and at the north end, the Cheyennes.

Warriors were seen running out of the camp. Cries of *Washichu!* ("white men!") rang out from among the Unkpapa warriors.

The battalion saw several warriors riding around in circles, a signal that the enemy was in sight or a challenge to fight.[11] The soldiers fired at the nearest tepees and seemed to have caused great disorder in the Lakota camp, as the braves hurried to find their ponies. Some warriors approached on Reno's left flank; others crossed the river and moved on the opposite bank. Some held back or retreated, as if attempting to entice the soldiers into an ambush. Waves of Unkpapa warriors and the other tribes kept pouring out of the encampment in increasing numbers.

Reno sent two messengers[12] back to Custer with a report that the enemy was in considerable strength.[13] Thus far, the warriors had not attacked but seemed to be waiting for the soldiers to advance.[14]

With a wide plain on which to deploy, Reno ordered the column to *Form line of battle!* positioning two companies in front and one in reserve. The line extended a few hundred yards.[15] Five yards were spaced between riders and fifteen yards between squads. G Company was brought up to the line, as the troopers galloped down the valley. The Arikaras left the line and approached the village stealthily. They rode down some Unkpapa women and children and seized a few ponies, but when the warriors appeared, they withdrew.[16] Among the Lakota killed were two wives and three children of the Unkpapa war chief, Gall.[17]

The warriors circled the advancing line, trying to find favorable positions to attack but remained outside of carbine range. The line advanced for three hundred yards up to a dry wash. Reno saw heads emerging in the ravine and began to suspect an ambush. Although not an experienced Indian fighter, Reno was acquainted with the warrior subterfuge of enticing the soldiers to move forward by pretending to withdraw and then falling on them from all sides. Quite reasonably, Reno called a halt and ordered his troops to dismount and form a skirmish line. De Rudio believed that if they had ridden five hundred yards further, they would all have been butchered. Three hundred yards ahead of them was a ditch several feet deep and three yards wide in which warriors had been concealed.[18] This landmark is not present today, because of changes wrought by farming, as well as by railroad and road construction.

The order was given: *"Dismount and prepare to fight on foot!"*[19] Cavalry often dismount for combat, since accuracy is poor on horseback and the men are easy targets. The revised *Manual of Cavalry Tactics*, published in 1874, calls for the mounted charge to be used only for initial shock, giving the cavalryman the opportunity to choose his ground for dismounted battle.[20] While dismounting, two troopers were carried off to the village to certain death, when their horses scented danger and became unmanageable.

Reno formed up a dismounted skirmish line a few hundred yards long,[21] with companies A and M in front and G Company in reserve. Three out of each four men remained on the skirmish line; the fourth held the horses and led them into the woods. The skirmish line was anchored on its right end to a stand of timber one hundred yards from the river bank and the left end, held by eight to twelve scouts[22] before their departure, extended out, "floated" toward the wide plain. They were then about two miles north of the Ford A. Their expectation was that Custer would cross down river and attack the village from the north.

After having dismounted, the line advanced on foot a brief distance and then halted. The firing grew fiercer. Warriors rode out of the village, signally each other with their bone whistles, which terrified the army horses.[23] Many warriors were stretched out flat on their ponies or bent over the far side of the pony. They raced and whooped around the dismounted riflemen, firing at them.[24]

The soldiers tried to make use of whatever cover was available, since they feel more secure when firing behind an object, no matter how trivial. Some used the little cones of earth of the prairie dog town as breastworks.

G Company, in reserve, was ordered to take up a position on the line, to replace the Arikara who had left to cut out the Sioux ponies grazing to the west.

Reno now began to understand he was in trouble. His raw command had been firing imprudently. At two to three shots a minute, their fifty rounds would soon be depleted and they would have to draw from the fifty rounds in their saddle bags. Some of the carbines jammed. This might have been caused by the heat generated from rapid fire, or dirt creeping into the lock, or the softness of the copper cartridges.[25] Another cause might have been the verdigris deposit caused by the cartridge rubbing against the leather loops in the belt. For this reason, veteran soldiers often replaced the leather belt with one made from canvas, known as a prairie belt.

Major Reno later testified that six of the three hundred eighty breech blocks had failed to close. The extractor had torn into the soft copper cartridge during ejection, leaving a cartridge in the chamber, which had to be cut out with a knife.[26] This rate of misfire does not appear to have been wildly excessive. More than thirty-eight thousand Springfield cartridges and three thousand revolver cartridges appear to have been fired during the entire engagement.[27]

Reno passed up and down the line, reassuring the men and urging them to reduce their fire to preserve the ammunition. Men were sent in succession to collect ammunition from their saddle bags.[28] Thus far, the men were in good spirits.[29]

Reno looked around for the "whole regiment support" Custer had promised him. Custer was last sighted high up on the east bank bluffs, leading his column in the down river direction, as if searching for another ford. A few claimed to have seen him waving his hat from a ridge across the river. De Rudio was one of them, but without binoculars, it is unlikely he, or anyone else, could identify a figure on horseback from that distance.

Where was Custer going? To the downriver Ford B? Certainly Custer had no thought of crossing at Ford A or of bringing his five companies up behind Reno. Passing through the minds of the soldiers in Reno's battalion was Custer's reputation for turning his back on his men. He abandoned the battlefield at Washita, leaving behind Major Elliot's party of twenty a scant two miles from the battleground. Near Ft. Wallace in July 1867, Custer did not take the time to look for the sergeant and six men whom he had sent to search for his mare.

Meanwhile, warriors were infiltrating their position. Some had crossed the river and moved upstream along the opposite bank, then recrossed to come up to Reno's rear, working themselves into position for a rush on Reno's horses. The enemy fire increased and great numbers of warriors flanked the troops, circling to the rear. This could be done with little difficulty, since the skirmish line was short. Troopers began to fall.

Ammunition was running low.[30] Some troopers were down to the last five cartridges in their belt.[31] On average, they had fired forty rounds a man.[32] An officer pleaded with a scout to take a message to Custer. "No man could get through that alive!" the scout retorted.

Word was brought to Reno that the warriors were infiltrating the wood, in an effort to cut out the horses. De Rudio was sent into the timber with some horse holders. Later, Reno ordered G Company off the line and into the wood copse to further protect the animals and prevent an attack on his flank. He extended the position of A Company to the left, to fill the gap. This put further pressure on the left flank. Up until now, the skirmish had been going on for only ten minutes[33] and there had been few casualties.[34]

Whether by command, or from a perceived danger of attack from the rear, the line began to wheel clockwise.[35] The left end of the line fell back several hundred yards to a stand of cottonwood timber. Troopers on the line now had their backs to the river. Throughout the timber were dense underbrush, narrow animal paths, willows, rushes and thickets.[36] Beavers had damned the mouth of the river bend and converted the pinched off pocket into a swamp. At one time the river had run close to their position, but had changed its course, leaving a deep ditch at their backs.

The dismounted soldiers took a position at the edge of the wood.[37] The horse holders, who had gone into the timber with the animals, were soon joined by G Company. They saw a two acre clearing where lodges had been earlier stood,[38] and it was there they brought the horses. Horse holders were a favorite target of the warriors.[39]

More warriors rode up, screaming, infiltrating the flanks. Others rode around, out of the Springfield carbine range of three hundred yards, sizing up the troops and their position. Reno now began to understand that he was facing a disaster. One hundred dismounted troopers were pitted against huge numbers of determined warriors, who were defending their encampment and families.

Reno's supply of ammunition was dwindling. At the present rate of fire, he might have sufficient cartridges for another hour. Help from Custer now seemed illusory. One of his officers told him frankly, "I think we better get out of here!" It was at this point that a bullet tore into the head of one of the scouts, and his brains splattered over Reno. As the story goes, this settled the matter for Reno.

Reno gave the order to *Mount up!* and get to the bluffs on the other side of the river. "We have to get out of here! We've got to charge them!" he was heard to say.[40] He rode along the line saying: "any of you men who wish to make your escape, follow me." Cries of "Charge, charge, we're going to charge (retreat)" were heard.[41] Reno was reported by some to have ordered "mount" and "dismount" three times;[42] others once.[43] Rather than indicate indecision on Reno's part, it might suggest that warriors may have infiltrated his position and had to be dealt with by dismounted soldiers before they could retreat. Others heard the battalion commander order them to mount in column of four facing upstream. Reno had no trumpeter and the noise of the firing, shouts and the shrill cries of the Lakota were deafening,[44] but word circulated to *Mount and move out!* The soldiers ran to their mounts. Some holders inexpertly released the horses, so that the troopers had difficulty mounting.[45] A few wounded horses broke away and ran, leaving some soldiers without transport. Many animals were too terrified to be mounted. Soldiers grabbed whatever mount was near. The dead and wounded were abandoned. Troopers and civilian scouts were left behind. Either they did not hear the order to mount, or, if they did, their horse was wounded, taken by another, or had run away.[46]

Mounted and in column of fours, the troopers broke out of the woods, first at trot, then at gallop.[47] Some say A Company was on Reno's right, G on his left and M behind, but this tidiness is unlikely. The warriors gave way, but promptly closed on the right flank of the retreating column,[48] firing from a distance of fifty to one hundred yards. They held their rifles across the pommels of their saddles, finger on the trigger, and pumped the Winchester rifles into the retreating soldiers.[49] Other warriors clung to the far side of their pony, known as "squaw riding," and fired under the animal's neck. Reno made no effort to post a squad to cover his retreat, but Captain Thomas Henry French, riding a mount with four white legs, was seen wheeling his horse around to protect the soldiers trying to flee.

Emerging from the woods, Reno led his men along the edge of the open plain, skirting the woods and bogs. A few of his men rode through the bogs and woods, perhaps following an old buffalo trail.[50] Across the river they saw a high bluff, and knew that it could not be mounted. At this point, Reno was two miles from Ford A, where he had made his crossing. It was apparent that he could not travel the two miles across the plain, with lively warrior ponies in pursuit. His only hope was to find a closer ford. By now, Crazy Horse and his Oglala warriors had arrived, breathing fire into the warriors attack and were charging straight into the Reno's line. Other warriors began to follow suit.

A few hundred yards south of where they had emerged from the woods, Reno saw, or was told about, a cleft in the bluffs. The scouts may have earlier used this crossing before reporting to him at Ford A. Reno led his command back through the woods to the riverbank. There was a six to eight foot drop into the water. The horses were reluctant to make the plunge, but were spurred on by the press of the mounts behind them. Warriors were on both banks of the river and on both flanks of the column, picking off the men. Some warriors rode into the stream, firing at the stampeding soldiers.[51] There was hand-to-hand fighting, and soldiers were pulled off their mounts. Sabers might have been useful at this point. The charge (if this were one) turned into a retreat and the retreat into a rout. Twenty-nine men and three officers were killed in the crossing; seven enlisted were wounded. One officer, one interpreter and fourteen soldiers and scouts were unaccounted for.[52] Here again, dead and wounded were abandoned.

The battalion crossed the swift flowing river and then mounted an eight-foot embankment. Fortunately, the soft bank collapsed after several riders, making the ascent easier. The troopers then retreated in single file up the bluff through a narrow ravine to a hill overlooking their battleground. Many horses, overcome with fatigue, would not mount the bluff with their riders.[53] Warriors fired at them from both sides of the river. Chief Gall started to block the retreat up the bluffs, but when he learned of the approach of another column, he gathered his men to attend to Custer.[54] An exhausted Reno arrived at the top of the ridge with only sixty effectives.[55]

By chance, Reno had come to a semicircular ridge

surrounding a shallow depression that sloped downward to the east. Within the depression was a meadow. Reno ordered rifle pits to be dug around the ridge. Since their tools were with the pack train, the men had to dig with tin cups and eating utensils. The horses were placed in the saddle and here the surviving contract physician set up his aid station.

Fortunately, the doctor had chloroform; for he was later called on to perform an amputation. The usual wisdom is that he used "sanitary whiskey,"[56] but it is unlikely, if not inconceivable, that he did not have one bottle of chloroform in his supplies. Also, there had been many arrow wounds. It is not known whether the surgeon removed the arrows, and, if so, what method he employed. In those days, most arrow heads were made of barbed iron, fashioned from barrel hoops or trade articles. Because of the barb, the arrowhead tears tissue as it is being withdrawn. Moreover, the longer it remains in the soft parts, the more likely it will become adherent to adjacent tissue, so that when late attempts are made to extract it, the arrowhead may detach from the shaft. One contemporary medical authority recommended looping a wire around the tip, to extract the arrowhead,[57] but most surgeons would have found it easier to enlarge the wound and extract it under direct vision.

Reno's position was barely adequate for defense, and especially vulnerable to warrior sharpshooters. Also, the adjacent ravines allowed the dismounted warriors to approach undetected. The attack began, as hundreds of warriors invested Reno's position at distances of two to five hundred yards[58] and engaged it in heavy fire. Reno's situation was becoming perilous. At about 4:30 p.m., twenty minutes after Reno had taken up his position, Captain Benteen's battalion was seen in the distance.

As Benteen approached Reno Hill, he heard heavy gunfire and saw scores of dismounted soldiers scrambling up the bluffs, pursued by mounted warriors. He immediately formed a mounted skirmish line and raced toward the hill with drawn revolvers. When Benteen reached Reno Hill, Major Reno blurted out that half his men were casualties[59] and that he desperately

Reno's Battles 239

needed assistance. Benteen was left with little choice. To leave a battalion, hotly engaged, with many wounded, little ammunition and in imminent danger of annihilation, in order to go off to report to his commanding officer without even the mule train in hand, would have been unimaginable folly. Benteen joined Reno, at least pending the arrival of the mule train. He ordered his men to share their ammunition and sent word to hurry the pack train. Noting that the position was somewhat extended, Benteen compacted the defensive line and set up improvised breastworks.

Reno, in turn, used the timely arrival of Benteen as an opportunity to search for the body of his adjutant, killed while climbing up from the river. Assembling a small party of volunteers with canteens, he climbed down the bluff toward the river. Several troopers were wounded in the effort.[60] Nearly the same brave action the next day resulted in the awards of Medals of Honor. On the way back, just when the party was particularly vulnerable, the firing began to slacken. The warriors had departed to attend to Custer.

It had been an hour since Reno's men had first engaged the enemy on the west side of the river.[61] Soldiers later reported hearing heavy gunfire in the distance, which they attributed to Custer. At any rate, the warriors heard something, or received a message, for hundreds of them rode off toward Custer Hill. An officer of Benteen's battalion later claimed that he, too, heard gunfire coming from Custer's direction. If so, it was all the more remarkable, for the officer had defective hearing.

Years later, a test was conducted in which an infantry company fired three rifle volleys and a 12 pounder on the Custer Battlefield. None of these were heard on Reno Hill.[62] Perhaps Reno's soldiers had heard warrior rifle fire in the vicinity, but it appears unlikely that they heard firing from Custer's troops.

Lt. Thomas Weir, a Custer protégé, whose commission Custer had once rescued,[63] sallied forth from the fortified position in a show of bravura, to search for Custer, with a company trailing behind him. Without adequate ammunition, Reno and Benteen held back. Then the van of the pack train arrived, moving in typical fashion with the front mules at a dogtrot and the rear pulled with lariats and whipped with blacksnakes.[64] Ammunition was quickly distributed. An additional twelve men of Reno's battalion joined the command soon thereafter. These were soldiers who had been left behind, dismounted on the west bank. They had succeeded in crossing the river and had made their way up to Reno Hill with surprisingly little difficulty.[65]

With the arrival of the first of the mule train, Benteen felt obliged to join Custer. Without Benteen to support him, Reno, too, had to reluctantly abandon his position. Benteen left first, since his troops had taken no casualties. Then Reno's battalion left, in a column of two's a hundred fifty to two hundred yards long,[66] dragging the wounded on four to six man horse blanket stretchers. Moving the wounded must have been an agonizing effort, which Reno was compelled to undertake with his sixty effectives, only because Benteen had left him. One doubts he got far. They struggled in the direction of a hill, now called Weir Point, one and a half miles away, which Weir had reached. From that point, many warriors could be seen rushing around in the distance, but no definite sign of Custer.

Having climbed the Weir hillock on a clear day and looked, withour binoculars, toward Custer Hill, I think that an impending battle three miles away would be barely visible over the undulating terrain. But a cloud of smoke and dust certainly could have been seen, and it would have lingered for *at least* ten minutes after the battle, easily recognizable to the old Civil War hands, who could spot an active battlefield a few miles away. But this is not what was generally reported, so one is tempted to presume that the Custer battle was well over by the time the troopers on Weir Point viewed the battlefield, and if any smoke or dust were present, it was not in sufficient concentration to suggest a recent battle.

When the soldiers finally did spy the enemy, the warriors had already left the Custer battlefield and were rushing towards them. Reno had the trumpeter sound *Halt!* "continuously and assiduously."[67] The two battalions quickly fell back to Reno Hill. Lt. E. S. Godfrey covered their retreat; his meritorious action went unmentioned in the later report of Major Reno. Shockingly, a wounded farrier, who could have been evacuated with a little effort, was abandoned by Captain Weir (who later leveled charges of cowardice against Reno)

Within the next hour the rest of the pack train arrived at Reno Hill, carrying with it a few shovels to entrench and bury the dead. Two of Custer's troopers mysteriously appeared around this time.[68] They reported that their horses had become lame, and they could not keep up with the Custer march. Before an alternate explanation is suggested, it should be noted that one of them would win the Medal of Honor for bravery the next day.[69] Also, the Arikara scouts turned up,[70] as well as three of Custer's Crows, who had been dismissed by Custer prior to the engagement. They could have left the battlefield, but chose to remain. Lastly, an additional twenty-four men from F Company in Custer's command appeared.[71] These men remain a mystery. Nightingale suggests that Custer left "the lost patrol" at Weir's Point to protect his advance.[72] It seems likely that they were Custer stragglers, whose horses had been disabled by the grueling march. They could not join Reno until after the warriors had left.

Once the Lakota warriors returned, they began a vigorous attack on the Reno position, which continued through the evening and subsided only after nightfall. The soldiers worked frantically to perfect their defenses, digging rifle pits and heaping up cases, bread boxes, sacks of bacon, hay, oats, and dead animals for breastworks. The animals were grotesquely bloated.[73] Only three shovels were available to dig pits, so cups and hands had to be used. A horseshoe-shaped line was finally established. There was no time to properly attend to the living animals. They were hobbled with lariats to weights and boxes. Not until late in the night were the horses unsaddled and the mules unloaded.

Benteen walked the line, as he directed the construction of

the defenses. Brave and imperturbable, he showed himself to be a professional soldier of the highest calling, moving about seemingly without fear. The warriors, now more than a thousand, approached to one to three hundred yards, occupying all the threatening positions. The circumference of their position was probably four thousand yards.[74] Ravines permitted them to creep up undetected until close to the defensive line. One warrior approached close enough to count coup.[75]

About forty to eighty percent of the warriors had modern weapons. In all, they used at least forty-one different kinds of firearms. For his handgun, the warrior had Remington, Colt or Smith and Wesson revolvers in .31 to .45 calibers.[76] Some revolvers could fire the Winchester rifle cartridge. The army revolvers were bought from traders or deserters.[77] For their long gun, many warriors had the lever-action 44/40 Winchester 73, an improved version of the Henry, which shot accurately to two hundred fifty yards, up to sixteen times a minute. Others had earlier versions of the Henry -Winchester, firing cartridges of twenty-five to forty grains. The range was less than the Springfield, especially since the Winchester primer was of *rimfire* type and required a twin firing pin to overcome the primer's unreliability. The army's single shot, center-fire Springfield, on the other hand, might fire up to sixteen shots a minute *on the firing range*, but less than three per minute when fired in battle by a recruit. The Bureau of Ordinance had concluded that the shortness of its range and the unreliability of the rimfire cartridge made the Winchester inferior to the centerfire Springfield, but this judgment predated the science of operation analysis, which established the importance of rapid fire. Some warriors had muskets, which may have better answered their needs.[78]

Warrior sharpshooters, firing from what is now known as Sharpshooter Ridge, used the Springfield .45/70 rifle, captured from Crook's infantry; or the mighty 15 pound 50/90 Sharp centerfire buffalo rifle.[79] A sergeant had one such Sharp rifle with a 2x telescopic sight, which he had packed in the mule train.

Reno's Battles 243

It helped discourage fire from Sharpshooter Ridge. Although the warriors probably did not use the iron sights,[80] they had uncanny accuracy, honed from practice with the bow and arrow. The troopers heard "Zip" for the rifle fire and "Zing" of carbine fire.

Where was Custer? In vain the scouts put their ear to the ground, to listen for the sound of hoofbeats. The whole command came to believe that Custer had gone off to join General Terry, leaving the rest of the regiment in the lurch. Trumpet calls were heard and initially the men were deceived into believing reinforcements were near. In fact, the trumpet calls came from the warriors themselves, who blew the notes on captured instruments. Exhausted and terrified, some troopers began to hallucinate, seeing columns of troops.

All through the night, the position came under sporadic fire. The men continued to dig rifle pits, however they could manage it, but the ground was hard, so the pits were shallow. A few drops of rain fell. The men were plagued with thirst; yet dare not leave their position to go to the river. Great bonfires shown from across the river, and the men heard the shouts and songs of the warriors dancing in camp. They celebrated Sitting Bull's vision and lamented the dead. Several times Benteen and Reno had to drive skulkers from the safety of the animal picket back onto the line.

By morning, two distant shots heralded the resumption of the attack. A furious barrage of gunfire erupted, greater than Major Reno had ever experienced in the Civil War.[81] Warrior sharpshooters continued to fire from the distance with the captured Springfield rifles. Some tricked the troopers into revealing their position by raising a hat or blanket on a stick to provoke fire. Others created panic by sending a pony into the line on which they had mounted a stuffed dummy dressed in buckskin.[82] Warriors raced around the perimeter, firings so furiously that they cut down the sagebrush in front of the Reno's position.[83]

Then the mounted charges began, as hundreds of horsemen warriors rushed up to the line, firing at the shallow rifle pits and improvised breastworks. Some of them wore captured cavalry uniforms and waved guidons and battle flags.[84] Arrows, shot into the air like mortar rounds, landed in the depression on the horses and the wounded. A few warriors fought hand-to-hand, touching the men with the coup stick. Benteen estimated that there were two thousand warriors surrounding their position and a thousand others waiting along the river for an opportunity to join the battle.[85] The sagebrush and deep grass offered good camouflage for a creeping warrior.

Benteen realized that only a bold attack could keep the warriors from overrunning their position. He assembled chosen men from three companies and, together with Reno, charged the nearby warriors sheltered in a protective ravine, driving them back, almost to the river.[86] It was costly in ammunition, but the warriors withdrew. Not one soldier was hit by enemy fire in the counterattack. There is no reliable estimate of the number of warriors killed around Reno Hill, but their dead were probably considerably less than the soldiers. Despite their whooping and shouting, warriors were remarkably prudent when attacking a fortified position, modern perceptions notwithstanding.

By now, the need for water was desperate, but the warriors commanded the approaches to the river.[87] The call for volunteers went out and twenty-four men offered to fetch water. The men began their descent through a ravine that led to the river, when a lively barrage of gunfire and arrows started up. Six troopers were shot during the mission. Two trips were made, and several canteens were brought back for the wounded. One man made four trips.[88] Many of these men were later awarded Medals of Honor. The selection was probably arbitrary. Augusto De Voto of B Company went for water but did not make the list. A Certificate of Merit might have been more welcome by some, since it meant an extra two dollars a month in pay.[89] In 1917 the criteria for the Medal of Honor award were reexamined and the requirements were increased.

During the early afternoon another furious attack by large numbers of unmounted warriors was beaten back. This signaled the end of the mass attacks, but the sharpshooting continued. During all this time, Benteen had been on his feet, moving about and encouraging the men.[90] Finally, around six in the evening, the firing stopped and a strange formation was sighted across the river.

The soldiers observed a long column of Lakota moving upstream toward the Bighorn Mountains. Their herd of ponies was the largest ever seen, estimated to be twenty thousand, six or eight to a man.[91] The warriors set fire to the grass behind them to prevent pursuit. This gave the soldiers hope.

Attention could now be given to the long-suffering animals. The horses were unsaddled, unbridled, watered and turned out to graze. Camp was relocated for easier access to water. Reno had Martini, the trumpeter, sound *Retreat! Recall!* and *March!*, so that any soldier in the ravines would hear the calls and report in.[92]

Eighteen men had been killed on the hill, forty wounded. Reno's total butcher's bill was fifty killed, fifty wounded. Reno ordered the dead to be buried, as best as was possible. That night four more stragglers turned up, De Rudio among them.

Notes

1. War Department, <u>Annual Report of the Secretary of War</u>. 1876, House Executive Document, No. I, Serial Vol. 1742, pp. 476-480.
2. Douglas D. Scott, P. Willey, and Melissa A. Connor, *They Died with Custer*, (Norman: University of Oklahoma, 1991), p. 38.
3. E. A. Brininstool, *Troopers with Custer* (Lincoln and London: University of Nebraska, 1952), p. 153.
4. Interview with Lt. Luther Hare, February 7, 1910. Kenneth Hammer, ed., *Custer in 76* (Norman and London: University of Oklahoma, 1988), p. 65; "With Colonel Charles A. Varnum," Chapter 4. Brininstool, p. 97.
5. Testimony of Lt. G. D. Wallace. W. A. Graham, *The Reno Court of Inquiry* (Mechanicsburg, PA: Stackpole, 1995), p. 17, Testimony of J. S. Payne. Graham, *Reno,* p. 89.
6. Testimony of J. S. Payne. Graham, *Reno,* p. 89.
7. "With Colonel Charles A. Varnum," Chapter 4. Brininstool, p. 94; "A Thrilling Escape – De Rudio and O'Neill," Chapter 5. Brininstool, p. 161.
8. "A Trooper's Account of Battle," Chapter 2, Pvt. William C. Slaper. Brininstool, p. 48.
9. Wayne Mitchell Sarf, *The Little Bighorn Campaign* (Conshohoken, PA: Combined Books, 2000), pp. 201, 101.
10. The testimony of De Rudio before the Court of Inquiry is quoted. Brininstool, p. 161.
11. Sarf, p. 199.
12. Testimony of Major M. Reno. Graham, *Reno*, p. 212.
13. Testimony of Major M. Reno. Graham, *Reno*, p. 212.
14. Testimony of George Herendeen (civilian). Graham, *Reno*, p. 81.
15. Testimony of Lt. George Wallace. Graham, *Reno*, p. 16.
16. Sarf, p. 203.
17. Interview with Lt. Luther Hare, February 7, 1910. Hammer, p. 66.
18. Testimony of Lt. George Wallace. Graham, *Reno*, p. 18.
19. "A Thrilling Escape – De Rudio and O'Neill," Chapter 5. Brininstool, p. 130; Testimony of Lt. C. De Rudio. Graham, *Reno*, p. 105.
20. Charles M. Robinson III, *A Good Year to Die. The Story of the Great Sioux War* (New York: Random House, 1955), p. 180.
21. Sarf, p. 2.
22. Brininstool, p. 99.
23. Jason Hook and Martin Pegler, *To Live and Die in the West* (Oxford: Osprey, 1999), p. 62.
24. Edward L. Daily, *Custer to MacArthur* (Paducah, KY: Turner, 1995), p. 71.
25. Evans S. Connell, *Son of the Morning Star* (New York: Harper Perennial, 1984), p. 306.

Reno's Battles 247

26. Testimony of Lt. C. C. De Rudio. Graham, *Reno*, p. 116.
27. Sarf, pp. 116, 117.
28. Richard Upton, *The Custer Adventure* (Ft. Collins, CO: Old Army Press, 1978), p. 38.
29. Interview with Thomas F. O'Neill (no date). Hammer, p. 106.
30. Testimony of Lt. Charles Varnum. Graham, *Reno*, p. 49.
31. "With Colonel Charles A. Varnum," Chapter 4. Brininstool, p. 93.
32. Testimony of Lt. Luther Hare. Graham, *Reno*, p. 95; Brininstool, p. 179.
33. Interview with Charles De Rudio, February 2, 1910. Hammer, p. 84.
34. Brininstool, p. 179.
35. Testimony of F. F. Girard (civilian). Graham, *Reno*, p. 39.
36. Letter from Theodore W. Goldin to Albert W. Johnson, December 8, 1928. John M. Carroll, *The Benteen-Goldin Letters on Custer and his last Battle* (New York: Liveright, 1974), p. 22.
37. "A Thrilling Escape – De Rudio and O'Neill," Chapter 5. Brininstool, p. 131.
38. Interview with Charles De Rudio. Hammer, p. 85.
39. Hook and Pegler, p. 62.
40. Testimony of Dr. H. R. Porter. Graham, *Reno*, p. 65.
41. John Upton Terrell, and George Walton, *Faint the Trumpet Sounds* (New York: McKay, 1966), p. 166.
42. Connell, p. 9.
43. Sarf, p. 207.
44. Testimony of Captain M. Moylan. Graham, *Reno*, p. 70.
45. "A Trooper's Account of Battle," Chapter 2. Brininstool, p. 5.
46. Brininstool, p. 154.
47. Testimony of Captain M. Moylan. Graham, *Reno*, p. 70.
48. Interview with Pvt. Thomas F. O'Neill (no date). Hammer, p. 107; Brininstool, p. 111.
49. Brininstool, p. 111, 182.
50. Testimony of Captain F. Benteen. Graham, *Reno*, p. 154.
51. "A Trooper's Account of Battle," Chapter 2, Pvt. William C. Slaper. Brininstool, p. 52.
52. Paul Andrew Hutton, *The Custer Reader* (Lincoln and London: University of Nebraska, 1992), p. 288.
53. "A Trooper's Account of Battle," Chapter 2, Pvt. William C. Slaper. Brininstool, p. 53.
54. Marguerite Merington, *The Custer Story* (Lincoln: University of Nebraska Press, 1987), p. 319.
55. Sarf, p. 211.
56. John S. Gray, *Centennial Company* (Ft. Collins, CO: Old Army Press, 1976), p. 279.
57. Sarf, p. 122.
58. Testimony of Lt. C. A. Varnum. Graham, *Reno,* p. 57.
59. Terrell and Walton, p. 168.
60. Testimony of Sgt. F. A. Culbertson. Graham, *Reno*, p. 125.
61. John S. Gray, *Custer's Last Campaign* (Lincoln and London: University of Nebraska Press, 1991), p. 290.
62. Letter from T. Goldin to A. Johnson, January 15, 1930. Carroll, *Benteen-Goldin*, p. 28.

63. Terrell and Walton, p. 71.
64. Letter from F. Benteen to T. Goldin, 1890. Carroll, *Benteen-Goldin,* p. 199.; Testimony of Capt. T. M. McDougall. Graham, *Reno,* p. 195.
65. Daily, p. 63.
66. Testimony of Lt. G. D. Wallace. Graham, *Reno,* p. 33; Interview with Luther Hare. Hammer, p. 66; Robert Nightingale, *Little Bighorn* (U.S.: Far West Publications, 1996), p. 13.
67. Narrative of F. Benteen [1890?]. Carroll, *Benteen-Goldin,* p. 186.
68. Interview with Richard P. Hanley, October 4, 1910. Hammer, p. 127.
69. Daniel Magnussen, *Peter Thompson's Narrative of the Little Bighorn Campaign of 1876* (Glendale, CA: Clark, 1974), p. 238.
70. Letter from Fred Dustin to Theodore Goldin, November 10, 1891. Carroll, *Benteen-Goldin,* p. 107.
71. Nightingale, p. 127; Magnussen, p. 121.
72. Nightingale, p. 129.
73. Interview with George Herendeen. Hammer, p. 225.
74. Testimony of Major M. Reno. Graham, *Reno,* p. 225.
75. Brininstool, p. 84. "Captain Benteen's Own Story," Chapter 3; Sarf, p. 123; Robinson, *Good Year,* p. xxix.
76. Stephen Longstreet, *War Cries on Horseback* (Garden City, NY: Doubleday, 1970), p. 214.
77. Don Rickey, *Forty Miles a Day on Beans and Hay* (Norman and London: University of Oklahoma, 1963), p. 166.
78. John S. DuMont, *Custer Battle Guns* (Ft. Collins, CO: Old Army Press, 1974), p. 46.
79. Scott, *Memories,* p. 79.
80. Sarf, p. 124.
81. Testimony of Major M. Reno. Graham, *Reno,* p. 279.
82. Interview with Pvt. Edward D. Pigford. Hammer, p. 144.
83. Interview with Pvt. Stanislas Roy. Hammer, p. 114.
84. Nightingale, p. 8.
85. Testimony of Captain F. Benteen. Graham, *Reno,* p. 141; Magnussen, p. 187.
86. Merington, p. 316.
87. "A Trooper's Account of Battle," Chapter 2, Pvt. William C. Slaper. Brininstool, p. 57.
88. Magnussen, p. 234.
89. Sarf, p. 84.
90. Interview with George W. Glenn. Hammer, p. 136.
91. Testimony of Lt. W. S. Edgerly. Graham, *Reno,* p. 165.
92. Testimony of Pvt. John Martin (Martini). Graham, *Reno,* p. 132.

XII
DE RUDIO'S ADVENTURE[1]

Even before Reno had ordered his battalion to dismount, De Rudio had taken a squad of men into the timber to the river bank, to guard against warriors infiltrating from across the river. He was then joined by G Company, which had been detailed to guard the horses.

The right side of the first skirmish line had extended to a clump of cottonwood trees and bushes and had passed over a dry, gravely creek bed, left over from high water. De Rudio could not see the skirmish line, nor did he know what was happening, until a trumpeter brought up his horse and told him the men were leaving the timber. The troopers quickly mounted up. In their haste they abandoned the G Company guidon at the side of the creek. The creek bed has since been obliterated by farming and road and rail track construction. When De Rudio ordered them to retrieve it, they called back: "To hell with the guidon, don't you see the Indians are coming in?" De Rudio picked it up and mounted his horse, but as he rode through the dense wood, the guidon became entangled in the tree branches and was pulled out of his hand. As he dismounted to retrieve it, a bullet struck his mount and the horse ran off, leaving De Rudio to face three hundred Sioux fifty yards away. The account given to Camp by De Rudio has slight variations, but the differences are inconsequential.[2]

De Rudio took cover in the thicket. There he encountered

Private Thomas O'Neill of G Company, whose horse had also been hit. O'Neill from Dublin, Ireland, had been a cook for his company commander. With O'Neill were Fred Girard, the interpreter, and William Jackson, a scout, as well as a party of twelve soldiers who, like O'Neill and De Rudio, were without mounts. De Rudio took command. His first task was to find them concealment from warrior fire. Later, when the fire subsided, De Rudio told them it was the duty of all to rejoin the command at the first safe opportunity. Led by George Herendeen, a dismounted scout, he and the twelve men immediately went down to the river and recklessly crossed it, then made their way on foot up the bluff to the ridge.[3] By this time, most of the warriors had left to do battle with Custer. After a brief exchange of fire with five mounted warriors, the soldiers were able to rejoin the command, just as they were were returning to Reno Hill after abandoning their advance towards Weir Point. There was no way forty-four year old De Rudio could have kept up with them on foot, let alone lead them back up the bluff. Girard and Jackson, both experienced frontiersmen, also held back.

Fearing that the mounts would betray their position, De Rudio suggested to the civilians that they drive away the horses. Predictably, the owners refused. De Rudio crawled into a hollow place in the bank of the dry creek, where a cottonwood stump had rotted, intending to cross the Little Bighorn at nightfall and rejoin the command.[4] Within ten minutes, he heard pistol shots nearby and the voices of several Lakota women. He cautiously peered out and saw them scalping a live soldier who had fallen in battle.

After the scalping, the warriors set fire to the woods. As he left his hiding place, someone called, "Lieutenant!" He saw the three men he had encountered earlier. They had followed him into the dry creek bed, after concealing the horses. The fire continued to burn until 5 p.m., when the wind changed direction and a light rain fell. Gunfire was heard up and downriver. The four remained in the creek bed, barely able to contain themselves, when the warriors passed close by.

After nightfall, they left their hiding place and started off toward Ford A. To reach it, they would have to travel two miles along the open plain. Girard and the scout mounted their horses, and De Rudio and Pvt. O'Neill each took hold of a tail. The horses were acting badly. One was stallion, the other a mare. To make them more manageable, the owners tied their heads together.[5] Girard assured De Rudio that if they had to rush off, they would notify the command of their whereabouts. Frank Girard was born in the Sandwich Islands and had been a trader. Captured by the Sioux, he had lived among them for five years and even claimed to have once shared a tepee with Sitting Bull.[6]

The sky was cloudy and the night dark, as they moved along the plain. Several mutilated bodies lay on the ground, stripped of their clothing. They heard the warriors returning to their village but could not see them.

De Rudio and O'Neill left Girard and Jackson and made their way to the river, to search for a closer ford. They saw only an insurmountable bluff on the eastern side. Both tried to cross the river, but the water was too deep and the current too swift. Instead, they filled their canteens and quenched their thirst. Returning to Girard and Jackson, the four men continued upriver, in search of a place to cross. They came to one likely prospect, and Frank Girard cast his watch into the water as an offering to the Great Spirit for a safe passage, praying in Sioux, "Help us to cross safely here." To Girard's surprise, the river was unexpectedly shallow. The party had to keep from laughing at the loss of Girard's watch.[7] But then, to their chagrin, they found they had crossed a bend in the river and were still on the west bank! Across the river, the bluffs were still insurmountable, almost two hundred feet high.

Suddenly, a party of several mounted warriors appeared. Girard and Jackson rode off like lightening, while De Rudio and O'Neill ran for cover into the bushes. Fortunately, the warriors had seen only the mounted men.

After the warriors left, they decided to find a better hiding place to await the return of the regiment, but their path was blocked by water. Beavers had dammed off the meandering bends of the river. They saw beavers diving into a pond and they most likely used the beaver dam to cross to the adjacent bank. (The author crossed a river bend by this method while exploring the west bank). In the thick underwood and briars near the river, they found a hiding place and passed the night in terror, listening to the faraway cries from the Lakota encampment.

Towards dawn, a loud, clanking of horseshoes was heard and then the splashing of water.[8] De Rudio carefully made his way to the river edge and looked out. He saw several men on the east bank with military blouses and white hats, mounted on gray horses. Some were starting up the bluffs toward Reno's position. One of them wore buckskin jacket, top boots and white hat and looked like Captain Tom Custer.

"Tom! Don't leave us here!" De Rudio called out.

He was answered by yells and a three hundred shot fusillade, cutting the brush in every direction. The two took cover in the bushes and tried to crawl off, but the warriors aimed at the movement of the branches, striking the logs around them. Fortunate for them, the braves did not cross the river. They were on their way to Reno Hill. But the shots drew the attention of other warriors close by.

De Rudio and O'Neill tried to slip away. They had gone fifty yards when they saw a party of mounted warriors galloping toward them. As they drew near, the two bolted and ran for their lives. Their sudden movement spooked the horses, which reared and plunged about. De Rudio and O'Neill took cover behind two twisted cottonwood stumps. In kneeling position they waited, De Rudio with Benteen's revolver, O'Neill with his carbine, as the warriors approached in single file.

When the warriors were ten yards away, De Rudio and O'Neill opened fire, killing at least two. The others hastily withdrew. During this time the remaining warriors across the river kept up their fire, but after the two warriors had been killed, the gunfire slackened. De Rudio remained in his defensive position, awaiting another attack. Across the river, from the direction of Reno Hill, they could see picketed horses and warrior sharpshooters in prone position. They also heard the troopers yelling, amidst the gunfire.

The warriors decided to burn them out. Fire was set, compelling them to change their position. They tried crawling out of the wood, but the flames blocked their escape. Nearby was a pile of trees, felled by beavers and stacked by the flood waters. They crept into it, mindless of the danger of rattlesnakes. This proved an ideal breastwork. O'Neill gave De Rudio some of his revolver ammunition, and they lay back and waited. As the flames crept closer, they smothered the fire with their gauntlet gloves. Around them, they could see warriors, one of who, seventy yards away, appeared to be directing the action. And so they passed the night.[9]

By sunrise, the warriors seemed to have forgotten about the two white men, hidden in the log breastwork. De Rudio and Pvt. O'Neill spent the morning watching the warriors mass for an attack on Reno Hill.

At 4 p.m. a warrior picket fired four revolver shots into the air at regular intervals, which appeared to be a signal. After this, a savage cry was repeated four times. They saw two hundred warriors leave the bluff and ford the river, abandoning Reno Hill. A half-hour later the same signals were repeated, and more warriors galloped away. Then the rest withdrew. Late afternoon, great bands of women and children passed them, moving upriver along the plain towards the mountains. Women and babies were mounted straddle-fashion and the children, six years and older, rode their own ponies, all dragging travois packed with the cooking utensils and provisions. The warriors followed the women and children -- more than a thousand of them, passing in haste only a hundred fifty yards from the two terrified observers. Lastly, came an immense herd of twenty-five thousand ponies.[10]

By 6 p.m. the dust had settled and all was quiet. Both men were ravenously hungry. De Rudio assumed that the regiment had left and that they would have to make their way to the Yellowstone River. They waited until 10 p.m. before crossing the Little Bighorn, pausing on the east bank to wring water from their uniforms.[11] They then scrambled up the high bluffs onto the broken high country and proceeded slowly and cautiously southward, to where they had seen the warriors pressing their attack.

After traveling a quarter mile, they saw a fire in the distance and made their way toward it stumbling over the body of a dead warrior. A mule brayed and they could hear indistinguishable voices. As they crept closer, they heard another bray and the voice of a sentry:

"Halt! Who goes there?"

De Rudio called out: "Picket, don't fire; it's Lieutenant De Rudio and Private O'Neill," and they started to run toward the sentry. Lt. Varnum rushed out to guide them in. At 2 a.m. they were greeted with cheers by the troopers.[12]

Lt. Varnum got them coffee and hardtack, but De Rudio could not eat, nor sleep. He learnt that Girard and Jackson had also reached the camp in safety a few hours before them, after abandoning their horses. The two related their adventures to the command. Benteen listened attentively and at first with his usual skepticism. Benteen wrote his wife: "He has a thrilling, romantic story -- made out already -- embellished, you bet. Far more of the truth will be found in the narrative of O'Neill. At any rate, it is not all colored, as he [O'Neill] is a cool level-headed fellow -- and tells it plainly and the same way all the time -- which is a big thing towards convincing one of the truth of a story."[13] One of the important factors in helping the 7th Cavalry to accept De Rudio's account is its similarity to the story related by Pvt. O'Neill, who was fulsome in his praise for De Rudio.[14] As time went on, Benteen became more critical: "He [De Rudio] deserves no credit for being caught in the woods, after being left there -- kept there." A fortnight later, he remarked to his wife "I think that had De Rudio made as good use of his eyes as fifteen or twenty of the men did -- he would have gotten out as they did..."[15]

Next morning, June 27 at 8 a.m., the troopers saw clouds of

De Rudio's Adventure

dust five miles to the north. Reno sent some scouts to investigate. Later, Gibbon and Terry rode into the camp, and the weary men wept like children.

It was not until the afternoon that H Company and a party of officers visited the Custer battlefield. The group included Captain Benteen, who was detailed to supervise the burial detail, and De Rudio, who had borrowed a horse from a wounded sergeant, so that he could accompany the party. Also in the detail were Martini and De Voto, who doubtless expressed their horror in their native tongue, as they witnessed the awful scene.

The party was guided to the battlefield by one of the officers of the Terry column who had first stumbled upon the battlefield. The burial party followed the ridge and then the Medicine Trail Coulee, which led to Ford B, where they supposed Custer tried to cross. From an inspection of the tracks, the party assumed at first glance, that Custer had been repelled at the ford and driven up Deep Coulee to the ridge.

On the battlefield, they inspected the bloated and decaying remains of the soldiers and horses and they put down the wounded army mounts. Keogh's body was identified by the *Medalglia di Pro Petri Sede* (For the Chair of Peter) medal given him by Pope Pious IX.[16] Comanche, his Morgan horse, was covered with flies, wounded in the neck, fore shoulder and hindquarters. Custer's body was identified, with his back braced up by the bodies of two others.

On viewing the body, Benteen murmered: "There he is, God damn him! He won't fight anymore."

In the company of Pvt. De Voto, De Rudio came upon the scattered corpses of E and F Company in the gully. His feelings may well be imagined as he reflected on the circumstances that kept him from serving with E Company.

De Rudio acted as a kind of recording secretary. He counted two hundred twelve bodies, of which approximately two hundred two or eight were troopers, the rest civilians. To this number must be added Reno's losses, bringing the military deaths to two hundred sixty-six. Warrior losses could not be estimated, since the bodies had been removed from the field. Only two dead warrior ponies were found.

The dismal task of burying the dead was next undertaken, but lacking pick and shovel, the troopers could only make tentative arrangements. Not until five years later was an appropriate monument erected.

By Wednesday, the enemy had retreated south toward the Rosebud Mountains in a column of dust, which Reno compared to a cavalry division on the march. They then turned east to the Powder and the Tongue rivers.

Meanwhile, the need for medical attention was urgent. Seven of the wounded had already died since Terry's arrival. The relief column struck camp and slowly made its way down the Little Bighorn.[17] The fifty wounded were carried by a variety of transport including four man litter, mule litter and travois litter. Few of the wounded had kind words for the four man litter. Lt. Gustavus C. Doane, of the Second Cavalry, favored the two mule litter;[18] the Crows, the travois litter.[19] The travois has two poles, with a blanket or horsehide stretched between them. One end of the pole is fastened to the horse's shoulders; the other end drags on the ground. For the transport of the badly wounded Commanche, an ingenious bellysling had been devised.

At the mouth of the Little Bighorn, the relief column met the *Far West,* which had been hastily transformed into a hospital ship. The wounded were transported down the Yellowstone to Bismarck, a distance of seven hundred ten miles through treacherous sandbars and innumerable snags and floating debris, in the incredibly record time of slightly over two days. Often, the head of steam hovered at the limit of safety. The twenty-six year old civilian surgeon, who had survived the battle with Reno, administered to the wounded day and night with great diligence. The ship arrived at Lincoln on July 5, with its flag at half mast and derrick and jack staff draped in black.[20] There, twenty-six women learned that they were widows and had to make plans to vacate their quarters.[21]

The shocking news of the Custer massacre reached Ft. Rice

July 5 by way of three Sioux, who had collected the news by the "moccasin telegraph." The wives gathered in the quarters of motherly Eliza De Rudio, who "put her brood to bed" and distributed pillows to the ladies. Since there were insufficient chairs, some of the women had to lie on the floor.[22] The frantic wives spent the night listening to the coyotes, as they awaited details. Finally, in the morning a steamboat appeared, bearing the sad news, together with messages from the surviving husbands.

News of the massacre swept the country and startled the Centenary Celebration in Philadelphia: CUSTER AND FIVE COMPANIES ANNIALATED BY SAVAGES! Sheridan tried to defend Custer's leadership, but General Grant was quick to call it a useless sacrifice of men for the exclusive benefit of Custer. Sturgis and Sherman were no less critical.[23]

The public was quickly caught up in the event, and much was written about the courage of Custer and the treachery of the red man. Even the economy-minded Democrats were galvanized into action. Enlistments of an additional twenty-five hundred cavalrymen were quickly authorized.[24]

De Rudio's adventures appeared in the New York *Herald* July 30, 1876 and in other newspapers. According to De Rudio, he had given the account to Major James S. Brisbin, Second Cavalry, in Col. Gibbon's column, with the understanding that it would not be published. Despite his promise, Brisbin sold the story to the newspaper. De Rudio disavowed some details. He complained that Brisbin was paid a pretty penny for his story, while De Rudio never saw a cent.

DE RUDIO'S ESCAPE

**A Thrilling Narrative by a Lieutenant
Of Custer's Cavalry Troop**

**The Indian Demons on the Trail--
Covered and Fired Upon**

**Thirty-Six Hours of Imminent Peril--
a Miraculous Deliverance.**

The 7th Calvary was retained in the Bighorn area under Terry's command and the surviving companies were consolidated. De Rudio was given command of the newly formed E Company, built around the men of that company who had been serving in the mule train. It was Benteen who had made the recommendation to Reno, but in his own perverse fashion, he made no mention of it to De Rudio.[25] At the same time, Benteen fretted to his wife that his letter to her was almost delayed because De Rudio had failed to notify him of outgoing mail. The long-delayed post from Lincoln finally caught up with them. Eliza had written before the battle that their son, Hercules, was being employed in the Subsistence Department at the fort. Also, that one of the wives had delivered twins.[26]

Colonel Nelson Miles and his 5th Infantry arrived by steamship to reinforce Terry's troops. He brought along with him cavalry recruits, horses and supplies for the badly depleted 7th Cavalry.[27] After remaining for four weeks camped at the mouth of Big Horn, Terry's command marched to Rosebud River, to meet up with General Crook.

General Crook had not learned of the Custer's disaster until

De Rudio's Adventure

sixteen days after the event,[28] although his scouts had known of it within hours, by mirror, smoke and runner. Crook was then ordered to proceed north with his two thousand soldiers to join Terry in an effort to trap the Lakota-Cheyenne. When he finally caught up with Terry on August 10, the tribes were nowhere to be seen. They had divided into small bands and scattered into the Yellowstone basin.

Both armies set off in different directions to run the warriors down. Each had its own objective. Coming from the Department of the Platte, Crook was more concerned with Crazy Horse and the Oglalas, the southern Lakotas. Terry, from the Department of the Dakotas, was more interested in Sitting Bull and Chief Gall of the Unkpapas, who ranged north of the Yellowstone all the way up into Canada.[29] Crook pursued his quarry for fifty-two days on starvation rations and was able to achieve a small, but well-publicized victory at Slim Buttes on September 9,1876. The army of General Terry sparred with the Sioux, but accomplished little. Winter was approaching. A battalion of the 7th Cavalry was sent back to Lincoln and the remaining cavalry and infantry, under Colonel Nelson Miles, were ordered to encamp on the Yellowstone with little hope that anything could be accomplished in the cold weather.

Meanwhile, several important events had occurred, which would have as great an impact on the Sioux and Cheyenne nations as the military campaigns. The construction of three forts was ordered, including Ft. Keogh on the Tongue and Ft. Custer on the mouth of the Little Bighorn. Supplies could now be stockpiled. In addition to demoralizing the warrior, these forts improved army mobility and provided the military with a longer working year. Moreover, the reservations were now placed under the army control, so that the warrior could no longer slip away unnoticed, nor procure ammunition from a lenient Indian agent. Troops were ordered to confiscate weapons and ponies. Most important, the government ordered that supplies be withheld from the Sioux until they ended hostilities and surrender claim to the Black Hills and the rail corridor. Accordingly, a select number of reservation Lakota were maneuvered into an "agreement," ceding the Black Hills and the rights of way. Unlike a treaty, the agreement did not require consent of three-fourths of the warriors, nor approval by two-thirds of the U.S. Senate. Having finally obtained title, the Northern Pacific was back on the road to solvency.

The attack on the Sioux-Northern Cheyenne nations continued through the cold months, led by the subordinate officers of Crook and Terry. Ronald S. Mackenzie, of Crook's command, met the Cheyenne at Crazy Woman Fork in the Powder River Valley on November 22, 1876 and sent the warriors fleeing naked into the snow. On the battlefield a pair of binoculars was found, together with 7th Cavalry equipment.[30] One wonders if the binoculars could have belonged to De Rudio.

Colonel Miles in Terry's command relentlessly dogged the enemy with his infantry. Miles, who commanded the 5th Infantry, was an ambitious non-West Point officer. A farm boy, then a crockery clerk, he entered the Civil War as a second lieutenant in a company of volunteer infantry and left as a brevet major general. Married to the niece of General William T. Sherman and Senator John Sherman, he had distinguished himself in the Red River War and was about to put the infantry to important use during the Sioux campaign. According to Miles, the infantry moved faster than the cavalry -- in the long run. Miles insisted that after the fourth's day march, the cavalry and infantry have equal speed, but after the seventh day, the foot outmarches the horse.[31] Nevertheless, although the foot soldier could keep up with the retreating hostiles, he could not easily maneuver the enemy into position for battle, without cavalry to herd them.[32] But Miles was not hidebound. He also made good use of cavalry and put his infantry on mounts, whenever possible.[33]

Throughout the winter Miles pursued Sitting Bull, Crazy Horse and the other tribes with his infantry ("heep walk men") and some companies of the 7th Cavalry. He destroyed their provisions, captured their horses, frightened their game and occasionally engaged them in skirmishes. The tribes held a

De Rudio's Adventure

loosing hand. The buffalo was scarce, and ammunition was in desperately short supply; but most ruinous of all, was the warriors' inability to rest up through the lean months of winter. Miles, following Crook's example, had an extensive system of Lakota spies, which kept him informed of the hostile movements. In January, Miles routed Crazy Horse at Wolf Mountain and in May, he defeated Lame Deer's Miniconjou.

One by one, the tribes surrendered. The reservation warriors returned to their agencies for their alotments and three thousand free-roamers and their families turned themselves in at reservations selected by Washington.[34] Sitting Bull and Chief Gall fled with the Unkpapa to Canada. By July 17, 1877 Sherman could say that he "regarded the Sioux Indian problem, as a war question, as solved,"[35] and by September 1877, the very last hostile had laid down his arms. Construction had been completed at Ft. Keogh and Ft. Custer. It had been an expensive war. Someone has calculated that it had cost $1,000,000 for each warrior killed and $2,000,000 to maintain a regiment for a year.[36]

Soon the worst fears of the Cheyenne and Sioux were realized. Unaware that the Northern Cheyenne could not thrive in the same climate as their southern brethren, the government plucked a thousand Northern Cheyenne from their accustomed lands and sent them in August 1877 to the Indian Territory and north Texas. There they proceeded to starve and die of disease.

Crazy Horse chose to surrender his eight hundred Oglala warriors to Crook, rather than to Miles, relying on Crook's honorable reputation and believing he would get better terms. He ended up in Camp Robinson in the Red Cloud Agency, where he grew dissatisfied with the promises made to him. For one thing, he had been promised a separate reservation for his people. Hundreds of families were camped within three miles of Camp Robinson, without sanitary facilities.[37] He felt no joy in a life where canvas tents replaced the skin tepee and where warriors and women wore *Washichu* clothing. Worst of all, ponies and guns were taken away. When the Nez Perce war broke out,

Crazy Horse was suspected of discouraging his warriors from enlisting in the army as government scouts. Part of the misunderstanding may have come from the faulty translations of Fred Girard. Girard was a wheeler-dealer, and what he was up to is anyone's guess. Crazy Horse was arrested in the first summer of his captivity and in the scuffle, sustained a knife or bayonet wound, which caused an agonizing death. Sadly, his burial place is unknown, but an astonishing monument is being raised to his memory.

Sitting Bull, Gall and the Unkpapas fled into Canada, "the old woman's (Queen Victoria) country," where Sitting Bull remained for five years, while his specter loomed over the northern plains. In Canada, the buffalo was scarce, and his people starved. The Unkpapa received no allotments from the Canadian Government and were pointedly encouraged to return to the United States. In July 19, 1881 Sitting Bull re-crossed the "British Line" and surrendered. He and his followers were sent by chartered steamboat down the Missouri, ending up at Ft. Randall. There, he was held as a prisoner of war for two years, before being sent in 1883 to Standing Rock Agency on the Missouri in Dakota Territory.

Notes

1. Interview of Charles De Rudio. Kenneth Hammer, ed., *Custer in 76* (Norman and London: University of Oklahoma, 1988), pp. 82-88; Interview of Thomas F. O'Neill, Hammer, pp. 106-110; "A Thrilling Escape – De Rudio and O'Neill," Chapter 5. E. A. Brininstool, *Troopers with Custer* (Lincoln and London: University of Nebraska, 1952), pp. 131-151; "A Thrilling Tale," *New York Herald*, 30 July 1876; George Herendeen's interview, *New York Times,* 8 July 1878; Interview of George Herendeen. Hammer, p. 219; "An Incident in the Little Bighorn Fight," *Harper's Weekly,* September 25, 1897; "De Rudio's Thrilling Escape," *Hunter, Trader-Trapper,* February 21, 1933.
2. Hammer, p. 85.
3. Interview of Henry Petring. Hammer, p. 133.
4. *Ibid.,* p. 85; Evans S. Connell, *Son of the Morning Star* (New York: Harper Perennial, 1984), p. 24.
5. Interview of Frederick F. Girard. Hammer, p. 233.
6. William O. Taylor, *With Custer on the Little Bighorn* (New York: Viking, 1996), p. 185.
7. Connell, p. 24.
8. Testimony of Lt. C. De Rudio. Graham, *Reno,* p. 111.
9. "A Thrilling Escape – De Rudio and O'Neill," Chapter 5. Brininstool, p. 145.
10. "Pvt. George Berry's Experiences," Chapter 18. Brininstool, p. 302.
11. "A Thrilling Escape – De Rudio and O'Neill," Chapter 5. Brininstool, p. 148.
12. "With Col. Charles A. Varnum," Chapter 4. Brininstool, p. 151.
13. Letter from F. Benteen to Mrs. Benteen, July 4, 1876. John M. Carroll, *Camp Talk* (Mattituck, NY: J. M. Carroll, 1983) p. 24.
14. Letter from F. Benteen to Mrs. Benteen, July 1, 1876, John M. Carroll, *The Benteen-Goldin Letters on Custer and his last Battle* (New York: Liveright, 1974), p. 156.
15. Carroll, *Camp Talk,* p. 44.
16. Edward S. Luce, *Keogh, Comanche and Custer* (Private Edition, 1939), p. 16.
17. "Pvt. George Berry's Experiences," Chapter 18. Brininstool, p. 302.
18. John S. Gray, *Centennial Campaign* (Ft. Collins, CO: Old Army Press, 1976), p. 274.
19. Wayne Mitchell Sarf, *The Little Bighorn Campaign* (Pennsylvania: Combined Books, 2000), p. 120.
20. *Ibid.,* p. 263.
21. Patricia Y. Stellard, *Glittering Misery; Dependents of the Indian Fighting Army* (Ft Collins, CO: Presidio Press, Old Army Press, 1978), p. 41.
22. Daniel Magnussen, *Peter Thompson's Narrative of the Little Bighorn Campaign of 1876* (Glendale, CA: Clark, 1974), p. 294; Katherine

Gibson Fougera, *With Custer's Cavalry* (Lincoln and London: University of Nebraska, 1986), p. 264.
23. Robert M. Utley, *Cavalier in Buckskin* (Norman and London: University of Oklahoma, 1988), p. 6.
24. Robert M. Utley, *Frontier Regulars. The United States Army and the Indian, 1866-1890* (New York: Macmillan, 1973), p. 176; John M. Carroll, ed., *I. Varnum* (Glendale, CA: Arthur H. Clark Co., 1892), p. 77.
25. Letter from F. Benteen to Mrs. Benteen, July 10, 1876. Carroll, *Camp Talk*, (Mattituck, NY: J. M. Carroll, 1983), p. 31.
26. *Ibid.*, p. 69.
27. Ronald H. Nichols, *In Custer's Shadow: Major Marcus Reno* (Norman: University of Oklahoma, 1999), p. 227.
28. Brininstool, p. 104.
29. John S. Gray, *Custer's Last Campaign* (Lincoln and London: University of Nebraska Press, 1991), p. 217.
30. Charles M. Robinson III, *A Good Year to Die. The Story of the Great Sioux War* (New York: Random House, 1955), pp. 290, 300.
31. Utley, *Frontier*, p. 59.
32. Robinson, *Good Year*, p. 278.
33. Utley, *Frontier*, p. 298.
34. *Ibid.*, p. 287.
35. Nelson A. Miles, *Personal Recollections and Observations of General Nelson A. Miles* (Lincoln and London: University of Nebraska, 1992), I:255.
36. Ralph K. Andrist, *The Long Death* (New York: Macmillan, 1964), p. 295.
37. James Welch and Paul Stekler, *Killing Custer* (New York: Norton, 1994), p. 245.

XIII
SOLDIERING

Following the junction with General Crook in August, Benteen persuaded General Terry, over Col. Miles' objections, to allow a battalion of 7th Cavalry to return to Bismarck as an escort for party of captured Northern Cheyenne. Benteen further arranged to have all the married officers sent with them. Along the way, the officers held a birthday party for Captain Benteen and Lt. Rudy. De Rudio was celebrating his forty-fourth birthday, Benteen his forty-second. After first completing a scouting assignment along the northern bank of the Yellowstone, they arrived in Lincoln on September 26, where they were met by the tears of the widows and the joyous greetings of their own wives and children.

It was a bitter, back biting group of officers who gathered nightly in the trader's hut. Reno was acting post commandant, in the absence of Colonel Sturgis, who had remained behind with Colonel Miles. Reno had begun to drink furiously, without a wife to restrain him. The trader recorded his purchase of large quantities of spirits. Soon after his return to Lincoln, Reno became embroiled in a heated argument with a young lieutenant, and they ended up struggling on the floor. When they had sobered up, the fight seemed to have been forgotten. De Rudio was one of the officers who had witnessed the encounter. With his family at Ft. Rice, he probably spent more time in the trader's hut, than had been his custom.

The regiment tried to repair itself, but lacking many officers and non-coms, the task was difficult. In October, the available troops in Ft. Lincoln were ordered to the Standing Rock Agency, sixty miles to the south, to confiscate firearms and horses. De Rudio was in command of A Company. Many Lakota families had by then returned to the Agency to draw rations for the winter.

The lodges were thoroughly searched, and muskets, sabers, revolvers and breech loading rifles were confiscated. Given the opportunity, the warriors would surrender obsolete weapons and conceal their best firearms under the skirts of the women. Rarely was a metallic cartridge handed over.[1] Nor were the ponies gracefully surrendered. It had been necessary to fire the Rodman and the Gatling guns to forestall trouble. With the confiscation of the ponies and weapons, the warrior's emasculation was virtually complete.

The detachment returned to Lincoln on November 3, 1876, driving a herd of warrior ponies six abreast, towed by lariat. Of the three thousand ponies confiscated at Standing Rock, only nine hundred arrived, the rest succumbing to the bitter cold and the soldiers' inexperience. The battery was the first to cross by ferry, but during the night the river began to freeze. By daybreak, the ice was too thin to support the weight of the cavalry, and too thick for the ferry to penetrate. The impatient battalion had to wait a week before the ice froze sufficiently to bear the weight of the horses.

The winter of 1876-77 was especially dreary and uncomfortable at Ft. Rice. Because of the severe cold, drills could not be conducted outdoors. The entire supply of forage and hay had to be moved into the stables, which were in shambles. Wood was in short supply, since the regular wood-cutter, Isaiah Dorman, a black frontiersman and scout, had accompanied the 7th and had been killed during Reno's first battle. The men had to travel for miles upriver just to find cottonwood, and even that was full of sap and difficult to burn.

Desertions and infractions of discipline were rampant at Ft.

Rice. Ten percent of the soldiers were in the guardhouse for offences committed while drunk. Garrison punishments might include bread and water, solitary confinement, whipping, iron collar and spikes, forced march with a knapsack of bricks or suspension by the wrists.[2] "Bobtail discharges" were common, so-named because the character clause was clipped from the discharge certificate, giving the paper a bobtail appearance.[3] This would correspond to today's dishonorable discharge. A deserter usually received a sentence of five years of prison, with another two years added for the theft of a horse. Those convicted of serious offences were sent to Ft. Leavenworth. Payday at Ft. Rice brought little relief from boredom, but at Lincoln, three hundred soldiers would descend on Bismarck, in search of mischief.[4]

In December 1876, upon Colonel Sturgis' return, Major Reno was sent to Ft. Abercrombie,[5] a small fort on the Red River, thirty miles south of Fargo and two hundred twenty rail miles from Bismarck. This might have been an attempt to get him away from Lincoln, perhaps for his drinking habits. At Ft. Abercrombie Reno had a confrontation with a vixen of an officer's wife and was accused of affronting her. Her husband was compelled, somewhat reluctantly, to demand that Reno be court-martialed. Reno was found guilty of conduct unbecoming an officer. His final sentence was suspension without pay for two years. Other charges involving the previous drunken brawl in Lincoln were also prepared, but the matter was dropped, at the insistence of General Terry. Among the witnesses to the charges in Lincoln were De Rudio and Moylan. "Rudy," as De Rudio was now called, was beginning to be noticed.

De Rudio left on furlough to Yankton from February 18-23, 1877, where he was joined by his wife and family. Once again, the publicity from the Brisbin article pursued him. From Eliza, he learned that one of the eastern newspapers had identified him as an Orsini conspirator, who had been released from French Guyana, in return for giving evidence against the others. The article had been reprinted on August 18 in the widely-read Red

River *Star* (Moorhead, Minnesota)[6] and had become a popular subject of conversation. De Rudio had never made any effort to conceal his part in the assassination attempt, nor of his escape from Ile Royal. On the contrary, he frequently related the details to his fellow officers. He was proud to be thought an Italian patriot and by now De Rudio had learned to live with the wildly inaccurate reports.

When he returned from furlough, De Rudio was given a disagreeable collateral duty in Lincoln, of inventorying the private property of the dead soldiers and of forwarding the possessions, wherever possible, to the heirs. Among the effects was a footlocker belonging to a John S. Hiley, of E Company. Hiley was discovered to be a Scottish baron, who had left for the United States because of gambling debts. De Rudio wrote to his mother and arranged for the trans-shipment of her son's belongings through the English ambassador in Washington. Those effects including a faro bank that could not be dispersed were auctioned off, and the handsome sum of $5,500 was raised for the regimental fund.[7]

Throughout the winter, A Company remained at Ft. Rice, performing regular garrison duties, while time and events passed them by. From newspapers, magazines and reports brought back by returning officers, tidings from the outside world filtered through. William W. Belknap, Secretary of War, was being impeached for receiving bribes. Womens' skirts were shorter. Thomas A. Edison invented the mimeograph. New York was marveling at the *can-can*, brought over by Jacques Offenbach from Paris. A train had completed the journey from New York to San Francisco in three and a half days. The National League of professional baseball players was founded. Girls were cascading their hair over their foreheads. A voluptuous dance was reported from the Sandwich Islands called the *Hula Hula*. The Emperor of Brazil was visiting the United States.[8]

But at the frontier fort, the routine seldom varied:

At first light *Mess Call,* then *Assembly*
7:30 *Mess*
8 *Fatigue Call*
9 *First Call for Guard mounting,* then *Assembly of Guard Details* and *Trumpeters;* guard inspected
10 *Water and Stable Calls*
12 *Recall & First Sergeant's Call*
12:30 *Mess Call*
1 pm *Fatigue Call*
2:30 *Drill Call;* Dismounted and mounted drill
4 *Recall*
4:30 *Water and Stable Call*
6 *Mess Call*
Sunset: *First Call, Assembly Retreat;* Evening gun fired
8:30 *First Call Tattoo, Assembly*
9 *Taps;* Quiet, "except for the click of billiard balls in the officers' club"[9]

Winter brought no respite from the drudgery of shoeing, grooming, saddle-bridle-halter repair, construction, stable fatigue and endless inspections. Suddenly, spring grass pushed up through the snow, and the regiment prepared to take to the field. Back to the Powder River country!

The first day out of Ft. Rice, the Benteen battalion, including A Company, marched an easy eighteen miles before setting up camp. In late afternoon, while De Rudio and the other officers were resting comfortably on folding cots in their Sibley tents, *Fire call!* sounded. Flames swept the plains engulfing the camp. Pup tents were unbuttoned and the sections used to smother the flames. A few of the tents were damaged and later had to be replaced.[10]

The battalion reached Ft. Lincoln and settled in on the campground two miles from the fort. Command of the 7th

Cavalry had reverted to Colonel Samuel D. Sturgis. On May 1, a departure parade was held in Bismarck, in honor of the former regimental commander. It took five exhausting hours to ferry the regiment and the wives across the Missouri. To the tune of the now popular *Custer's Last Charge*, the regiment marched in columns of four's down the main street. Then it was back across the Missouri and off to the field. The regiment took with it a new kind of armored stage wagon, mounting a two pound Mountain Howitzer on top and housing twelve riflemen inside, each armed with a Winchester repeater. The wagon was called a Black Hill Stage and may have reminded De Rudio of the armored carriage of Napoleon III.[11]

The next day De Rudio was given temporary command of E Company. The march started out as a romp for the regiment's five hundred young recruits, but they soon grew weary. When it rained, they had no change of clothing and could only roll up the wet garment and placed it in their saddle blanket, where it absorbed the horse's sweat and odor. The regiment passed Ft. Stevenson, but lingered only long enough for the officers to get a drink. They passed the Berthal Indian Agency, where the soldiers could buy milk and potatoes; and whiskey, for a dollar a half-pint. On Sundays, the soldiers fished for catfish and suckers, using bacon fat for bait. Hoards of mosquitoes descended on them when they came to the mouth of the Yellowstone, where it enters the Missouri. Here the *Far West* waited with supplies, brought upriver from Lincoln. Eggs sold for fifty cents a dozen.[12] The ingenious troopers found a way to fry the eggs, using trench spades as frying pans. Since wood was scarce, they made use of buffalo chips, whenever available.

With the temperature hovering in the 90's, men fainted from sunstroke. Then, abruptly, a light dusting of snow fell, and the men shivered. Sickle-billed curlew and paired grass plover covered the prairies.[13] Further on the march, hoards of grasshoppers descended on the column, blotting out the sun like an eclipse and chewing holes in the tents, blankets and overcoats. At long last, the regiment reached Sunday Creek, three and a half miles from Ft. Keogh, the Tongue River Cantonment, arriving there on June 22, seven weary weeks out of Lincoln. The first task was to rid the camp of rattlesnakes. A few adventurous troopers had learned to eat them, which they found to be sweeter than eel. Always, the dismounted soldier guarded against hostile attacks. He unbitted his horse, so it could graze, but kept it saddled, as a precaution.[14]

Nearby Sunday Creek was Miles City, with its glut of tents, log houses and rough board huts, which doubled as saloons, gambling halls and brothels. Since the paymaster's visit had been delayed, the soldiers could not fully yield to temptation. Items of necessity could still be bought from the trader, who received payment on payday. Soldiers complained that the trader charged them more than the officers. In July, E Company escorted Colonel Miles to Glendive station on the lower Missouri. Although a pleasant diversion for the men, it was a hardship for the horses, some of which responded poorly to the spur and had to be led.[15]

The regiment was next ordered to take up permanent station at Cedar Creek, sixty miles to the east, far removed from the temptations of Miles City. Along the way it endured a hailstorm, which terrified the horses and exhausted the men. In the same storm, five hundred Crow ponies stampeded over a cliff into the Yellowstone, and a thousand glass panes were destroyed at Ft. Lincoln.[16]

The weary 7th arrived at Cedar Creek and set up camp. In all, they had marched 1,732 miles,[17] more than halfway across the United States. The men built sunshades over their tents and relaxed, but kept a sharp lookout for hostile attack. During their leisure hours, the soldiers were allowed to hunt. In those days, dense buffalo herds still roamed the region.[18]

Little did the 7th Cavalry realize that they were about to be embroiled in another war, not with their familiar enemies, but with a tribe few had heard of.

Notes

1. Hugh Lenox Scott, *Some Memories of a Soldier* (New York: Century, 1928), p. 37.
2. Ronald H. Nichols, *In Custer's Shadow: Major Marcus Reno* (Norman: University of Oklahoma, 1999), p. 233.
3. John Upton Terrell, and George Walton, *Faint the Trumpet Sounds* (New York: McKay, 1966), p. 204
4. Nichols, p. 241.
5. Ani Frank Mulford, *Fighting Indians in the 7th Cavalry* 2nd ed. (Fairfield, WA: Ye Galleon Press, 1972), p. 39.
6. Cesare Marino, *Dal Piave al Little Bighorn* (Belluno: Tarantola, 1996), p. 258.
7. Kenneth Hammer, ed., *Custer in 76* (Norman and London: University of Oklahoma, 1988), p. 87.
8. Dee Brown, *The Year of the Century 18 76* (New York: Scribner, 1966).
9. Mulford, p. 46.
10. *Ibid.*, p. 62.
11. *Ibid.*, pp. 65, 68.
12. *Ibid.*, pp. 71-76.
13. Scott, *Memories*, p. 46.
14. Mulford, p. 110.
15. *Ibid.*, pp. 97, 111.
16. Scott, *Memories*, p. 50.
17. Edward L. Daily, *Custer to MacArthur* (Paducah, KY: Turner, 1995), p. 72.
18. Scott, *Memories*, pp. 51, 52.

XIV
NEZ PERCE

The Nez Perce, whose name was derived from an earlier practice of inserting ornaments through their pierced noses, are remembered for their benevolent assistance to Lewis and Clark. They dwelt in Idaho, Oregon and Washington in a rather advanced aboriginal culture. Some lived on the reservation in well-built houses, others on non-treaty lands, including the Wallowa Valley. They had missionary schools and were comfortable and prosperous.[1] The Nez Perce were especially noted for horse breeding. Their horse was the Appaloosa, a hardy mount usually reconginzed by it's distinctive multi-colored spotted coat. The tribe practiced selective breeding and was famous for its fine stock and horsemanship.

Since the buffalo did not range west of the Rockies, parties of Nez Perce hunters were accustomed to cross the Continental Divide and spend spring and summer hunting the buffalo with the Crow people, to whom they had become closely allied by marriage and trade.

After the Civil War, prospectors and ranchers invaded the non-treaty country of the Nez Perce and a familiar story was repeated. The terms of their treaty of 1863 was unilaterally abrogated.

General Otis O. Howard, newly arrived to the Oregon Territory in September 1874, commanded the military Department of Columbia. He had previously served in the southwest, where, after a brilliant effort, he had concluded a peace agreement with the Chiricahua chief, Cochise, at Dragon Springs on October 12, 1872, apparently accomplishing in a few days, what his predecessors had not been able to do in twelve years.[2] It remained for Crook to end the campaign at Tonto Basin some months later.

Under pressure from the settlers and the War Department, Howard issued an ultimatum in May 1877, ordering the Nez Perce to abandon their non-treaty lands and report within thirty days to the Lapwai Reservation across the Snake River in Idaho.

The young warriors rebelled and killed several farmers, some of whom had been abusive to the Nez Perce. With great reluctance, the chiefs were compelled to support the warriors; among them the six foot two inch tall and powerfully built Chief Joseph. Until then, Chief Joseph had never fired a weapon at another human being.[3] Fighting broke out and the government lost no time in preparing repressive measures. Perceiving that his people were about to receive savage punishment, Joseph and the other chiefs in the non-treaty lands decided to move their people away from the region. Thus began an epic odyssey of almost seventeen hundred miles, which concluded thirty-five miles from the Canadian border.

June 22, 1877 Howard's column of four hundred men took to the field in pursuit of the hostiles. The Nez Perce, numbering about two hundred fifty warriors and four hundred fifty women and children, fled into the Rocky Mountains. Howard encountered the Nez Perce at Clearwater River on July 11, 1877. The tribe defended their camp from cavalry attack and Howitzer and Gatling gunfire, by constructing breastworks of timber and earth. Through a rear-guard action, they succeeded in escaping. The chiefs then led their tribe over the Lolo Trail into Montana, known to them from their annual hunting parties. By now, Howard's mounts were exhausted and barely able to move sixteen miles a day. Unlike the warrior who had five or more ponies to share the burden of the forced march, the soldier had only one horse, which was entirely dependant on the rapidly depleting supply of grain feed. Sheridan was outraged at the escape and ordered Howard to continue the pursuit. The Nez Perce paced Howard, stopping when he stopped, speeding ahead when he rushed along. Rarely did the army lag more than two to three days behind.[4]

Once over the Divide, the Nez Perce were in the Department of the Dakotas. General Terry was alerted and sent Colonel Gibbon to meet them. On August 9, Gibbon's hastily organized party surprised the Nez Perce at Big Hole on the western edge of Montana. He was able to bring his Mountain Howitzer into action, but the Nez Perce repulsed the attack, inflicting thirty dead and forty wounded and forcing Gibbon to ignominiously request help from the governor. Gibbon remained pinned down until relieved by Howard's troops. Once again, the Nez Perce had managed to slip away.

The Nez Perce pushed on, pursued by Howard and his weary column. In a brilliant ploy at Camas Meadows, the Nez Perce entered Howard's camp at night in columns of four's, disguised as Shoshoni scouts, and made off with Howard's mules.

They continued east toward the Yellowstone National Park, opened for tourism only five years before. General William Sherman, who had been vacationing in the park,[5] had left a few days previously, but several other tourists were captured, and some were wounded by the young braves, to Chief Joseph's dismay.

Yellowstone National Park in the upper western corner of Wyoming was a box with several openings. To the North, lay the Washburn Range, through which the Yellowstone River flows. Beyond the northern boundary lay Ft. Ellis, on the outskirts of the Crow Reservation, extending from the Musselshell River to Judith's Basin. To the east, the park is bordered by the Absaroka Range, through which flow the Clark's Fork and the Stinking Water (Shoshone) Rivers, each with steep, narrow canyons. South of the park is the Teton-Wind River Range, where the forces of Colonel Merrill were positioned.

The Nez Perce entered the Yellowstone National Park on August 22 through the west entrance, pursued by General

Howard. Their general object was to enlist the aid of their close allies, the Crows. Failing that, they would try to move to Canada to join Sitting Bull and the Unkpapa.

These were good times for the Crow. Their enemy, the Lakota Sioux, was no longer of concern. The Crow had three hundred fifty-four lodges and a herd of ten thousand horses.[6] They lived in fine dwellings, covered by buffalo hides so well smoked that the sun could not penetrate, but light enough to discourage the flies. Buffalo were still plentiful on the northern plains, and the Crow did their best to insure their survival. They conducted buffalo runs only at specified times and killed only limited numbers, which left the herds undisturbed.[7]

A young lieutenant of the 2nd Cavalry named Gustavus C. Doane was stationed at Ft. Ellis, near the Crow Reservation. Instead of immersing himself in wontonness and drink, so common among the frontier officers, he had spent his time in exploration, studying the flora and fauna and learning the Crow language and customs.[8] Doane had been in the original Yellowstone Expedition in 1870, whose work led to the establishment by Congress of the Yellowstone National Park. He was well liked by the Crows, even though he had banned spirits from the reservation. More than a good officer, he was a thorough plainsman.

Lt. Gustavus C. Doane was not a West Point graduate. He rose from the ranks during the Civil War and had been commissioned in the regular army in 1868. Assigned to the 2nd Cavalry, he remained with them throughout his military career.[9] On July 14, 1877 he had recruited four hundred Crow allies for scouting, and issued them three months rations and one hundred rounds of ammunition per man. This was done in response to the rumor that Sitting Bull was planning to reenter the United States.

Doane happened to be at Cedar Creek near the Tongue River Cantonment, when word was received of the approach of the Nez Perce. Miles immediately alerted Colonel Sturgis and Lt. Doane. Doane was ordered to return to the Crow reservation,[10] recruit Crow scouts[11] and proceed to the Musselshell River-

Judith Basin area, to watch for the Nez Perce. This was Crow hunting ground. Lt. Doane let it be known that he needed a company of cavalry to go with him.[12] The call went out, and Lt. Charles De Rudio offered the services of E Company, since the mission was supposed to be uncomplicated and would relieve his company from fatiguing and monotonous patrols. Interestingly, Colonel Miles ordered that if sufficient carbine cartridges were not available, rifle cartridges would be issued to Doane.[13] This reflected the urgency of the situation, since firing rifle ammunition in a carbine resulted in horrid recoil and could only be justified by an emergency.

Orders were cut on August 2: "1st Lieut. C.C. De Rudio, 7th Cavalry, will report for duty with his Co "E" to Lieut. G.C. Doane, 2nd Cavalry, by command of Colonel N.A. Miles." De Rudio met Doane and appraised him of their orders "to burn grass to drive the game further westward," in order to deny food and fodder to the Nez Perce.[14]

Benteen, with his customary sarcasm, thought that Doane "will manage affairs as well as they can be. De R would blox everything."[15] Like most old hands, Benteen had serious reservations about volunteering for anything. He also remarked, "if Lt. Doane wants to avoid Rudio killing him with his usual stories, make sure he stops up his ears." Years later, when in his waspish mood, Benteen wrote that when De Rudio found out he might have to stay out in the field for several months, De Rudio no longer wanted the assignment, but by then it was too late to back out.[16]

This banter was typical for Benteen. Irascible and critical as he was in his private letters, he never failed to help, when De Rudio needed assistance.

Col. Sturgis received his orders on August 11, after the defeat of Colonel Gibbon at Big Hole. He was instructed to proceed with six companies to "intercept or pursue and capture or destroy" the Nez Perce from the north and to rely on the advice of Lt Doane. Miles further added: "Please communicate with him [Doane] and spare no pains or effort to so employ the entire force."[17] Colonel Sturgis might have been miffed at being ordered to confer with a lieutenant, but Colonel Miles had a shrewd appreciation of Doane's qualifications.

Doane, De Rudio and E Company left in forced march for the Musselshell River and Judith Basin, in accordance with orders from Colonel Miles.[18] This was a distance of one hundred miles in straight line and double that by march route. They brought with them supplies for the miners of Virginia City, which somewhat impeded rapid progress. Along the way, they acquired a recent West Point graduate, 2nd Lieut. Hugh L. Scott, who managed to get himself attached to De Rudio's command by offering Doane a bottle of walnut pickles and a tin pail.[19] In his memoirs of later years, Scott had little to say of De Rudio, but is lavish in the description of his own activities.

At first, the Crow were reluctant to join Doane's party, since they were allies of the Nez Perce, but eventually forty-two braves agreed to sign on to the Nez Perce campaign.[20] A messenger brought word that the Nez Perce were heading in their direction, and Lt. Doane did his best to dissuade the Crow from giving aid. He made the chiefs agree to take the Crow warriors -- other than those whose services he required -- back to the reservation, to keep them out of trouble.

A terrible hailstorm arose, pummeling the company with baseball-sized hailstones. Worn out by the rapid march, Doane thought it best to revittel and reshoe at Ft. Ellis, at the same time enabling him to deliver the miners' supplies. Meanwhile, the Musselshell-Judith Basin order was superseded.

Doane was certain that Chief Joseph's route would take him either to the Yellowstone exit or to the Clark's Fork or Stinking Water River exits. But the Yellowstone escape could be easily blocked off by a small party of soldiers stationed on the bluffs of the lower canyon. So the probabilities were that the Nez Perce would choose either the Clark's Fork or Stinking Water River exit, especially if they wanted to contact their Crow cousins or Sitting Bull in Canada. On balance, Doane suspected the Clark Fork exit.[21]

On August 25 Sturgis directed Doane to "occupy a position at, or in the vicinity of, the lower canon (of the Yellowstone River), so as to hold the enemy in check should he come that way."[22] Doane and E Company departed Ft. Ellis the day that the Nez Perce entered the Yellowstone National Park. Doane marched the company south to the Yellowstone River. On August 29 Sturgis wrote Doane: "all my information points to probability that the hostile Indians will emerge from the mountains by way of Clark's Fork or vicinity." He ordered Doane to join him the moment he was no longer needed to guard the Yellowstone Route,[23] as if one company would make a vital difference in the forthcoming battle. On the same day Sturgis again wrote Doane:

".. in the meantime I desire that you remain with your cavalry, and such Crows as may not be required for scouting, at the *lower canon of the Yellowstone*...Should the Indians come own the Yellowstone, I can then, on timely information from you, concentrate at that point; but should they take the Clark's Fork route, then you would be in position to join me.."[24]

Doane, De Rudio and the detachment consisted of E Company, forty-two scouts, and thirty civilian volunteers, many of them miners. They reached the junction of Gardiner River and the Yellowstone on at the north entrance of the Park on September 1. The orders were to remain in the lower canyon of the Yellowstone and report the movement of the Nez Perce, should they head toward the Absaroka Mountains, and to block their escape, if they tried to leave by the Yellowstone Canyon. Doane set fire to the grass to impede the northward escape.[25] Sturgis repeated his tiresome request that Doane join him, if his presence were no longer required.[26] To meet up with Sturgis, Doane would have had to move through one of the two canyons, whichever route the main body of Nez Perce did not take, and then try to locate Sturgis' command before the anticipated battle.

On station in the lower canyon, Doane and De Rudio were in excellent position to observe the direction of the Nez Perce movements.

By September 8, the Nez Perce were boxed in within the Park.[27] The chiefs must have taken stock of their options. They could go north through the lower Yellowstone canyon where Doane and De Rudio were in wait. In such a circumstance, a single company could easily block their passage through the canyon. Moreover, the grass had been set afire, so that their ponies would have little to eat. Or, they could move through the Clark's Ford or the Stinking Water River canyons. Sturgis was waiting somewhere near the exits.

The Nez Perce chose the longer Clark's Fork trail. They did not know that they had a further advantage. E Company, which was in position to report hostile movements to Colonel Sturgis, had been recalled from the lower Yellowstone canyon by an ill-advised senior officer.[28]

It came about this way. Impatient with the failure of General Howard, General Sherman wanted him replaced with Lt. Col C.C. Gilbert of the 7th Infantry. Lt. Colonel Gilbert appeared at Ft. Ellis and unaware of the importance of Doane's station, ordered him to abandon his position and report to General Howard's command,[29] where Gilbert, himself, was planning to go to relieve Howard. Gilbert's appointment was later rescinded. Although Gilbert is usually blamed for Doane's removal from his strategic position, Colonel Sturgis was also at fault. Sturgis had received a bizarre report that the Nez Perce had moved south to the Wind River or Snake River.[30] On the basis of this report, Colonel Sturgis on September 2 formally ended De Rudio's assignment[31] and ordered E Company to join his command. He suggested that Doane do the same.[32]

In vain, Doane pleaded with tears in his eyes[33] to remain in the lower canyon, while the Nez Perce were skirting the northern part of Yellowstone Lake and heading east. His plea fell on deaf ears. Reluctantly, Doane and De Rudio returned to Ft. Ellis, and so E Company lost its chance to boast that it had participated in the defeat of the valiant and resourceful Nez Perce.

Benteen in his sardonic fashion wrote "if the tribe (Crows) had decided to unite with the Nez Perce, I am certain De Rudio would end with a great fright and would have left his scalp, if it were not for the fact that Lt. Doane is in charge and succeeded in controlling the situation as best he was able."[34]

It fell to Colonel Sturgis to suffer the consequences of Gilbert's imprudent order. Sturgis had moved from the Musselshell to intercept the Nez Perce.[35] Of the two exits to the Yellowstone Park, Sturgis chose the more likely Clark's Fork, with its incredibly steep walls -- the old Lewis and Clark exploration trail.[36] Chief Joseph was quick to discern what lay in store for his people. He had the warriors fasten sagebrush to their lariats and sent them riding furiously along the Stinking Water River Canyon, raising a great dust cloud. The three army scouts who might have seen through the deception fell into the hands of the Nez Perce and were killed. The information Sturgis received was that Joseph was moving his party along the Stinking Water River. Believing that he was pursuing the main band, Sturgis moved his troops to the Stinking Water River in a futile forty mile pursuit.[37] This allowed the Nez Perce to pass undetected through Clark's Ford Canyon. They emerged from the Absaroka Mountains on September 9. Had Doane been able to keep him informed, Sturgis might not have fallen victim to this ruse. Then again, Doane's messengers might never have reached Colonel Sturgis, since their movement would have been blocked by the main body of the Nez Perce in Clark's Ford Canyon or their scouts in Stinking Water Canyon, both canyons being steep, narrow and easily obstructed. But all this is speculative, since messengers have great ingenuity. At any rate, Chief Joseph and his people escaped the ambush and had gained fifty miles on their pursuers.[38]

For Colonel Sturgis, this escape was an unmitigated disaster. His reputation lay in shreds. The ever-resourceful Benteen showed him a way to recoup. He advised Sturgis to pursue the Nez Perce with forced marches: "40 miles today; 50 miles tomorrow if necessary!"[39] By now, Sturgis and his weary and hungry troopers were exhausted and already living on mule meat,[40] but Sturgis did exactly what Benteen suggested. He began a forced march without food supplies, butchering captured ponies for meat. The Nez Perce were overtaken on September 13 at Canyon Creek, Montana, ten miles north of the Yellowstone River, near present day Billings. In the erroneous belief that the Nez Perce were anxious to engage his three hundred fifty soldiers, Sturgis dismounted and attacked. The warriors quickly occupied the high ground, which the troopers could not clear, and by firing down on the soldiers, succeeded after furious fighting, in disengaging and withdrawing. Captain Benteen's charges were especially valiant, for which he was belatedly breveted. Captain Thomas French, later a foe of De Rudio, also distinguished himself. The Crow scouts managed to seize nine hundred ponies, but some were later recaptured by the Nez Perce braves. The weary soldiers kept up a running battle with the retreating warriors, but exhaustion soon forced Sturgis to abandon the chase.

But there is another twist to the Doane-De Rudio story. Doane, De Rudio and E Company crossed the Yellowstone and were en route to Ft. Ellis, when they encountered Chief Joseph's scouts. According to Scott, the Nez Perce mistook the party for an advanced force and made a detour to the west. It was this detour that delayed the Nez Perce and, as will be seen shortly, permitted Miles to overtake them.[41] Some might dismiss this conjecture as fanciful, since, had the Nez Perce continued east, they might have run into Colonel Miles sooner.[42]

Colonel Miles had been confined to the Tongue River Cantonment because of a report that Sitting Bull had left Canada and was traveling south to the Musselshell River to come to the aid of the Nez Perce. Col. Sturgis was doubtful of this,[43] and in fact, the report proved to be false. Upon learning of Sturgis' defeat, Miles gathered three companies of 7th Cavalry and mounted his 5th Infantry on captured Indian ponies.[44] This must have been a challenge, since these spirited mounts were not

Nez Perce

accustomed to the white man and paniced at the scent. Moreover, they are mounted on the right side.[45]

The column raced to intercept the Nez Perce before they could cross into Canada. Their march led over foothills and grassy plains, so that progress was rapid.

The army surprised the Nez Perce at Bear Paw Mountain September 30, 1877, thirty-five miles from the Canadian border. The warriors quickly occupied the crests of the twenty foot bluffs and carefully picked off the officers and the NCO's wearing chevrons. Companies repeatedly charged into the camp, sustaining enormous losses. The 7th Cavalry alone had fifty-three casualties in a force of one hundred fifteen officers and enlisted.[46] Only one officer escaped death or injury! Two of the dead officers were Little Bighorn veterans.

The battle continued for five days. The warriors dug ingenious rifle pits, which were almost unassailable. The Nez Perce bravely fought on, until it became clear that Sitting Bull was not coming to their rescue. Having lost their pony herds, upon which their very existence depended, Chief Joseph was compelled to surrender his one hundred warriors. As he approached the victors, they saw his clothes had been pierced by more than a dozen bullet holes.[47] Some ninty-two warriors under Chief Looking Glass succeeded in escaping to Canada with their families.

General Howard and his column arrived toward the close of the battle. As an illustration of Howard's generous character and in deference to the nephew of the Commanding General, he allowed Miles to accept the surrender in order to improve his chances of obtaining a brigadier's star. But today, the fame of the generals is largely eclipsed by the thrilling saga of Chief Joseph and his seventeen hundred mile fighting exodus.

Notes

1. Don Rickey, *Forty Miles a Day on Beans and Hay* (Norman and London: University of Oklahoma, 1963), p. 226.
2. John A. Carpenter, *Sword and Olive Branch* (Pittsburgh: University of Pittsburgh, 1964), p. 216.
3. Stephen Longstreet, *War Cries on Horseback* (Garden City, NY: Doubleday, 1970), p. 258.
4. John Tebbel and Keith Jennison, *The American Indian Wars* (New York: Harper, 1900), p. 284.
5. Nelson A. Miles, *Personal Recollections and Observations of General Nelson A. Miles* (Lincoln and London: University of Nebraska, 1992), I:260.
6. Mark H. Brown, *The Flight of the Nez Perce* (New York: Putnam, 1994), p. 308.
7. Hugh Lenox Scott, *Some Memories of a Soldier* (New York: Century, 1928), pp. 52, 59.
8. *Ibid.*, p. 59.
9. I am indebted to Mr. Kim Allen Scott, of the Montana State Library, for the biographical material on Lt. Gustavus Doane.
10. Brown, *The Flight*, p. 308.
11. Bruce Hampton, *Children of Grace* (New York: Holt, 1994), p. 246.
12. Letter from Lt. G. C. Doane to Gen. N. Miles, 3 August 1877, Doane Letters, manuscript collection, Burlingame Special Collection (BSC), Montana State Library, Billings, MT. I owe great thanks to its curator, Kim Allen Scott, for providing me with photocopies of the letters.
13. Hampton, p. 246.
14. Thomas Marquis, *Custer, Cavalry and Crows* (Ft Collins, CO: Old Army Press, 1975), p. 126.
15. Letter from F. Benteen to Mrs. Benteen, August 11, 1877. John M. Carroll, *The Benteen-Goldin Letters on Custer and his last Battle* (New York: Liveright, 1974), p. 85.
16. *Ibid.*, p. 83.
17. Miles to Sturgis, 11 August 1877, BSC.
18. Marquis, *Custer, Cavalry*, p.136.
19. Scott, *Memories*, p. 54.
20. Marquis, *Custer, Cavalry*, p. 126; Miles to Doane, 11 August 1877, BSC.
21. Doane to Miles, 21 August 1877, BSC; Hampton, p. 248.
22. Sturgis to Doane, 25 August 1877, BSC; Miles to Doane, 25 August 1877, BSC.
17. Miles to Sturgis, 11 August 1877, BSC.
18. Marquis, *Custer, Cavalry*, p. 136.
19. Scott, *Memories*, p. 54.
20. Marquis, *Custer, Cavalry*, p. 126.

Nez Perce

21. Doane to Miles, 21 August 1877, BSC; Bruce Hampton, *Children of Grace The Nez Perce War of 1877.* (New York: Holt, 1994) p.248.
22. Sturgis to Doane, 25 August 1877, BSC; Miles to Doane, 25 August 1877, BSC.
23. Sturgis to Doane, 29 August 1877, BSC.
24. Sturgis to Doane, 29 August 1877, BSC.
25. Doane to Gilbert, 1 September 1877, BSC.
26. Sturgis to Doane, 5 September 1877, BSC.
27. Merrill D. Beal, *I Will Fight No More Forever* (Seattle: University of Washington Press, 1963), p. 185.
28. Gilbert to Doane, 2 September 1877, BSC.
29. Gilbert to Doane, 2 September 1877, BSC.
30. Sturgis to Doane, 21 August 1877, BSC.
31. Sturgis to Doane, 2 September 1877, BSC.
32. Sturgis to Doane, 2 September 1877, BSC.
33. Hampton, p. 248.
34. Letter from F. Benteen to Mrs. Benteen, August 11, 1877. Carroll, *Benteen-Goldin*, p. 85.
35. Doane to Miles, 21 August 1877, BSC.
36. Marquis, *Custer, Cavalry,* p. 135.
37. Beal, pp. 187, 188.
38. *Ibid.*, p. 195.
39. Carroll, *Benteen-Goldin*, p. 202.
40. Rickey, p. 264; Ani Frank Mulford, *Fighting Indians in the 7th Cavalry* 2nd ed. (Fairfield, WA: Ye Galleon Press, 1972), p. 126.
41. S. L. A. Marshall, *Crimsoned Prairie* (New York: Scribner, 1972), p. 212.
42. Scott, *Memories,* p. 65.
43. Sturgis to Doane, 17 August 1877, BSC.
44. Rickey, p. 224.
45. Miles, *Personal Recollections*, p. 252; Helen Addison Howard and Dan L. McGrath, *War Chief Joseph* (Lincoln: University of Nebraska, 1941), p. 269.
46. Howard & McGrath, p. 273.
47. *Ibid.*, p. 282.

XV
COURT OF INQUIRY

Following the battle of Bear Paw Mountain, De Rudio and E Company scoured the countryside for wounded warriors as well as for Nez Perce families. They conveyed them in six-mule teams to Ft. Buford, on the Missouri, arriving November 9, 1877.[1] The fort served as a collection point for the prisoners of war. From there Chief Joseph and the Nez Perce survivors were transported down the Missouri on large mackinaws to Ft. Lincoln, where they were greeted by the blowing of steam whistles and the booming of cannons.[2] Chief Joseph was paraded down Main Street on a pony and feted as "honored guest" at an evening banquet.[3] Contrary to promises made to them, the Nez Perce were not sent back to their homes in the Northwest, but put into railroad cars and transported to the Indian Territory. There, they remained for eight years, before being allowed to return to Washington State, but never to their beloved Wallowa Valley in Oregon. The white settlers who had usurped their land, made quite sure of that.

A month later E Company was called on for another lugubrious duty. From December 19-30 they escorted Northern Cheyenne prisoners, en route to the Indian Territory. Thereafter, the company returned to Ft. Lincoln, where they remained a month, before being detached to Ft. Rice for winter quarters. Exhausted, De Rudio took two month's furlough in February 1878.

In the spring of 1878, De Rudio and his company were ordered to the Black Hills, two hundred twenty five miles to the southwest. A report had been received that three hundred lodges of Sioux warriors had broken out of the Pine Ridge Reservation and were planning to join Sitting Bull. This proved to be an exaggeration. In truth, small parties of warriors were raiding farms, ranches and stagecoach lines. They struck and then vanished. In one instance, the warriors had captured a treasure coach from Deadwood but lacked the means to open the safe. The warriors were overtaken and persuaded to return to the reservation.[4]

The Black Hills had been undergoing great demographic changes. A new generation of prospectors had appeared since the Colorado gold strikes fifteen years earlier. Gone were the overland travels in prairie schooners across deserts and over the Rockies. Now the prospectors traveled in Union Pacific or Northern Pacific railroad cars, swilling whiskey and playing cards. They left the tracks at Bismarck or Cheyenne and traveled by stagecoach across rugged terrain. Yankton, Pierre and Sidney were also crowded with prospectors, clamoring for space on the newly established stagecoach lines.[5]

Much of the prospecting initially took place in the southern part of the Black Hills in the vicinity of Custer City, but by the fall of 1875 a rich strike had been reported from the north, and the stampede was redirected. Deadwood swelled almost overnight to a population of ten thousand with a long straight street of log and frame houses.[6] The city quickly acquired a Grand Central Hotel, theaters and a variety of frontier entertainment. The aging frontiersmen flocked to Deadwood, for their last opportunity for riches. Wealthy investors lost no time in buying up claims, and from the beginning, modern mining supplanted the old placer and hydraulic methods.

Nowhere in the Dakota Territory was the fear of warrior raids more evident than in the newly established towns in the Black Hills. The Black Hills had been wrested from Indian control by an "agreement," imposed upon the Sioux by a peace commission in 1876, which added to Lakota resentment. In fact, 1877 was the bloodiest year in the hills since the beginning of the white settlement.[7] Military detachments were rushed from Forts Lincoln and Totten. They set up small camps to patrol the area, but it soon became apparent that a permanent fort would spare them hundreds of miles of march.

A lively dispute arose as to the best site for the fort. Bear Butte, near Deadwood City, now a city of twenty-five thousand people finally won out. The site had a stream, ample timber and grass and was situated near the convergence of roads from Bismarck, Pierre and Sidney.

Colonel Sturgis arrived at Bear Butte after a twelve day march from Ft. Lincoln with eight companies, including E Company. They set up camp and were soon joined by General Sheridan. Escorted by De Rudio's company, Sheridan scouted the region for a post site, while the other companies sat around or watched the Benteen Nine play baseball with a Deadwood team.

A site was chosen on a plain fronting a gap in the foothills near the head of Bear Butte Creek, fourteen miles northeast of the temptations of Deadwood. It was eventually named Ft. Meade. Plans called for a reserve enclosure of six miles by two miles. A first lieutenant of Infantry (Engineers) supervised construction. As many as a hundred civilian workers from Deadwood were hired to begin work, and they reported with tools and bedding.[8] De Rudio's company was assigned to help.

In September 1878, the regiment was called out to intercept the Northern Cheyenne, who were fleeing north from the Indian Territory. Their flight has come to be known as the *Cheyenne Autumn*, a sad chapter in American history. Exiled to the Indian Territory in Oklahoma after their defeat, the Northern Cheyenne sickened in great numbers during the winter of 1877. Finally in autumn of the next year, they quit the territory and began an epic trek northward, pursued by ten thousand soldiers and three thousand civilian militiamen. Reaching the Spotted Tail and Red Cloud Agencies in Nebraska, they discovered that these familiar reservations had been closed. The tribe then separated. The followers of Dull Knife were inhumanely imprisoned at Camp Robinson and decimated during an escape attempt. The followers of Little Wolf were cornered and sent to Pine Ridge Agency in South Dakota, where they were eventually joined by the remnants of Dull Knife's band. After untold hardships, the Northern Cheyenne were settled in a new agency on the Tongue River.

E Company remained on Black Hills patrol until November then returned to Ft. Rice for the winter quarters. No rest for the weary troopers. In February 1879 E Company was ordered out in the dead of winter to pursue a band of Lakota warriors that had attacked a wagon train. The company marched two hundred miles in fiercely cold weather.

Meanwhile, work on Ft. Meade had been progressing rapidly and reasonably well, thanks to civilian craftsmen and a good selection of timber from the Black Hills. The guardhouse was the first structure completed and immediately put to use. With temptation close at hand, desertion, drunkenness and absence without leave were endemic.[9] By December, barrack and stable buildings were begun, with local sandstone and pine used in both constructions. Last to be erected were the officers' quarters. On the first floor, each unit had a parlor, a sitting room, a dining room and a kitchen; and on the second floor, four bedrooms with closets.[10] After the shoddy construction of Ft. Rice, the new quarters must have seemed like paradise, with doors and windows that could open and close. In addition to his E Company duties, De Rudio was assigned to the Administration Council, which dispensed funds for garden seed plantings and other important projects.

But if 1879 promised to be a quiet year in the Department of the Dakotas, it was not so in the east. A Custer controversy had erupted in the press. A magazine writer named Frederick Whittaker had published in 1876 his *Complete Life of General George A. Custer*,[11] strongly critical of Major Reno. His premise was that Custer's demise was caused by the failure of Major

Reno and Captain Benteen to come to Custer's aid. Unfortunate for the two officers, the book was tolerably well written.[12] Libby Custer, an attractive widow who was to outlive her husband by fifty-seven years, publicly supported the author. For the remainder of her long life, she was to defend her husband from criticism and tirelessly promote his reputation.

There was no need for Major Reno to respond, since President Grant, General Terry and General Sherman had found no fault with him, but Major Reno -- still under suspension for his encounter with the officer's wife -- chose to apply for a Court of Inquiry. A Court of Inquiry is not quite the same as a Court Martial. No charges had been brought against Reno, or against anyone else. It was Reno, himself, that sought the inquiry, annoyed by the gossip around him. Much of this was the result of personal animosity and a desire to irritate, rather than a reflection of his military judgment in the Little Bighorn affair. Under pressure from the press, President Rutherford B. Hayes ordered a Court of Inquiry, to publicly review the accusations against the officers of the 7th Cavalry.

Courts of Inquiry can be a wonderful diversion for a frontier officer from the monotony of his work. It means leaving the tedium of field or garrison life and going to a city, where he would be lodged and fed at government expense. Most officers who start out believing that they have nothing to conceal, welcome an appearance at a Court of Inquiry. Later they come to see that their actions receive minute scrutiny, and their reputations, even if not the primary concern of the inquiry may come to suffer. Many an officer has been unexpectedly ruined.

Before leaving for Chicago, De Rudio was interviewed on January 14 by a reporter for the Chicago *Times*. Astonishingly, he told him that Reno had committed a fatal error when he decided to leave the wood! This was a serious and brash indiscretion, in advance of a public inquiry, an indiscretion that he would shortly regret. What the statement implied was that if Reno had stood fast on the west bank battlefied, the warriors could not, or would not, have mounted a *concerted* attack on the eight companies of Custer and Benteen. Supporters of Whittiker doubtless applauded this opinion, while Reno defenders must have questioned a perspective from someone who was not even on the firing line.

Officers summoned before a Court of Inquiry, in which they not a primary subject of investigation, often arrive at a common understanding before being called to give testimony. De Rudio had already jumped the gun. A tacit consensus was quietly emerging among the officers of the 7th that Reno's reputation was to be preserved. Girard, the Sioux interpreter himself a witnesses, reported that there was much dining and wining during the trial and conferences to discuss the nature of the forthcoming testimony.[13] To be sure, there was still an undercurrent of resentment against Reno, who, except for his praise of Benteen, had failed to mention any of the other officers in his official report of the Little Bighorn battle.[14] Such omissions were highly impolitic and bitterly resented. Had he cited the performance of a few of the officers, how different and less contentious might have been his fate!

The Court convened on January 13, 1879 at the Palmer House in the heart of downtown Chicago at Monroe and State Streets, a quintessential Victorian Hotel with mahogany bars, paneled dining rooms, excellent dining and a barbershop tiled with silver dollars. Rebuilt after the great fire of 1871, it held itself out as the only thoroughly fireproof hotel in the United States. Rudyard Kipling was unimpressed. He described it as a "guilded and mirred rabbitwarren...cramed with people talking about money and spitting everywhere."

The trial lasted a month. The Court, consisting of two cavalry colonels and an infantry colonel, heard twenty-three sworn witnesses, including officers of the 7th, scouts, teamsters, packers, two non-commissioned officers and the trumpeter.

The two packers and Girard testified that Reno had been drunk during the engagement. The remaining witnesses supported Reno.[15] Benteen testified he had observed Reno at fifteen or twenty minute intervals and that "there was no time during the 25th or 26th when there was any indication of drunkenness on the part of Major Reno."[16] Benteen tried to denigrate the testimony of the packers by stating that they had stolen from him and that they had concealed skulkers who had left assigned positions on the line.[17] Reno testified that he had once discharged Girard for stealing, but that Custer had reinstated him.[18]

Captain Thomas B. Weir, the most outspoken of Reno's critics, did not testify at the trial. This was the man whom Colonel Sturgis had once charged before a Benzine Board with "not only of dissipated and dissolute habits, but ... a low, vulgar man, devoid of moral principles and unfit to associate with officers and their families."[19] Weir had died of pneumonia during an episode of severe depression, while on recruiting duty in New York. Nor did Captain Thomas Henry French testify. He had earlier stated that Reno hid during most of the fight, but at the time of the Court of Inquiry, French himself was undergoing a court martial, brought about when Eliza De Rudio reported him for drunkenness while on duty.[20] Just as well for De Rudio that he was absent. French had developed an implacable hatred for that "black-hearted Italian."[21]

De Rudio's testimony was given chiefly on January 29, 1879. His reputation had preceded him. The press identified him as an Orsini conspirator and described as "rather small and thin, with moustache and with streaked gray hair."

De Rudio was nervous when he gave his testimony. At times he was verbose and did not always answer directly. Often his account of the battle seemed incomplete and difficult to reconcile with the reports of others, nor were his descriptions able to be plotted on the official map used by the court.

De Rudio's answers seemed to provoke laughter on many occasions, not because of their subject matter, but because of his manner of delivery. But De Rudio was no fool. His insight was surely as shrewd as any in the courtroom. He had needed sagacity to survive. In view of the newspaper interview given before his testimony, at odds with the consensus, it is possible that his purpose in seemingly acting the clown was to divert attention from the inconsistency of his previous statement to the journalist.

At the end of his direct testimony, De Rudio was cross-examined by Reno's attorney.

By this time, De Rudio's opinion had undergone a complete turn-about from the newspaper interview. He now stated that Reno's conduct was exemplary and that Reno was correct in ordering a halt. "I said 'good for you' because we would have been massacred if we continued for another four hundred meters," he told the court.

The prosecution called Captain E. J. Mathey, the pack train officer, to rebut De Rudio's testimony. He testified that in the previous year De Rudio had told him that had they not been commanded by a coward, they would all have been killed.[22] The captain was then cross-examined by Reno's attorney, who extracted from him an admission that the story of De Rudio's escape had been doubted by some officers.[23] Captain Mathey did not recall their names. Reno's attorney hinted to the Court that De Rudio's accusations of cowardice might have been misapplied.[24] Thus, De Rudio learned the hard way that a Court of Inquiry is never a frolic.

At the end of the inquiry, the Court found no cause for further judicial action. It concluded, in effect, that the Custer disaster could not be attributed to Reno and that Custer alone was responsible.

Following their court appearances, the officers dispersed. None had gained much from the proceedings. After the bright lights and excitement of Chicago, De Rudio returned to the humdrum life of a cavalry officer in a frontier fort. Through attrition, De Rudio was slowly advancing in the regimental social hierarchy, but Captains Moylan and French continued to despise him.

De Rudio remained at Forts Lincoln and Rice until the summer of 1879 when the regiment was transferred to Ft. Meade, near the Black Hills, which would be its permanent station for five years. By then, construction had been completed. Ft. Meade now had ten companies and a telegraph line. There were fifteen officer quarters south of the parade ground and five barracks to the north, as well as the other familiar buildings and the stables. Comanche was brought to Ft. Meade from Ft. Lincoln, where he would live for another twelve years, rejuvenated by generous amounts of beer fed him by the soldiers on payday.

Major Reno returned to duty with the 7th Cavalry in May 1879, with his two years' suspension and the Court of Inquiry behind him. He was delegated to serve as executive officer to Colonel Sturgis at Ft. Meade.

Tragedy soon overtook Major Reno. He fell in love with Colonel Sturgis's twenty-one year old daughter. He, a forty-four year old widower, was considered ineligible. A heavy drinker, he spent much of his spare time in the company of the junior officers, who were often boisterous and unruly, after an evening of carousing. On several occasions, Reno had been involved in fistfights with subalterns. The fights went unreported until one evening, after many hours of drinking he peered through a parlor window at Colonel Sturgis' daughter and tapped on the pane. Both father and daughter were outraged, and charges were promptly brought against Reno.

Colonel Sturgis should have learned to be more forgiving. In Memphis, during the Civil War, he had been accused of passing his arm around a girl's waist after a drinking bout.[25] To make matters worse, he was defeated shortly thereafter by the weaker forces of Nathan Bedford Forrest at Bryce Cross Roads. In the Board of Investigation that followed, Sturgis was accused of being intoxicated during the battle. He was denied another combat assignment for the remainder of the war.[26]

Reno was court martialed in November 1879. Several officers testified against him. Although Captain Benteen predictably gave spirited testimony in Reno's behalf, Reno was found guilty and dismissed from the service. Despite the appeals for clemency from several members of the Court and the Judge

Advocate, President Hayes upheld the sentence choosing to disregard irregularities in the sentencing procedure. The President had had a run-in with Reno during the Civil War, when Brevet General Marcus Reno publicly criticized Colonel Hayes for allowing his regiment, the 23rd Ohio, to scavenge a farmer's haystacks for bedding.[27] Reno never returned to duty. He died in poverty from an agonizing tongue cancer in 1889 and was buried in an unmarked grave. In 1967, the charges against him were dismissed for want of merit, and his body was disinterred and reburied in the cemetery at Little Bighorn Battlefield, where he lies today, sadly without special distinction.

In September, upon the return of E Company's regular commander, De Rudio was relieved of command and made acting commissary officer at Ft. Meade, a post that he held for several years. He had a capacity for meticulous record keeping and honest work, which enhanced his reputation as an able administrator. He remained on the books as an officer of E Company and from time to time went out on patrol and escort duty.

There were no large attacks by the Lakota Sioux or Cheyenne in 1880, although raids were frequent, and the troops at Ft. Meade were often called out in pursuit. In their spare time, officers were allowed hunting leave, but required to turn in relief maps of the area. Buffalo still roamed the northern plains in 1882, but ruthless slaughter, sod breaking and barbed wire fences relentlessly decimated their numbers, so that within two years, the buffalo had vanished from the plains. The Indians believed they had gone underground to rest.[28] Small herds briefly persisted in the Texas panhandle, but these too were swiftly exterminated.[29] A few were kept in the Yellowstone National Park and in the Bronx Zoo, where the artist, James Earle Fraser, was able to find a subject for the buffalo nickel.

During the next two years, the activities of the regiment were hardly noteworthy. Besides its regular garrison duties, the regiment returned small bands of wandering Lakota to their reservations[30] and provided escort and protection for the

Northern Pacific Railroad crews working in Montana.[31] Work on the railroad had resumed after the stoppage in 1875, and by 1880, the track reached Ft. Pierre. This was only of negligible benefit to the garrison at Ft. Meade, since travel from Pierre to Meade still took seven days on a hard, incredibly uncomfortable and expensive ride by stagecoach.

While De Rudio was serving in this frontier fort, the Orsini affair had again erupted in the American press. De Rudio had apparently given out, or sold, to the New York *Times* an article about the assassination attempt on Napoleon III. In it, he mentions that a third bomb was thrown, but does not name the person who threw it. The article was printed on March 20, 1881 in the New York Sunday *Times*.

ORSINI AND NAPOLEON III

SECRET HISTORY OF THE ATTEMPT AT ASSASSINATION

TOLD BY ONE OF THE CONSPIRATORS, WHO IS NOW ALIVE--NAPOLEON'S TREACHERY--

Astonishingly, two days later an editorial appeared in the same newspaper, in which an anonymous writer asks if it is possible that an officer in the 7th Cavalry could be the assassin mentioned in the Orsini affair:

> **"If it is demonstrated that De Rudio was the traitor of the conspirators, he should not stay another day in the United States Army...If De Rudio is really the man who as assassin was hired for 500 francs, it would be better if he were immediately thrown out of the army."**

The *Evening Post* and other newspapers picked up the story. A few days later, the *L'Echo d'Italia* replied to the invectives by staunchly defending De Rudio. It associated the attack on him with Italian xenophobia: "[De Rudio] had served in the Union army, entering as an enlisted man and for acts of value and true heroism, reached the rank of lieutenant of cavalry, which if he had been American or Irish, he would now be a general or at least a colonel." *L'Echo d'Italia* was the faithful watchdog and spokesman for the Italian community, quick to defend its beleaguered members.[32]

De Rudio made no public response. As is often the case, the polemics quickly subsided. He was accustomed to these attacks, but now, for the first time, he had support from an unexpected quarter.

Notes

1. Hugh Lenox Scott, *Some Memories of a Soldier* (New York: Century, 1928), p. 73.
2. Geoffrey C. Ward, , *The West* (Boston: Little Brown, 1999), p. 303.
3. Ani Frank Mulford, *Fighting Indians in the 7th Cavalry* 2nd ed. (Fairfield, WA: Ye Galleon Press, 1972), p. 126.
4. Scott, *Memories,* p. 88.
5. Albert N. Williams, *The Black Hills* (Dallas, TX: Southern Methodist University Press, 1952), p. 58.
6. John R. Finerty, *War-Path and Bivouac* (Norman: University of Oklahoma Press, 1961), p. 10.
7. Robert Lee, *Fort Meade and the Black Hills* (Lincoln and London: University of Nebraska Press, 1991), p. 10.
8. *Ibid.,* pp. 26, 31.
9. *Ibid.,* p. 38; Scott, *Memories,* 107.
10. Lee, p. 40.
11. Frederick Whittiker, *A Complete Life of General George A. Custer: Major General of Volunteers, Brevet Major General, U.S. Army and Lt. Colonel, U.S. Cavalry,* 2 vols. (New York, Sheldon, 1876).
12. For a different opinion see letter from Dustin to Goldin, February 26, 1934. John M. Carroll, *The Benteen-Goldin Letters on Custer and his last Battle* (New York: Liveright, 1974), p. 114.
13. Girard in Kenneth Hammer, ed., *Custer in 76* (Norman and London: University of Oklahoma, 1988), p. 238.
14. Ronald H. Nichols, *In Custer's Shadow: Major Marcus Reno* (Norman: University of Oklahoma, 1999), p. 220.
15. E. A. Brininstool, *Troopers with Custer* (Lincoln and London: University of Nebraska, 1952), p. 156.
16. John Upton Terrell, and George Walton, *Faint the Trumpet Sounds* (New York: McKay, 1966), p. 254.
17. Testimony of Captain Benteen. W. A. Graham, *The Reno Court of Inquiry* (Mechanicsburg, PA: Stackpole, 1995), p. 188.
18. Testimony of Major Reno. Graham, *Reno,* p. 143.
19. Terrell and Walton, p. 71.
20. Robert Nightingale, *Little Bighorn* (U.S.: Far West Publications, 1996), p. 170.
21. Cesare Marino, *Dal Piave al Little Bighorn* (Belluno: Tarantola, 1996), p. 406, n. 176.
22. Testimony of Captain E. G. Mathey. Graham, *Reno,* p. 205.
23. Benteen mentions this to his wife, Carroll, *Benteen-Goldin,* p. 148.
24. Testimony of Captain E. G. Mathey. Graham, *Reno,* p. 206.
25. Lee, p. 69.

26. Robert Selph Henry *'First with the Most' Forrest* (New York: Bobbs-Merrill, 1944), p. 302.
27. Hans L. Trefousse, p. 28.
28. Scott, *Memories,* pp. 123, 125; W. Nye, *Carbines and Lance* (Norman: University of Oklahoma Press, 1943)
29. Stephen Longstreet, *War Cries on Horseback* (Garden City, NY: Doubleday, 1970), p. 189.
30. Edward L. Daily, *Custer to MacArthur* (Paducah, KY: Turner, 1995), p. 76.
31. Lee, p. 75.
32. Jerre Mangione and Ben Morreale, *La Storia* (New York: Harper Perennial, 1993), p. 16.

XVI
CAPTAIN

De Rudio was promoted to captain on December 17, 1882, while serving at Ft. Meade.[1] This was a significant advancement in the peacetime army. Better living quarters and higher social standing could only have make life more pleasant. The De Rudio family had put all their resources into the education of their children. Plans were made to send Hercules, age 22, to college to study mining engineering and the girls, ages 12 to 15, to a convent school.[2] The girls were described as "olive-skinned and sparkling eyed, almost heartbreakingly lovely."[3] A French military proverb has it that a second lieutenant runs up debts, a first lieutenant pays them off and a captain puts money in the bank; but in De Rudio's case, the maxim is quite optimistic. At times, when De Rudio was financially pinched, Benteen had lent him money.[4]

Promotion also came to Benteen in February 1883, while on recruiting duty in New York. Promotion to field grade usually means transfer to another regiment. With the majority came word that he had been assigned to the 9th Cavalry (colored). Benteen was outraged. He had rejected a major's commission in the *same* regiment in 1868, prior to his assignment to the 7th Cavalry. He tried to circumvent his transfer by circulating a petition, but most of the officers refused to sign it.[5] Benteen, by this time, was a very heavy drinker and quite irascible. Service in a frontier fort was trying enough for the officers, without having to put up with extra bother. Besides, a junior officer cannot move up, if a senior officer remains in place. One need not presume that racial bias was the reason for Benteen's reluctance to accept a post with a black regiment. The black soldier gave his officer less trouble with drunkenness and desertion and his reenlistment rate was higher than that of the white soldier. Furthermore, the Army had reached a point where service with a black regiment no longer adversely affected advancement of an officer's career Benteen had served with credit as a Lt. Colonel in the 138th United States Colored Troop from July 1865 to January 1866 and probably felt that now, at the very least, he was entitled to command a regiment. Besides, since he had only a few years to serve before retirement, he was reluctant to exchange the comforts of Ft. Meade and the command of his beloved H Company for service at a more primitive fort, which is what he could expect with his new assignment and which, in fact, was what he got.

De Rudio, age fifty-one, was given command of H Company on February 1, 1883. This occasioned the bitterness Benteen would show in later years towards his comrades in the 7th Cavalry and towards De Rudio in particular. "Count No-Count," he called him.[6]

Benteen's career declined rapidly. At Ft. Du Chesne, Utah he continued to drink heavily and appeared intoxicated while on duty. Worse, he is said to have reviled the Mormon religion and insulted a Mormon trader. It is likely that he encurred the enmity of the local builders, who found him unyielding and unwilling to condone their "arrangements." Charges were brought against him for drinking on duty and conduct unbecoming an officer. A court martial suspended him from rank and duties at half pay for one year. Upon his reinstatement in 1888, he retired from active service and went to live in Atlanta. One source of solace for Benteen was his investments. He was as shrewd a businessman as he was a gambler. When stationed in Atlanta after the war, he had purchased two hundred acres of productive farmland, which his father ran for him. Benteen himself built a home in Atlanta, where he spent his last years supervising his estate. In 1890, he was brevetted to the rank of Brigadier General, for gallantry at Little Bighorn and at Canyon Creek in the Nez Perce war. He died in Atlanta in 1898 at the age of sixty-three and is buried in the National Cemetery at Arlington. His wife, Kate, died six years later. In his later years, Benteen had become querulous in his letters, criticizing many officers, among them De Rudio. "Though I knew he was an out and out shyster, I treated him like a gentleman--which he was not!"[7] Characteristically, even in retirement, Benteen never criticized in public, nor did he give out interviews to the press.

In 1883 the regiment performed the usual garrison duties. It pursued warrior raiders and marched to Ft. Pierre to fetch horses and recruits. Around this time, the cavalry began to substitute the terms "troop" for "company" and "squadron" for "battalion,"[8] although many, like Custer, had long used the terms unofficially.

Racial strife was destined to appear in Ft. Meade during 1884-86 when a black regiment, the 24th Infantry, arrived at the fort. One of its privates killed a civilian doctor, who had been defending a black prostitute, and the private was lynched by a civilian mob. Later, cavalrymen from H Troop fired into the black brothel, killing one man. Several soldiers were apprehended, tried and sentenced. All but one escaped, and he was sent to the penitentiary, where he died. The controversy gradually subsided.[9]

Captain De Rudio was absent during the fracas. After selling his property[10] and turning over H Troop to Lt. Varnum, he left for New York in September 1884 for a two year tour of recruitment duty. These assignments were made not only to accommodate an officer and his family, permitting them to exchange the hardship and monotony of a frontier station for the pleasures of the big city, but also to provide a means for procuring recruits for the regiment, commensurate with the recruiting skills of the officer.

Someone had alerted The New York *Times* to De Rudio's arrival in that city. On October 2, 1884 the newspaper observed:

ONCE MORE

"An officer of the United States Army is expected to be a gentleman. It is therefore clear that a man who is a cowardly-assasin, or who claims to be such, has no right to wear the United States uniform."

Again, De Rudio refrained from a reply and allowed the flume to vent itself. Is it possible Libby Custer might have had a hand in bringing the matter to the attention of the newspaper? Elizabeth Custer, then seventy-one years old, was living in New York at 71 Park Avenue. At her husband's death, she had been left in dire financial straights, but had recouped her fortunes handsomely with her three well-written books about her adventures as an army wife and a series of successful lecture tours. She surely must have learned that De Rudio was in the city, but so far as is known, made no attempt to contact her late husband's junior officer. De Rudio's loyalty to Reno in the Court of Inquiry doubtless made him unwelcome. Of interest is an illustration appearing in her 1885 edition of *Tenting on the Plains*,[11] in which the author describes an excitable messenger delivering a letter. The illustration shows a soldier with goatee and mustache who closely resembles De Rudio. Perhaps this was her way of inflicting a sly hurt.

During their stay in New York, the De Rudio family may have promenaded or traveled by elevated railroad over that great engineering masterpiece, the Brooklyn Bridge, which had opened a year earlier. Another marvel they beheld was the electric lighting system, newly installed in lower New York. Perhaps they attended the recently opened Metropolitan Opera House, where 65 Italian musicians performed in the orchestra. Doubtless, they visited Battery Park, to watch progress on the Statue of Liberty, now nearing completion. It was here, close to the landing, that a miserable steerage passenger came ashore two decades earlier, vowing to succeed.

While in New York, De Rudio had an opportunity to meet the Italian community, which had grown to twelve thousand in the past two decades.[12] Immigration to the United States had increased ever since the failure of the Italian fruit crop and following the terrible Yellow Fever epidemic in Brazil, which cut off travel to that country.[13] The immigrants now were more likely from the *mezzogiorno*, or southern Italy, rather than from northern regions, as before. Many congregated around Mulberry Street, along with the Corkians.[14] In contrast to the previous immigrants, the newcomers were more apt to be illiterate *contadini*, scorned by the northern Italian. But there were exceptions. Achille La Guardia, father of the future mayor of New York, also from the *mezzogiorno*, accepted a bandmaster's appointment in the U.S. Army and moved west with his family, to spend the rest of his life in backwater army forts. Many arrived without their women, planning to send for them or to return to their homeland after they had made their fortunes.[15] Italian restaurants, clubs and social events lent an appealing flavor to the city. It could only have been pleasurable for Captain and Mrs. De Rudio to be received at the home of important Italian-American citizens, and to exchange recollections of Italy.

De Rudio remained with his wife and family in New York on recruiting duties until the spring of 1886. If anything like his fellow officer's service, De Rudio "examined, enlisted, reached and shipped recruits every day but Sunday."[16] His tour of duty apparently was highly successful, since it was cited repeatedly in his later efficiency reports. The prospective recruit, often of foreign birth, evidently responded to the blandishments of an officer who was foreign-born -- and one who had served with Custer! On his return to Dakota, De Rudio stopped off in Chicago, where his stay at the Leland Hotel was mentioned in the Italian newspaper *L'Italia* on April 28, 1886. Once again, the Orsini history was recalled.[17]

In the summer of 1886 a Little Bighorn reunion was held at Ft. Custer, constructed on the bluff above the confluence of the

Big Horn and Little Big Horn rivers. Benteen attended, as did a few other participants in the battle. Also present were Chief Gall and the Crow scout, Curly. Sitting Bull was on tour with the Buffalo Bill Cody's Wild West Company.[18] De Rudio did not attend.

By autumn, De Rudio was back at Ft. Meade, Dakota Territory, with H Troop. Colonel James W. Forsyth now commanded the regiment. A West Point graduate and Civil War *aide de camp* to General Sheridan, he had replaced Sturgis on his retirement.

In October, H Troop was transferred to Ft. Yates, near the Standing Rock Reservation. The fort was built on a timbered tableland, but over the years the surrounding woods had been consumed by the needs of the steamships and construction. While at Ft. Yates, De Rudio got to know Sitting Bull, who maintained his leadership role. He had recrossed from Canada in July 1881, surrendered at Ft. Buford, Dakota Territory[19] and, after two years of loose surveillance while camped near Ft. Randall, was sent by steamboat to the Standing Rock Reservation. There he remained, apart from his one year tour with the Wild West Show of Buffalo Bill Cody, a saddened witness to the decline of the Lakota nomadic society.

With the extermination of the northern buffalo, the Sioux and Cheyenne had no reasonable choice but to accept the reservation, leaving the 7th Cavalry with little to do. In accordance with the army's fixed policy of rotation, the 7th Cavalry was ordered back to Kansas, to supervise the tribes of the southern plains. The all too familiar preparations were repeated. Colonel Forsyth and two of his troops were the first to leave for Ft. Riley, Kansas, where the regiment had been organized.

Next to leave was H Troop and then the remainder of the regiment. After a month's stay at Ft. Riley, H Troop and four others were sent on to Ft. Sill in southwest Oklahoma, in sight of the Wichita Mountains. The nearest railroad station for Ft. Sill was Henrietta, Texas, sixty-seven miles to the south. From there, the families had to travel by stagecoach or four mule ambulance[20] through flat, open countryside, with high winds and abrupt changes in temperature.

Ft. Sill was in sorrowful condition. The stone gables of the officers' quarters had collapsed, the plaster was crumbling, the flooring rolled, the roofs leaked badly and the building foundations required bracing. The sewerage system was primitive, generating odious smells. Undrained marshes around the fort were a breeding ground for mosquitoes and malaria. To add to the hardships, fuel was scarce. Elm, cottonwood, and oak had long since vanished along the streams and even pecan and walnut were being felled.[21]

The 7th Cavalry watched over the reservations of the Kiowa, Comanche and Plains Apache. They also kept the Texas ranchers from running long horn cattle across the reservations during the long drives, in an effort to halt the spread of tic-borne "Texas Fever."[22]

Two decades had passed since the crafty Chief Satanta had ravaged the plains, using the environs of Ft. Sill as his base. The tribes had recently begun to adjust to reservation life.[23] They proved adept at farming, and their small plots became marvels of productivity. In the absence of buffalo, the families learned to supplement their rations with quail, turkey and fish and to lease out part of the reservation for grazing. Not all could appreciate their progress. To one not too perceptive an officer, they were still "blanket Indians, quite primitive in every way."[24]

Captain De Rudio spent 1888-1892 at Ft. Sill. Despite his pay raise to $2,400/annum, money must have been difficult to come by, and the more difficult to hold on to, with the pressing demands of his children. He had to caution Eliza from overspending, an easy temptation for a mother with three pretty teen-aged girls.

De Rudio and H Troop were present at the first historic

Oklahoma Land Rush on April 22, 1889, when 100,000 people, "boomers," waited on the Arkansas and Texas borders for the signals that would allow them to cross the boundary lines to lay claim to two million acres of "unassigned" lands. Even with the prohibition of the sale of alcohol, violence was sometimes difficult to control. The Indian Territory had long been the haven for vicious desperadoes, and not for another year would the territorial and local governments be established. Meanwhile, although forbidden to act as peace officers (*posse comitatus*), the army found subtle ways to restrain the hooligans and to keep land disputes from escalating into murder.[25] To add to his troubles, De Rudio came down with malaria during his Oklahoma service, which required a lengthy sick leave.[26]

The same year, the first full-scale peacetime army maneuvers were conducted under General Wesley Merritt on the Kansas border near Arkansas City. They were humorously called "the bloody war of 1889," with reference to the hoards of insects, but, in truth, the day of the plains wars was past. The troops made practice marches and held field maneuvers in the Indian Territory, lasting twenty-one days.[27] De Rudio's performance was evaluated by his commanding officer in the recently introduced efficiency report: "sense of duty, discipline of his men, care and attention to their well being: very good. General conduct: excellent. Well prepared both for field operations, as well as barracks. Particularly disposed to taking charge of recruiting."[28]

It was during De Rudio's tour of duty at Ft. Sill, Oklahoma that the shocking news was received about the events at Wounded Knee.

Confined to their ever-shrinking reservation, the forlorn plains warriors ecstatically embraced the "ghost dance" religion. According to the tenets, frenzied ritual dance would summon a messiah, who would rid the plains of the white man and bring back the buffalo and the old ways.[29] Onto this vision, the Lakota superimposed a belief that a ghost shirt would protect the wearer from the white man's bullets. Forewarned of the unrest, the army dispatched eight troops of the 7th Cavalry to guard against an uprising. H Troop was not among them. They left Ft. Riley by rail and arrived on November 27 at the Pine Ridge Agency in southern South Dakota. The soldiers were as green as the men who had fought at Little Bighorn.[30]

Sitting Bull, living in the Standing Rock Reservation in North Dakota after his year tour with Buffalo Bill Cody, was thought to subscribe to the ritual ghost dance, and an incompetent Indian agent ordered his arrest. When Sitting Bull resisted, he and eight supporters were killed by the Sioux policemen. Upon learning of this tragedy, many Miniconjous Sioux fled the Cheyenne River Reservation.

Colonel George A. Forsyth, commanding the 7th Cavalry, overtook the tribe and herded it back toward the reservation, stopping en route at Wounded Knee Creek. As the warriors were being disarmed, a shot rang out, whereupon the warriors, in an apparently pre-arranged plan, withdrew their Winchesters from behind their blankets and fired at the soldiers. Concealing weapons under a blanket was a common warrior ploy, ever since the days of Pontiac. The soldiers quickly returned the fire. Eighty-four warriors were killed, many believing that their ghost shirt would repel bullets. The four Hotchkiss cannons, each capable of firing fifty rounds a minute, fired point blank into the village.[31] The soldiers then pursued and fired at the fleeing tribe, littering two square miles with as many as three hundred seventy bodies. The 7th Cavalry also suffered losses. One officer and twenty-five enlisted were killed, and two officers (including Captain Moylan) and thirty-nine soldiers wounded.[32] For both sides, the episode was a sorrowful disaster, even if not a deliberate massacre. Once again, as if protected by a talisman, De Rudio and H Troop were thankfully removed from this sad event.

In Ft. Sill, when news of the Wounded Knee disaster was received, some feared that the local tribes would create problems. Thought was given to disarming the warriors, but happily they were left alone and the trouble subsided.[33]

December 12, 1890 De Rudio was granted a six month leave of absence on a surgeon's certificate of disability, with permission to leave the Department of the Missouri. His efficiency report states that De Rudio was "well posted in field and garrison duty. Fitted for recruiting detail." This was written by his immediate superior, in the absence of Colonel Forsyth. When Forsyth returned from Wounded Knee, he insisted on writing his own fitness report, based upon an interval of twenty days of service in his command: "sense of duty, professional ability, his men's discipline care and attention to their comfort: good. General conduct: excellent. *Excitable, as he is Italian by birth and education.* Fitness to field operations not noted."[34]

This was a mean evaluation of an officer who did his best and gave his superiors no trouble. The comment of "excitable" seems curious coming from a man who was directly responsible for the events at Wounded Knee, through some misguided fear of the mystical ghost dance. Forsyth may have been in poor humor when he wrote the evaluation. Following the events at Wounded Knee, he had been temporarily relieved of command and a Court of Inquiry ordered. No charges were brought against him, but General Miles accused Forsyth of "incompetence" and "entire inexperience."[35]

H Troop spent the year 1891 in garrison duties at Ft. Sill. By now, the frontier had come to an end, and the unsettled regions were no longer connected to each other. "Old Rudy" was now in his fifty-ninth year, worn out by his duties in the field. On January 23, 1891 Captain Blair D. Taylor, a sympathetic Assistant Surgeon, notified the Adjutant General that Charles De Rudio was "unfitted for active service in the field, on account of failure of the heart's action, muscular rheumatism, orbital neuralgia, weak eyes and a general failing of the vital powers."[36] This long litany of illness may have been compiled at De Rudio's own request. Medical officers can be easily swayed by a polite, middle age officer with grey-streaked hair.

If De Rudio hoped to be assigned more sedentary duties, he was to be sorely disappointed. Wounded Knee had left the regiment short of seasoned officers. His choice was field duty or retirement, and De Rudio was in no financial position to retire. This left him with no alternative but to soldier on. In April and November, H Troop made two marches of one hundred thirty-six miles to the Texas cattle crossing to keep the longhorns off the reservations. Meanwhile the regiment was again thrown into confusion when a train en route to Ft. Riley, carrying several troops of the 7th Cavalry, collided with another train near Florena, Kansas, seriously injuring two officers and fifteen enlisted men. Now, more than ever, the regiment required his services.

The following year, H Troop performed its usual garrison duties at Ft. Sill then left for patrol in the Cheyenne and Arapaho Reservations. De Rudio was excused from patrol duty and from field maneuvers. Col. Forsyth wrote in his efficiency report: "Efficiency unknown" In October, Captain De Rudio and H Troop, together with two others, were ordered to Ft. Riley, in Kansas. The families packed their belongings and boarded the train.

Ft. Riley was situated on a treeless plateau, four miles east of Junction City on the Kansas Pacific track, not far from the old Chisholm Trail. Buildings were made of sandstone, quarried in the Wichita Mountains. An ocean of buffalo grass surrounded the fort, extending far out to the horizon. Fierce winds swept the plains and raked the compound, shredding flags and lifting the womens' skirts over their heads as they crossed the parade ground. Some wives weighed their hems with strips of lead.[37] Patrols were long and tiring, the plains monotonous, and the river crossings endless. Life within the fort was equally oppressive, with boredom relieved by rare visits to nearby Junction City. Eliza and the other wives watched the days go by and the lines in their faces deepen into furrows.

Notes

1. Kenneth Hammer, ed., *Custer in 76* (Norman and London: University of Oklahoma, 1988), p. 88.
2. De Rudio to Gen. Geo. D. Ruggles, June 12, 18 95. ACP, Charles C. De Rudio, CF D345 CT 1864, NAB.
3. Charles K. Mills, *Charles C. De Rudio* (Mattetuch and Bryan, NY: J. M. Carroll, 1983), p. 16.
4. Narrative of F. Benteen. John M. Carroll, *The Benteen-Goldin Letters on Custer and his last Battle* (New York: Liveright, 1974), p. 149; W. A. Graham, *The Custer Myth* (Harrisburg, PA: Stackpole, 1953), p. 159.
5. Robert Nightingale, *Little Bighorn* (U.S.: Far West Publications, 1996), p. 43.
6. Letter from Benteen to Barry, April 1, 1898, manuscript collection, White Swan (Little Bighorn) Library.
7. *Ibid.,*
8. Daniel Magnussen, *Peter Thompson's Narrative of the Little Bighorn Campaign of 1876* (Glendale, CA: Clark, 1974), p. 35.
9. Robert Lee, *Fort Meade and the Black Hills* (Lincoln and London: University of Nebraska Press, 1991), pp. 81-84.
10. Hugh Lenox Scott, *Some Memories of a Soldier* (New York: Century, 1928), p. 125.
11. Elizabeth B. Custer, *Tenting on the Plains* (New York: Webster, 1889), p. 673.
12. Edward Roff Ellis, *The Epic of New York City* (New York: Coward-McCann, 1966), p. 419.
13. Jerre Mangione and Ben Morreale, *La Storia* (New York: Harper Perennial, 1993), p. 14.
14. Edwin G. Burrows and Mike Wallace, *A History of New York City to 1898* (New York and Oxford: Oxford, 1999), p. 746.
15. Ellis, p. 419.
16. Scott, *Memories,* p. 124.
17. Cesare Marino, *Dal Piave al Little Bighorn* (Belluno: Tarantola, 1996), p. 292.
18. Evans S. Connell, *Son of the Morning Star* (New York: Harper Perennial, 1984), p. 316.
19. Don Rickey, *Forty Miles a Day on Beans and Hay* (Norman and London: University of Oklahoma, 1963), p. 12.
20. Scott, *Memories,* p. 127.
21. *Ibid.,* p. 137.
22. *Ibid.,* p. 139.
23. Rickey, p. 15.
24. Scott, *Memories,* pp. 127-129.
25. *Ibid.,* p. 132.
26. Letter from De Rudio to Gen. Geo. D. Ruggles, June 23, 1895, ACP, Charles C.

De Rudio, CF D345 CT 1864, NAB
27. Edward L. Daily, *Custer to MacArthur* (Paducah, KY: Turner, 1995), p. 77.
28. Annual Evaluation, 1889, ACP, Charles C. De Rudio, CF D345 CT 1864, NAB
29. Robinson, p. 345. which title?
30. Robert M. Utley, *Frontier Regulars. The United States Army and the Indian, 1866-1890* (New York: Macmillan, 1973), p. 26.
31. Robinson, *Good Year*, p. 345.
32. Wayne Mitchell Sarf, *The Little Bighorn Campaign* (Pennsylvania: Combined Books, 2000), p. 195.
33. Scott, *Memories*, p. 146.
34. Annual Evaluation, ACP, Charles C. De Rudio, CF D345 CT 1864, NAB
35. Robert Wooster, *Nelson A. Miles and the Twilight of the Frontier Army* (Lincoln: University of Nebraska, 1993).
36. ACP, Charles C. De Rudio, CF D345 CT 1864, NAB
37. Marguerite Merington, *The Custer Story* (Lincoln: University of Nebraska Press, 1987), p. 195.

XVII
FINAL DAYS

The inevitable could not be postponed. In June 1893, De Rudio was ordered to turn over command of H Troop to Captain Edward S. Godfrey, a veteran of Little Bighorn and Wounded Knee, who had been badly injured at Bear Butte and in the train collision in 1891. De Rudio was assigned to D Troop, which was stationed at Ft. Sam Houston in Texas.

De Rudio traveled to Austin, Texas on government railroad warrant, with his family at half-fare. They arrived in August and went on to Ft. Sam Houston. Built for fifteen companies, the fort was the largest military installation that De Rudio had served in. It had a lively social life and was considered a preferred permanent post. The De Rudios could only have been delighted with their new station.

D Troop was assigned to border patrol. Rustlers, criminals and small bands of Kickapoos, Lipans and Mescalero Apache raiders had long been disturbing the countryside on both sides of the border. After a decade of pursuit, the raiders had been largely contained, but small bands continued to slip across the Rio Grande River. From June 30, 1894 to October 5, 1895, De Rudio and D Troop patrolled the countryside and border[1] with little expectation of an encounter with the illusive raiders. In addition, the troops sought out gangs of irregular soldiers, raised by a Texan editor named Cararino E. Gargo, men who were intent on invading Mexico to overthrow the government of Portino Diaz.

The commandant of the fort, not his commanding officer Colonel Forsyth, evaluated his services: "sense of duty and general behavior: excellent. His men' discipline, care and attention to their comfort: very good. Ability of command: good. No particular fitness for field operations. A faithful officer."[2]

By now, De Rudio suffered greatly from "rheumatism of the arms and legs." His medical reports detail many visits to the medical officer. The condition must have been a sequel to camping outdoors for a quarter century in extremes of weather. Or he may have suffered from disc herniation, after years in the saddle. Or perhaps both. At any event, the symptoms were quite painful. Moreover, De Rudio had developed troublesome asthmatic attacks. The statement "No particular fitness for field operations" confirms that De Rudio had difficulty in carrying out the patrol assignments. This pitiful circumstance was the consequence of a man of field officer age required to perform a company officer's duties.[3]

Nothing noteworthy seems to have occurred in 1894 on patrol or in garrison. Unlike service in the north, the commands were active during the winter months. Two of the troops had been sent to Chicago during the Pullman Strike, but D Troop remained in Texas.

Another article about De Rudio appeared in the Washington *Post* on August 29, 1894. It would seem that by now he was always good for a story. The article was prompted by a member of Congress who was attempting to forestall an attempt to expel assassins from American soil:

> "Not all the bombers that land on these beaches from the old and worn-out monarchies of Europe keep on following their temperament
> ...The free institutions of the United States contributes to the process of improvement of human nature and to redeem one..."

In other words, De Rudio may have once been bad, but there

was still hope.

At Ft. Sam Houston and at Austin, Captain De Rudio had become a celebrity. He and Eliza moved in elevated military circles and were sought after in the homes of Texas society. His gold hilt saber was often shown to an admiring audience, and he was doubtless ready to comply with any request for an account of his adventures at Little Bighorn.

Colonel Forsyth was less than impressed. He wrote his efficiency report: "a perfectly willing subordinate officer of some intellectual ability and not an efficient soldier or instructor."[4] At least there was no further repetition of the "excitable Italian" remark, suggesting that Colonel Forsyth may have been rebuked for his previous comment.

In 1895, the 7th Cavalry was transferred to the Arizona Territory. D Troop left by rail on a two day trip to Ft. Bayard, an old Apache fort in southwest New Mexico, ten miles east of Silver City. The post was of modest size, housing seven companies, five of them from the 24th Infantry. This was the same regiment that had been stationed at Ft. Meade. Happily, there was no recurrance of the racial difficulties. One of the soldiers described his quarters: "Huts of logs and round stones, with flat dirt roof that in summer leaked and brought down rivulets of liquid mud; in winter, the hiding place of the tarantula and the centipede, with ceilings of 'condemned' canvas..."[5] Although some found the climate hot, dry and dusty, to most it was surprisingly mild and gentle, so that in later years, it was thought beneficial for soldiers afflicted with tuberculosis. De Rudio might even have noted some improvement of his asthma.

In the distant past, Geronimo had harassed the ranches of Arizona and Mexico, before agreeing to surrender to Crook at Canyon de los Embudos in Mexico on March 25, 1886. Most of his tribe returned to the reservation, but Geronimo and a few of his followers escaped, only to be captured by Miles on September 4, 1886 at Skeleton Canyon in Arizona. Miles had required the services of one-fifth of the entire U.S. Army to capture the handful of warriors. Always the improviser, Miles had built fifteen heliographic stations for rapid communication, but in the end had to rely on Apache scouts, as did Crook. With the surrender of Geronimo, the last of 243,000 Native Americans had finally been confined to one hundred eighty-seven reservations.[6]

But Apache habits and traditions die slowly. A Chiricahua Apache, named Massai (Big Foot), was implicated in raids against ranchers. After surrendering with Geronimo in 1886, he had escaped from the train en route to Florida and made his way back to Arizona, a distance of fifteen hundred miles, where, for twenty years,[7] he raided and ambushed settlers on both sides of the Mexican border.[8] Since many acts of violence were attributed to him, often with uncertain justification, his notoriety grew quickly.

Another band of Chiricahua Apaches had also been stealing livestock and property, killing ranchers and stealing women from the reservations Their leader was an Apache first sergeant scout, called the Apache Kid,[9] who killed the man responsible for the murder of his father. Tried by a general court martial, he served eight months in Alcatraz, before receiving a presidential pardon. He was arrested and convicted of another shooting but escaped while on the way to Yuma Prison. In the escape, the sheriff and another peace officer were killed. Thereafter the Apache Kid was a marked man, roaming the countryside with a handful of followers, attacking ranches and prospectors, raping and murdering. Following Geronimo's example, he and his band made their way over mountain and desert and across the Mexican border, hiding in the Sierra Madre mountains in Old Mexico. There they committed depredations on the Mexican population before stealing back across the border to continue their raids. As with Massai, he was blamed for nearly every crime in the Arizona Territory. Rewards of fifteen thousand dollars were offered for his capture.[10]

The cavalry was instructed to "pursue, intercept, capture or destroy" the bands of outlaws, whose numbers ranged from four to seventeen members.[11] For a decade the army sent out

Final Days

innumerable patrols, which searched unceasingly for the two desperados. Their mission was made more difficult by the refusal of the Mexican minister to allow the United States troops to cross the border. A treaty to permit both countries to cross the border had been in force briefly in 1882, but the terms were so restrictive[12] that the treaty was seldom invoked. Mercifully, after leading the army on a merry chase for many years, the Apache Kid eventually ceased his operations, for reasons not known.[13] He was last heard from in 1924 in Sonora, Mexico. His fate is uncertain; he may have died from tuberculosis.[14] Massai, too, gradually wound down his operations and faded into myth.

D Troop went on a two hundred mile scout in December. This was Captain De Rudio's last patrol, and Ft. Bayard would be his final memory of army service.

De Rudio took a terminal furlough the following year, travelling by train to San Diego, where he celebrated his sixty-fourth birthday. Having reached the maximum age for military service,[15] Captain De Rudio was retired on August 26, 1896, in accordance with Special Orders # 201.

He took up residence in San Diego but remained there for less than two years, before moving to Los Angeles.[16] Upon learning of the outbreak of hostilities with Spain in 1898, he immediately requested recall to active service. No action was taken on his request. The 7th Cavalry did not see combat in Cuba. It arrived in Havana in January 1899 and spent two and a half years in garrison duty on the island.[17]

Suddenly, from the recesses of oblivion, Antonio Gomez emerged. Word was reported in the press in 1901 that at long last Gomez had been freed from French Guyana. De Rudio was again fair game. The St Louis *Republic* wondered if Gomez would ever try to contact De Rudio, since criminals often flock together. The Washington *Post* of September 4 repeated the canard: "to speak of the escape of that man [De Rudio] from isolation of Devil's Island in a miraculous test of courage and tenacity is pure nonsense. His escape was orchestrated by the authorities to compensate him for his betrayal..."[18]

In fact, Gomez had been freed fourteen years earlier but the news was slow to reach the attention of the American press. He could have been released in 1876, after the fall of the Second Empire, when amnesty was granted to the political prisoners of Napoleon III. Tibaldi was released after thirteen years of imprisonment, but the imprisonment of Gomez continued until his plight was discovered by a visiting French Senator, who brought it to public notice. The President of France pardoned Gomez on March 3, 1887.

In an attempt to supplement his meager pension, De Rudio tried to procure army employment. He requested on March 23, 1904 an assignment in the now-centralized recruiting office of Los Angeles. He wrote, with great imagination, "I am in good and vigorous health and fully able to faithfully perform the duties of office."[19]

No action was taken on this request, but on April 23, 1904 the War Department promoted De Rudio to the retirement rank of Major. With it came an increase in his army pension.

De Rudio was honored in his retirement. A long article about the Little Bighorn adventure appeared in Harper's *Weekly* on September 25, 1897. The American Cyclopedia of American History in 1898 also cited his exploits. He was a member of the Liberal Club, Indian War Veterans's Club, Loyal Legion of the United States and honorary president of practically every Italian organization in Los Angeles. By this time, the wave of Italian immigration had seeded the United States, and especially California, with large colonies of Italians. His three daughters had married and also lived in Los Angeles: Mrs. H.C. Scott at 819 W. 8th Street, Mrs. N.B. Vickrey at 2909 Raymond Avenue and Mrs. S.E. Adair at the New England Avenue home. He had three grandchildren, one of who, Samuel De Rudio Adair, indicated a desire to enter West Point. His son, Hercules, was a mining engineer in Signal, Arizona. He participated in the sale of the then defunct Great McCraken Silver Mine, once assayed at a thousand dollars per ton and negotiated for the purchase of other claims, traveling around the countryside in a steam automobile.

Final Days

Hercules appears to have had the familial explosive temper and was highly regarded as a man who hated injustice. He was tried and acquitted for publicly thrashing a man who had beaten his own mother.[21]

In his decorated cottage at 1034 S. Figueroa Street, Los Angeles, Charles and Eliza celebrated their golden anniversary, in a lavish party reported in the Los Angeles *Times* on December 5, 1905. Eliza, dressed in black velvet, wore around her neck a necklace of imported Italian coral, given as an anniversary present by her husband. At the end of the meal, Major De Rudio, in dress uniform, cut the cake with his thirty-five year old sword, presented to him by G Troop in Kansas. On the wall hung a portrait of the beloved Francisco Calvi.

De Rudio might have expected to spend the remainder of his years enjoying a tranquil retirement. Even the American press had halted their pursuit. But peace was still to elude him.

An Italian historian and Orsini biographer had written De Rudio, asking for an account of the famous assassination plot, to be used in connection with a celebration of the ninetieth anniversary of the birth of Orsini.

De Rudio was loath to reply, since he himself had intended to publish his memoirs, but he finally relented and sent a letter to the historian. The account was published in six installments in a Bolognese newspaper, *Il Resto di Carlino,* beginning August 9, 1908.

The letter recounted the history and details of the plot. In it, De Rudio charged for the first time that FRANCESCO CRISPI HAD THROWN THE THIRD BOMB! The accusation fell like a thunderbolt on the unprepared Italian public.

Francesco Crispi[21] had come a long way since the fateful day of the Orsini assassination attempt. Until his death in 1901, he had been a venerated public figure. He had supported Garibaldi in the successful Sicilian campaign and, after the reunification of Italy, served as president of the Chamber, cabinet minister and finally Premier during two terms of office. His revolutionary activities were relegated to the past, as he rose in the establishment to become monarchist, imperialist and (some say) reactionary. The history of the new Italy had become magisterial, and his many supporters now abhorred stories of bombs and assassinations.

A torrent of Italian newspaper abuse greeted the publication of the De Rudio letter. Various details in the account were meticulously examined and ridiculed, especially by Alexander Luzio, director of the Royal Archives of Mantua, in an article appearing in the *Corriera della Sera* on August 15, 1908. He scoffed at De Rudio's story of his providential rescue in the courtyard of the guillotine, and derided many other statements, but it is quite evident that his real object was to discredit the accusation against Crispi.

Support for Luzio came from many disparate sources. The "evidence," detailed by Marino, is at times quite unconvincing.[22] A lawyer friend of the brother of Felice Orsini, related that Cesar Orsini had told him that Crispi had a part in the conspiracy but did not throw the bomb (*Corriere d'Italia,* August 14).

Tommaso Palmalenghi-Crispi, the nephew of Crispi, refuted the charge of complicity by alluding to certain secret papers not available for public inspection. (*Messaggero* August 13, 1908).

Mrs. Ernestina Orsini, only daughter of Orsini, is quoted in *Gionale d'Italia* on August 23, 1908 as expressing doubts about certain documents compromising Crispi, said to have been in the possession of her uncle, Cesar Orsini.

Rosalita Montmassan, the ex-wife of Crispi, reported to the *Figaro* of August 19, 1908 that she accompanied Crispi on several trips when he had carried bombs, but those bombs had been made in Sicily. She affirmed that Crispi had nothing to do with the Orsini bomb or the attempt on the life of Napoleon III.

Count Carlo Galateri in the *Gionale d'Italia* on August 23, 1908 stated that Crispi's nephew, Felice Caralozzolo, told him that Crispi was opposed to the Orsini attempt and wanted to stop it.[22]

Even Antonio Gomez was brought into the controversy. In a series of four articles beginning in the *La Stampa* of Torino on

Final Days

August 24, 1908, a correspondent briefly related Gomez's recollections of the famous *attentat* and quoted him as saying that he had no knowledge of Crispi's participation.[23]

And on it went. In the absence of a reply from De Rudio, his sister Luigia living in Venice, ever faithful to the memory of Fortunato Calvi, felt compelled to defend her brother in an article reprinted in the *Il Resto di Carlino* on August 20, 1908. She vigorously denied that money was the reason for his participation in the conspiracy.

De Rudio's letter was finally received and published by the *Resto di Carlino* on October 4, 1908. His answers to the charges made by Luzio seem quite plausible. More to the point, he was able to identify Crispi and place him at the scene, since he had known Crispi in Genoa and in London and could easily recognize him. He quoted Orsini's statement at the trial that Orsini had given a bomb to an Italian in the Rue Lepelletier and noted that Orsini had spoken to only one Italian-- Francesco Crispi.

The polemics continued for several years and the issue is still unsettled. De Rudio had been in poor health, suffering with asthma, congestive heart failure and overweight, from the retention of body fluids. In October 1910 his medical status deteriorated, and he was forced to take to his bed in his new home on 1839 S. New England Avenue, Los Angeles.

Word was sent to his family and close friends, and Hercules was summoned from Signal, Arizona. Dr. Bartholomew Sassilla, his physician for ten years, attended him at the bedside. In his last days, The Sunday *Star* (Washington, D.C.) published a biography of De Rudio on October 16, 1910, always an ominous sign.

Major De Rudio died November 1, 1910. The cause of death was "acute bronchopneumonia catarrh and a weak heart, chronic." Reports of his death were printed in the Los Angeles *Daily Times*, the New York *Times* and by many other newspapers across the land. Five of his fellow officers at Little Bighorn survived him.

Charles De Rudio was cremated on November 3 at the Los Angeles Crematory, and his ashes transported by his family to San Francisco for burial in the officers' section of the National Military Cemetery of the Presidio in Plot 109 6, not far from the grave of Charles Varnum, his old comrade-in-arms. A simple military headstone stands at the head, with a cross in base relief and the words:

Charles C. De Rudio
Major, 7th Cavalry
November 1, 1910

Hercules De Rudio never married. He had a successful career in Signal, Arizona as a mining engineer and investor. After 1913, nothing further is known of his whereabouts. He was buried on November 4, 1938 at the Presidio. Charles De Rudio's grandson did not receive an appointment to West Point. Efforts to trace living descendents have been unsuccessful.[24] The family in Italy has been extinguished.

Eliza De Rudio applied for a widow's pension. She received the equivalent of a soldier's pay of twelve dollars per month until her death on January 9, 1922.[25] She was cremated and her remains buried near her husband.

And so the story ends. The trumpet is stilled and the sounds of the march fade into memory.

Notes

1. Kenneth Hammer, ed., *Custer in 76* (Norman and London: University of Oklahoma, 1988), p. 88.
2. ACP, Charles C. De Rudio, CF D345 CT 1864, NAB.
3. Robert M. Utley, *Frontier Regulars. The United States Army and the Indian, 1866-1890* (New York: Macmillan, 1973), p. 21.
4. Annual Evaluation. ACP, Charles C. De Rudio, CF D345 CT 1864, NAB
5. Utley, *Frontier*, p. 84.
6. Geoffrey C. Ward, *The West* (Boston: Little Brown, 1999), p. 324.
7. Edward L. Daily, *Custer to MacArthur* (Paducah, KY: Turner, 1995), p. 88.
8. Carl Waldman, *Biographical Dictionary of American Indian History to 1900* (New York: Checkmark Books, 2001), p.236.
9. Dee Brown, *The American West* (New York: Scribner, 1966), p. 324.
10. Phyllis De la Garza, *The Apachie Kid* (Tucson: Westernlore, 1995), pp 28-162; Jay Robert Nash, *Encyclopedia of Western Lawmen and Outlaws* (New York: Da Capo, 1994), p. 10.
11. Scott, *Memories,* p. 193.
12. Stephen Longstreet, *War Cries on Horseback* (Garden City, NY: Doubleday, 1970), p. 92.
13. Frank Richard Prassel, *The Great American Outlaw* (Norman and London: University of Oklahoma Press, 1993), p.205.
14. Jason Hook and Martin Pegler, *To Live and Die in the West* (Oxford: Osprey, 1999), p. 151.
15. Maurice Matlof, *American Military History* Office of the Chief of Military History, 1969 (revised 1973), Government Printing Office, p. 315. p. 290.
16. Hammer, p. 88.
17. Daily, p. 93.
18. Cesare Marino, *Dal Piave al Little Bighorn* (Belluno: Tarantola, 1996), p. 297.
19. ACP, Charles C. De Rudio, CF D345 CT 1864, NAB
20. news article, *Mohave County Miner*, 2 November 1908, 23 April 1910.
21. Encyclopedia Britannica, 15th edition, 1988, s.v. "Francesio Crispi."
22. Marino, pp. 301-345.
23. Ugo Ricci, "Il Memorials Inedito di un complice d'Orsini," Gomez A. *La Stampa*, 24 August 1908, 27 August 1908, 30 August 1908, 13 September 1908.
24. Italia Adair d. Oct. 2, 1923, Los Angeles; Carlotta Vicery d. Nov. 10, 1962 Los Angeles; Roma Wilcox d. Dec. 1, 1968 Santa Clara, CA.
25. ACP, Charles C. De Rudio, CF D345 CT 1864, NAB

BIBLIOGRAPHY

Adams, Alexander B. *Geronimo*. New York, NY: Da Capo, 1971.
Allen, Olivis. *New York*. New York: Athenium, 1990.
Alexander, Bevin. *Robert E. Lee's Civil War*. Holbrook, MA: Adams Media, 1998.
Andrist, Ralph K. *The Long Death*. New York: Macmillan, 1964.
Appointment, Commissions, Personal (ACP) File: Charles C. De Rudio, consolidated File D 345 Ct 1864; Pension File: Charles C. De Rudio (Elizabeth Booth de Rudio). National Archives. Washington D.C.
Aronson, Theo. *The Fall of the Third Napoleon*. Indianapolis and New York: Bobbs-Merrell, 1970.
Ashworth, W. *London*. London: Macgibbon & Kee, 1864.
Athearn, Robert G. *Forts of the Upper Missouri*. Englewood Cliffs, NJ: Prentice Hall, 1967.
Aubry, Octave. *The Second Empire*. Philadelphia and New York: Lippincott, 1940.
Baker, Paul R. *The Fortunate Pilgrims*. Cambridge, MA: Harvard University Press, 1964.
Barnard, Edward S., ed. *Story of the Great American West*. New York and Montreal: Readers Digest, 1977.
Barnard, Sandy. *Custer's First Sergeant John Ryan*. Terre Haute, IN: AST Press, 1996.
Barnard, Sandy. *Ten Years with Custer. A 7th Cavalryman's Memoirs*. Ft. Collins, CO: Citizen Printing, 2001.
Barnard, Sandy. *Digging into Custer's Last Stand*. Huntington Beach, CA: Ventana, 1998.
Barnes, Frank. *Cartridges of the World*. Wisconsin: Krause, 2000
Barschak, Erna. *The Innocent Empress*. New York: E. P. Dulton, 1943.
Beal, Merrill D. *I Will Fight No More Forever*. Seattle: University of Washington Press, 1963.
Beales, Derek. *England and Italy 1859-60*. London: Nelson, 1961.
Berlin, Ira, ed. *Freedoms*. Cambridge, London: Cambridge University, 1982.
Bolitho, William. *Twelve against the Gods. The Story of Adventure*. New York: Readers Club, 1929.
Bowers, Claude G. *The Tragic Era*. Cambridge, MA: Houghton Mifflin, 1929.
Bradley, James H. *The March of the Montana Column*. Norman: University of Oklahoma, 1961.

Briggs, Asa. *Victorian Cities.* New York and Evanston: Harper and Row, 1963.
Brininstool, E. A. *Troopers with Custer.* Lincoln and London: University of Nebraska, 1952.
Brown, Dee. *The American West.* New York: Touchstone (Scribner), 1994.
Brown, Mark H. *The Flight of the Nez Perce.* Putnam N.Y., 1994.
Buckmaster, Henrietta. *Freedom Bound.* New York: Macmillan, 1965.
Burns, Michael. *Dreyfus.* New York: Harper Collins, 1991.
Burrows, Edwin G. And Mike Wallace. *A History of New York City to 1898.* New York and Oxford: Oxford, 1999.
Burton, William L. *Melting Pot Soldiers.* Ames: Iowa State University Press, 1988.
Bury, J. P. T. *France.* Philadelphia: University of Pennsylvania Press, 1949.
Butler, W.F. *The Great Lone Land.* London: Low, Marston, Low & Searle, 1873.
Carpenter, John A. *Sword and Olive Branch.* Pittsburgh: University of Pittsburgh Press, 1964.
Carroll, John M. *The Benteen-Goldin Letters on Custer and his last Battle.* New York: Liveright, 1974.
Carroll, John M. *Camp Talk.* Matetuch, NY: J. M. Carroll, 1983.
Carroll, John M., ed. *I. Varnum.* Glendale, CA: Arthur H. Clark Co., 1892.
Carroll, John M. *They Rode with Custer.* Matetuch, NY: J. M. Carroll, 1993.
Castelot, Andre. *The Turbulent City: Paris.* New York: Harper and Row, 1962.
Chandler, Melbourne C. *Of Gary Owen in Glory.* Annadale, VA: Turnpike Press, 1960.
Chapman, J. M. and Brian Chapman. *Life and Times of Baron Haussmann.* New York: Brentano, 1920
Coffeen, Herbert. *The Custer Battle Book.* New York: Carlton Press, 1964.
Collier, Richard. *The General Next to God.* New York: Dutton, 1965.
Connell, Evan S. *Son of the Morning Star.* New York: Harper Perennial, 1984.
Coppa, Frank J. *The Origins of the Italian Wars of Independence.* London and New York: Longman, 1992.
Corley, Thomas, and Anthony Buchanan. *Democratic Despot. A Life of Napoleon III.* London: Barrie & Rocliff, 1923.
Crespi, Cesare. *Per la Liberta!* San Francisco: Canessa Printing, 1913.
Current, Richard Nelson. *Those Terrible Carpetbaggers.* New York and Oxford: Oxford, 1988.
Custer, Elizabeth B. *Boots and Saddles.* New York: Harper, 1885.
Custer, Elizabeth B. *Following the Guidon.* Lincoln and London: University of Nebraska Press, 1994.
Custer, Elizabeth B. *Tenting on the Plains.* New York: Webster, 1889.
Custer, G. A. *My Life on the Plains.* New York: Citadel, 1874.
Cutler, William G. *History of the State of Kansas.* Chicago: Andreas, 1883.
Daily, Edward L. *Custer to Mac Arthur.* Paducah, KY: Turner, 1995.
Dictionary of American Biography, Scribner: N.Y., 1936.
Dobak, W. A. and Thomas D. Phillips. *The Black Regulars 1866-1898.* Norman: University of Oklahoma Press, 1995.
Dore, Gustave and Jerrold Blanchard. *London, a Pilgrimage.* New York and London: Benjamin Blom, 1872.
Du Mont, John S. *Custer Battle Guns.* Ft. Collins, CO: Old Army Press, 1974.
Dunbar, Seymour. *A History of Travel in America.* New York: Tudor, 1937.

Bibliography

Ellis, Edward Roff. *The Epic of New York City.* New York: Coward-McCann, 1966.
Farcaras, Dana & Michael Pauls. *Venetia and the Dalamites.* London: Cardogan, 1999.
Finerty, John R. *War-Path and Bivouac.* Norman: University of Oklahoma Press, 1961.
Foner, Eric. *Reconstruction. America's Unfinished Revolution 1863-1877.* New York: Harper & Row, 1988.
Fougera, Katherine Gibson. *With Custer's Cavalry.* Lincoln and London: University of Nebraska, 1986.
Frazer, Robert W. *Forts of the West.* Norman and London: University of Oklahoma, 1988.
Geer, Walter. *Napoleon the Third, The Romance of an Emperor.* NY: Brentano, 1920.
Gilliard, Charles. *A History of Switzerland.* London: Allan and Unwin, 1955.
Glatthaar, Joseph T. *Forged in Battle.* New York: Macmillan, 1990.
Gooch, G. P. *The Second Empire.* Westport, CT: Greenwood Press, 1960.
Gorce, Pierre de la. *Histoire du Second Empire.* Vol. II. New York: AIMS Press, 1969.
Graham, W. A. *The Reno Court of Inquiry.* Mechanicsburg, PA: Stackpole, 1995.
Graham, W. A. *The Custer Myth.* Harrisburg, PA: Stackpole, 1953.
Gray, John S. *Centennial Campaign.* Ft. Collins, CO: Old Army Press, 1976.
Gray, John S. *Custer's Last Campaign.* Norman and London: University of Nebraska, 1991.
Greene, Jerome A. *Battles and Skirmishes of the Great Sioux War.* Norman and London: University of Oklahoma, 1993.
Guyana. Visual Geography Series, Lerner Publication Corp., Minneapolis, MN: Lerner Publication Corp., 1988.
Hale, William Harlan. *Horace Greeley.* New York: Harper, 1950.
Hales, Edward Elton Young. *Mazzini and the Secret Societies.* New York: Kennedy, 1956.
Hammer Kenneth, ed. *Custer in 76.* Norman and London: University of Oklahoma, 1988.
Hampton, Bruce. *Children of Grace.* New York: Holt, 1994
Hargrove, Hondon B. *Black Union Soldiers in the Civil War.* Jefferson, NC: McFarnand, 1988.
Hattaway, Herman. *The Sable Arm.* Lawrence KS: University of Kansas Press, 1987.
Herbert, Christopher. *Rome The Biography of a City.* New York and London: Norton, 1985.
Henry, Robert Selph. *'First with the Most' Forrest.* New York: Bobbs-Merrill, 1944.
Henry, Robert Sellph. *The Story of Reconstruction.* Indianapolis and New York: Bobbs-Merrill, 1938.
Hibbert, Christopher. *Garibaldi and his Enemies.* Boston and Toronto: Little Brown and Co, 1965.
Higginson, Thomas Wentworth. *Army Life in a Black Regiment.* New York: Penguin Books, 1997.

Hinkley, Edyth. *Mazzini. The Story of a Great Italian.* Port Washington, NY and London: Kennekat, 1924.
Hook, Jason & Martin Pegler. *To Live and Die in the West.* Oxford: Osprey, 1999.
Howard, Helen Addison and Dan L. McGrath. *War Chief Joseph.* Lincoln: University of Nebraska, 1941.
Hoxie, Frederick E. *Encyclopedia of North American Indians.* Boston and New York: Houghton Mifflin, 1998.
Hunt, Frazier and Robert Hunt. *"I Fought with Custer."* New York and London: Scriber, 1947.
Hutton, Paul Andrew. *The Custer Reader.* Lincoln and London: University of Nebraska, 1992.
Jackson, Kenneth and T. Jackson, ed. *The Encyclopedia of New York City.* New Haven: Yale University Press, 1995.
Jones, Mary Ellen. *Daily Life on the Nineteenth Century American Frontier.* Westport, CT: Greenwood, 1988.
Jordan, Jr., Ervin L. *Black Confederates and Afro-Yankees in the Civil War.* Charlottesville, VA: Virginia University Press, 1955.
King, Bolton. *A History of Italian Unity 1814-1871.* Vol I. London: Nesbet, 1934.
Knapton, Ernest John. *France.* New York: Scribner, 1971.
Kurtz, Harold. *The Empress Eugenie.* Boston: Houghton Mifflin, 1964.
Lanning, Michael Lee. *The African American Soldier.* Secaucus, NJ: Carol, 1997.
Lee, Robert. *Fort Meade and the Black Hills.* Lincoln and London: University of Nebraska Press, 1991.
Longstreet, Stephen. *War Cries on Horseback.* Garden City, NY: Doubleday, 1970.
Luce, Edward S. *Keogh, Comanche and Custer.* Private Edition, 1939.
McClernand, Edward J. *With the Indian and the Buffalo in Montana.* Glendale, CA: Clark, 1969.
McKay, Ernest. *The Civil War and New York City.* Syracuse, NY: Syracuse University Press, 1990.
McPherson, James M. *The Negro's Civil War.* Urbana, Chicago: University of Illinois, 1982.
Maddocks, Melvin. *The Atlantic Crossing.* Np; Time-Life, 1981.
Magnussen, Daniel. *Peter Thompson's Narrative of the Little Bighorn Campaign of 1876.* Glendale, CA: Clark, 1974.
Mangione, Jerre and Ben Morreale. *La Storia.* New York: Harper Perennial, 1993.
Marcy, Randolph B. *The Prairie Traveler 1859.* Bedford, MA: Applewood, 1993.
Marino, Cesare. *Dal Piave al Little Bighorn.* Belluno: Tarantola, 1996.
Markowitz, Harvey, ed. *American Indians.* Pasadena, CA and Englewood Cliffs, NJ: Salem, 1995.
Marquis, Thomas. *Custer on the Little Bighorn.* Lodi, CA: Marquis, 1967.
Marquis, Thomas. *Custer, Cavalry and Crows.* Ft. Collins, CO: Old Army Press, 1975.
Marraro, Howard R. "Italians in New York in the 1850's." N.Y. History 30, no. 2. April-July, 1949.
Marshall, S. L. A. *Crimsoned Prairie.* New York: Scribner, 1972.
Matlof, Maurice. *American Military History.* Office of the Chief of Military History, 1969 (revised 1973). Government Printing Office.
Merington, Marguerite. *The Custer Story.* Lincoln: University of Nebraska Press, 1987.

Meyers, Augustus. *Ten Years in the Ranks of the U.S. Army.* New York: Arno, 1979.
Michno, Gregory. *The Mystery of E Troop.* Missoula, MT: Mountain Press, 1994.
Miles, Alexander. *Devil's Island. Colony of the Damned.* Berkley, CA: Ten Speed Press, 1988.
Miles, Nelson A. *Personal Recollections and Observations of General Nelson A. Miles.* Vol. I. Lincoln and London: University of Nebraska, 1992.
Mills, Charles K. *Charles De Rudio.* Mattetuch and Bryan, NY: J. M. Carroll, 1983.
Mont, John S. Du. *Custer Battle Guns.* Ft. Collins, CO: Old Army Press, 1974.
Morreale, Ben and Robert Carol. *Italian Americans: The Immigrant Experience.* Hong Kong: Hugh Lauter Levin, 2000.
Mulford, Ani Frank. *Fighting Indians in the 7th Cavalry.* 2nd ed. Fairfield, WA: Ye Galleon Press, 1972.
Murphy, Richard W. *The Nation Reunited.* Alexandria, VA: Time-Life Books, 1887.
Nash, Jay Robert. *Encyclopedia of Western Lawsmen and Outlaws.* New York: Da Capo Press, 1994.
Nichols, Ronald H. *In Custer's Shadow: Major Marcus Reno* Norman: University of Oklahoma, 1999
Nightingale, Robert. *Little Bighorn.* U.S.: Far West Publications, 1996.
Official Army Register for 1908. Washington D.C.: Government Printing Office.
Osgood, Samuel M. *Napoleon III.* Boston: Heath, 1963.
Packe, Michael St. John. *The Bombs of Orsini.* London: Secker and Warburg, 1957.
Panzeri, Peter. *Little Bighorn 1876.* Botley, Oxford: Osprey Publishing Co., 1995.
Pellegrini, D. Francesco. *Codice Diplomatico.* Venezia: Antonelli, 1869.
Phisterer, Frederick. *New York in the War of the Rebellion 1861-1865.* Albany: Lyon, 1912.
Prassel, Frank Richard. *The Great American Outlaw.* Norman and London: University of Oklahoma Press, 1993.
Price, Roger. *The French Second Republic, A Social History.* Ithaca, NY: Cornell University Press, 1972.
Procacci, Guiliano. *History of the Italian People.* New York: Harper and Row, 1968.
Quarles, Benjamin. *The Negro in the Civil War.* Boston: Da Capo, 1953.

Randall, J. G. & David Donald. *The Civil War and Reconstruction.* Boston: Heath, 1961.
Returns [personnel reports] from Regular Army Cavalry Regiments, 1833-1916: The Seventh Cavalry, 1866-1896 Microfilm 744, Rolls 71-74, National Archives. Washington, D.C.
Returns [personnel reports] from U.S. Military Posts, 1800-1916 Ft Lincoln N. Dakota 1872- 1902 Microfilm 617, Rolls 628-629, National Archives. Washington, D.C.
Rheinardt, E. A. *Napoleon and Eugenie.* New York: Knoff, 1931.
Rickey, Don. *Forty Miles a Day on Beans and Hay.* Norman and London: University of Oklahoma, 1963.
Ridley, Jasper. *Garibaldi.* New York: Viking Press, 1974.
Robinson III, Charles M. *A Good Year to Die. The Story of the Great Sioux War.*

New York: Random House, 1955.
Robinson, Elwyn B. *History of North Dakota*. Lincoln: University of Nebraska Press, 1967.
Sandoz, Mari. *The Battle of Little Bighorn*. Philadelphia and New York: Lippincott, 1966.
Sarf, Wayne M. *The Little Bighorn Campaign*. Pennsylvania: Combined Books, 2000.
Scott, Douglas D. Scott and Richard A. Fox, Jr., *Custer Battle*. Norman: University of Oklahoma, 1987
Scott, Douglas D & Melissa A Connor. *They Died with Custer*. Norman: University of Oklahoma, 1991.
Douglas D. Scott and Richard A. Fox, Jr., *Custer Battle* (Norman: University of Oklahoma, 1987)
Scott, Hugh Lenox. *Some Memories of a Soldier*. New York: Century, 1928.
Secretary of War. *Annual Report 1876*. 54th Congress, First Session, Executive Document No. 1, Serial Vol. 1742 p. 2-8
Sedillot, Rene. *An Outline of French History*. New York: Knopf, 1967.
Sencourt, Robert. *Napoleon III: The Modern Emperor*. Freeport, NY: Librarie Press, 1933.
Shaw, Frederick. *One Hundred and Forty Years Service in Peace and War: History of the Second Infantry*. Detroit and Fullerton, CA: Strathmore, 1930.
Shunt, Frazier and Robert. *I fought with Custer*. New York and London: Scribner, 1947.
Simpson, F. A. *Napoleon and the Recovery of France*. London: Longmans Green, 1951.
Simpson, Frederick Arthur. *The Rise of Louis Napoleon*. London: Cass, 1968.
Slaughter, Linda. *Fortress to Farm or 23 Years on the Frontier*. New York: Exposition, 1972.
Smith, Denis Mack. *Mazzini*. New Haven and London: Yale University Press, 1994.
Smith, William Herbert Cecil. *Napoleon III*. New York: St. Martin Press, 1973.
Sommers, Richard J. *Richmond Redeemed*. Garden City, NY: Doubleday, 1999.
Sprigge, Cecil J. S. *The Development of Modern Italy*. New Haven: Yale University Press, 1944.
Stellard, Patricia Y. *Glittering Misery; Dependents of the Indian Fighting Army*. Ft. Collins, CO: Presidio Press, Old Army Press, 1978.
Stewart, Edgar I. *Custer's Luck*. Norman and London: University of Oklahoma Press, 1955.
Sutton, Horace. *Footloose in Switzerland*. New York and Toronto: Reinhart, 1935.
Tarbox, Increase. *Missionary Patriots. Memoirs of James H. Schneider and Edward M. Schneider*. Boston: Massachusetts Sabbath School Society, 1867.
Taylor, William O. *With Custer on the Little Bighorn*. New York: Viking, 1996.
Tebbel, John and Keith Jennison. *The American Indian Wars*. New York: Harper, 1900.
Terrell, John Upton and George Walton. *Faint the Trumpet Sounds*. New York: McKay, 1966.
Thayer, William Roscoe. *A Short History of Venice*. Boston and New York: Houghton Mifflin, 1908.

Bibliography

Thompson, J. M. *Louis Napoleon and the Second Empire.* New York: Norton, 1955.
Tibaldi, Paolo. *Da Roma a Cayenna: lotte, esigli, deportazione/ narrazine di Paolo Tibaldi.* 3rd edit. Roma: Tipagrafico Italiano, 1888. Widener Lib. (Harvard Univ.) Film W 13029.
Todd, William. *The 79th Highlanders.* Albany, NY: Biandow, Barton, 1880.
Trefousse, Hans L. *Rutherford B. Hayes.* New York: Time Books and Holt and Co., 2002.
Trevelylan, Janet Penrose. *A Short History of the Italian People.* New York: Pitman, 1956.
Trudeau, Noah Andre. *Like Men of War.* Boston: Little Brown, 1998.
Upton, Richard. *The Custer Adventure.* Ft. Collins, CO: Old Army Press, 1978.
Utley, Robert M. *Frontier Regulars. The United States Army and the Indian, 1866-1890.* New York: Macmillan, 1973.
Utley, Robert M. *Cavalier in Buckskin.* Norman and London: University of Oklahoma Press, 1988.
Van de Water, Frederick F. *Glory Hunter.* Lincoln and London: University of Nebraska, 1934.
Vaughn, J. W. *Indian Fights.* Norman: University of Oklahoma Press, 1956.
Viola, Herman and Susan P. Viola. *Guiseppi Garibaldi.* New York, Chelsea, 1988.
Vistal, Stanley. *The Missouri.* New York and Toronto: Ferrar and Rinehart, 1945.
Waldman, Carl. *Biographical Dictionary of American Indian History to 1900.* New York: Checkmark Books, 2001.
Ward, Geoffrey C. *The West.* Boston: Little Brown & Co., 1999.
War Department, Bureau of Military Justice. Case of 2nd Lieut. C.C. De Rudio. Statement of Case and Claim of Rank, made by 2nd Lieutenant C.C. De Rudio, 7th U.S. Cavalry, 1872 in ACP File, C. C. DeRudio.
War of the Rebellion, A Compilation of the Official Records of the Union and Confederate Armies. 130 vol. Washington D.C.: Government Printing Office, 1880-1901.
Welch, James and Paul Stekler. *Killing Custer.* New York: Norton, 1994.
Wesley, Charles A. and Patricia W. Romero. *Negro American in the Civil War.* New York: Publishers Co., 1967.
Wert, Jeffrey D. *Custer.* New York: Simon & Schuster, 1996.
Wexler, Alan. *Atlas of Western Expansion.* New York: Facts on File, 1995.
White, Lonnie J. *Hostiles and Horse Soldiers.* Boulder, CO: Pruett, 1972.
Williams, Albert N. *The Black Hills.* Dallas, TX: Southern Methodist University Press, 1952.
Williams, Roger L. *Gaslight and Shadow.* New York: Macmillin, 1957.
Wooster, Robert. *Nelson A. Miles and the Twilight of the Frontier Army.* Lincoln: University of Nebraska, 1993.

NEWSPAPERS AND PERIODICALS

Bismarck *Tribune Extra*, 6 July 1876.
Colliers Weekly, 15 March 1920.
Los Angeles Daily *Times*, 1 November 1910.
Los Angeles *Sunday Times*, 10 December 1905.
Milan *Il Resto del Carlino*, 9, 10, 12-13 August 1908.

Mohave County *Miner*, 1 June, 2 November 1907; 11 January, 11 April, 14 October 1908; 9 April, 11 April, 24 October 1908; 9 April, 16 April, 23 April 1910.
New York *Herald*, 30 July 1876.
New York *Times*, 20-22 March 1881; 21 October 1884.
Turin *La Stampa*, 24, 27, 30 August and 13 September 1908.
Washington *Post*, August 29, 1894; 3-4 September 1901.
Washington *Star*, 16 October 1910.
Wild West, June 1999.

INDEX

----, Apache Kid 318-319
----, Eliza 70
----, King Bomba, 6 9
1ST FOREIGN RIFLES, 99
2ND CAVALRY, 256-257 276 276-277
2ND INFANTRY, 123 126-127 140 Co F 125
2ND U S COLORED TROOPS, 108 110-111
2ND U S COLORED TROOPS (INFANTRY), 106-107
3RD CAVALRY DIVISION, 111
4TH U S ARTILLERY BATTERY B, 144
5TH CAVALRY, 137
5TH CORPS OF THE ARMY OF THE POTOMAC, 123
5TH INFANTRY, 258 260 282
5TH MILITARY (LOUISIANA-TEXAS) DISTRICT, 135
5TH MILITARY DISTRICT, 174
7TH CAVALRY, 131-136 139-142 146 153 156 158 161 164 166 173 187-188 190 192 203 207 254 258-260 265-266 269-271 277 282-283 291-292 295 297 301-302 306-307 309 311 317 319
7TH INFANTRY, 280
9TH ARMY CORP, 106
9TH CAVALRY (COLORED), 301
9TH CORPS, 105
11TH NEW YORK CAVALRY, 99
16TH INFANTRY, 127
17TH INFANTRY, 122
24TH INFANTRY, 303 317
39TH NEW YORK (GARIBALDI) REGIMENT, 99
39TH NEW YORK INFANTRY REGIMENT, 98
47TH PENNSYLVANIA, 109
54TH MASSACHUSETTS, 118
79TH HIGHLANDERS, 103
79TH NEW YORK HIGHLANDERS, 104
79TH NEW YORK INFANTRY, 105
79TH REGIMENT, 106 109
137TH U S COLORED TROOP (INFANTRY) 133

ABSAROKA MOUNTAINS, 275 279 281
ACADEMY OF MUSIC, 98
ACKERMANN, Karen 13
ADAIR, Mrs S E 320 Samuel De Rudio 320
AFRICA, 84
ALABAMA, 172
ALBERT, Prince of ? 43
ALEXANDER II, Czar of Russia 90
ALEXIS, Grand Duke of Russia 146
ALGERIA, 26 29 54
ALICANTE, 26
ALLSOP, Mr 54-55 Thomas 53 61 88
AMAZON RIVER, 76
ANTI-PAPISTS, 98
ANTIETAM, 103
APACHE, 317-318
APPALOOSA (HORSE), 273
APPOMATTOX COURT HOUSE, 111
ARAPAHO, 135-136
ARAPAHO RESERVATION, 311
ARDA RIVER, 44
ARDO RIVER, 1 4 38
ARGENTINA, 16
ARIKARA, 190 192 197 200 229 231 233 241
ARIZONA, 317-318
ARIZONA TERRITORY, 317-318
ARKANSAS, 308
ARKANSAS CITY, 308
ARKANSAS RIVER, 132 134
ARLINGTON HEIGHTS, 107
ARLINGTON NATIONAL CEMETERY, 303
ARMY OF THE POTOMAC, 97 104-105 174
ARMY OF THE UNITED STATES, 104
ARMY OF VIRGINIA, 104
ASH BARRACKS TENNESSEE, 146 148
ASH, Brev Brig Gen 120
ATLANTA GEORGIA, 302-303
ATLANTIC OCEAN, 74 86 119
AUGUSTUS, 1
AUSTERLITZ, 27
AUSTIN TEXAS, 315 317

336 Index

AUSTRIA, 4 7-8 46 67 80 122 Duke of 1
BACON, Elizabeth 133
BAD LANDS, 193
BAIRD, Andrew D 104
BALEN, 76
BARCELONA SPAIN, 26
BAROZZI, Bastiano 4-5 10 30 37-38 Father 37 43
BASSI, Ugo 98
BATIGNOLLE, 27
BAY PORT, 109
BEAR BUTTE, 196 289 315
BEAR BUTTE CREEK, 289
BEAR PAW MOUNTAIN, 283 287
BEDINI, Gaetano 98
BELFIORE, 36
BELGIUM, 57
BELKNAP, Secretary of War 166 187 William W 268
BELLOWS, Dr 112 Henry W 100 Rev 100-101 Rev Dr 117
BELLUNO, 1-2 2-4 6 10-11 31 37-39 39 41 43 89 91 100 175
BELUNUM, 1
BENTEEN, Capt 137 141-143 147 160 164-166 170 175-176 187-189 193 199 201-204 207-210 217 219 221 229 238-241 243-245 252 254-255 255 258 265 269 277 281-282 291-293 295 301-303 306 Catherine Louse 171 Freddie 143 170 Freddy 172 Frederick W 133-134 Kate 143 303 Mrs 137 159
BENZINE BOARD, 127 143 293
BERBICK RIVER 83-84
BERNARD, Simon Francis 51-54 56 64 70 73 87-89
BERNE, 45
BERTHAL INDIAN AGENCY, 270
BIG, Foot 318 Hole 275 277
BIGHORN, 258
BIGHORN MOUNTAINS, 245 River 155 182 195-197 210 258 306
BILLINGS, 282
BINGHAM, John A 100
BIRMINGHAM, 51 53 55 88
BISMARCK, 159 164-166 265 267 270 288-289 River 256
BLACK HILLS EXPEDITION, 160
BLACK HILLS SOUTH DAKOTA, 153 155 167-168 175 181-183 193 196 259-260 288 290 294
BLACKFEET, 153-154
BLUFF CREEK, 135
BOGESS, Howard 221 224
BOLZANO, 40

BONAPARTE, 174 Napoleon 1 3 53 132
BOOT HILL, 138
BOOTH, Elizabeth 46-47 Jane 88 William 46
BORDEAU, 60
BOULOGNE, 5
BOURBON, 2 28
BOUYER, Mitch 206-207 218
BOWDOIN COLLEGE, 112
BOYLE, Edward T 47
BOZEMAN, 185
BOZEMAN TRAIL, 154-155 184
BOZEMAN WAR, 184
BRAZIL, 15 74 82 305 Emperor of 268
BREAUX BRIDGE LOUISIANA, 172 174
BRESCIA, 8
BRISBIN, James S 257 267
BRITAIN, 35 45 47 51
BRITISH GUYANA, 83-84
BRONX NEW YORK, 103
BRONX ZOO, 296
BROOKLYN NEW YORK, 98 103
BROWNING, Robert 35
BRULE, 154
BRUSSELS, 36 53-54 56 62
BRYCE CROSS ROADS, 295
BUENOS AIRES, 16
BULL RUN, 123
BULL RUN, First Battle 103
BUREAU OF COLORED TROOPS, 105
BUREAU OF ORDINANCE 242
BREAU OF REFUGEES, FREEDMEN, AND ABANDONED LANDS, 112
BURRASCA, 37
BUTLER, Benjamin 118
BYRON, Lord 5 28
CADERE, 37
CADORE, 10 37
CAIRO ILLINOIS, 156
CALAIS, 27 60-61
CALHOUN, 224 James 191
CALHOUN HILL, 221-224
CALIFORNIA, 181 320
CALVI, 34 38-39 43 47 Col 10 12 14 31 36-37 40-41 Fortunado 30 Fortunato 10 323 Francisco 321
CAMAS MEADOWS, 275
CAMBDENTOWN, 54
CAMP ROBINSON, 261 290
CANADA, 259 261-262 276 278 282-283 306
CANADIAN BOUNDARY COMMISSION, 139
CANARY ISLANDS, 74
CANYON CREEK MONTANA, 282 303

Index

CANYON DE LOS EMBUDOS MEXICO, 317
CAPRERA, 89
CARALOZZOLO, Felice 322
CARBONARI, 5 13 15 68
CARONTI, Filippo 41-44 48 53
CARPENTER, O A 110
CARROLTOWN, 148
CARTHEGENA SPAIN, 26
CASELLA, Giovanni 168
CASEY, 105 Silas 101-102
CASEY BOARD, 101
CASTELNUOVA, 8
CASTLE GARDEN, 93
CAVEDALIS, Giovanni 14 Minister 14
CAVOUR, Count 80
CAYENNE, 74 81
CEDAR COULEE, 219
CEDAR CREEK, 271 276
CENTURY CLUB, 100
CHANNING, Rev 106
CHARLES, Albert King of Piedmont Savoy 7-9 13 25
CHARLES X, King of? 3 28
CHENEY, Eliza 54 63-64
CHEYENNE, 134-136 145 155 167 206 231 259 261 296 306
CHEYENNE (NORTHERN), 154 182 184 196 218 260-261 265 287 289-290
CHEYENNE RESERVATION, 311
CHEYENNE (TOWN), 288
CHEYENNE RIVER RESERVATION, 309
CHICAGO ILLINOIS, 127 291-292 294 305 316
CHINA, 84
CHIOGGIA, 14
CHIPPEWA, 153
CHIRICAHUA, 274
CHIRICAHUA APACHE, 183 318
CHISHOLM TRAIL, 137 311
CIRCLE OF HEAVEN, 27
CIVIL WAR, 98 124-125 131-133 139 141 148 160 183 187 189 211 240 243 260 273 276 295 306
CIVITA VECCHIA, 15-16 21
CLARK, 154 273 281
CLARK'S FORK CANYON, 281
CLARK'S FORK RIVER, 275 278 278-281
CLEARWATER RIVER, 274
CLOTHILDE, 90
CLOUET, Francoise 174 Gen 174
COBLENZ, 80
COCHISE, 183 274
COCKRELL, Senator 140
CODY, Buffalo Bill 306 309

COLD HARBOR, 104 123
COLOGNE, 80
COLORADO, 126 131 131 154 181 288
COLT REVOLVER, 191 242
COLUMBIA COLLEGE, 98
COMANCHE, 144 307
COMAMCHE (HORSE), 204 255-256
COMMITTEE OF ITALIAN POLITICAL REFUGEES, 97
COOKE, William 207
COUNCIL OF VIENNA, 84
COUP OF 1851, 28
COUP OF 1852, 42
COUSINS, 79-83
CRACOW, 4
CRAZY HORSE, 184 224 231 237 259-262
CRAZY WOMAN FORK, 260
CRIMEAN, War 41 43 47 70
CRISPI, Francesco 58 321-323
CRITTENDEN BARRACKS KENTUCKY, 125
CROOK, Gen 182 187 196-197 202 211 242 258-261 265 274 317-318 George 183-185
CROW, 153 182 184-185 197 200 203-207 209-210 217 221 224 229-230 271 273 276 276-279 281-282 306
CROW RESERVATION, 275-276
CROW'S NEST, 205-206
CUBA, 319
CULLUM, George Washington 100
CURLY, 221 306
CUSTER, Boston 191 205 219 Elizabeth 133 304 George Armstrong 111 132-135 135-139 141-147 157 160-162 165-166 171 175 181 185 187-190 193-195 197-211 217-224 229 231-232 234-235 237 239-241 243 250 255-258 290 292-294 303 Libby 139 143 157-159 164 291 304 Mrs 156 191 Tom 161 164 191 205 252
CUSTER BATTLEFIELD, 223 239
CUSTER CITY, 288
CUSTER HILL, 223-224 239-240
CUSTOM SERVICE, 173
CUSTOZZA, 9
DAKOTA, 305
DAKOTA SIOUX, 153
DAKOTA TERRITORY, 153 167 262 288
DALMATIA, 4
DANA, Charles A 106 Mr 106 Under Secretary of War 118
DASYLVA, Antonio 60 Jose Antonin 54
DAWES, Henry 117
DEAD CANYON GORGE, 185

Index

DEADWOOD, 288-289
DEADWOOD CITY, 289
DECASALI, G F Secchi 97
DECESNOLA, Luigi 99
DECOLLET, M 69
DEDANINI, Elisabetta 3
DEEP COULEE, 221 224 255
DDEP RAVINE, 224
DELADROME, Mathieu 64
DELAWARE, 106
DEMOCRATIC CONVENTION, 191
DEMOCRATIC PRESIDENTIAL CONVENTION, 187
DEMONTIJO, Eugenie 42 59 67-69
DENVER COLORADO, 146
DER, 277 Mrs 171
DERBY, 88
DERUDIO, 2 265-266 268-270 298 302 304-306 308 310 315 1st Lt 189 2nd Lt 125-127 Achille 3-5 7 10-11 America Carlotta 148 Assassination Attempt on Napoleon III 51-70 297-298 321-323 C C 106 121 277 Capt 303 305 307 311 317 319 Carlo 5-7 10-11 38 100 126 149 Carlo Camillo 4-5 40 90 Carlotta 148 Charles 104 123 277 310 321 324 Charles C 103 120 175 324 Charles Camillus 117 Conspirator in Italy 25-48 Count 38 41 85-86 142 Countess 39 Death 323-324 Elisabetta 3 Elizabeth 47-48 52 54 59 64 67 69 86-89 92 103 109-110 126 143-144 148 157 159 171-172 175-176 257-258 267 293 307 311 317 321 324 Ercole 3 25 37-38 41 48 51 Ercole Placido 3 Guistiniano 4 38 Hercules 48 103 110 258 301 320-321 323-324 Italia 148 Italia Luigia 126 Lt 159 204 254 Luigia 4 10 14 38-41 89 323 Maj 321 323 Mr 112 Mrs 171-172 305 Obtains a Regular Army Commission 117-128 Participation in Attack on Nez Perce 273-283 Participation in Black Hills Patrol 287-290 Participation in Court of Inquiry 290-297 Participation in Little Bighorn Massacre 181-212 217-225 229-245 249-262 Partipation in the American Civil War 97-113 Prisoner in French Guyana 73-93 Promotion to Captain 301 Promotion to Major 320 Pvt 105 Retirement 320-321 Roma 143 148 172 Roma Elisabetta 122 Rudy 267 310 Service as Cavalry Officer in the 7th Cavalry 131-149 Service in Dakota Territory 153-176 Sgt 11 14

DERUDIO (continued)
  Youth and Teenage Years 4-21
DESMET, Pierre Jean 167
DEVIL'S ISLAND, 75 319
DEVOTO, 255 August 168 Augusto 244 Pvt 255
DEWEY, Maj 117
DIAZ, Portino 315
DICKENS, 35
DIJON, 27
DIRUDIO, 2
DISECCI, Carlos 100
DJON, Edward H 121
DOANE, G C 277 Gustavus C 256 276 Lt 276-277 277-282
DODGE, 135
DOMINI, Col 4-5 Fortunado 4
DORMAN, Isaiah 266
DRAGON SPRINGS, 274
DRUSO, 1
DUBLIN IRELAND, 250
DUCHIES, 81
DULL KNIFE, 290
DUTCH GUYANA, 74 82
EARLY, Jubel 133
EDISON, Thomas A 268
ELIZABETHTOWN KENTUCKY, 146
ELLIOT, Maj 234
ENGLAND, 27 48 53-55 67 70 89 97 100
FARGO, 267
FERDINAND II, 17
FERDINAND II, King of Naples 9 12
FERDINAND II, King of Naples-Sicily 6 58
FETTERMAN, William 184
FIRST UNITARIAN CHURCH OF NEW YORK, 100
FLORENA KANSAS, 311
FLORIDA, 318
FLORIDA MILTIARY ACADEMY, 111
FORD A, 230 232 234 237 251
FORD B, 217 219-222 234 255
FORREST, Nathan Bedford 147 295
FORSYTH, Col 306 310-311 316-317 George A 309 James W 306
FORTS, Abercrombie 267 Abraham Lincoln 161 164 Bayard 317 319 Benton 154 159 Buford Dakota Territory 287 306 Custer 259 261 305 Dodge 137 Du Chesne Utah 302 Ellis 185 275-276 278-280 282 Fetterman 182-184 Fisher 187 Harker 137 Hays Kansas 105 137-138 140-141 144 Keogh 259 261 271 Leavenworth 135 144 267 Lincoln 158-159 161 161-164 166-171 182 185 187-190 229 266 269 271 287 289 294-295

FORTS (continued)
  Meade Dakota Territory 289-290 294-297 301-303 306 317 Monroe Virginia 104 Myers Florida 110 Phil Kearny 184 Pierre 296 303 Randall 175 175-176 262 306 Rice 157-159 161 163 167-171 176 188-189 256 265-269 287 290 294 Riley Kansas 131-132 134 306 309 311 Sam Houston Texas 315 317 Shaw 157 182 Sill Oklahoma 307-310 Stedman 103 Stevenson 270 Sumter 103 Taylor 108 110 Totten 289 Wallace 234 Yates 306 Zachary Taylor 108
FORTY THIEVES, 189
FOSCHINI, 48
FOSTER, C W 102 106
FRANCE, 2 21 29 42 47 55 73-74 80 President of 320
FRANCESCO, Sforza 32
FRASER, James Earle 296
FREDERICKSBURG, 103 123
FREEDMAN'S BUREAU, 112
FREEMASONS, 15 98-99 165
FRENCH, Capt 294 Thomas 282 Thomas Henry 236 293
FRENCH GUYANA, 29 54 73-74 76 79 84 89 175 267 319
FRIENDS OF ITALY SOCIETY, 35
FUMAGALLI, Angelo 44 46-47
GAETA, 12-13
GALATERI, Carlo 322
GALL, 184-185 222 224 231-232 237 259 261-262 306
GARDINER RIVER, 279
GARGO, Cararino E 315
GARIBALDI, 13 89-90 92 97-98 219 321 Anita 19-21 21 Giuseppe 15-18 20-21 25
GARIBALDI LEGION, 99
GARRYOWEN IRELAND, 203
GATLING GUN, 161 192 195 198 201 266 274
GENOA, 10 25 25 33 99 323
GEORGIA, 107
GERMANY, 93 124
GERONIMO, 317-318
GETTYSBURG PENNSYLVANIA, 99 123 133 185 203
GIBBON, Col 185-186 193-195 197 199 204 255 257 275 277 John 185-186
GILBERT, C C 280 Lt Col 280-281
GIOVINE, Italia 13
GIRARD, 254 292-293 Frank 251 Fred 189 250-251 262
GLEN, Elder 145

GLENDIVE, 271
GODFREY, E S 241 Edward S 315
GOLD DISCOVERED, 126 131
GOMEZ, Antonio 55-58 60 62 65-69 73-75 77 79 319-320 322-323
GOOSE CREEK WYOMING, 184
GRAHAM, 222 224
GRANT, Gen 257 President 167 173 181 187-188 291 Ulysses S 97 104 111
GRATZ AUSTRIA, 8-9
GRAVESEND, 87
GRAY, J S 209 218
GREAT SPIRIT SPRING KANSAS, 144
GREELEY, Horace 99-100 102 106 117 121
GRILLANZONI, Count 44
GULF OF MEXICO, 108
GUYANA, 86
HAM, 5 68
HANCOCK, Gen 134-135 174 Winfield Scott 174
HANCOCK'S WAR, 134
HAPSBURG, 2 7
HART ISLAND, 103 120
HARTMANN, Rosina 55 62
HARVARD CLUB, 100
HAUSSMANN, Gen 28
HAVANA CUBA, 319
HAYES, President 296 Rutherford B 291
HAYS CITY, 137 144
HEART RIVER, 159
HEINTZELMAN, S P 122
HENRIETTA TEXAS, 307
HENRY RIFLE, 242
HERENDEEN, George 250
HICKOK, Wild Bill 137
HILEY, John S 268
HODGE, T D P 53
HOLYOAKE, 88-89 92 George 103 George Jacob 53
HOMONYMON RIVER, 144
HORNED HORSE, 218
HOTCHKISS CANNON, 309
HOWARD, Gen 112 118 275-276 280 283 Oliver Otis 112-113 Otis O 273-275
HOWITZER GUN, 274
HUGO, Victor 28 45 74
HUNGARY, 6 9
HUNTSVILLE ALABAMA, 148
IDAHO, 126 273-274
ILE ROYAL, 74-75 77-78 80 268
ILES DU SALUT, 78
INDIA, 84
INDIAN TERRITORY, 131 261 287 289 308

INDIANA, 106
INDUSTRIAL REVOLUTION, 45
INTRA ITALY, 33
INVISIBLE CIRCLE, 147
IRELAND, 124
ISLE OF JERSEY, 45
ISLES DU SALUT, 75
ITALIAN GUARD, 99
ITALY, 2 4 7 10 26 30-31 33-34 36 43 81 89-90 90 97 146 219 305 321 324
   Kingdom of 89 122
JACKSON BARRACKS, 172-173
JACKSON, William 250-251 254
JAMES RIVER, 104
JEFFERSON BARRACKS MISSOURI, 125
JOHNSON, President 121 135
JOSEPH, 274-275 278 281-283 287
JUDITH BASIN, 277-278
JUDITH'S BASIN, 275
JUNCTION CITY, 311
KANSAS, 131 153 308 321
KANSAS PACIFIC RAILROAD, 132 137 146 311
KELLOGG, Gov 173 William P 173
KELTON, D C 120 G C 121
KENT, 61
KENTUCKY, 106
KEOGH, Capt 203-205 223 255 Myles 203
KEY WEST FLORIDA, 106 108-111 111
KICKAPOO, 315
KINNER, Mr 88
KIOWA, 135 144 307
KIPLING, Rudyard 292
KNAPP, F V 101 Frederick Newman 106
KNIGHTS OF THE WHITE CAMELLIA, 147
KOSSUTH, 6 36
KU KLUX KLAN, 147-148 173
LADIN, 1
LAFAYETTE LOUISIANA, 174
LAFAYETTE, Marquis De 139
LAGUARDIA, Achille 305
LAKE COMO, 44 44
LAEK GARDA, 10
LAKE MASSIORE, 33-34
LAKE SUPERIOR, 156
LAKOTA COUNTRY, 161
LAKOTA RIVER, 208
LAKOTA SIOUX, 153 153-155 158-159 165 167 176 182 184-186 193-194 196 203 206-207 218 231 241 245 250 259 261 266 276 290 296 306 308
LAME DEER, 261
LAPWAI RESERVATION, 274

LEBANON KENTUCKY, 126-127
LEE, Gen 111 Robert E 133
LEEDS, 88
LEONI, 46-47
LEVY COUNTY, 110
LEWIS, 154 273 281
LEXINGTON KENTUCKY, 147
LIGURIAN DISTRICT, 25
LINCOLN, 188 195 200 207 256 258-259 265-268 270-271
LINCOLN, Abraham 99 106 Pres 106
LIPAN, 315
LITTLE BIGHORN, 145 229-230 250 283 291-292 303 305 309 315 317 320 323 Battle of 200
LITTLE BIGHORN BATTLEFIELD, 296
LITTLE BIGHORN RIVER, 161 184 196-197 204-209 211 217 254 256 259 306
LITTLE BIGHORN VALLEY, 210 217
LITTLE MISSOURI RIVER, 193
LITTLE WOLF, 290
LIVERPOOL, 92 103
LIVINGSTON ALABAMA, 148
LOCARNO SWITZERLAND, 33-34
LOLO TRAIL, 274
LOMBARDI, Frances 168
LOMBARDY, 2 31 81
LOMBARDY-VENETIA, 6
LONDON ENGLAND, 21 35 45-47 51-52 54 61 86-88 90 93 144 323
LOOKING GLASS, 283
LOS ANGELES CALIFORNIA, 319-321 323
LOUIS NAPOLEON, 29 42 52 68
LOUIS PHILIPPE 28 74
LOUIS XVIII, King of ? 28
LOUISIANA, 171 173 175
LOUISVILLE KENTUCKY, 123 125 146-147 156
LUCERN, 30
LUGANO SWITZERLAND, 31 34 44 90
LUGO, 48
LUZIO, Alexander 322
MACKENZIE, Ronald S 260
MAGENTA, Battle of 80
MAINE, 112
MALGHERA, 11 14
MANCHERINI, 88 Mr 46 Mrs 47 Sarah 46
MANCHESTER, 88
MANTUA, 9 41 47 51 61
MARGE, William L R 125
MARGHERA, 10
MARINO, 48 322
MARONI RIVER, 74
MARSEILLES, 15 26 55 73

Index

MARTINI, 245 255 Giovanni 168 219
  Trumpeter 220
MARX, Karl 35 70
MARYLAND, 106 108
MASACHUSETTS, 118
MASSAI, 318-319
MATHEY, Capt 294 E J 294
MATTERNICH, 6
MAYON, Richard 67
MAZZINI, 13 15 17 21 26 31 33-36 38 41-43 47-48 51-53 80 87 89 92 97 99-100 Guiseppi 90 Joseph 91
MCCLELLAN, George 203
MCCLELLEN SADDLE, 188
MEADE, Gen 133
MEDICINE LODGE TREATY, 132
MEDICINE TAIL COULEE, 219
MEDICINE TRAIL COULEE, 221 255
MELVILLE, Mr 84
MEMPHIS TENNESSEE, 156 295
MERRILL, Col 275
MERRITT, Wesley 308
MESCALERO APACHE, 315
MESTRE, 11-12
METTERNICH, 2
MEXICAN WAR, 101 132
MEXICO, 182 315 317-318
MILAN, 5-9 31-34 80 85 Duke of 1
MILES, 283 317 City 271 Col 260-261 265 271 277-278 278 282 Gen 310 N A 277 Nelson 258-259
MILITARY ACADEMY OF SAN LUCA, 7
MILITARY ACADEMY OF ST LUCA, 5 85
MINICONJOU, 154 261
MINICONJOU FORD, 219
MINICONJOU SIOUX, 309
MINNELLI, D 98 103
MINNESOTA, 153
MISSISSIPPI, 108 147
MISSOURI, 133 153 166
MISSOURI RIVER, 123 154 156-159 164 175 190 197 262 270 271 287
MOBILE GULF 108
MODOC, 157
MONTAGNE, D'Argent 74-76 78 85-86
MONTAIGNE, D'Argent 75
MONTANA, 126 184 274-275
MONTEVIDEO, 16
MONTMASSAN, Rosalita 322
MOORE, William G 121-122
MOORHEAD MINNESOTA, 268
MORBIOLI, 78-79
MORBIOLO, 81-82
MORELLI, 79-81
MOSCOW, 67
MOUNT JANICULUM, 16
MOUNT SERVA, 1
MOUNTAIN HOWITZER, 198 270 275
MOYLAN, Capt 193-194 207 218 229 267 294 309 Myles 141 189
MUD CREEK, 203
MUSSELSHELL RIVER, 275-276 278 281-282
NAPLES, 6 18 Kingdom of 89
NAPOLEON, 90 Jerome 60 90 Louis 5-6 15 27
NAPOLEON II, 29
NAPOLEON III 29 42-43 51-52 54 56 58-60 64 67-68 79-80 146 167 270 297 320 322
NASHVILLE TENNESSEE, 146 148
NATIONAL ITALIAN COMMITTEE 35
NATIONAL LOAN BONDS, 35
NATIONAL MILTIARY CEMETERY, 324
NATIONAL REVOLUTIONARY COMMITTEE, 44
NATURAL BRIDGE VIRGINIA, 111
NEBRASKA, 289
NETHERLANDS LEGION, 99
NEVADA, 127
NEW AMSTERDAM, 83-86
NEW MEXICO, 317
NEW ORLEANS LOUISIANA, 108 156 172 174
NEW RAMSLEY OHIO 132
NEW YORK, 92-93 98 100 103 108 110 119 121-122 160 165 187 268 293 297 301 303-305
NEW YORK CITY, 120 191
NEW YORK RIOT, 1863 102
NEW YORK UNIVERSAL EXPOSITION, 98
NEWPORT, 110
NEWPORT BARRACKS KENTUCKY, 123-124
NEWTON, Gen 117
NEZ PERCE, 199 261 273-275 275-277 277-283 287 303
NICE, 15 81
NIGHTINGALE, 241
NORADANO, 2
NORTH CAROLINA, 185
NORTH PACIFIC RAILROAD, 260
NORTH PLATTE RIVER, 155
NORTHERN PACIFIC RAILROAD, 153 155-159 288 296
NOSADANI, 2

NOSODANO, 2 Carlo 90 Count of 90 104
NOTTINGHAM ENGLAND 47-48 51-52 67 87-88 92 103
NOVARA, 13 25
O'NEILL, Pvt 251-254 Thomas 250
OFFENBACH, Jacques 268
OGLALA, 154-155 184 224 231 237 259 261
OJAPOCK RIVER, 75
OKLAHOMA, 289 307
OKLAHOMA LAND RUSH, 308
OPAPOK RIVER, 76
OREGON, 273
OREGON TERRITORY, 273
ORLEANS, Louis Philippe Of 3 6
ORSINI, Andrea 68 Cesar 322 Ernestina 322 Felice 11-12 41 44-45 51-70 74 87-89 91 120 267 293 297 321-323
OSOPPO, 37
OUDINOT, Gen 17-19 21 Nicholas 15
OXFORD MISSISSIPPI, 147-148
OYAPOCK RIVER, 74
PADUA, 11
PAIUTE, 183
PALE FACES, 148
PALMALENGHI-CRISPI, Tommaso 322
PALMANOVA, 4
PALMERSTON, Lord 70
PARIS, 6 27-29 42 54-56 62 65-66 77 98 Cardinal Archbishop of 67-68
PARIS FRANCE, 268
PELLICO, Silvio 68
PENNSYLVANIA, 125
PETERS, Willie 205
PETERSBURG, 103-104 109 111
PHILADELPHIA EPNNSYLVANIA, 101 105 171
PIANCIANI, Luigi 36 43 45-46
PIAVE RIVER, 1 10
PIAVE VALLEY, 37
PIEDMONT, 41 51 80 90 Kingdom of 89
PIEDMONT SARDINIA, Kingdom of 8
PIEDMONT SAVOY, 21 25 47 80 King of 13
PIERI, Guiseppe Andrea 55-57 59-62 66-68 Mr 61
PIERNEY, Andrea 60
PIERRE, 288-289 297
PINE RIDGE AGENCY SOUTH DAKOTA, 290 309
PINE RIDGE RESERVATION, 288
PIOUS IX, Pope 3 9 11-12 15 255
PIUS IX, Pope 7
PLAINS APACHE, 307
PLATTE RIVER, 134

POINT RASSA, 109
POLAND, 90
POLISH LEGION, 99
PONCA INDIAN AGENCY, 175
PONTIAC, 309
PORTUGAL, 84
POWDER RIVER, 155 182 184 194-197 211 256 269
POWDER RIVER VALLEY, 260
PRUSSIA, 80 146
PUNTA ROSSA, 111
QUADRILATERAL, 8
RADETSKY, Count 7 Field Marshal 7
RADETZKY, 8-9
RADONICH, Enrico 33-34
RAPPAHANNOCK RIVER, 104
RAVENNA, 14-15 21
RED CLOUD, 155 181
RED CLOUD AGENCY, 261 289
RED CLOUD TREATY, 175-176
RED CLOUD'S WAR, 155
RED RIVER, 267-268
RED RIVER WAR, 260
REE, 200
REMINGTON REVOLVER, 242
RENAULT, Philippe 139
RENO CREEK, 208 210-211
RENO HILL, 218 238-241 244 250 253 253
RENO, Maj 160 187 192-193 195 197-198 200 210-211 217-222 225 229-241 243-245 249 252 255-256 258 265 265-267 290-296 304 Marcus 132 Marcus Albert 139 143 Mark 139 Mary Hannah 139 160
REVOLUTION OF 1848, 6 11 25-26 31 41 55 58 99
RICE, 188
RICHMOND, 111
RIO GRANDE, 315
RIPETTI, Alexander 99
ROCKY MOUNTAINS, 274 288
RODMAN GUN, 266
ROME, 1 7 12-17 19-21 21 26 90 98 146 Republic of 13
ROSEBUD DIVIDE, 208
ROSEBUD MOUNTAINS, 256 River 186 195-197 197 199 202 204-205 207-208 258
ROSEBUD VALLEY, 200
ROSEBUD-TONGUE RIVER, 184
ROSS, Mary Hannah 139 William B 103
ROSSI, 87-88
ROUEN, 74
RUDIO, 230 277 Capt 118 Charles 91 93 Mr 122

Index

RUDY, Lt 265
RUSSIA, 3 47 66 Czarina of 73
SAINT ANTOINE, 27
SAINT GEORGE, 41 76
SAINT GOTHARD'S PASS, 30
SAINT JOSEPH, 75
SAINT LAURENT, 74 83
SAINT LOUIS, 142 174
SAINT MARK, Republic of 7
SAINT MARKS FLORIDA, 110
SAINT MORITZ SWITZERLAND, 44
SAINT PAUL, 157 159 161 166-168
SAINT SIMONIAN SOCIALISTS, 15
SAMARIA, Countess 54
SAN ARCS, 154
SAN DIEGO, 319
SAN FRANCISCO, 127 268 324
SANDRI, Antonio 33
SANDWICH ISLANDS, 251 268
SANTA CRUZ, 74
SANTA FE TRAIL, 131
SANTEE SIOUX, 153
SARDINIA, 89
SASSILLA, Bartholomew 323
SATANTA, 307
SAVOY, 81 House of 8
SCHNEIDER, James 107
SCHRIVER, Gen 118
SCOTT, 282 Hugh L 278 Mrs H C 320
SEATTLE WASHINGTON, 156
SECOND EMPIRE, 42 320
SECOND REPUBLIC, 6 42
SECRETARY OF WAR, 101 118-119 127 140
SEINE RIVER, 59
SHARP RIFLE, 242
SHARPSBURG, 123
SHARPSHOOTER RIDGE, 242-243
SHENANDOAH, 111 133
SHERIDAN, Gen 111 133 139 174 184 257 289 306 Philip 132-133 Philip H 135-136
SHERMAN, Gen 107 111 135 182-183 257 261 280 291 John 260 William 275 William T 260
SHIP ISLAND, 108
SHOSHONE, 182 184
SHOSHONE RIVER, 275
SHOSHONI, 275
SIBLEY TENT, 194 269
SICILY, 58 89 322
SIDNEY, 288-289
SIERRA MADRE MOUNTAINS, 318
SIGNAL ARIZONA, 320 323-324
SILVER CITY, 317
SILVER DISCOVERED, 127
SIOUX, 134 182 196 206 221 233 249 251 259-261 288 292 306 309
SIOUX CITY, 169
SIOUX COUNTRY, 182
SIOUX NATION, 153
SIOUX WAR, 154
SITTING BULL, 185 196 202 243 251 259-260 262 276 278 282-283 288 306 309
SKELETON CANYON ARIZONA, 317
SLIM BUTTES, 259
SLOAN, M J 120
SMITH & WESSON REVOLVER, 242
SMITH, Andrew J 132
SMOKEY HILL TRAIL, 137
SMOKY HILL TRAIL, 131
SNAKE, 184
SNAKE RIVER, 274 280
SOLFERINO, Battle of 80
SOLOMON FORKS, 144-145
SONORA MEXICO, 319
SOUTH CAROLINA, 147
SOUTH DAKOTA, 155 290
SOUTH PLATTE RIVER, 154
SOUTH SIDE RAILROAD, 104 111
SPAIN, 319
SPENCER RIFLE, 136
SPOTTED BULL HORN, 221-222
SPOTTED TAIL AGENCY, 289
SPOTTSYLVANIA VIRGINIA, 103-104 123
SPRINGFIELD RIFLE, 110 191-192 199 233 235 242-243
STANDING RIVER SIOUX RESERVATION, 161
STANDING ROCK, 266
STANDING ROCK AGENCY, 262 266
STANDING ROCK RESERVATION NORTH DAKOTA, 306 309
STANLEY'S STOCKADE, 160-161 190
STANTON, Edwin 99 112 Secretary of War 121
STATEN ISLAND NEW YORK, 21
STINKING WATER CANYON, 281
STINKING WATER RIVER, 275 278 280-281
STINKING WATER RIVER CANYON, 281
STRAITS OF GIBRALTAR, 119
STRASBOURG, 5
STURGIS, Col 143 160 257 265 267 276-282 289 293 295 306 Samuel 132
Samuel D 270

Index

SUMMIT SPRINGS COLORADO, 137
SUMNER, Charles 100 118 121 Senator 118
SUN DANCE, 196 202
SUNDAY CREEK, 270-271
SURREY, 47
SWITZERLAND, 1 4 29-31 35 40-41 97
TALLAHASSEE FLORIDA, 110-111
TAMPA, 109
TAUSZKY, Dr 121 R 120
TAYLOR, Blair D 310 Foundry 53 57
TENNESSEE, 103 147
TERRY, Alfred 153 Alfred H 182-183 Gen 166 186-190 192-197 199-200 203-204 243 255-256 258-260 265 267 275 291
TETON, 154
TETON-WIND RIVER RANGE, 275
TEXAS, 123 131 261 296 308 316-317
TEXAS FEVER, 307
THACKERAY, 35
THAMES RIVER 87
TIBALDI, Paolo 53-54 320
TIBER RIVER, 16 18
TIBERIUS, Emperor of? 1
TIBOLDI, Paolo 79
TICINO RIVER, 32
TONGUE RIVER, 182 186 194-197 256 259 290
TONGUE RIVER CANTONMENT, 271 276 282
TONTO BASIN ARIZONA, 183 274
TORINO, 322
TORROCFALDA, Baron 53
TOSCANY, 81
TOULON, 21 73
TOWNSEND, E D 140
TRANSLYVANIA, 4
TRANSTEVERE, 19
TRANSYLVANIA, 41
TREATY OF FORT LARAMIE, 155 167 181
TRENT, 37
TRESSOLDI, 45-46 Mr 35
TREVINA, Duke of 1
TREVIS VALLEY, 40
TRIESTE, 4
TROLLI, 26-30
TULLAHOMA TENNESSEE, 147
TULLOCK'S CREEK, 203
TURIN, 30 32 42 99 164
TURKEY, 47
TWO KETTLES, 154
TYROL, 1
UDINE, 2
UNION LEAGUE CLUB, 100

UNION PACIFIC RAILROAD, 288
UNITED STATES ARMY, 98 155 175 185 196 217 219 304-305 317
UNITED STATES COLORED TROOPS, 107 110 302
UNITED STATES INDIAN BUREAU, 182
UNITED STATES SANITARY COMMISSION, 100-101
UNKPAPA, 154 185 196 224 231-232 259 261-262 276
UNTAMED HORSE, 184
URBAN VIII, Pope 16
URUGUAY, 16
VALENCIA, 26
VALETTRI, 17
VALTELLINA ITALY, 44
VARESE ITALY, 30 34
VARNUM, Charles 206 324 Lt 206 254 303
VENETIA, 2 4 10 90 122
VENEZUELA, 86
VENICE, 1-2 7 9-13 13-15 21 30 323
VENITIERI, Felice 164
VERONA, 8-9 31
VICKREY, Mrs N B 320
VICKSBURG, 103
VICTOR EMANUEL II, King of? 90 King of Piedmont Savoy 13 43 51 80 89 146
VICTORIA, Queen of England 67 69 262
VIENNA, 6 9-10 29 80 Congress of 2
VILLA CORSINI, 16 18-19
VINCENZA, 9-10
VINITIERI, Felice 167
VIRGINIA, 133
VIRGINIA CITY MONTANA, 154 159 181 278
WALLOWA VALLEY OREGON, 273 287
WALTER, John 67
WASHBURN RANGE, 275
WASHINGTON, 273 287 Dc 97 100-101 106-108 112 122 153 155 174 181 191 261 268
WASHITA, 138 144 192 199 217 Battle of 137
WASHITA RIVER, 136
WATKINS, E C 182
WEIR, Capt 241 Point 240 250 Thomas 239 Thomas B 146
WEIR'S POINT, 218
WEIT, Thomas B 293
WEST INDIES, 84
WEST POINT, 112 118 123 132 134 139 183 185 260 276 278 306 320 324
WHISKEY POINT, 165
WHITE LEAGUE, 147 173
WHITE MAN'S CROW'S NEST, 206

WHITTAKER, Frederick 290
WHITTIKER, 292
WICHITA MOUNTAINS, 307 311
WICKIUP, 202
WILD WEST COMPANY, 306
WILDER, John 109 117
WILDERNESS, 103-104 123
WILLIAMSPORT, 133
WILMINGTON NORTH CAROLINA, 110 187
WINCHESTER RIFLE, 192 242
WIND RIVER, 280
WOLF MOUNTAIN, 203 261
WOUNDED KNEE, 308-310 315
WOUNDED KNEE CREEK, 309
WYOMING, 126 154 197 275
YANKTON DAKOTA TERRITORY, 156-159 168 170 175 267 288
YANKTON SIOUX, 153
YELLOW FEVER, 77 109 305
YELLOWSTONE, 182
YELLOWSTONE CANYON, 279
YELLOWSTONE EXPEDITION, 159-161 276
YELLOWSTONE LAKE, 280
YELLOWSTONE NATIONAL PARK, 275-276 279-281 296
YELLOWSTONE RIVER, 156 160-161 185-186 190 194-195 197 253 256 259 265 270-271 275 278-279 282
YELLOWSTONE VALLEY, 155 158
YOUNG ITALY, 13 15 26 91
ZAPPA, Mr 42
ZLINCK'S STATION, 104
ZURICH, 36-37 40-43 48 88

www.ingramcontent.com/pod-product-compliance
Lightning Source LLC
Chambersburg PA
CBHW050835230426
43667CB00012B/2002